Ottawa

SOCIAL ANTHROPOLOGY OF PEASANTRY

SOCIAL ANTHROPOLOGY
OF
PEASANTRY

JOAN P. MENCHER

SOMAIYA PUBLICATIONS PVT. LTD.
BOMBAY • MADRAS • NEW DELHI

Published by S. G. Nene
for Somaiya Publications Pvt. Ltd.
172, Mumbai Marathi
Granthasangrahalaya Marg
Dadar, Bombay 400 014.
INDIA

First Edition 1983

Rs. 150/-

Phototypeset and Printed by N. S. Ray
at. THE BOOK CENTRE LIMITED
103, Road No. 29,
Sion (East)
BOMBAY 400 022.
INDIA

CONTENTS

Acknowledgments   vii

Contributors   ix

Introduction   1

PART I : GENERAL THEORETICAL ISSUES,
CONCEPTS AND METHODS

The Concept of Peasant and the Concept of
Culture — *Sydel Silverman*   7

Peasants into Proletarians from the Household
Out : An Analysis from the intersection of Anthro-
pology and Social History — *Rayna Rapp*   32

On Peasant Rent — *Eric R. Wolf*   48

Defining Peasants : Conceptualization and De-
Conceptualizations : old and new in a Marxist
Debate— *Teodor Shanin*   60

The Growth of Capitalism and the Peasant
Economy : Some Problems on the Transference
of Surplus — *Eduardo P. Archetti*   87

Discussions   104

PART II : SOME SPECIFIC STUDIES FROM EUROPE,
AFRICA, LATIN AMERICA, AND CHINA

Peasant Production and Population in Mexico
— *Arturo Warman*   121

Social Conditions of Production and Technical
Change in Venezuelan Agriculture
— *Hebe M. C. Vessuri*   130

The Problem of Arab Peasant Kinship : Superimposed, Structure Collectivity and Descent, Politicized, Marriage and Patriarchal Property Control
—*Henry Rosenfeld*   154

Political Consciousness and Struggle Among an
African Peasantry — *Joan Vincent*   177

Cognitive Aspects of Peasant Livelihood in
Hungary — *Tamás Hofer*   191

The People's Commune and the Socialist Transformation of the Chinese Peasantry — *Tse Ka-Kui*   204

Discussion   228

PART III : SOME VIEWS OF THE INDIAN PEASANTRY

The Evolutionary Status of Caste in Peasant India
— *Gerald D. Berreman*   237

Agrarian Conflict and Peasant Movements in
Twentieth Century India — *Walter Hauser*   251

Peasant Transformation in a Fringe Village : A
Study in the Process— *U.S. Misra & B.R.K. Shukla*   262

Peasants and Neo-peasants in Northeast India : and
their new Dimension — *M. C. Goswami*   266

Agricultural Labour in Thanjavur —
— *Kathleen Gough*   276

Agricultural Labourers in Peasant Societies : The
Case of South Asia — *Joan P. Mencher*   291

The Conditions of the Peasantry in Bangladesh
— *Shapan Adnan*   313

Agrarian Movements in Tamil Nadu— *Gopal Iyer*   320

Discussion   328

PART IV : A SUMMING UP — *Eric R. Wolf*   345

ACKNOWLEDGMENTS

This volume owes its existence to a number of organizations and people. First of all, I would like to thank the Smithsonian Institution for so generously providing funding for the travel and accommodation of most of the non-Indian participants in the Post-Plenary session held in Lucknow, India. Specifically, I would like to thank Ms. Francine Berkowitz and Ms. Betty Wingfield as well as the Smithsonian Travel department for their help.

Thanks also go to the members of the Ethnographic and Folk Culture Society of Lucknow for all that they did to make our stay so pleasant, including all of the conference arrangements, meeting the participants, transporting them to their hotels, arranging for bussing to the meetings, and a number of other details. Without their help, the conference and the book would not have been possible.

The following people deserve thanks for work connected with preparation of the book: Deborah D'Amico and Pamela Wright for transcribing the tapes of the Conference Discussion, and Franklin C. Southworth for extensive help with the editing and proof-reading.

Contributors

Silverman. Sydel : Associated with Queens College, City University of New York, since 1962; Executive Officer of the Ph. D. Programme in Anthropology, City University Graduate School, since 1975. Author of *Three Bells of Civilization* (1975) and other works on rural and urban society in central Italy, editor of *Totems and Teachers: Perspectives on the History of Anthropology* (1981).

Rayna Rapp : She obtained her B. A., M. A. and Ph. D. degrees from the University of Michigan in 1968, 1969, and 1973 respectively. She is currently an associate Professor at the New School for Social Research. Her publications include : "Sex and Society : A Research Note for Anthropology and Social History" in Comparative Studies in Society and History Vol. 23 :

1. 51-72 (written along with E. Ross) 1981

2. "Review Essay : Anthropology" in Signs Vol. $ 3,497-513, 1979

3. (Along with E. Ross and R. Brindenthal) "Examining Family History" in Feminist Studies, Vol. 5, No. 1, pp. 174-200. 1980

4. *(Ed.) Toward an Anthropology of Women* Monthly Review Press, 1975

Eric R. Wolf : B. A. Queens College, L. K., New York, Ph. D. Columbia University, New York (1951). Major fieldwork in Puerto Rico (1948-49) Mexico (1951-52) and the Italian Alps (1960-61). Associated since 1971 with H. Lehman College, City University of New York. Author of *Peasants* (1964) and *Peasant Wars of the 20th Century* (1969), among other books and articles dealing with complex societies and peasant problems.

Shanin. Teodor : Professor of Sociology, Manchester University, Author of the Oxford Class, editor of "Peasants and Peasant Societies", "The Rules of the Game", member of editorial team of Jl. of Contemporary Asia.

Archetti. Eduardo P. : Studied at the University of Buenos Aires, Argentina, M. A. (Sociology) : University of Paris, Ph. D. (Social anthropology), Assistant Professor, University of Santa Fe, Argentina, 1974: Fellow, University of Oslo, 1975-80: Assistant Professor, University of Oslo, 1980-Author of *Explotacion Familiar y Acumulacion de Capital en el Campo Argentino,* 1975: *Estructura Agraria y Campesinado en America Latina,* 1981.

Arturo Warman : first came into contact with the peasantry of his country through work with state agencies concerned with agrarian issues, and through a major interest in popular music and arts. Field work in various regions of Mexico earned him an M. A. in anthropology from the Escuela Nacional de Anthropologia in 1968 and his doctorate in anthropology from Universidad Iberoamericana in 1975. He has written extensively and critically on the problems of the peasantry; his major study of the peasantry of Morelos and its relation to the national state has been published in English under the title *We Come to Object* (Johns Hopkins Press, 1980). Warman is currently associated with the Universidad Nacional Autonoma de Mexico.

Hebe M. C. Vessuri : was educated at the University of Buenos Aires (1960-62) and at Oxford University (B. Litt., 1964., D. Phil., 1971). She has served as Director of the Centre of Sociological Research of the National University of Tucuman (1971-74) and has taught at that University. She has also taught at Dalhousie University. (1966-68), the University of Victoria (1968-69), Simon Fraser University (1970) and the Central University of Venezuela (1976 to the present). She is currently Head of the Science and Technology Area of the Center for Development Studies (CENDES) of the Central University of Venezuela.

Henry Rosenfeld : has done field work among Arab villagers and city people, in collective settlements (kibbutzim), among Jewish immigrants in a development town, and the Jewish Middle class in Israel, and has published on different subjects related to these groups. He teaches at the University of Haifa and has taught at Brooklyn College, Manchester University (as a Simon senior Fellow), and at Rutgers University as (Distinguished Visiting Professor). Recent publications include *"The Class Situation of the Arab Minority in Israel"* and *"The Privatization of Public Means, the State-made Middle class,* and *the Realization of Family Value in Israel"* (in collaboration with Shulamit Carari).

Joan Vincent : B.Sc., (Econ.) London School of Economics and Political Science; M.A. University of Chicago; Ph.D., Columbia University, 1968. Professor of Anthropology, Barnard College, Columbia University, since 1975. Lecturer in Political Sociology Makerere University 1966-67. Fellow, East African Institute of Social Research, 1966-67. Field research in Uganda (1966-67, 1970) and Northern Ireland (1975 to the present).

Tamas Hofer : is Head of the Department of Social Anthropology in the Ethnographic Institute of the Hungarian Academy of Sciences. He was educated at the University of Budapest (M.A. 1953, Ph. D. 1958). He was affiliated to the Hungarian Ethnographic Museum (1952-1980), taught at Budapest University and was a visiting professor at the University of North Carolina, Chapel Hill (1971). His main research interest is peasant social organization and peasant cultural traditions in Hungary and East Central Europe.

Tse Ka-Kui : Graduated from the Department of Sociology, Chung Chi College, the Chinese University of Hong Kong in 1974. Pursued post-graduate studies at the University of Manchester, U. K. under Professors Peter Worsley and Teodor Shanin and awarded M.A. in 1975 and Ph. D. in 1978. Worked at the Department of Sociology, University of Hong Kong from 1976-1980. Since March 1980, joined Lam Soon (HK) Ltd. as its Personnel Manager and Head of Industrial Engineering Division. Published extensively in English and in Chinese including such journals as Monthly Review (N.Y.) Dialectical Anthropology, Social Praxis, Eastern Anthropology, Hong Kong Manager and Economic Management (Beijing).

Gerala D. Berreman : has done his B.A. and M.A. in anthropology, University of Oregon; Ph. D. social anthropology, Cornell University. Research and Publication on Aleutian Islands, Alaska (1952, 1962); Garhwali village of Dehra Dun District of U.P. Himalayas, India (1957-59, 1968-69, 1972) research on urban social relations and social history of Dehra Dun (1968-69, 1972, 1981-82) Professor, University of California, Berkeley, 1959 to present; visiting Professor Stockholm (1972) Delhi (1968-69). Hon. doctorates University of Stockholm (1978) Garhwal University (1979). Major research and publication; *culture and society of India, comparative social inequality, methods and ethics of research, social and cultural change..*

Walter Hauser : is on the faculty of the Department of History at the University of Virginia and was until recently the Director of the Centre for South Asian Studies at that institution. His research and publications have focussed on the nature and role of peasant movements in the North Indian Gangetic plain in the twentieth century. His forthcoming book is titled *"Control, Conflict and Political Mobilization in Rural India : A Study of Peasant Movements in an Agrarian Society".* He is the co-editor (with Dr. James Manor) of a volume of essays based on recent Bihar and Karnataka scholarship.

B. R. K. Shukla : is affliated with the Anthropology Department of the Lucknow University. He is the Honorary Secretary of the Ethnographic and Folk Culture Society of Lucknow which was the host for the post-pleninary session where these papers where first presented. He has written a number of papers both along and with various co-authors on his research in Uttar Pradesh.

U. S. Mishra : Department of Anthropology, Lucknow.

M. C. Goswami : Specialised in socio-cultural, anthropology. Retired as Professor of anthropology of the University of Gauhati, Currently attached to

Law Research Institute, Gauhati High Court, on a project entitled "Customary Laws and Practices of selected tribes of N.E. India", where he carried on extensive field work. Co-authored *Social Institutions of the Garos of Meghalaya* and edited the *Bulletin of the Department of Anthropology* till retirement in 1978. Sectional President of the I.S.C.A. (1971) and the Oriental Conference (1956). Cochairperson in two sessions of the Xth ICAES.

Kathleen Gough : is a Research Associate in anthropology at the University of British Columbia. She has done extensive fieldwork in South Indian villages. With David M. Schneider she co-authored and co-edited *Matrilineal Kinship*, University of California Press, 1973, and with Hari P. Sharma, *Imperialism and Revolution in South Asia*, Monthly Review Press, 1973. She is the author of *Ten Times more Beautiful: the Rebuilding of Vietnam*, New Star and Monthly Review Presses, 1973, and of *Rural Society in Southeast India*, Cambridge University Press, 1981.

Joan P. Mencher : Professor of Anthropology at Lehman College and City University of New York Graduate Center since 1968. Field research in India 1958-60, 1962-64, 1966-67, 1971-72, 1975-76 and 1980-81 (primarily in Kerala and Tamil Nadu, also in West Bengal). Author of *Agriculture and Social Structure in Tamil Nadu* (1978); and numerous articles on socio-economic problems in India as well as problems of peasant society.

Shapan Adnan : is affiliated with the Bangladesh Institute for Development Studies in Dacca. He has worked at the Centre for South Asian Studies at Cambridge University in England. His research has focussed on problems of agrarian relations and development, and he has published a number of papers and edited volumes through the Institute in Dacca.

Dr. Gopal Iyer : Worked as Lecturer in Sociology in Patna University from 1966 to 1974; as a Research Fellow in National Labour Institute from 1975 to 1978; and presently working as a Reader in Sociology in Punjab University, Chandigarh. Published a number of articles on agrarian situation in India including agrarian movements.

Introduction

The papers collected in this volume were presented at a post-plenary session which met in Lucknow, India, following the Tenth International Congress of Anthropological Sciences in New Delhi, India, in December 1978. The purpose of this three-day session was to explore in depth some of the crucial issues that have emerged in the study of peasant societies world-wide. Though the field of peasant studies has been of great interest to anthropologists, at least since the 1930s, a number of crucial issues have stood out as unresolved, and this session was designed to address some of these issues. The organizers feel that the papers presented here, as well as the lively discussion which followed each day's set of papers, have helped us to come to grips with these. The intent of the conference was to bring together people with a wide range of viewpoints and a diversity of field experience to discuss these common concerns — without, of course, expecting any definitive resolution of any of them. Thus, we hope that the papers in this volume, along with the discussion following each section, will succeed in clarifying a number of important issues.

The questions that were raised fall into a few basic categories: (1) questions of definition, (2) questions of time scale, (3) questions of comparison, (4) the question of contemporary changes going on in peasant societies, and (5) the study of peasant consciousness as an aspect of class consciousness — and related to this, the question of peasant rebellions (both in the past and today). Some of the papers in this volume deal primarily with one of the above categories, some with more than one, but all in one way or another touch on these basic issues.

Questions of definition dominate the first part of the book. It is clear from any study of political economy that definitions of peasantry play an important role in how we conceptualize them. Do they include, for example, traditional agricultural labourers? (Note that we find landless or semi-landless agricultural labourers only in some parts of the world, primarily Asia, but to some extent also in Europe and Egypt prior to the sixteenth century). Do they include herdsmen? (This again is more important in some parts of the world than in others.) The question of identification or classification of peasants led to considerable debate, with differences depending (at least in part) on the area of the world best known to the speaker.

Another major topic of theoretical debate was concerned with how we can handle the complex question of social classes within the peasantry. Far too often writings about peasants seem to implicitly accept the idea of a relatively homogeneous group of people in a given area, but we know that in fact, in most of the world, there were and are today social class distinctions in village society. Several of the papers in this volume touch on this differentiation of the peasantry in a number of different ways, including its probable origins. The discussions following the first and the last day of the conference deal with this in some detail, and go into the reasons why it has occurred more in some areas than in others. Some have used Marxist classifications, while some have used other schemes; on the whole, the Marxist classification (if not applied too rigidly, and if allowed to take into account specific local situations) appears to be the most useful.

One of the major questions underlying the entire symposium was the extent to which the peasantry of one world area can be considered comparable to that of another. Ancillary to that is the question of how theoretical models developed in one world region can be applicable to other areas. How necessary is it to develop different kinds of models, and in what ways can the same models be used in these diverse regions? Though not dealt with explicitly in any one paper, a good part of the general discussion from the floor revolved around this crucial question as specialists in European, African, or Latin American studies held a dialogue with those who have worked in South Asia, China, and the Middle East.

Rayna Rapp raised the question of the time frame to be used. This matter was also dealt with by Vincent, Archetti, Vessuri and others, who pointed to changes among peasants over time. This led to another major focus of the conference, which was that of change in peasant societies: In what ways does it come about? What has been the impact of the colonial experience? Related questions include peasant rebellions (When and under what circumstances do they occur?), and the even more complex question of raising peasant consciousness. Some of the papers, especially from China and eastern Europe, deal with changes that resulted from peasant rebellions, while those from western Europe deal more with gradual evolution and the effects of the industrial revolution; those from South Asia focus on what has been happening as a result of over 25 years of independence.

The discussion following the papers focused not only on substantive matters but also on the use of concepts and definitions, and perhaps helped to clarify some of the confusions that exist in present terminology. Though none of the papers deals directly with the question of peasant consciousness, many of them raise implicit questions relating to peasant "rebellions". The majority of the papers, rooted as they are in specific concrete historical situations, bring to light some of the underlying reasons why there have or have not been rebellions in particular parts of the world. From this perspective, it was extremely useful to have papers from both socialist and capitalist societies.

About one-third of the book deals with South Asian society, which is in large part due to the fact that the symposium was held in India. However, this also served to put South Asian studies into a wider context than is the case at many conferences, where people who work in South Asia rarely get to talk to Latin Americanists or European specialists. The exchange of views between the two was highly provocative and generated many useful ideas.

A common theme of all the papers in this volume is that they look at the forces which energize the peasantry and at the circumstances under which this energy can be either blocked or freed to explore new avenues of change. All the authors also showed a clear awareness of the relationship between their detailed studies and the wider socio-economic and historical structures in which the societies studied were located, in both time and space. Thus, although not all of the papers were influenced by a theoretical Marxian approach, they nevertheless tend to relate particular studies to the mode of production of the country or region in question.

While most of the papers focus on the materialist aspect of peasant societies, the discussion did also raise other questions. Some key points may be briefly noted here. It was pointed out that in talking about change (especially socialist change) in peasant societies, one must also look at the issue of social justice; that a socialist revolution is not only a matter of technology (and by implication economics), but also social and ideological in nature. Several participants, both in their papers and in discussion, pointed out that a strength of the anthropological approach is its ability to focus on the study of socio-economic conditions — the mode of production — as well as the question of consciousness, as it relates to socio-political possibilities in a given time frame.

There was also considerable concern with the interrelationship between belief structures and socio-economic change. During the last day, one of the questions that hung in the air (though not the primary focus of any paper) was the relationship between caste and peasant uprising in the South Asian subcontinent, particularly the role of caste in keeping people from uniting on the basis of class.

Though we touched on many issues during the three-day conference, it was also clear that we have not exhausted the range of issues to be explored in peasant studies. We hope, however, that this volume will help to raise, and perhaps partially clarify, some of the main current issues in the field.

PART : I

GENERAL THEORETICAL ISSUES, CONCEPTS AND METHODS

The Concept of Peasant
and
The Concept of Culture

SYDEL SILVERMAN

Perhaps the most tiresome topic in the anthropology of peasantry is the seemingly endless debate over the definition of "peasant". Shanin's comment in 1971 that "there is something amusing, if not grotesque" in the failure of scholars to reach agreement on the concept (Shanin 1971 : 12) would hardly be phrased more sanguinely today in view of the continuing literature on the issue throughout the 1970s. Yet definition is not merely an exercise in pedantry. A definition represents a parsimonious statement of a theoretical stance, a selection of the features that are to be regarded as analytically primary. Definitions of "peasantry" must therefore be as varied, as changing, and as much subject to debate as are the theoretical views in peasant studies.

An analogous but far more pervasive debate has raged in American anthropology since its inception — the debate over the definition of "culture". This concept has played a historical role as an integrative theme of anthropology in the United States, because it embodies a number of assumptions that have imparted a unity to the discipline. These include assumptions about the evolutionary context of the human species, the distinction between genetic patterning and learning, the role of symbolic processes in human behaviour, and the relationship between the unity of the species and behavioural variability. Overlying this common framework are competing definitions of culture, which reflect different positions on a range of theoretical issues — not least of them the issue of what is the proper subject-matter of the discipline. Indeed, the debate over culture continues even as many anthropologists find the concept increasingly problematical, precisely because of the common assumption that what culture "is" determines what anthropology can and should study.

I shall argue that varying concepts of "peasant" among American anthropologists are closely linked to their varying concepts of culture. I shall argue further that within the anthropological study of peasantry two formative figures, Robert Redfield and Julian Steward, taking their departures from contrasting notions of culture, established fundamentally different views of peasantry. These differences, I contend, created divergent directions in peasant studies. Although many students have attempted to reconcile them, they rest on different premises and point to different research problems and modes of analysis. Thus, unravelling the two threads may reveal some order in what appears to be the diversity of approaches in contemporary peasant studies, and perhaps help clarify some of the confusions in attempts to define the concept of peasant.

DEVELOPMENT OF THE ANTHROPOLOGY OF PEASANTRY

Anthropology did not invent the study of peasants, but in a sense it discovered the subject for itself, for peasant studies in Anglophone cultural and social anthropology developed independently of earlier scholarly interests in peasants. Historians of medieval Europe, jurists and political theorists, Russian economists and "rural statisticians" who carried out studies of peasants on a national scale, eastern European ethnographers of folk-life, rural sociologists stimulated by LePlay to record family budgets, and others had written about peasants long before Robert Redfield's first field trip to Mexico in 1926. These scholarly traditions produced theory and data of immense value to contemporary peasant studies, but they do not constitute the historical background of the social anthropology of peasantry. To the extent that they dealt with peasants, the point of reference of such traditions was specific peasant groups, usually the politically significant peasantry of particular nations. The roots of the anthropological interest in peasants were elsewhere, in the comparative study of the human condition.

This comparative interest led anthropologists to do field studies in settlements of small-scale agriculturalists within civilized, state societies — and sometimes to refer to their subjects as "peasants" — long before they treated peasants as an analytic category. The central issue to which the early studies were addressed was the nature of human communities; they were, first of all, village studies, and only incidentally studies of peasants.

The community-study approach to settlements that would later be described as "peasant" was the product of links between certain trends in sociology and functionalist anthropology. The ground-breaking work in community study — Robert and Helen Lynd's *Middletown* of the mid-1920s — was, of course, not a peasant study at all but a description of small-town America (Lynd and Lynd 1929, 1937). Redfield's *Tepoztlan* (1930) emerged out of the "human ecology" school of urban sociology developed at the University of Chicago under the auspices of Redfield's father-in-law, Robert E. Park. However, Radcliffe-Brown's influence was crucial, for his definition of social anthropology as "comparative sociology" was an invitation to extend the theoretical framework of his structural-functionalism into the study of literate societies. Warner brought this approach to Harvard in 1929, developing both his long-term project on Yankee City and the social-anthropological phase of a Harvard study on Ireland, which was continued by Conrad Arensberg and Solon Kimball (Arensberg 1937; Arensberg and Kimball 1940). At the University of Chicago, a direct link to Chicago sociology was forged by Radcliffe-Brown's sojourn there (1931 to 1937), followed by the appointment of Warner. Among the early "peasant" studies that came out of Chicago are the works of Redfield and his associates in Yucatan (with Villa Rojas 1934; Redfield 1941, 1950), of Charlotte Gower Chapman in Sicily (written in 1935 and published in 1971), of John Embree in Japan (1939), and of Horace Miner in Quebec (1939). Malinowski's role during this period was important too, both through the theoretical and methodological influence of his functionalism and through his training of students such as Fei Hsiao-Tung (1939) and Hortense Powdermaker (1939). Note should also be taken of the extensive work done by anthropologists in rural communities of the United States during the 1930s, for the U.S. Bureau of Agricultural Economics.

These developments were basically an extension into civilized nations of the functionalist enterprise, which both Radcliffe-Brown and Malinowski saw as building a universal science. Anthropological field methods could be applied to the small, bounded unit of a "community", and the holism of Malinowski's "culture" and Radcliffe-Brown's "social structure" guided the inclusion of "all the details of [the community's] life" within "an integrated social study" (quotes from Radcliffe-Brown's and Embree's prefaces to *Suye Mura*).The communities studied in this period — American factory towns and rural seats in the Midwest and Deep South and New England, as well as peasant villages of several countries — tended to be treated as a common type. Sometimes the type was contrasted with primitive tribesmen. Sometimes, as in early Redfield, the type subsumed primitives and was contrasted with urban communities as depicted by Louis Wirth. Surprisingly little contrast was drawn among the communities, as diverse as they were. Further theoretical content was given to this work by Redfield's development of the "folk" depiction. He, and others after him, applied the term to both societal and cultural dimensions of such communities; "folk society" and "folk culture" were not systematically distinguished but were used interchangeably or simply according to preference.

The term "peasant" appears frequently but casually in the rural studies done in the quarter-century after Tepoztlan. The titles of the landmark books emphasize that these are studies of "villages" or studies of "life in" certain kinds of places: Redfield's *Tepoztlan: A Mexican Village, A Study of Folk Life; Chan Kom : A Maya Village* (with Villa Rojas); and *The Folk Culture of Yucatan;* Arensberg's

The Irish Countrymen and *Family and Community in Ireland* (with Kimball);
Chapman's *Milocca : A Sicilian Village;* Embree's *Suye Mura : A Japanese
Village:* Fei's *Peasant Life in China : A Field Study of Country Life in the
Yangtze Valley;* Lewis's *Life in a Mexican Village : Tepoztlan Restudied* (1951);
Beals's *Cheran : A Sierra Tarascan Village* (1946); Foster's *Empire's Children :
The People of Tzintzuntzan* (1948); and so on. The villagers may or may not be
described as "peasants"; the term is rarely defined but rather is used as if it were
self-explanatory, with the common dictionary meaning of rustics who work the
land. Peasantry is not problematical in this literature. Thus, *Suye Mura* has no
index listing for "peasant" but it does for "peasant community". *Family and
Community in Ireland* indexes "Peasants" with the notation, "see Farmers".
(The study is submitted as a description of contemporary Irish "folk culture", but
the quotation marks suggest a certain skepticism about the concept.) Fei never
defines the "peasant" of his title, but he does take pains to explain his taking "the
village" as his unit of study. In a later article on peasantry and gentry in China,
Fei offers a brief description of peasantry as "a way of living, a complex of formal
organization, individual behaviour, and social attitudes, closely knit together for
the purpose of husbanding land with simple tools and human labor" (1946 : 1-2).
Although the statement is phrased in general terms, he clearly has China in mind
rather than a broader analytic category.

Outside of anthropology, a number of studies of this period did refer to
"peasants" in their titles, such as W.I. Thomas and F. Znaniecki's early *The
Polish Peasant in Europe and America* (1918), and Doreen Warriner's *The
Economics of Peasant Farming* (1939). Invariably, however, such works dealt
with particular groups of peasants, usually European. "Peasant" was not taken
as an analytic category, or even as a term that called for definition.

Perhaps the first analytic use of the peasant concept was that of Raymond
Firth in *Malay Fishermen : Their Peasant Economy* (1946). Here Firth's aim is to
use the term for "a socio-economic category", and he justifies its application to
non-cultivators. His explicit criteria are economic: small-scale producers with
non-industrial technology relying primarily on what they produce for their
subsistence. Thus, he includes in the category small-scale producers other than
cultivators who share the "same kind of simple economic organization" (1951 :
87). He adds, however," . . . and community life", and then goes on to talk about
the "folk" character of these communities. In a later statement about "peasant"
economics, Firth explains that he extended the term to "other [non-agricultural]
'countrymen' also, who share the social life and values of the cultivators ... "
because "they are part of the same social system" (1964 : 18). Thus, Firth
essentially abandoned his intention to build an analytic category on the basis of
specific criteria, and instead absorbed into his category generalizations from the
prevailing interest in the life and values of the "folk". At the same time, his

unconventional extension of the term "peasant" to non-agriculturalists limited his influence on other students of peasantry.

Kroeber (1948) is usually credited with setting forth "peasantry" as a concept for anthropology. The much quoted reference to peasants as "part-societies with part-cultures" appears in a section of his massive text entitled "Rural and Urban—Folk and Sophisticate Facets" (1948 : 280-86). The peasantry are introduced in explication of the "folk-sophisticate polarity"; peasantry occupy an intermediate place in it. Thus, Kroeber's view of peasantry did not go beyond that of most other students of the time.

It was only in the mid-1950s that the "peasant" was established as an analytic category and a subject-matter in its own right. In his *Primitive World and Its Transformations (1953)*, Redfield discussed "the peasant . . . as a human type". (Still, this appears in a chapter called "Later Histories of the Folk Societies", in which he continues to talk of "the folk society" and even "the folk man" [1953 : 29, 39, and *passim*.].) Redfield's 1954 lecture at the University of Chicago on "The Peasant's View of the Good Life" stimulated the philosopher F.G. Friedmann to organize a continuing symposium-by-correspondence entitled "The Peasant : A Symposium Concerning the Peasant Way and View Life", which began with an exchange of letters among nine scholars. In 1956 Redfield published this lecture along with three others as *Peasant Society and Culture,* which became a text for the anthropology of peasantry. In 1955 Eric R. Wolf published in the *American Anthropologist* the article "Types of Latin American Peasantry : A Preliminary Discussion", which began with a section on "The Peasant Type" that developed a definition of "peasant" on the basis of three distinctions. From this time on, references to the "folk" diminished and were replaced by "peasant", and discussions generally began with the problem of definition and with attention to the implications of different definitions.

This time also saw the beginning of a geometric growth in studies of peasants by anthropologists. Fostered by Western political interests in the rural inhabitants of the Third World and the corresponding availability of research funds, and with the impetus of modernization and development theory, the anthropologists were soon joined by a variety of other disciplines. Theoretical as well as linguistic boundaries, however, tended to limit interdisciplinary communication among students of peasantry. It was only with the late 1960s that both linguistic and disciplinary boundaries in peasant studies effectively broke down, the result both of increased publication of translations and of the emergence of common theoretical ground among Marxist scholars and others emphasizing political-economic and historical aspects of peasantry. While it can be argued that there is still a distinctly anthropological approach to the study of peasants, the "anthropology of peasantry" has given way to a more inclusive "peasant studies".

REDFIELD

Although Robert Redfield is the ancestral figure in the anthropological study of peasants, he did not use the concept until it was common parlance in the 1950s. He referred to both Tepoztlan and Chan Kom as "peasant villages", but his key term was "folk" — "folk life" in the book on Tepoztlan and "folk culture" (or "the basic folk culture") in the works on Chan Kom. Initially, his reference to "folk" was as casual as his use of "peasant". As he explains after the Lewis restudy of Tepoztlan was published, he did not have a concept of folk culture or folk-urban continuum in mind when he described Tepoztlan; this conception, he says, was developed several years later (1955 : 147).

> . . . I had at most in mind the simple thought that Tepoztlan was a kind of
> community intermediate between primitive tribal group and town or city,
> and that changes were occurring in Tepoztlan which moved it along a road
> of transition from one to the other.
>
> I think it is simply true that without benefit of any well-considered
> scheme of theoretical idea at all, I looked at certain aspects of Tepoztecan
> life because they both interested me and pleased me . . . In writing my book
> I emphasized these things because they came to my particular interest and
> taste . . . I was saying, "Look! Here is an aspect of peasant life you people up
> there may not be thinking about . . . ." (1955 : 135).

The first monograph on Chan Kom has a brief opening discussion of "gradients of civilization in Yucatan" (Redfield and Villa Rojas 1934: 1-2) which foreshadows the folk-urban continuum. The idea is fully developed in *The Folk Culture of Yucatan* (1941). However, Redfield had already made the "folk" concept explicit, as indicated by comments that he presented to a seminar in 1934:

> . . . Whether an element of rural Mexican custom is Indian in historical
> orgin or is Spanish . . . is never as important as is the quality of the mode of
> life and attendant behavior of the villages who live under such customs . . .
> [Indian and Spanish elements of culture combine in these villages] to form
> a round of life, a pattern for living that is in certain respects like all the
> patterns for living cut out by the cultures of nonliterate peoples
> everywhere, and that is in these respects different from the modes of life to
> be found in cities everywhere, especially in our modern Western cities. To
> include under one term peasant and tribal native . . . they and their mode of
> life may be denoted "folk" . . . The essential contrast is then, between folk
> and city, between folkways and city ways (1962 : 176).

Redfield's formal statement on "the folk society and culture" as a comparative type, apart from any specific cultural setting, appeared first in 1940 — appropriately enough, in a volume edited by Louis Wirth (Redfield 1940). Publication of "The Folk Society" in the *American Journal of Sociology* in 1947 then spawned a large literature on folk-urban and rural-urban types and continua both in anthropology and in sociology.

Later scholars would find a shift in terminology from "folk" to "peasant" an easy step to take; for instance, Foster commented in 1967 that when he had talked about "folk" in his 1953 article "What is Folk Culture?", in fact he was talking about "peasants" (1967 : 4). However, the term "folk" addressed a specific set of interests, which are not identical to the range of interests encompassed by "peasant" studies. Redfield's corpus of writing reveals consistent themes: the recurrent references to "life in" a place, "the way of life", and "the good life"; the stress on values, meanings, and understandings; and the view of social relations primarily as a vehicle of communication of ideas. When he devotes himself specifically to social dimensions, he reveals an evaluative framework. There is no doubt about his preferences as between "the folk society" and "urbanism as a way of life", and the social polarities in the folk-urban continuum carry implicit evaluations; clearly, organization is more valued than disorganization, sacred ways more than secular ways, group relationships more than individualized ones. The central interest of Redfield's work, I submit, was in the quality of life and the quality of human relations, as these are shaped in communities of different kinds and in different phases of the human career.

This interest marks Redfield's fully developed work on "peasants" as well as his early thoughts on the "folk". In his 1956 book, he adopts the term "peasant" for "folk", and accepts Wolf's criteria of agricultural producers who control their land. Even so, Redfield's definition retains his major concerns: peasants cultivate their land "as part of a traditional way of life" and "look to or are influenced by gentry . . . whose way of life is like theirs but in a more civilized form" (1956a : 19-20). Thus, the notions of "tradition", "way of life", and peasant-elite relationships seen in terms of ideational influence remain central.

Redfield's position is based on his general approach to the concept of culture. There are only a few explicit definitions of culture in his writings, but they are quite consistent over a period of many years. In 1940 and 1941 he refers to "an organization of conventional understandings . . . persisting through tradition" (cited by Kroeber and Kluckhohn 1952 : 61). In 1956 Redfield speaks of culture as "the body of conventional meanings made known to us through acts and artifacts". In the same piece, he defines "a society" as "people with common ends getting along with one another", and goes on to talk about "a society as people sharing convictions about the good life", "a plan of life", and "people feeling solidarity with one another" (1956b: 345-48). It is noteworthy that he moves back and forth between "society" and "culture" with little change of focus, as is the case in his use of "folk society" and "folk culture". When definition is required, "society" is reserved for groups of people and "culture" for meanings, but there is a one-to-one relationship between the two concepts. The connection between society and culture is made as follows in this essay :

> Society operates because its members have around them a universe which to them makes sense. Moreover, this plan is not merely a pattern without moral meaning: it is a plan for right conduct, an organization of conceptions as to the good, the true, and indeed the beautiful. The body of conventional meanings . . . is . . . called "the culture" of a community . . . (1956b : 347).

He then goes on to talk about how, over the course of human history, the "wholeness" of cultural meanings that characterizes primitive societies gives way. In modern urban society "the sense of the meaning of life tends to be lost; men experience uncertainty, insecurity, and confusion". At the same time, "the basis for the operation of society" tends to shift "from tradition to deliberate social invention and thoughtful choice" (1956b : 347-48).

In speaking specifically of peasantry, Redfield sets society and culture side by side (1956a). Culture (which here includes great and little traditions, values, and world-views) is the plan and meanings that hold society together. Society (social relations, particularly peasant-elite relations) gives culture a vehicle and means of communication, a "social organization of tradition". This view of the relationship of society and culture is compatible with a variety of theoretical positions: those that emphasize values or world-view and those primarily interested in social relations; those that take into account many "aspects" of society or culture without commitment to any theory as to how they are related, and those that see society or culture as systemic or integral.

Redfield's position, at once holistic in the range of social and cultural phenomena that may be brought into an analysis and non-committal on the question of causal relations, is congenial with several of the theoretical approaches that have dominated American anthropology in different phases of its history. One such approach I would identify as an "additive" conception of culture. This is basically a legacy of Tylor's highly influential definition, although as Stocking (1966) has shown, the Boasian period brought considerable change in the meaning of the culture concept. The term "additive" is meant to include various definitions of culture that encompass a large number of aspects or components but take no position on priorities among them and do not emphasize their interconnections. For instance, Kroeber's textbook definition reads: "Now the mass of learned and transmitted motor reactions, habits, techniques, ideas, and values — and the behavior they induce — is what constitutes *culture*"(1948: 8). The compromise statement that Kroeber and Kluckhohn reach after their exhaustive survey of all extant uses of the culture concept is similarly all-inclusive, covering patterns "of and for" behaviour, symbols, and artifacts. Although "the essential core of culture" is assigned to "ideas and their attached values", they take a clear stand against causal priorities, since cultural systems are both "products of action" and "conditioning elements of further action" (Kroeber and Kluckhohn 1952 : 181).

A second approach to the concept of culture I would call "integrative". This approach is the legacy of functionalism. While the historical particularists repeated Tylor's phrase "that complex whole", their emphasis lay in what the whole included — especially belief, art, custom, and certain other of the "capabilities and habits acquired by man as a member of society" — rather than in the nature of the whole. In contrast, Malinowski's definition begins with "the integral whole" and the integration of the whole is his central concern (1944).

A major part of contemporary American anthropology can be viewed as the combination of both these legacies. The most common approach to culture today is eclectic. The "holism" beloved of anthropologists is retained in the sense that it is assumed that all "aspects" of culture (the material, the social, the ideational, etc.) should somehow be taken account of and regarded as potentially of interest, although particular problems will dictate the emphases of any endeavour. The "whole" is taken to be integrated in some degree, but not everything is expected to "fit". To the extet that systemic interconnections can be detected they will be drawn; to the extent that some cultural phenomena cannot be placed in neat relation to others, these will simply be described, that is, accounted for additively.

The "integrative" approach of functionalism also led in another direction in American anthropology, producing a genealogy from social anthropology (a British development but imported into the United States under the auspices of the University of Chicago) to symbolic anthropology. Both kinds of anthropology represent a separation between culture-as-ideas and social structure; they differ mainly in the choice of one or the other as the primary focus of interest. In both, society and culture are analytically separated as a first step, but then placed back in relation to each other. Indeed, the basic concept of social status in British anthropology contains a "moral" dimension, and social anthropologists regularly draw on values and ideas in describing social relations. Similarly, symbolic anthropology attempts to account for social life by cultural analysis. The definitive statement of the separation and mutuality of culture and society (or social system), which in effect established the programme of symbolic anthropology in the United States, was the announcement of the jurisdictional treaty between Kroeber and Talcott Parsons (Kroeber and Parsons 1958). As

befits a peaceful settlement, neither side was granted priority. Thus, the various
approaches that separate but juxtapose society and culture tend to deny (or at
least do not insist upon) a causal order between the two and see them either as
functionally related or as two sides of a coin.

Redfield's strategic role in the anthropology of peasantry was due to historical
precedence but, even more, to the fact that he filled a theoretical vacuum. The
ideas in *The Folk Culture of Yucatan* were a point of departure for some and a
point of contention for others, but in both ways they dominated discussions of
peasantry for two decades. However, long after he joined his critics in laying the
folk-urban continuum to rest, his influence has continued. I have suggested that
this is partly due to the fact that his general views of peasant society and culture
are consistent with the approaches that have dominated American anthropology
and, indeed, the social sciences in general. In addition, I think his influence rests
in his use of certain key notions: "community", "tradition", and "way of life".
These terms have been so widely adopted — and have seemed so self-evident and
persuasive — that they now make up a basic vocabulary of the peasant literature,
both in anthropology and outside of it. As Redfield used these terms, they
entailed theoretical positions that are not at all self-evident. However, the
inherent ambiguity contained in each of these terms has invited other scholars
(even those who challenge Redfield's explicit theories) to adopt his language. In the
process, many of Redfield's underlying theoretical assumptions have persisted.

The term "community" is generally used in the peasant literature
interchangeably with "village" or other units of settlement. However, Redfield's
usage was not casual; it formed part of a complex theory of "a human whole"
(note the subtitle of Redfield 1955). Anthony Leeds has aptly pointed out the
difference between "community" as a settlement and "community" as a
specification of the kinds of relationships that are assumed to exist; because the
latter meaning is so enmeshed in the term, he uses only the neutral word
"locality" (Leeds 1973). Most uses of "community" merge the two meanings and
absorb Redfield's assumptions about the *nature* of small communities.

The term "tradition" for Redfield referred to civilizational content, that is,
culture in the sense of *meaning*. However, "tradition" has a broader significance
in American anthropology. It has long been equated with the idea of social
heritage in the context of one of the basic arguments to which the culture concept
was addressed — genetic versus non-genetic transmission of behaviour patterns.
This notion of culture as tradition is so fundamental to anthropological thinking
that other assumptions contained in the term are rarely examined: the
assumptions that patterns will be perpetuated unless something acts to disrupt
them, that it is the interruption rather than the "traditional" which needs
explanation, and that culture is fuelled by an internal dynamic rather than
historically situated. Those who follow Redfield in stressing "tradition" among

peasants (and the elite who influence them) tend to see change, but not tradition, as problematic, as well as to adopt Redfield's own meaning in using the term — culture content and patterns of ideas.

Finally, the phrase "way of life" enjoys the same centrality to the culture concept, and the same immunity from examination, as does "tradition". In American anthropology, the holistic property of culture is often expressed as a "way of life". This emphasizes the inclusion of subsistence modes as well as artistic achievement, daily routines as well as elaborate ideas — in other words, the anthropologist's homely and inclusive "culture" as distinct from the lay meaning of the word. Redfield's frequent reference to "way of life" thus seems straightforward. In fact, his concern was with *way* of life: in using the phrase he was placing theoretical emphasis on conventional understandings, world-views, styles of living, and, above all, quality of life.

Thus, Redfield's definition of peasantry as entailing "a traditional way of life" is not merely a summary description. Similarly, his interchangeable use of "peasant society", "peasant village", and "peasant community"(e.g. 1956a : 24) is not simply imprecision of terminology. These are loaded theoretical positions.

STEWARD

Julian Steward did not become directly involved in studies of peasants until after World War II, and this was not the central concern of his career. Nevertheless, the theoretical orientations he developed out of the study of primitive societies and out of his interests in archaeology and culture history were to exert a major influence on the field of peasant studies. Above all, Steward offered a concept of culture that contrasted with the prevailing views in anthropology, and one that outlined a different approach to peasants. The contrast lay in his belief in an order of priority among the components of culture, which rested upon his view of cultural causality. He never developed a particular, elaborated theory, and his work reveals a good deal of inconsistency, but the major themes that mark his contribution to peasant studies are present throughout his writings.

Steward saw an essential distinction among the aspects, traits, or institutions of culture, which he referred to as *core* and *secondary, primary* and *secondary,* or variations of these terms. He assigned causal priority to those features "most closely related to subsistence activities and economic arrangements" or "most closely involved in the utilization of environment in culturally prescribed ways" (1955 : 37). What distinguishes Steward from most of his contemporaries, as early as the 1930s, is not the particular way he defined the culture core (which shifted a good deal), but the fact that he differentiated within the cultural whole and specifically rejected attempts "to give equal weight to all features of culture" (1949 : 7).

Curiously, Kroeber and Kluckhohn do not treat the question of causal priority as a significant issue in their review of concepts of culture. They assign Steward's definition of culture to their category D-II, "Psychological Definitions, Emphasis on Learning" (1952 : 58), since he had referred to "learned modes of behavior which are socially transmitted . . . and which may be diffused"; they remark about this quote that his "emphasis on diffusion" is "characteristically anthropological" (1952 : 59). (In fact, Steward's argument — made repeatedly — was that only secondary features are subject to diffusion, and moreover, that "diffusion" actually explains nothing but must itself be accounted for.) Kroeber and Kluckhohn ignore his specification that *behaviour* is at issue (compare their own conclusion that "the essential core of culture" consists of ideas and values). Moreover, elsewhere they repeat one of Steward's clearest statements of his position on the priorities among cultural components — a statement that appears in italics — yet they neglect his major point. His passage (from Steward 1949 : 6) reads:

> If the more important institutions of culture can be isolated from their unique setting so as to be typed, classified, and related to recurring antecedents of functional correlates, it follows that it is possible to consider the institutions in question as the basic or constant ones, whereas the features that lend uniqueness are the secondary or variable ones.

The message that Kroeber and Kluckhohn take from this is that there are few if any absolute uniformities in culture content unless one states the content in extremely general form (1952 : 164).

Steward's view of causal priorities within culture was based upon a "concept and method" of cultural ecology. Robert Murphy has suggested that Steward's ecology had little to do with environment as such, but that its central interest was in the social organization and social implications of work. The cultural-ecological nexus is the trinity of labour, resources, and technology, with labour being the most important element. Given an environment with certain resources and given a certain technology, the implementation of this technology upon these resources involves limitations in the cycling and organization of labour, that in turn impinge upon the social system (Murphy 1981). For instance, in an early paper attempting to formulate "something akin to cultural law" to explain the occurrence of band types (1936 : 331), Steward discussed environment only in the most general terms. Rather, he looked at the interrelations among resources, population density, the organizational requirements of food-getting with a given technology, the size and composition of groups that can exist in different territories — in short, the social consequences of different hunting and gathering economies.

Steward did not arrive at "laws" of social types, but what is important is where he looked for explanation: in the "organic connection of the components of a culture and their environmental basis" (1936 : 344). In a later piece, however, in which he attempted to formulate stages in the development of civilization, he de-emphasized the environmental basis as such. He stressed instead "basic socio-economic institutions", which are "adapted to the requirements of subsistence patterns established in particular environments" (1949 : 24).

This conception of culture is significant not only for its position on causal priorities but also for its emphasis on the organization of social activity rather than in the normative sense of culture — above all, in the way people interdigitate their efforts in search of a livelihood (Murphy 1981). Steward's interest in subsistence activity, born out of his work with the Basin Plateau Shoshone, became in his paper on early civilizations a broader concept of "basic" institutions, taking in social, political, economic, and religious patterns; in his work on modern peasants, it became "productive complexes". Throughout, however, his point of departure remained social action, and specifically action geared to subsistence requirements. Although Steward himself argued that cultural-ecological considerations become less important with the evolution of culture, his influence on the anthropology of complex societies lay precisely in his calling attention to the definitive role of productive arrangements.

The link between Steward's work with primitive societies and his interest in modern communities is probably in his role within the Bureau of American Ethnology of the Smithsonian Institution, where he was employed for over a decade (1935-46). In 1943 he helped create the Institute of Social Anthropology, which sponsored a series of community studies in Mexico and Peru. As Steward stated it at the time, the research interest of the Institute centred upon "broad, social science studies of selected communities which represent samples of the basic populations of the country in question". While these studies would principally concern peoples who are partly or wholly Indian, biologically and culturally, they would follow "certain modern trends in the analysis of contemporary cultures, which they seek to understand in terms of the environmental, historical, and other processes that have produced their modern content and organization . . . " (1944 : ix). A major effort of the Institute was the study of a particular region, the Tarascan area of Mexico, which consisted of an interdisciplinary programme as well as four community studies; Steward later referred to these, critically, as "standard ethnographic descriptions" of the "variant types of local culture", with each community treated "as if it were a locally self-contained and integrated whole" (1950 : 60-62). Although Steward's role in the project was only an indirect and administrative one, the Tarascan experience was for him a school for the study of regions in complex societies and a background for his subsequent Puerto Rico study. (See his review and critique of the Tarascan programme in 1950 : 57-66).

Turning his attention to complex societies, Steward rejected monolithic views of modern nations and proposed instead a more differentiated concept of levels of socio-cultural integration (1951). He was critical both of acculturation studies that saw a uniform tribal culture confronting a uniform national culture, and of national-character studies that assumed shared behaviour and common characteristics among the members of the nation. He argued that "cultural and social interaction take place on different levels" and he identified national, community, and family levels (saying that there are other levels as well that are significant for certain problems). In doing so, he effectively placed community studies in a context that excluded their being regarded as microcosms of a nation, and called for separate treatment of the national level. At the same time, he devised a general framework for studying "a national sociocultural system". He saw such a system as composed of different kinds of interdependent parts, which need to be studied separately and then related to each other: (1) localized socio-cultural subgroups or communities; (2) "horizontal" subgroups, i.e. social, occupational, ethnic, and other special groups that cut across communities and regions, and when arranged in hierarchical relationships are known as "classes"; and (3) formal national institutions, which constitute the binding and regulating forces of the whole (1950 : 140-41; 1955 : 64-67). While this framework appears to us today as mechanistic, it represents a significant advance over the Redfieldian approach to Yucatan, in which the unit of analysis was whole communities and in which diversity within the region was accounted for by linear differences along a bipolar continuum.

Steward devised this framework while designing a project to study the social anthropology of the island of Puerto Rico, which he hoped to understand "as an entity with respect to both its internal structure and function and its external relations" (1950 : 127). Because it was so complex an entity, his strategy was to record the major variations in community and regional subcultures, which then had to be seen as parts of an insular whole subject to influence by the various national institutions, "and the Island as a whole had to be seen in relationship to other areas, especially the United States" (1950 : 129). (Note that Steward was specifically concerned to relate community studies to the "larger whole", and that he was well aware of the significance of Puerto Rico's dependency status, two points on which the project is often criticized today.) Because Puerto Rico was overwhelmingly agrarian and rural, the chief task was to study the major regional variants of the farm population. Then, in an effort to understand "the Island as a whole rather than merely as a composite of communities and farm regions", a special study was made of the culture and the social, political, and economic role of the upper class of San Juan, on the grounds that it was a focus of much power within the island.

The hypothesis that guided the selection of communities and the analysis as a whole clearly was derived from Steward's earlier thinking:

> . . . Principally it was assumed that, while the broad patterns of Puerto Rican life were determined by the Hispanic heritage and by the colonial position and subtropical nature of the Island, regional cultural differences resulted from adaptations of the productive complexes, that is, land use, to different local environments . . . The very great local differences could be explained only by cultural-ecological processes — the processes by which production, social patterns, and related modes of life are selectively borrowed from outside sources and adapted to local needs in each natural region. More concretely, it was suspected that . . . the way of life in the coffee area, the tobacco and mixed crops area, and in the several sugar areas would differ profoundly . . . (1955 : 133-34).

The "productive processes" — land use, land ownership, organization of production, and related phenomena — were taken as primary; variations in "the way of life" were assumed to be corollaries of these processes (1955 : 134).

Four communities were chosen as localized (vertical) socio-cultural segments of the society. Steward recognized that most Puerto Rican communities had class divisions and that there were horizontal segments other than class that cross-cut regions. However, he left it to a "final synthesis of the insular whole" to account for these, because he thought that in Puerto Rico, "sociocultural segments had greater local than horizontal integration". He also intended to systematically study the national institutions, but the interdisciplinary effort that he hoped for did not materialize; nevertheless, the plan for the community studies specifically included "local aspects" of these formal institutions. The study of the San Juan upper class developed as a rather limited focus on "the prominent families" and their Americanization. This effort may have suffered from the weight of Steward's initial expectation that this subculture would provide a key to the integration of the national system. While the Puerto Rico project never achieved the "synthesis of the insular whole" that Steward hoped for, it realized his theoretical framework in a more fundamental way. It used the community-study approach not merely to produce a series of well-rounded descriptions, but also to begin to account for social and cultural patterns in terms of productive arrangements (Steward *et al.* 1956).[2]

AFTER PUERTO RICO

While the basic conception of the Puerto Rico project was Steward's, the field work was carried out, analysed, and synthesized by the participants, separately and in communication with one another. Steward provided the initial theoretical orientation, but his students carried it forward in ways that Steward himself neither anticipated nor perhaps even fully understood.[3]

Steward's view of the regional subcultures as consequences of different "productive complexes", which he had conceived as mainly in terms of land use and the productive requirements of different crops, proved insufficient. Correspondence between Sidney Mintz and Eric Wolf during the field work focused instead on what we would now call political economy: the economic and social situation of those who produce and those who live off of the crops, and the relationship of the local productive arrangements to the larger processes of colonialism and capitalist development that shaped them. For them, the significant contrasts among the regions were not in the character of the crops but in productive relations, and in the interplay among aspects of the labour force, resources, capital, and other factors within particular political-historical contexts. Thus, in an early communication, Mintz expressed concern that he could not characterize his area in terms of Steward's "productive complexes"; the basic features of the area consisted not only in the dominant crops but also in the facts of "big-scale production, American capital, large landholdings, central-administered land, high mill grinding capacity, etc.". A little later, he drew the distinction between sugar and coffee, "or any *plantation* crop versus any *non-plantation* crop within the colonial system", by their respective roles within colonial production. Exchanges between Mintz and Wolf on the similarities and contrasts between haciendas and plantations, which continued for several years, clearly placed these forms in the context of European capitalist development and world market competition. For instance, it specifically rejected views of the hacienda as merely a prestige item or — as Steward had viewed the coffee hacienda — as a "survival of old Hispanic patterns" (1950 : 138).

Steward had presented the regional subcultures as a synchronic typology. While he argued the importance of research on cultural history, he referred to this history only in the general terms of "the Hispanic heritage" and "Puerto Rico's changing colonial status", and his main point was that history could only explain commonalities of the island as a whole and not regional differences (1950: 133-134). In a synthesis drawn up by Wolf in 1951, however, the regional subcultures were treated as the specific outcomes of three historical stages, which were drawn with reference to the needs and policies of the colonial powers and the development of Puerto Rico as "a capitalist, agrarian and dependent country". Wolf saw the synchronic typology to be, in fact, the result of historical developments interacting with specific local environments.

While the treatment of history by Wolf, Mintz, and others on the project differed considerably from Steward's, it nevertheless remained close to his basic theoretical orientation. When the chapter on Puerto Rican culture history was challenged by a historian for its neglect of humanitarian sentiments and the influences of European liberalism, Wolf and Mintz reaffirmed the team's conviction that the material motive should be stressed over the ideological motive. When criticized for their emphasis on political unrest, they responded that the historian's "picture of peace and quiet", in which "everything is gained by reform and legislation", ignored the realities of conflict.

During his six years at Columbia (1946-52), Steward provided a focus for the materialist interest of a large number of students, many of them returned veterans and many of them with radical political commitments. However, the influence of these students on each other was at least as important as Steward's own influence on them. Several of Steward's students formed a group in which they discussed their developing research. Calling themselves the Mundial Upheaval Society, the initial group in 1950 included Mintz, Wolf, Stanley Diamond, Morton Fried, Elman Service, and John Murra (whose formal graduate education had been at Chicago, but who was in Steward's orbit through his work on the Puerto Rico project). The topics that came under discussion in the group were those for which these anthropologists are now best known. Their interests in such problems as comparative state development, nation formation, and the relationship of kinship structures to political-economic and historical contexts were compatible with Steward's approach but were by no means direct outgrowths of it.

In their subsequent work on peasantry, Mintz focused on other islands of the Caribbean and on plantation systems in general, while Wolf turned to field work in Mexico and Europe and to comparative peasant studies. Wolf's writings trace an evolution of his materialist perspective. In the "Types of Latin American Peasantry" article (1955), his definition of peasants used economic criteria: agricultural production (differing with Firth's inclusion of non-cultivators in "peasant economy"), control of land, and production for subsistence rather than reinvestment. Although Wolf opted for an emphasis on "structural relations" rather than culture content, he defined his subject-matter as "peasant part-cultures" and repeatedly referred to "the culture" of "peasant segments". The concept of culture he was using was holistic, but one that saw a clear order of priorities among the components of culture. He justified this order on empirical rather than theoretical grounds.

> In selecting out certain structural features rather than others to provide a starting point for the formulation of types we may proceed wholly on an empirical basis. The selection of primarily economic criteria would be congruent with the present interest in typologies based on economic and · sociopolitical features alone. The functional implications of these features are more clearly understood at present than those of

other features of culture, and their dominant role in the development of the organizational framework has been noted empirically in many studies of particular cultures (1955 : 454).

If peasants are segments of a larger whole, then a basic issue is how they are integrated into it. Wolf's answer was that "peasants function primarily within a local setting . . . the peasantry is integrated into the sociocultural whole primarily through the structure of the community . . . In other words, a typology of peasants must include a typology of the kinds of communities in which they live" (1955 : 455).

Thus Wolf, in common with other students of peasantry of the time, still retained an interest in communities and a conviction that the community was the key to understanding how peasants are integrated with the outside world. However, Wolf's approach to communities, unlike Redfield's, saw them as outcomes of larger political-historical processes. The "closed corporate community" was not a "way of life" but a creation of processes of colonialization—processes repeated in the Spanish conquest of America, the Dutch conquest of Java, the internal colonization of pre-1861 Russia, and in other cases (1955, 1957). The community was still a reference point in a 1956 paper, but the direction of interest there was outward. Communities were viewed as "the local termini of a web of group relations which extend through intermediate levels from the level of the community to that of the nation. In the community itself, these relationships may be wholly tangential to each other" (1956 : 1065). In Wolf's later work, the interest in communities gave way increasingly to a concern with relations between peasants and their larger matrix, between local settings and national-level (or wider) phenomena (1959, 1966b).

In his 1966 book, Wolf outlined a concept of peasants that differed from his 1955 definition. The emphasis now was on the role of the state—a "crystallization of executive power" that serves to maintain asymmetrical power relations in the social order and to guarantee claims over the cultivators'"fund of rent" (1966a : 10-11). On the one hand, this concept was a rejection of "the city" as the key to understanding peasantry, which still dominated the literature, a heritage from Redfield and those of his critics who shared his premises (e.g. Foster 1953; Sjoberg 1955). On the other, Wolf's 1966 concept made *power* central; economic (and ecological) processes were still very much at issue, but they were seen simultaneously as relations of power.

The move towards an explicit concern with power marks the progression of Mintz's work as well. His continuing interest in plantation systems and their historical aftermaths is phrased in his most recent work as a concern with "sugar and power". It should be noted that this dimension is lacking in Steward no less than in Redfield. Neither of these two seminal figures pursued the political implications of his theories, or went very far in studying the modern world. However, it may be suggested that Redfield's approach led in the direction of modernization theory, while Steward's led towards interests in power, political economy, and Marxist theory.

That these divergent lines within the anthropology of peasantry correspond to different uses of the culture concept is pointed up by some comments made by Mintz in a paper on the problem of defining peasants (1973). Mintz argues for developing typologies of rural socio-economic groupings rather than abstract definitions of "the peasantry". In the process he takes issue with certain conceptions of culture, and thus exposes the approach to culture that he and Wolf, whom he cites, follow (1973 : 96-97). First, he rejects cognitive views of culture and insists that "what men see is at least to some degree a function of their stakes within a structure of power, wealth, status and authority". Culture is behaviour as well as values; social position and social action have causal priority over the "way of perceiving". Second, he rejects assumptions of homogeneity in "culture", and specifically inquires into the diversity concealed by references to "peasant culture" or the "small community"—which implies a homogeneous group carrying a homogeneous body of conventional understandings (1973 : 97). Third, he criticizes notions of culture as "blind custom" and stresses instead the element of *manoeuvre,* i.e. the way in which individuals manipulate and use cultural forms rather than simply "carrying" them. Fourth, he attacks the idea of the "traditional", the assumption that culture is something "surviving" or "conserved" from the past. In contrast, his concern is with culture as *historically-derived* patterns of behaviour. While historicity does not exclude generalization, social and cultural patterns must be understood in the first instance as products of specific historical events and conditions. On each of these issues, there is clear contrast with Redfield's view of peasant culture, which emphasizes cognition, while rejecting priorities between social action and values; assumes an essential homogeneity of "common understandings"; stresses culture as the property of a group, allowing little latitude to individual manipulation; and focuses on the continuity of "tradition".

DEFINING PEASANTS

These two approaches have influenced the development of conceptions of peasantry in quite different ways. Redfield's approach has directed attention to a search for relationships among societal and ideational patterns that form part of coherent schemes of meaning, while Steward's has led to efforts to ground such patterns in productive systems and the relations of power within which they exist. This is not to say that these correspond to a discrete opposition among students of peasantry. Many have combined the approaches, sometimes in an explicit attempt to reach consensus definitions. Such efforts tend to obscure rather then to clarify the issues, for to average out the diversity among scholars is to eradicate significant differences in their theoretical positions. Rather, it is useful to embrace dissensus and to disentangle the threads of influence in contemporary peasant studies.

Because of its compatibility with the predominant concepts of culture and society both in the United States and in Britain, the Redfieldian approach has continued to be highly influential, even among scholars who emphasize the economic and political dimensions of peasantry. In particular, three elements deriving from Redfield are so common to definitions of peasants that they are rarely treated as issues in their own right. First, there is the assumption that peasants (or peasant societies) are characterized by certain "cultural" attributes, in the sense of attitudes, values, and other ideational elements. The key contributions by Foster (1953) and Marriott (1955) gave these attributes a central place. Similarly, Fallers (1961) argued explicitly for a "cultural" definition in questioning whether African cultivators should be called "peasants". For Fallers, "cultural semi-autonomy" was the critical feature of peasant society, that is, the presence of a differentiation into "high" (literary) and "folk" cultures, and corresponding attitudes of rustics and elites towards each other. More recently, the political scientist John Duncan Powell proposed a definition that he believed represented the points of agreement among all scholars of peasantry (specifically including Steward, Wolf, Wittfogel, and others not in the Redfield tradition). It read:

> A peasant society is composed of settled rural peoples, engaged for the most part in agricultural production, whose productive activities *and culturally distinct characteristics* are influenced, shaped, or determined to a significant extent by powerful outsiders. [1972 : 97; itàlics mine]

A second element of definitions reflecting Redfield's influence is the assumption that the study of peasants is the study of villages, i.e. that peasants inhabit particular kinds of *communities*. In much of the literature references to peasants are interchangeable with "villagers", "the local community", and so on. Thus, in the first reader published on peasant society, Foster introduced the concept of peasant with a "structural" definition; the "structural relationship" that was his "primary criterion for defining peasant society" was that between "the village" and "the city" (1967 : 5, 8, *passim.*). Reviewing various approaches to peasants, Foster repeatedly referred to "the village community", "the peasant community", and "village culture", but he never considered the use of such terms as an issue. Moreover, while he explicitly accepted Wolf's point about the *state* being the significant marker rather than the city, he continued to use "the city" throughout his discussion.

Finally, there is the assumption deriving from Redfield that peasants are "traditional", within a typological, ahistorical contrast between tradition and modernity. Gamst, for instance, placed peasant societies on a "continuum of modernization from a polar type of agricultural civilization to another polar type of industrial urban civilization" (1974 : 3).

These Redfieldian assumptions carry over into the definitions even of scholars who do not follow Redfield's approach. For instance, the sociologist Teodor Shanin compiled a reader that drew heavily on economc, political, and historical perspectives and paid relatively little attention to "culture" (a topic covered by four selections out of a total of twenty-eight). Shanin proposed a definition of peasantry with "four basic facets": the peasant family farm as the basic social unit; land husbandry as the main livelihood, providing most consumption needs; "specific traditional culture related to the way of life of small communities"; and the "underdog" position—domination by outsiders (1971 : 14-15). Like the notion that the basic organizational unit is the "family farm", the assumption that peasants live in "small communities" marked by a particular "way of life" and a "specific traditional culture" may derive from the fact that Shanin's own work has been with eastern European peasants. It is, however, the theoretical apparatus of the Redfield tradition, fully intact. Shanin exempted from his description only certain groups he considered to be "analytically marginal" (1971 : 15-16).

The direction pointed to by Steward would restrict definitions of peasantry to political-economic criteria. This is not an emphasis on "occupational" aspects of peasantry, a characterization first made by Geertz (1962) and repeated by others (Foster 1967; Powell 1972; van Schendel 1976). It is concerned not with the activity engaged in by people in order to earn their living, but with the organization of production and the nature of liens upon it. It is based on a theoretical commitment to the priority of certain aspects of culture, but this does not rule other aspects out of study. Unlike approaches that presuppose commonalities of world-view, settlement form, and quality of social relations among peasants—and thus take these as criteria for determining which cases are to be considered "peasant" and admitted into comparison—it makes the identification of such patterns the *object* of research, a matter of empirical determination. This tactic makes it possible to inquire into the diversity of attitudes and values, the different kinds of settlements, and the variable quality of social relations in them, under different conditions and different historical contingencies.

To illustrate this approach, for purposes of discussion, I would propose a definition that begins not with "peasants" but with peasant production: domestically organized agricultural production within state societies. No presumption is made in advance as to cultural attributes, forms of community, or social relations beyond those directly implied in this form of production. Focusing on production as a process rather than on *persons* allows one to deal with the very common situations in which peasant production is admixed with other activities in the same social setting, the same family, or the same individual, as well as those situations in which there is a shift from one kind of production to another within short time spans. "Domestically organized" means that production is geared to the resources, labour, and maintenance requirements of a domestic group. "Agricultural" is specified to point up the distinctive characteristics of the productive process entailed in cultivation, as compared with other kinds of activity. "Within state societies" refers to the existence of claims over the product, which are exercised by superordinate powers and are guaranteed by the state. One may then describe as "peasants" those persons who are substantially engaged in such production, and describe as "peasant communities" those places in which such production dominates. However, these derivative terms should be understood as deliberately imprecise, suggesting questions rather than answers. To proceed as if "the peasant" represents some basic or invariable type is to cut off inquiry precisely where it should begin.

NOTES

1. This paper was originally prepared for the Xth ICAES Post-Plenary Session. A slightly different version was published, under the title "The Peasant Concept in Anthropology", in the *Journal of Peasant Studies,* vol. 7, no. 1, October 1979. For help in clarifying the historical developments discussed in the paper, I am indebted to Conrad Arenberg, Sidney Mintz, Robert Murphy, and Eric Wolf.

2. The project participants included: Robert Manners, who worked in a mountain community of small farmers raising subsistence crops and tobacco; Sidney Mintz, who studied a rural-proletarian community in the corporate-owned sugar area; Elena Padilla Seda, who concentrated on a government-owned, profit-sharing sugar plantation; Eric Wolf, who worked in a coffee-producing community in an area of haciendas and small peasant holdings; Raymond Scheele, who did the study of the San Juan upper-class families; John Murra, who served as field director during the initial months of the field work; and several field assistants from the University of Puerto Rico (see Steward *et al.* 1956 : vii).

3. The interpretation of Steward's role in the Puerto Rico study offered in this paper is based on unpublished materials provided by Wolf and Mintz, including correspondence among some of the project participants during and after the field work period, drafts of theoretical statements, and notes on meetings of the team. This interpretation supports, in general, William Roseberry's recent analysis of *The People of Puerto Rico,* in which he argues that each of the participants departed from Steward's cultural ecology and moved instead toward a "cultural historical" approach (Roseberry 1978).

REFERENCES CITED

Arensberg, Conrad M. (1937): The Irish Countrymen : An Anthropological Study. New York: Macmillan.

Arensberg, Conrad M. and Solon T. Kimball (1940) : Family and Community in Ireland. Cambridge: Harvard University Press.

Beals, Ralph L. (1946) : Cheran : A Sierra Tarascan Village. Smithsonian Institution, Institute of Social Anthropology Publication No. 2.

Chapman, Charlotte Gower (1971) : Milocca : A Sicilian Village. Cambridge, MA: Schenkman.

Embree, John P. (1939) : Suye Mura, A Japanese Village. Chicago : University of Chicago Press.

Fallers, L.A. (1961) : Are African Cultivators To Be Called "Peasants"? Current Anthropology 2 : 108-110.

Fei, Hsiao-Tung (1939) : Peasant Life in China. London : Kegan Paul, Trench, Trubner and Co.

        (1946) : Peasantry and Gentry : An Interpretation of Chinese Social Structure and Its Changes. American Journal of Sociology 52 : 1-17.

Firth, Raymond (1946) : Malay Fishermen : Their Peasant Economy. London : Kegan Paul, Trench, Trubner and Co.

        (1951) : Elements of Social Organization. London : Watts & Co.

        (1964) : Capital, Saving and Credit in Peasant Societies : A Viewpoint from Economic Anthropology. *In* Capital, Saving and Credit in Peasant Societies. Raymond Firth and B.S. Yamey, eds. Pp. 15-34. Chicago : Aldine.

Foster, George M. (1948) : Empire's Children : The People of Tzintzuntzan. Smithsonian Institution, Insitute of Social Anthropology Publication No. 6.

        (1953) : What Is Folk Culture? American Anthropologist 55 : 159-173.

        (1967) : Introduction : What Is a Peasant? *In* Peasant Society: A Reader. Jack M. Potter, May N. Diaz, and George M. Foster, eds. Pp. 2-14. Boston : Little, Brown.

Gamst, Frederick (1974) : Peasants in Complex Society. New York: Holt, Rinehart and Winston.

Geertz, Clifford (1962) : Studies in Peasant Life : Community and Society. *In* Biennial Review of Anthropology 1961. Bernard Siegel, ed. Pp. 1-41. Stanford: Stanford University Press.

Kroeber, A.L. (1948) : Anthropology. New York: Harcourt, Brace.

Kroeber, A.L. and Clyde Kluckhohn (1952) : Culture : A Critical Review of Concepts and Definitions. Papers of the Peabody Museum of American Archaeology and Ethnology, Harvard University, Vol. 47, No. 1.

Kroeber, A.L. and Talcott Parsons (1958) : The Concepts of Culture and of Social System. American Sociological Review 23 : 582-583.

Leeds, Anthony (1973) : Locality Power in Relation to Supralocal Power Institutions. In Urban Anthropology. Aidan Southall, ed. Pp. 15-41.

Lewis, Oscar (1951) : Life in a Mexican Village : Tepoztlan Restudied. Urbana : University of Illinois Press.

Lynd, Robert S. and Helen M. (1929) : Middletown : A Study in Contemporary American Culture. New York : Harcourt, Brace.

        (1937) : Middletown in Transition : A Study in Cultural Conflicts. New York : Harcourt, Brace.

Malinowski, B. (1944) : A Scientific Theory of Culture. Chapel Hill : University of North Carolina Press.

Marriott, McKim (1955) : Little Communities in an Indigenous Civilization. *In* Village India. McKim Marriott, ed. Pp. 171-222. American Anthropological Association Memoir 83.

Miner, Horace (1939) : St. Denis : A French-Canadian Parish. Chicago : University of Chicago Press.

Mintz, Sidney (1973) : A Note on the Definition of Peasantries. Journal of Peasant Studies 1 : 91-106.

Murphy, Robert F. (1981) : Julian Steward. *In* Totems and Teachers : Perspectives on the History of Anthropology. Sydel Silverman, ed. Pp. 171-204. New York: Columbia University Press.

Powdermaker, Hortense (1939) : After Freedom : A Cultural Study in the Deep South. New York: Viking Press.

Powell, John Duncan (1972) : On Defining Peasants and Peasant Society. Peasant Studies Newsletter 1 : 94-99.

Redfield, Robert (1930) : Tepoztlan, A Mexican Village. Chicago : University of Chicago Press.

(1940) : The Folk Society and Culture. *In* Eleven Twenty-Six. Louis Wirth, ed. Pp. 39-50. Chicago : University of Chicago Press.

(1941) : The Folk Culture of Yucatan. Chicago : University of Chicago Press.

(1947) : The Folk Society. American Journal of Sociology 52 : 292-308.

(1950) : A Village That Chose Progress, Chan Kom Revisited. Chicago : University of Chicago Press.

(1953) : The Primitive World and its Transformations. Ithaca, NY : Cornell University Press.

(1955) : The Little Community : Viewpoints for the Study of a Human Whole. Chicago : University of Chicago Press.

(1956a) : Peasant Society and Culture. Chicago : University of Chicago Press.

(1956b) : How Human Society Operates. *In* Man, Culture, and Society. Harry L. Shapiro, ed. Pp. 345-368. New York: Oxford University Press.

(1962) : Folkways and City Ways. *In* Human Nature and the Study of Society : The Papers of Robert Redfield. Vol. I. Margaret Park Redfield, ed. Pp. 172-182. Chicago : University of Chicago Press. (Originally published 1935).

Redfield, Robert and Alfonso Villa Rojas (1934) : Chan Kom, A Maya Village. Washington, D.C.: Carnegie Institute Publication, No. 448.

Roseberry, William (1978) : Historical Materialism and *The People of Puerto Rico*. Revista/Review Interamericana 8 : 26-36.

Shanin, Teodor (1971) : Introduction. *In* Peasants and Peasant Societies. Teodor Shanin, ed. Pp. 11-19. Penguin Books, Ltd., Harmondsworth, Middlesex, England and Baltimore, MD.

Sjoberg, Gideon (1955) : The Preindustrial City. American Journal of Sociology 60 : 438-445.

Steward, Julian H. (1936) : The Economic and Social Basis of Primitive Bands. *In* Essays in Anthropology in Honor of Alfred Louis Kroeber. Cora DuBois, ed. Pp. 311-350. Berkeley : University of California Press.

(1944) : Preface. *In* Houses and House Use of the Sierra Tarascans. Ralph L. Beals, Pedro Carrasco, and Thomas McCorkle, eds. Institute of Social Anthropology Publication No. 1. Washington : Smithsonian Institution.

(1949) : Cultural Causality and Law : A Trial Formulation of the Development of Early Civilizations. American Anthropologist 51 : 1-27.

(1950) : Area Research : Theory and Practice. Social Science Research Council, Bulletin 63. New York.

(1951) : Levels of Sociocultural Integration : An Operational Concept. Southwestern Journal of Anthropology 7 : 374-390.

(1955) : Theory of Culture Change : The Methodology of Multilinear Evolution. Urbana: University of Illinois Press.

Steward, Julian H. *et. al.* (1956) : The People of Puerto Rico. Urbana : University of Illinois Press.

Stocking, George W., Jr. (1966) : Franz Boas and the Culture Concept in Historical Perspective. American Anthropologist 68 : 867-882.

Thomas, William I., and Florian Znaniecki (1918) : The Polish Peasant in Europe and America. Chicago : University of Chicago Press.

Van Schendel, Willem (1976) : Peasants as Cultivators? Problems of Definition. Peasant Studies 5 : 16-17.

Warriner, Doreen (1939) : The Economic of Peasant Farming. New York : Oxford University Press.

Wolf, Eric R. (1955) : Types of Latin American Peasantry : A Preliminary Definition. American Anthropologist 57 : 452-471.–

(1956) : Aspects of Group Relations in a Complex Society : Mexico. American Anthropologist 58 : 1065-1078.

(1957) : Closed Corporate Peasant Communities in Mesoamerica and Central Java. Southwestern Journal of Anthropology 13 : 1-18.

(1959) : Sons of the Shaking Earth. Chicago : University of Chicago Press.

(1966a) : Peasants. Englewood Cliffs, NJ : Prentice-Hall.

(1966b) : Kinship, Friendship, and Patron-Client Relations in Complex Societies. *In* The Social Anthropology of Complex Societies. Michael Banton, ed. Pp. 1-22. Association of Social Anthropologists Monograph 4. London : Tavistock.

Peasants into Proletarians from the Household Out : An Analysis from the Intersection of Anthropology and Social History

RAYNA RAPP

The social history of Europe provides particularly rich resources for anthropologists analysing popular culture. Over the past decade, the links between anthropology and social history have been strongly forged, and those of us interested in the transformation of peasantries into proletarians have benefited from the connection.[1] Class differentiation and class culture are topics well researched in European history. The most persuasive of European historians have ploughed this field for us, and we can easily glean from their harvest. They give us, on the one hand, complex and culturally laden accounts of agrarian social history, urban and labour history, and the classic treatises from Marx through E.P. Thompson and beyond on the making of the working class out of the unmaking of peasants and artisans. They also give us, on the other, creative discussions of family history, such as those presented by the Cambridge Group, descendants of Jules Henry and the Annales School, and recent scholars of family "modernization".[2] Both the work and the family lives of peasants becoming proletarians in villages, towns, regions, and nation-states are thus potentially available to us, and we should examine them with enthusiasm.

But when we do, we discover the same complex and ambiguous situations concerning the definition of peasants and proletarians in European history that we find in both historic and contemporary instances in other areas of the world. "Peasant" is a category we are learning to live without or, at least, live with as a descriptive rather than an analytic term. History is more complex than our peasant typologies have often allowed: As Mintz, Wolf, Roseberry, and debates raging in the pages of the *Journal of Peasant Studies* all point out, the term may describe the phenomenal reality of family-based subsistence farming, but the exact relations by which surplus is pumped out of village-based households into larger networks of economic circulation actually condition "peasant" social organization. Shifting relations of production and extraction have increasingly drawn the attention of anthropologists as we abandon the idea of peasant social organizations as timeless, and analytically distinct from the social formations in which it is embedded. We are increasingly able to see (in Europe, as elsewhere) the importance of changing, often non-waged forms of exploitation: rent and merchant capital may be analysed as forms of "concealed" surplus value, taxation and expropriation contribute to class differentiation within and between peasant households. The term "peasants" refers to a historical set of cultivators attempting to reproduce themselves through subsistence farming; in the process, they contribute to economic circuits far beyond their seemingly isolated villages. Complex relations of production are richly mystified and organised by ideological aspects of peasant livelihood: relations of kinship, community, patronage, and religion can be studied to reveal class differentiation within and between local units. As we pierce the notion of "peasants", we find a complex and far-reaching set of social relations of production which have conditioned their social organization, historically and in the present.[3]

Changing relations of production, then, have been the subject of significant, recent analysis. What I will argue in this paper is that changing relations of reproduction also require such centred analysis. As Edholm, Harris, and Young point out, the term reproduction is an anbiguous one in Marxist theory, and is currently a contested domain. "Reproduction" potentially conflates at least three different processes: the reproduction of people across generations (demography); subsistence and maintenance work to sustain people daily; and the complex issue of relations outside of production which are ideologically linked to conditions of production.[4] It is the first two uses of the term - demography and subsistence work - that concern me here, although their analysis contributes to an understanding of the more abstract question of ideology.

Classically, it is the reproduction of wage-labourers that is usually analysed by Marxist theorists. Capitalism in western Europe both required and created an army of wage-dependent workers. In so doing, it separated people from their means of production, leaving them only with their labour power to sell. The social relations of production of capitalism require that labour power be available, but they do not produce it capitalistically. The wage is a payment for the reproduction of labour power, but the actual work of reproduction is done outside of production itself, by people organised not simply as "free labourers" but as family members. Recent attention in both political economy and anthropology has thus turned to the ambiguities of reproduction of labour power which takes place via unwaged domestic relations. There is a growing concern with questions of female exploitation, housework, and the future of "the family" as capitalism evolves.[5]

In this context, another and related question arises: unwaged work to reproduce labour concerns not only the domestic arrangements of waged workers, but "domestic communities" of peasants which are themselves unwaged, incompletely waged, or waged below capitalist reproduction costs, i.e. not completely separated from their means of production. How do such relations of reproduction relate to capital accumulation? This question, rooted classically in the works of Luxemburg and Lenin, has been the subject of a decade of work by dependency theorists. Meillassoux's most recent book attempts a theory of imperialism based precisely on the notion of domestic communities providing necessary and cheap labour power to international capitalism. The same argument could be made regionally and historically for merchant, rent, and mixed agrarian forms of capital in the western European experience. That is, sectors which retain the ambivalent and vexing status of "peasantries" are linked to the wage-labour requirements of capital accumulation.[6]

In order to approach the question of reproduction and of unwaged work (both female and peasant), a lurking functionalism implicit in the literature must be noted: authors seem to assume that the families of proletarians and peasants must be reproduced for cheap labour to be available. It is not *people,* but the social relations of wage-labour to capital that must be reproduced. When we shift our perspective from concrete groups of people to abstract social relations, we see that any group of people is a contingency, because the capital/wage-labour relation is potentially reproduced anywhere, through the creation of the reserve army.[7] Viewed in this light, concrete social organizational forms are tools people use to reproduce themselves under conditions not of their own making. Given the analytic contingency of reproduction (which often means non-reproduction for some categories of prople), we should examine the domestic organizations of peasants and proletarians as a set of strategies for survival under conditions which are constantly shifting. Family forms, migration routes, marriage patterns are all attempts, as E.P. Thompson says of the "grid of inheritance", to project a set of secure relations across the generations under conditions which are continuously decomposing and recomposing (Thompson 1976). As class differentiation emerges and is reproduced in town and country, domestic relations serve as strategies for survival within the larger social relations in which peasants-turning-proletarians are embedded. In attempting to reproduce themselves, the reproduction of the larger social formation is also heavily implicated. How much labour-power is available, what its quality and mobility is, how rapidly population is increasing or decreasing in an area, for example, are questions whose answers depend in part on domestic strategies.

To sum up my argument thus far: capitalist accumulation alters the social relations of production of that complex category we gloss as "peasants"; its social relations of reproduction are necessarily altered as well. The form of that alternation is historically contingent, and responds not only to the technical requirements of a capitalist labour force, but also to the domestic strategies, struggles, and consciousness within which people emerge as semi — or full proletarians. The meaning of "the peasant family" as a unit of reproduction as well as a unit of production is thus important to:

(1) Revising the history of proletarianization of western Europe to understand how work and family relations interpenetrate. In so doing, the simultaneity of gender as well as class stratification should become clear.

(2) Dismantling a faulty developmentalist model drawn from the western European experience and projected onto the rest of the globe, where family economies are currently responding to capitalist penetration and transformation.

(3) Explicating the relation of women to development and exploitation, a relation which is found among peasants and proletarians, in western Europe, and in other areas of the world.

The implications of an analysis linking changing relations of production to those of reproduction are thus very large. My own goals in this paper are much more modest: I want simply to illustrate the sort of analysis of the subject which can be undertaken, once both the centrality and the contingency of reproductive strategies are seen. My examples will be drawn primarily from nineteenth-century England, with instances from France, Italy, and Spain thrown in for comparison. I will show that people respond to changing relations of production not simply as peasants or proletarians, but also as members of domestic units. They do so because self-reproduction is a strategy they create in response to capitalist penetration, and households are the locus of those self-reproducing relationships. "Free labour" is still tied to the social organizational forms within which it is reproduced, and "free labour" is mainly reproduced inside of families. So it is within families that people intimately internalize, accommodate to, and resist the changing relations of production which characterize their proletarianization.

The interdependence of changing relations of production and reproduction is best seen when we make a methodological distinction between household and family. In the demographically-oriented family history literature, the household is usually defined as a co-resident group while the family consists of those household members who also share kinship relations to one another.[8]

I will use the distinction slightly differently, focusing on the household as a locus of shared activities, and the family as providing normative recruitment to those household activities. I will argue that household activities are continuously part of the "larger" processes of production, reproduction, and consumption. They cannot be analysed as separate from the socio-economic relations of the societies in which they are embedded. Households are material units within which people pool resources and perform certain tasks. It is within households that people enter into relations of production, reproduction, and consumption with one another, and on one another's account.

The way in which people enter those household relations is of course through their family connections. As a concept, family is a bit harder to define than is household. In the family history literature, family usually means a group of kinsfolk minus servants, boarders, etc. who *should* be living together inside of a household. I want to focus on the "should" portion of that definition (that is, the idea of family-based households as normative) in order to reveal a key structure in our understanding of ideology. It is through their commitment to the concept of family that people are recruited to the material relations of households. Because people accept the meaningfulness of family, they enter into relations of production, reproduction and consumption with one another—they marry, beget children, work to support dependents; and accumulate, transmit, and inherit cultural and material resources. In all of these activities, the concept of family both reflects and masks the realities of household formation and sustenance. It also glosses over the variety of experiences that social categories of persons have within households. These experiences alter radically depending on class, gender, and generation. Factory workers, artisans, and owners; men and women; the old and the young officially participate in "the family", but their experiences in it may be quite different. This is because their seemingly private experiences in "the family" reflect the household activities in which their particular families are engaged.

For example, recent work by the Schneiders in the history of a nineteenth-century Sicilian agro-town reveals connections between changing productive relations, class differentiation, and the household and family patterns of its residents. As a rising gentry (or *civile*) assumed control over land tenure and marketing, they spawned new social relations of production in the artisan class which supplied them with consumption goods. The rise of both a town-dwelling peasantry and unskilled day-labouring proletarians is also linked to their ascendancy. The household activities of each of those four strata were self-organized in relation to the boom-and-bust cycles of a *civile*-controlled local economy, and family experiences intimately reflected that control and differentiation. In proletarian families, all household members were employed as early as possible, and usually without skills; wet-nursing, serving, and field work yielded cash, and marriage took place at an early age. Landed peasants and artisans passed on skills to their children, who had to accumulate labour-consuming dowries and trades which delayed their marriages. The families of the rich purchased the commodities produced by the skilled or unskilled labour of other classes; their daughters therefore acquired dowries and/or were sent to nunneries at early ages. The analysis suggests that socialization of children, marriage patterns and fertility, diet, and possibly even birth control varied with class-stratified household activities (P. Schneider N.d., J. Schneider N.d.). Family codes and ideologies privately organize recruitment to public relations of production and reproduction, when viewed from the household out. Such relations are extremely contingent, both analytically and historically—that is, self-reproduction is difficult work as capitalist production relations become dominant. Commitment to families helps people to share and survive by changing their reproduction strategies within their households. In the process, the meaning of family life changes as well.

People respond to changing relations of production in order to sustain the households in which they are family members. That is, they are recruited to specific relations of production "for the sake of the family". Entrance into labour relations is organized not only by capital's need for a changing labour force, but by the struggles which people organized within households wage for survival, using and changing their family forms. Attention to the family division of labour by age and sex illustrates this point. For example, Tilly and Scott help us to see that the young, unmarried women workers who entered service and textile production in both England and France in the early nineteenth century migrated not as "free labourers", but as expendable peasant daughters. They went to urban centres in order to remit wages, and to accumulate a dowry their families of origin were unable to provide. In the process, they entered into new relations of production which changed their relations of reproduction; they married at different ages, to different sorts of men, and/or entered free unions, depending on whether they went to mining, service, or industrial towns, where sex ratios and available work varied a great deal. Attempting to reproduce the peasant kin and community patterns which sent them into proletarian occupations, they actually participated in major household and family transformations (Tilly and Scott 1975, 1978).

Early factories may have depended on "free" labour, but it was free from the means of production only—it still depended then (as now) to a large extent on workers who were first and foremost self-defined family members. They entered those factories simultaneously as workers, and as men and women, children and adults, married and single members of families. Their class participation was simultaneously gender and generational participation, for these were the social

relations that were available and threatened with non-reproduction as people
became proletarians. Many social historians have described the familial nature
of the textile factories' work force. According to Smelser, whole families entered
British textile production, fathers hiring their own wives and especially their
children as assistants. Struggles to secure increased wages and to retain skilled
apprenticing in the 1820s were played out by fathers who wanted to both control
and protect their own children. Reddy's analysis of the power-loom linen
weavers in Armentieres at the turn of the twentieth century similarly sees
working-class solidarity as an artifact of kinship. It was families who organized
access to jobs, apprenticing, and militant strikes. Kinship categories took on
differential and changing meanings as they were turned into wage-labour
categories. As Minge-Kalman points out, the advent of public education
"rescued" child labourers from an increasingly non-kinship organized factory
work fórce in the late nineteenth century. This contributed to the enforced, full-
time housewifery of their mothers, who could no longer deploy their offspring as
a flexible work force to do child-minding.

Gareth Stedman Jones describes the struggles of skilled artisans over the
control of the education their children would receive as it contradictorily
liberated the young from both the factories, and the skills and job categories so
carefully passed down the generations. Humphries analyzes the fight for the
family wage in the 1820s and '30s in England in which men understood that the
incremental proletarianization of women and children cheapened their wage.
They therefore organized in factory after factory to exclude women and
children from work, and to obtain a wage which covered their subsistence. To
the extent that they succeeded, it was at the price of demobilizing other members
of the family, who were pushed back into the household as their dependents. A
household and class victory was thus implicated in the strengthening of
patriarchal relations inside of working-class families. Changing relations of
reproduction—in this case, the meaning and uses of sex and age categories inside
of families—were part of a strategic response to wage-labour/capital struggles.[9]

When we turn from recuitment to relations of production to changing
relations of reproduction, the importance of households organized by families is
quite clear. For labour-power is not usually reproduced by individuals, but by
collectivities representing the division of labour by age and sex. The concept of
reproduction, as noted earlier, is an ambiguous one. Most narrowly construed,
relations of reproduction organize a social context for demography: differing
sexualities, patters of nuptuality, fertility, etc. produce not only human beings
but also social participants in relations between the genders and generations.
Behind population explosions or the spread of birth control are people whose
consciousness and options are framed in a world of rapidly changing economic
relations. There may well be a link, for example, between the adoption of

contraception, age at marriage, and changing labour forms.

Franklin Mendals presented a pioneering thesis on proto-industrialization and the growth of population pressure in eighteenth-century Flanders; merchant-supervised cottage industry allowed more peasant offspring to marry, and to marry at a younger age. Their fertility as well as their nuptuality increased dramatically in relation to waged work. Levine's comparative study of four English towns from the sixteenth through the mid-nineteenth centuries reveals differential demographic regimes for nascent class sectors. In Shepshed, knitters created different family patterns for themselves than did peasants or artisans. They married earlier and had more children, as long as waged labour was booming, and children were employable. With the crash of their market in the 1830s and '40s, they readjusted their household and family patterns. Those knitters were illustrating Coontz' model of class-specific demographic regimes, sensitive to the demand for labour.

Fertility and its control are of course highly politicized issues; they respond to political power as well as to economic conditions. Henriques' research on the bastardy clauses which were attached to the new English poor laws (1824) reveals that malthusianism and class antagonism were major factors in their passage. The bastardy clauses made it very difficult for an unwed mother to get support from either the father of her child or the parish in which she lived. Both had been popularly available prior to the clauses, and were built into country courting customs. The babies of the poor were offically outlawed by the clauses, with contradictory results. In some areas, illegitimacy actually increased as young men could now skip out on what would have formerly been a community-wide obligation to marry their pregnant sweethearts. The clauses were enormously hated, and popular discontent was so extreme that they were eventually repealed, but not before they had wrought havoc with sex and marriage. Gillis feels that the decline of female lustiness expressed in popular ballads and stories between the late eighteenth and the late nineteenth centuries reflects the increasing risks which sexually active young women faced. Prior to the passage of the clauses, they could expect either to marry or to get aid in supporting their illegitimate infants. After the clauses, only "respectable" charity was available; declarations of basic chastity and erroneous seduction were required of the women to qualify for the aid. Babies born inside or outside of wedlock needed support. Tilly and Scott describe assorted practices of wet-nursing, drugging, and bottle-feeding infants so that their mothers could continue to work. Very high rates of infant mortality fluctuated in part with the employment of mothers. During the American Civil War, infants in Manchester, England, had an increased survival rate; the cotton blockade had put their mothers out of work, and they were being nursed (Mendels 1969; Levine 1977; Coontz 1957; Henriques 1967, Tilly and Scott 1975, 1978; Burgviere 1976).

Relations of reproduction concern more than the creation of the next generation: they refer to all the daily work through which subsistence occurs for household members. The activities that go into the daily reproduction of adult labourers are primarily performed by women in their capacity as wives, daughters, and mothers. Descriptions of peasant, shepherd, and rural proletarian households throughout western Europe shows us that kinship authority and domestic work are intertwined for women. Classically, relations between mothers and their daughters, and especially, between mothers-in-law and their daughters-in-law, organize subsistence labour processes. These relations organize household work, and hence reproduction.[10] There is much evidence that women reduced to wage-dependency on their husbands reproduce male and female labour power differentially. Oren, for example, found that there were separate standards of living for wives and husbands in the budgets culled from poverty surveys among urban workers in England in the 1880s. Men received more food, more health care, more recreational monies than their wives, who managed the meagre household budget by depriving themselves of food and of sleep. The women mediated the difference between the exchange value of their husbands' wages and the use values their families needed with their own bodies. While it is beyond the scope of this paper, the culmination of this crisis in family reproduction is instructive: the first family allowances bill in England, which was passed in 1945 after cross-class battles, provided direct payment to mothers. The bill for providing milk to nursing mothers and their children was in part paid by taxing those male commodities, alcohol and cigarettes. The state thus redistributed income between waged husbands and their wageless wives (Oren 1973).

Once we see households and the families that organize them as class-stratified, and continuously involved in relations of production and reproduction, other aspects of the changing social matrix in which peasants are turning into proletarians will become more sharply focused. The cultural component of the life cycle, domestic cycle, and the shifting bases of gender identity may be clarified. The life cycle, for example, incorporates progressive class differentiation into its stages when examined in modern western European history. Recently research on the history of childhood reveals that being a child has been a highly variable social position. Much of that variation reflects recruitment and socialization to class. A young apprentice placed in an artisan household had a different experience of his childhood than did peasant youth redistributed among farming families, or weavers' offspring sent into the textile mills.

Recalling the Schneiders' research in Sicily, "youth" was virtually non-existent for the labouring poor, was extended through apprenticing and dowry-production for artisans, and terminated in nunneries for at least some of the daughters of *civile*. Gillis' work on the history of age relations suggests that the very concept of youth is class-specific; it emerges only in the century between 1770 and 1870, when working-class youngsters are both contributing to the family economy and gaining early autonomy. At the same period, children of the middle class are kept from many sexual and social experiences as part of their education and training for professional status. By the turn of the twentieth century, middle-class youngsters are permitted to have an adolescence while their working-class peers are labelled juvenile delinquents for having autonomous social organisations. Courting, marriage, parenthood, and old age are other life-cycle positions that have undoubtedly differentiated with class fragmentation.[11]

The domestic cycle could also be examined for indications of class differentiation, e.g. Mendels' Flemish cottage weavers had different patterns of household fusion and fission than did the peasants he studied, and the number of offspring marrying, and their ages at marriage, varied between land-scarce and land-adequate Provençal peasants at the turn of the twentieth century. Both recruitment to household membership and inter-household links respond to proletarianization: Anderson's sensitive study of Lancashire textile workers in the nineteenth century shows nuclear families becoming more extended as they took in migrants, and pooled wages. Both nineteenth and twentieth-century sources reveal the ways in which women specifically organized their extended kinship networks and their neighbouring connections to do some of the work of reproduction in English towns and cities (Anderson 1971).[12] Timing of family fusion and fission (e.g. age at home-leaving, marriage, proclivity to share single or neighbouring households by stem and extended families) might be best reinterpreted in the light of changing relations of production and reproduction.

The very meaning of maleness and femaleness might be rescued from a misplaced, ahistorical naturalism if the relations between gender and class were better understood. E.P. Thompson and Gareth Stedman Jones have both written with great sensitivity about men. Segregation of male friendship and sociability accompanied proletarianization and later struggles to structure leisure life outside of factories (Jones 1974, 1971; Thompson 1967, 1963).[13] Brian Harrison's provocative article, "For Church, Queen and Family", describes the Girls' Friendly Societies of late nineteenth-century England. The GFS was a mass movement in which working-class girls were "saved" from "family disorganization" by being taught the virtues of chastity, thrift, and gentility. Mobilizing many more members than the suffrage movement ever drew, the GFS paired aristocratic lady volunteers with their working-class charges, whose attitudes towards sex, marriage, work, and politics they tried to shape (Harrison 1973). Dominant ideologies of what men and women *ought* to be may be transmitted and/or resisted in class-specific forms of organization. In such examples, the concept of reproduction moves us away from demography and maintenance work, and toward an understanding of ideology.

This paper has argued that peasants and proletarians must be analysed not only in terms of their production relations, but in terms of their reproduction relations as well. It has further urged that we view reproduction/production via a methodological split between households and the families that organize them. Neither in early capitalist accumulation nor now have the labour processes involved in reproduction been directly subsumed by capital; people must reproduce themselves outside of the production process, and they do so using their own historically available forms. It is in households that claims on subsistence and pooling of resources occur as family members share, strategize, and cope with the realities of class formation and differentiation. Seemingly "private" domestic arrangements must therefore be seen as an integral part of the larger political-economic relations of production and reproduction. Changing family forms are both a product of, and a resistance to, the processes of capital accumulation which turn peasants into proletarians. The making of the working class out of the unmaking of peasants and artisans took place, and continues to take place, not only in enclosures, on factory floors, in pubs and in unions, but in bedrooms and kitchens as well. Until we double our vision to see the simultaneity of production and reproduction, we will miss the systematic connections between work-place and home, between "public" social life and "private" family life It is precisely the connection of such seemingly separate realms of activity which has shaped our own innermost consciousness as well as that of the people we seek to study. *This* is one of the lessons to be gleaned at the intersection of anthropology and social history in western Europe.

NOTES

1. Products of this cross-disciplinary borrowing are seen in articles in *Past and Present, Journal of Social History, History Workshop,* and *Annales.* The borrowing has occurred mainly in one direction, as Charles Tilly points out (1978). A recent series of conferences on relations between the two fields has taken place in Europe, and a group of American Anthropologists presented a history-anthropology symposium at the American Anthropological Association Meetings, 14-19 November 1978, in Los Angeles.

2. Classic sources on working class history in England and France would include: Marx (1954, V.L, especially part 4, Chapter 15; part 7, Chapter 25; and part 8); E.P. Thompson (1967, 1963); Jones (1974, 1971); Hobsbawn (1964); Marcus (1974); Benevolo (1971); Polanyi (1957); Moore (1966); Foster (1974); and the journals *Past and Present, History Workshop, Annales, E.S.C.* Overviews on the history of the family would include Pleck (1976); Tilly and Scott (1975, 1978); Davidoff (1974); Humphries (1977); Rapp, Ross, and Bridenthal (1979); Hareven (1976); Vogel (1978); Laslett and the Cambridge Group (1972); Anderson (1971); Levine (1977); Forster and Ranum (1976).

3. This summary of recent debates in the peasant literature is illustrated in Mintz (1973, 1974, 1977); Ennew, Hirst, and Tribe (1977); Roseberry (1978a, 1978b); the question rages through the

Journal of Peasant Studies; it is also illustrated in the early works of Wolf (1955, 1957, (1955, 1957, 1966) on social organization and the articulation of peasantries, and underlies the recent debate in the *American Anthropoligist* on "peasant exploitation" initiated by Dalton who received numerous responses (1974). On social organizational forms which express class ideologies, see L. Li Causi (1975); Parish (n.d.); and Schneider (1978).

4. Edholm, Harris, and Young (1977) delineate the ambiguities and conflations in the term.

5. See, for example, "Women's Issue", *Critique of Anthropology* (1977), especially, articles by Bradby, Goddard, and Whitehead; see also Tilly (1979); summaries of a vast literature on the value of housework are found in Fee (1976) and Malos (1977).

6. The issue of cheap labour-power runs through the work of the dependency theorists writing over the past decade, i.e. Samir Amin, Andre Gunder Frank, Rodney Williams, etc.; Wallerstein (1975) and *Review,* the journal he has recently founded; it is central to the analysis of Meillassoux (1975); O'Laughlin (1977); and Rapp (1977).

7. My ideas on the contingency of reproduction under capitalism have been shaped by the personal communication and team-teaching I have been privileged to share with Gita Sen. Her work on the subject is available from the author, Department of Economics, Graduate Faculty, New School for Social Research.

8. Household/family is defined in Laslett's Introduction (1972). A discussion of the distinctions between quantitative and qualitative perspectives on family history is found in Berkner (1973) and Wrigley (1977). It is made explicit in Lees (n.d.) Examples of demographically-oriented, quantitative analyses include Laslett (1972), Berkner (1972), Wrigley (1969), and Hajnal (1965). Examples of a more qualitative orientation include works by psychohistorians, e.g. de Mause (1974), Aries (1962), Stone (1975, 1977), and Davis (1977). Both perspectives, of course, are generally considered important, and scholars increasingly attempt to integrate the two, e.g. Tilly and Scott (1978) and Hareven (1976).

9. My interpretations are based on the research presented in Smelser (1967, 1959), Reddy (1975), Humphries (1977a, 1977b), Tilly and Scott (1975, 1978); Minge-Kalman (1978a, 1978b); Jones (1974). For important theoretical work in economics on this subject, see Weinbaum (n.d., 1977, 1978).

10. Both tension and cooperation as kinship/work relations of female peasants and proletarians is widespread in the literature, e.g. Cornelisen (1977), Campbell (1964), and Réiter (1975).

11. European apprentices are discussed in Laslett (1965); peasant child exchanges in Berkner (1972), Gillis (1977).

12. I am indebted to Ellen Ross for this discussion of neighbourhood networks. She cites Young and Wilmott (1957), Roberts (1973), Meachem (1977), and Tomes (1978). See also Mendels (1969) and my own unpublished field notes,Provence, 1969, 1970, 1971, 1972.

13. Ellen Ross should once again be credited for her interpretation of these sources.

REFERENCES

Anderson, Michael (1971): Family strucure in 19th century Lancashire. Cambridge: Cambridge University Press.

Aries, Philippe (1962): Centuries of childhood. New York: Vintage Books.

Benevolo, Leonard (1971): The origins of modern town planning. Mass.: MIT Press.

Berkfner, Lutz K. (1972): The stem family and the developmental cycle of the peasant household : An 18th century Austrian example. American Historical Review 77:398-418.

        (1973): Recent research on the history of the family in Western Europe. Journal of Marriage and the Family 35:395-406.

Buguiere, Andre (1976): From Malthus to Max Weber : Belated marriage and the spirit of enterprise. In Forster and Ranum (eds.), Family and society : Selections from the *Annales*. Baltimore : The John Hopkins University Press, pp. 237-250.

Campbell, J.K. (1964): Honour, family, and patronage. Oxford : Oxford University Press.

Causi, L. Li (1975): Anthropology and ideology : the case of "patronage" in Mediterranean societies. Critique of Anthropology Vol. 2/3, Nos. 4/5, pp. 72-89. Coontz. p22.

Coontz, Sydney H. (1957): Population theories and the economic interpretation. New York: Humanities Press.

Cornelisen, Ann (1977): Women of the shadows. New York: Vintage.

Dalton, George (1974): "How exactly are peasants 'exploited'" American Anthropologist 76(4): 553-561.

Davidoff, Leonore (1974): Mastered for life : Servant and wife in Victorian and Edwardian England. Journal of Social History 8:406-428.

Davis, Natalie (1977): Ghosts, kin and progeny : Some features of family life in early modern France. Daedalus 106 : 87-114.

de Mause, Lloyd (ed.) (1974): The history of childhood, New York: Harper and Row.

Edholm, Felicity, Olivia Harris, and Kate Young (1977): Conceptualizing women. Critique of Anthropology 3 (9/10) : 101-130.

Ennew, Judith, Paul Hirst, and Keith Tribe (1977): Peasantry as an economic category. Journal of Peasant Studies 4(4): 295-322.

Fee, Terry (1976) : The value of housework and capitalist production. Review of Radical Political Economy 8(3).

Foster, John O. (1974): Class Struggle and the Industrial Revolution, London: Weidenfeld & Nicolson.

Foster, Robert and Orest Ranum, (eds.) (1976): Family and society : Selections from the *Annales*. Baltimore: The Johns Hopkins University Press.

Gillis, John (1974): Youth and history: Tradition and change in European age relations 1770-present. New York: Academic Press.

        (n.d.): Paper delivered at the International Conference in Women's History, University of Maryland, Nov. 16-20, 1977.

Hajnal, J. (1965): European marriage patterns in perspective. In Glass and Eversley (eds.), Population in history. London: Edward Arnold, pp. 101-43.

Hareven, Tamara (1976): The history of the family and modernization theory. Signs 2:190-206.

Harrison, Brain (1973): For Church, Queen and Family : The Girls' Friendly Society, 1874-1920. Past and Present 61:107-138.

Henriques, U.R.Q. (1967): Bartardy and the New Poor Law. Past and Present 37:103-129.

Hobsbawn, Eric (1964): Labouring men. London: Weidenfeld and Nicolson.

Humphries, Jane (1977a): Working class struggle and the persistence of the working class family. Cambridge Journal of Economics 1:241-258.

(1977b): The working class family, women's liberation and class struggles : The case of 19th century British history. Journal of Radical Political Economics 9(3): 25-41.

Jones, Gareth Stedman (1974): Working class culture and working-class politics in London, 1870-1900 : Notes on the remaking of a working class. Journal of Social History 8:460-508.

Laslett, Peter (1965): The world we have lost. London : Methuen.

(1972): Introduction : The history of the family. In Laslett (ed.), Household and family in past time. Cambridge: Cambridge University Press. pp. 1-90.

(1972): Household and family in past time. Cambridge: Cambridge University Press.

Lees, Lynn Hollen (n.d.): Alternative approaches to the history of the family; unpublished paper presented at the Conference on Social Theory and Social History, Columbia University, 19 February 1977.

Levine, David (1977): Family formation in an age of nascent capitalism. New York: Acxademic Press.

MacIntosh, Maureen (1977): "Reproduction and Patriarchy : A Critique of Claude Meillassoux 'Femmes, Greniers et Capitaux'" *Capital and Class* 9, pp. 119-127.

Malos, Ellen (1977): Housework and the politics of women's liberation. Socialist Revi8ew No. 37 (Vol. 8, 1): 41-71.

Marcus, Steven (1974), Engels, Manchester and the working class. New York: Vintage.

Marx, Karl (1954): Capital. Vol. 1, Moscow: Progress Publishers.

Meachem, Standish (1977): Life apart, the English working class, 1890-1914. Boston: Harvard University Press.

Meillassoux, Claude (1975): Femmes, greniers et capitaux. Paris : Maspero.

Mendels, Franklin (1969): Industrialization and population pressure in 18th century Flanders. Ph.D. Thesis, University of Wisconsin.

Minge-Kalman, Wanda (1978): The Industrial Revolution and the European family : The institutionalization of "childhood" as a market for family labour. Comparatrive Studies in Society and History, 20(3) : 454-468.

(1978) : Household economy during the peasant-to-worker transition in the Swiss Alps. Ethnology 17 : 183-196.

Mintz, Sidney (1973) : A note on the definition of peasantries. Journal of Peasant Studies 1(1) : 91-106.

(1974) : The rural proletariat and the problem of rural proletarian consciousness. Journal of Peasant Studies 1(3) : 291-325.

(1977) : The so-called world system : Local initiative and local response. Diaqlectical Anthropology 2 (4) : 253-270.

Moore, Barrington (1966) : The social origins of dictatorship and democracy. Boston: Beacon Press.

O'Laughlin, Bidget (1977) : "Production and Reproduction : Meillassoux's Femes, Greniers et Critique of Anthropology 2(8) : 3-32.

Oren, Laura (1973) : The welfare women in labouring families : England 1860-1950. Feminist Studies 1(3/4): 107-125.

Parish, Timothy (n.d.): Patrons, clients, and the world system. Unpublished ms. (Anthropology Program, New School for Social Research).

Pleck, Elizabeth (1976): Two worlds in one: Work and family. Journal of Social History 10: 178-195.

Polanyi, Karl (1957) : The great transformation. Boston: Beacon Press.

Rapp, Rayna (sée also under Reiter) (1977) : "Claude Meillassoux 'Femmes, Greniers et Capitaux'". *Dialectical Anthropology* 2 (4) : 317-324.

       Ellen Ross, and Renate Bridenthal (1979) "Examining family history." Feminist Studies 5(1) pp. 174-200.

Reddy, William (1975) : Family and factory: French linen weavers in the Belle Epoque. Journal of Social History 8 (3) : 102-112.

Reiter, Rayna (see also under Rapp) (1975) : Men and women in the south of France : Public and private domains. In Reiter (ed.), Toward and Anthropology of Women. New York : Monthly Review Press.

Roberts, Robert (1973) : The classic slum. Harmondsworth, England : Penguin.

Roseberry, William (1978a) : Rent differentiation and the development of capitalism among peasants. American Anthropologist 78(1) : 45-58.

       (1978b) : Peasants as proletarians. Critique of Anthropology 11 : 3-18.

Schneider, Jane (n.d.) : Proletarianization and dowries. Paper presented to the CUNNY Anthropology Program Seminar on Complex Societies, Spring 1978.

       (1978) : Of peacocks and penguins. American Ethnologist 6(3) : 413-337.

Schneider, Peter (n.d.) : Class formation, material culture and ideology in 19th century Sicily. Paper presented at the AAA Meetings, Los Angeles, Nov. 1978.

Sen, Gita (n.d.) Class struggle and the working class family : A comment. Available from the author, Department of Economics. Graduate Faculty, New School for Social Research.

       (n.d.) : Peasant production, domestic labor and the value of labor power. Available from the author, Department of Economics. Graduate Faculty, New School for Social Research.

Smelser, Neil J. (1959) : Social change and the industrial revolution. Chicago : University of Chicago Press.

       (1967) : The industrial revolution and the British working class family. Journal of Social History 1(1) : 17-36.

Stone, Lawrence (1977): The family, sex and marriage in England, 1500-1800. New York: Harper and
Stone, Lawrence (1975): The rise of the nuclear family in early modern England : The patriarchal stage. In Rosenberg (ed.), The family in history. Philadelphia: University of Pennysylvania Press.

       (1977): The family, sex and marriage in England, 1500-1800. New York: Harper and Row.

Thompson. E.P. (1963) : The making of the English working class. New York : Vintage.

       (1967 : Time, work-discipline, and industrial capitalism. Past and Present No. 38, pp. 56-97.

       (1976): The "grid" of inheritance : A comment. In Goody, Thirsk, and Thompson (eds.), Family and Inheritance. Cambridge : Cambridge University Press. pp. 328-360.

Tilly, Charles (1978) : Anthropology, History and the *Annales*. Review 1(3)/4): 207-214.

Tilly, Louise (n.d.) : Production and reproduction in Roubaix. Unpublished ms. (Department of History, University of Michigan).

and Joan Scott (1975): Women's work and the family in 19th century Europe. Comparative Studies in Society and History : 36-64.

(1978) : Women, work, and family. New York : Holt, Rinehart and Winston.

(1979) : The Family Wage Economy of a French Textile City : Roubaix, 1872-1906."Jl. of Family History 4 (4) : 381-394.

Tomes, Nancy (1978) : A torrent of abuse : Crimes of violence between working-class men and women in London, 1840-1873. Journal of Social History 11 (3) : 329-354.

Vogel, Lise (1978): The contested domain : A note on the family in the transition to capitalism. Marxist Perspectives 1(1) : 50-73.

Wallerstein, Immanuel (1975) : The modern world-system. New York: Academic Press.

Weinbaum, Batya (n.d.) : Kin categories in the economy. Paper delivered at the URPE Conference on Social Policy, Spring 1977.

(1977) : Redefining the question of revolution. Review of Radical Political Econimics 9(3) : 54-78.

(1978) : The curious courtship of marxism and feminism. Boston : South End Press.

Wolf, Eric (1955) : Types of Latin American peasantries : A preliminary discussion. American Anthropologist 57(3) 452-471.

(1957): Closed corporate peasant communities in Mesoamerica and Central Java. Southwestern Journal of Anthropology 13(1) : 1-18.

(1966) : Peasants. Englewood Cliffs, New Jersey : Prentice Hall.

Wrigley, E. Anthony (1969) : Population and history. New York and Toronto : McGraw-Hill.

(1977) : Reflections on the history of the family. Daedalus 106 : 71-86.

Young, Michael and Peter Wilmott (1957) : Family and kinship in East London. Harmondsworth, England: Penguin.

On Peasant Rent

ERIC R. WOLF

Peasant studies in American anthropology have taken two different approaches.
A first approach strove to explore the understandings in peasants' minds, aiming
at a definition of peasant values or world-view. The second took its departure
from the study of the material, economic, and political processes at work in
peasant life, and at constructing a political economy of peasantry. Central to the
first approach was the concern with the cultural encounter between city and
country, civilization and folk, "great tradition" and "little tradition." Central to
the second approach was the definition of mechanisms linking cultivators to
economy and polity, to market and state. To focus on these mechanisms, Wolf
(1966 : 10) introduced the concept of rent, arguing that "it is this production of a
fund of rent which critically distinguishes the peasant from the primitive
cultivator." He argued further that significant variations in the peasant condition
could be accounted for by the different ways in which rent was assigned and
transferred.

While the terms "rent" and "fund of rent" were accepted uncritically by some
social scientists, others resisted their introduction, perhaps because the author
made it insufficiently clear that the two terms were to be used in the classical
political economic sense which defines rent as "a payment made to the owner of a
monopoly over resources in return for access to these resources." The utility of
taking a classical approach in this context lies in the fact that its categories—
whether "capital", "rent", or "labour"—do not merely define factors of
production, but serve to exhibit classes and the relationships among them. Thus,
David Ricardo, in using the classical concept of "rent", attempted to show that
"the interest of the landlords is always opposed to the interest of every other class
in the community."

This classical interest in how different classes are initially endowed with
differential access to economic factors and services is not in the mainstream of
modern neo-orthodox economics, which takes its departure not from classes and
relationships among classes, but from "firms" (including households), variously
endowed with factors and services. This initial endowment is taken as given.
Interest focuses not on classes of "firms" and possible conflict among such
classes, but on their encounter in the market place where they exchange the

factors and services in their possession against economic inducements sufficient to initiate such exchange. In this perspective, rent appears not as a transfer of labour, product, or money to holders of economic or political power by virtue of existing relations of production, but as an inducement to firms holding the scarce factors of real estate or housing to release them for exchange. Such usage can illuminate consumer behaviour and consumer satisfaction in price-setting markets. It cannot, of itself, lead to an adequate anatomy of society.

In contrast to neo-orthodox usage, the classical categories can serve not only to visualize significant relationships among classes, but also to illuminate historically different combinations of classes and their changing relationships. The exploration of this possibility was, of course, Marx's contribution in his "critique of political economy" to the study of political economy. By postulating the existence of various historically distinctive modes of production, Marx also allows us to treat a category like "rent" as a category which changes its "content" or function in the shift from one mode of production to another. Rent in one mode of production may have a different role to play than in another mode of production. If we are able to define these distinctive roles, however, we may be able to say something not only about the relation between rent-payers and rent-receivers, but also about the wider constellation of classes of which these categories form a part.

It is a hall-mark of pre-capitalist modes of production based upon class divisions into producers of surpluses and takers of surpluses, that rent is captured by the surplus-takers at the end of the cycle of production. In social formations predicated upon such modes, the producer is granted usufruct of the means of production (called by Marx "possession" as opposed to property) but thereby becomes subject to the direct sway of a politically dominant taker of surpluses. "Under such conditions", says Marx of these producers, "the surplus-labour for the nominal owner of the land can only be extorted from them by other than economic pressure" (Marx 1967 (1894) : 791).

Once extorted, the rent is distributed among the various subdivisions of surplus-takers. Such differential allocation of rent among the rent-receivers is primarily a matter of political power. Centralization of power will cause rent to flow towards the apex of political power; fragmentation of power will spread rent receipts more widely among lower-level claimants to power. Rent under such conditions is outright tribute, whether paid in labour, kind, or money, and such modes may properly be called "tributary" modes of production (see Amin 1970). In such modes the economic and political components of rent overlap, and the allocation of rent to different strata among the power-holders is a function of the political relations among them.

What of rent under capitalist relations of production? For one thing, tributary rent changes its form. It becomes what Marx called "capitalized rent", where land is treated as capital and rent as "the interest on an imaginary capital" (Marx 1967 (1894): 623). Thus,

> if the average rate of interest is 5%, then an annual ground-rent of £200 may be regarded as interest on a capital of £4,500. . . If a capitalist buys land yielding a rent of £200 annually and pays £4,000 for it, then he draws the average annual interest on his capital of £4,000, just as if he had invested this capital in interest-bearing papers or loaned it directly at 5% interest.

At the same time, rent undergoes a change of function. This change of function has been particularly difficult to conceptualize, notably in its bearing on the analysis of peasantry. Marx distinguished three kinds of rent under capitalist conditions: differential rent, absolute rent, and monopoly rent (see Cutler 1975; Edel 1976: Murray 1977; Tribe 1977). Differential rent, in Cutler's pithy formulation (1975: 73), "arises in any situation where there is an unequal product from two equal applications of capital where the organic composition is constant". Such differential rent is by no means limited to agriculture; it appears also where availability or location favour one source of energy or raw material over another. Such differences constitute more than mere differences in the physical environment; their utilization also depends on the available means of production and the labour power which can be harnessed to set them in motion. Within the capitalist system, means of production and labour power are marshalled by capital, and differences in availability and location become socially manifest only in the competition between different capitals. Within the same capitalist system, however, such competition of individual capitals is ultimately determined by the intensity with which total social labour is exploited by total social capital. This intensity, measured by the ratio of surplus value to total capital outlay (c + v), constituted the overall rate of profit of the system. Differential rent thus appears only when different capitals embodied in different units of production receive their aliquot proportions of profit according to their different costs of production.[1]

Similar general theoretical considerations also underlie Marx's concept of absolute rent. Absolute rent feeds on two quite different conditions. The first of these is the existence of private property in land; the second consists in the low organic composition of capital in agriculture (low ratio of equipment to labour power). The low organic composition of agriculture keeps costs of production at a low level. The existence of private property, in turn, allows capitalist land owners to withhold their land from use, until a rent is paid on its utilization. This gives landowners an advantage over non-agricultural producers. In the non-agricultural sector of the economy, where both capital and labour are wholly mobile, the competition of individual capitals is governed by the overall rate of profit, constituted by the ration of surplus value of capital outlay. Commodity prices in this sector are thus set by the cost of labour power and plant, plus the average rate of profit for the economy as a whole $(c + v + p)$, by what Marx called "the price of production". Landlords, however are able to impede the free flow of a capital and labour into their sector, by fencing off their estates as private properties, and then taking advantage of any difference between their lower than average cost of production (due to low $c + s$) and the prevailing "price of production" $(c + s + p)$ in the non-agricultural sector. *This* difference is what Marx called absolute rent.

As Ricardo and Marx both realized, this produces a tendency to lower the rate of profit for capital and increase the cost of subsistence for labour. Put in another way, it results in an "unearned" transfer of surplus value from the non-agricultural sector to the sector dominated by landlords. If capital is to maximize its rate of accumulation, it must—at some historical conjuncture—move to break the power of the landlord class. Such a liquidation of the landlord class is, of course, a political as much as a purely economic problem, and therefore the outcome, at any determinate point in history, of shifts in the parallelogram of forces obtaining among the various classes of the society under study—peasants, artisans, and wage-workers, as well as landlords, merchants, and capitalists. Put in another way, our analysis of such conjunctures must move from the abstract formulation of modes of production to a analysis of the historical struggles among classes engendered by these modes (see Brenner 1976; Moore 1966).

These class confrontations are, however, quite variable both in the core regions of capitalist development and along its expanding frontiers. The capitalist mode does not come into the world full-blown and all-dominant, but develops by intermittent advances in its regions of origin, and by intermittent expansion beyond them. During its period of initial growth it must co-exist with other modes at home and enter into temporary agreeements with other modes abroad. In fact, as Pierre-Phillippe Rey has pointed out (1976), there was a period during which the capitalist mode benefited from a symbiotic articulation with tributary ("feudal") modes in its western European setting. Enhanced capitalist accumulation set in motion the capitalization of rent by landlords who, in turn, took to working their land with wage-labour, while at the same time expelling the tributary population characteristic of the previous mode and driving them to seek employment in the nascent industries. Similarly, the capitalist mode in its initial drive beyond western Europe for some time actually reinforced tributary modes in the affected regions, enlisting or installing tributary overlords to produce raw materials for the centre under non-capitalist relations of production. Nascent industrial capitalism in the home regions, with its tendency to augment the capture of surplus value by harnessing purchased labour power (v) to expenditures for ever-proliferating means of production (c), fed for a long time on raw materials produced by labour harnessed politically to means of production assembled without the intervention of capital.[2] Thus, the initial development of capitalism in its home provinces reinforced or created in the periphery classes of tribute-takers linked to the capitalist epicentre, but engaged in class confrontations of their own.

In regions once significant in the early beginnings of the capitalist mode, and later de-industrialized by the historic shift from the Mediterranean to northwestern Europe, moreover, capitalist advance in the north went hand in hand with an expansion of share-tenancy on the estates of capital-owning landlords. Unable to compete effectively with foreign competitors in the industrial realm, and dealing with a declining home market, owners of capital found it appealing to invest in agriculture. Cultivators, in turn, unable to move into industrial employment or by-employment, found it preferable to intensify their labour on the land, even at high rates of land rental. As a result of the share contract, the landlord could appropriate all or part of that surplus labour time in ways not possible within local industry. Such a conjuncture led to a stabilization of share rents until workers found new sources of employment or owners of capital discovered new outlets for investment (see Cutler 1975; 85).

While capitalism thus engendered, in its forward march, new tributary formations on its frontiers, as well as share-tenancy in regions of stunted industrial growth, it also encouraged a new phenomenon: the development of "independent", property-owning peasantries. While populations of cultivators holding rights of property in land existed on the margins and in the interstices of tributary formations here and there, the heavy increase of freehold or copyhold peasantries in most world areas (other than China) was largely a phenomenon of the nineteenth century. This makes the growth of such peasantries conterminous with the historic victory of the capitalist mode. What is the relationship between the two phenomena? To explain this conjuncture as due primarily to a generalization of property rights would seem to place too much of the burden of explanation on the role of "legal fictions" in effecting political and economic change. To interpret it as a linear consequence of capitalist development is to ignore the fact that the organic composition of capital in freehold peasant agriculture remained low until after World War II, probably even lower than in the tribute-taking landlord-operated agriculture which preceded it.

We are likely to find better explanations for the rise of such peasantry in the political realm, that is, in the political conjunctures produced by the changing relations of classes. In some cases, as in the French Revolution, the major political confrontation occurred between peasantry and tributary landowners. This confrontation ended the domination of landowners and brought to the fore an independent peasantry. If anything, however, the victory of this peasantry put a brake upon capitalist accumulation in France until well into the twentieth century. Elsewhere, efforts to institute land-holding peasantries were initiated "from the top down", by state policy rather than by peasant initiative. Such was the case in the movement to free the serfs in the Habsburg dominions and in Russia; the attempts to install *ryotwari* tenure in parts of India; and the Mexican Reform initiated by Benito Juárez. In Austria-Hungary and Russia, legal and land reforms were prompted by a wish to forestall peasant discontent and uprisings. In India, the ideology of the English utilitarians dovetailed with the desire to liquidate native land-owning classes. In Mexico the announced intention was to disestablish land-owning ecclesiatical corporations and closed corporate communities in order to create a Mexican yeomanry. It failed. The unannounced outcome of the Reform was instead the wholesale seizure of church and Indian lands by landowners.

If, on the one hand, the land reforms were an outcome of the confrontations between landowners and peasant cultivators, on the other hand, we must take note of the way in which they affected the development of the working classes produced by the processes of capitalist accumulation. The nineteenth century witnessed not only the victory of the capitalist mode, but also produced the realization that a strong peasantry could be used as a counterfoil against the emerging proletariat. In Europe, especially, the population earning a living by selling its labour power increased heavily in the course of the nineteenth century, from an estimated 90 million, or 47.3 per cent of the total population, in 1800 to 300 million, or 60 per cent of the total population, in 1900 (Tilly 1976:17). Installation of a freehold peasantry could offset the social and political consequences of this growth in several ways. Keeping part of the working class tied to the land diminished the costs of worker subsistence and support. At the same time, it served to inhibit or reduce tendencies towards increased worker solidarity by granting part-time workers a stake in the ownership of land. Finally, peasant interests could be played off effectively against worker interests on the political level.

At the same time, however, it must be noted that such political efforts to strengthen the peasantry amounted simultaneously to a political decision to slow or alter the rate of scope of capitalist development. Marx had recognized this possibility when he wrote that the development of capitalism

> encounters major barriers, when numerous and large-scale spheres of production which are not operated capitalistically (e.g. agriculture by small-scale cultivators) insert themselves between the capitalistically operated enterprises and connect themselves with them. (1967[1894]: 196).

A decision to favour the growth of peasantry, therefore, was also a decision to limit the mobility of labour and capital, and hence to inhibit the generalization of a system-wide rate of profit. This amounts in turn to the maintenance of niches, regions, and sectors of the political economy in which capitalist competition yields to political and economic monopolies which batten on the uneven development of capitalism, while contributing further to this unevenness.

This also has implications for the utilization of the Marxian concepts of "differential" and "absolute" rent in the study of peasantry. To the extent that these concepts were predicated upon a model of a "pure" or "abstract" capitalist system, they were not intended to illuminate conditions in which capitalist development becomes uneven and proceeds in archipelagic rather then continuous fashion. How, then, does peasant rent operate under such uneven conditions?

The first thing to note about a freehold peasantry is that it usually operates in the context of a market. A peasant household is certainly not a capitalist enterprise (getting its aliquot share of profit by laying out c + v, and appropriating surplus value). At the same time, total isolation from markets, and hence total isolation from the need to produce commodities for exchange in markets, is unusual. Indeed, and paradoxically, American farms between 1750 and 1850 may have approximated most closely to such a logically possible, but historically infrequent, condition (see Merrill 1977). Moreover, in the world system of capitalism, as it existed in the nineteenth century, commodity markets for peasant produce were not wholly dominated by the capitalist process of accumulation, and yet articulated with the field of relations set up by the burgeoning mode. The peasant thus entered markets affected, if not yet wholly dominated, by that mode, markets which were linked to that mode and yet constituted "major barriers" against its further development.

The peasant encountered these contradictory linkages in at least three ways: when he bought, sold, or mortgaged land; when he entered industrial by-employment; and—of course—when he sold his produce. In buying, selling, or mortgaging land he had to confront the fac that the land market was determined to a considerable degree by the fact that land had previously been owned by landlords who treated land as a source of "capitalized rent". As Kautsky pointed out (see Banaji 1976 : 36) the land-buying peasant may be concerned only with his needs or resources, but the level of the price he has to pay for land is set by the capitalized rent of his predecessors. When property is mortgaged, in turn, to obtain money or capital, the peasant sells his "imaginary capital", together with its rent, to a money-lender or bank. Capitalist property rights may indeed secure him possession of the holding, as long as he does not default, and its restitution when he repays his debt. Legally his title continues to mark him as an owner of property; analytically, he has become a tenant paying rent for occupance or possession of his "own" land. Put in another way, capitalized rent—as embodied in land prices—affected, first, the scale of his operation. Where he needed to seek out the assistance of others in order to maintain himself on the land, the level of capitalized rent affected the terms of his indebtedness.

While anthropologists and historians have recently paid a great deal of attention to the processes of inheritance in peasant households, they have been concerned much less with the effects of debt on the constitution and differentiation of peasantries. Yet the historical materials on peasantry are full of instances in which the institution of private property in land merely accelerated its disposal to third parties. Thus, "most historians of early and mid-nineteenth century France insist on the crucial role of the peasants' burden of debt"(Weber 1976:39). Growing peasant indebtedness was true of most German states where, characteristically, laws against usury were abolished in the 1860s (Treue 1970 : 399). One effect of this indebtedness in the eastern German states was that peasant land was bought up in huge amounts by *Junker* landowners, engaged in creating the *Gutsherrschaften* which were destroyed only after World War II. Junker monopolization of land unleashed a massive peasant migration westwards, into industry within Germany and into migration overseas, notably to the United States. In India, the British decision to render land private property brought on a massive transfer of holdings from the initial title-holders to money-lenders and new owners (Thorner and Thorner 1962 : 108-109). In Mexico, Guatemala, and the Caribbean, peasant indebtedness furnished one of the chief mechanisms for the transfer of peasant land to encroaching landowners.

Acceptance of industrial by-employment, ranging from the production of artisan commodities to the engagement in particular segments or phases of commodity production, constitutes a second point of peasant entry into the market. The associated responses run an extraordinary gamut of variation, at all points of capitalist expansion. Although the phenomena themselves are relatively well known, their relation to peasant needs for money and peasant indebtedness remains to be explored in further research. There may also exist a relation between industrial by-employment on the holding and full-time commitment to industrial wage labour in hidden or overt form.

In the third place, the peasant encounters the market when he sells his produce. Given the conditions of an uneven development of the capitalist mode, however, the peasant is apt to fall into the hands of middlemen whose margin of profit depends upon the initiation of unequal exchange, which requires that they acquire goods below their price of production and sell them above it. With regard to peasantry it works best when the peasant is constrained or limited in his choice of market, and when the recipients of his surplus product can funnel it into the market without inviting the competition of industrial capital. The essence of the link-up between merchant capital and peasantry is thus the establishment of oligopoly or monopoly in circulation.

The peasant, for his part, needs money to pay for instruments of production, taxes, or ceremonial expenditures. The merchant and his agents offer such funds as advances in exchange for exclusive rights over the disposal of the product. From such an original point of vantage, they may gradually invade the peasant's process of production, both through advances of capital (for tools, working animals, seed, and fertilizer) and through the establishment of quality controls over the product. All of this can be reinforced through the exercise of political power, coercing the peasant into commercial commitments, guarding the channels of circulation against competitors, and ensuring the inequities associated with unequyal exchange. Frequently the merchant, the money-lender, and the local strongman come indeed to be the same person, as in the figure of the Mexican *cacique-acaparador*.

Under such circumstances, not only does peasant rent pass to the merchant-money-lender as part of the repayment for advances, but the peasant in effect pays "protection rent" (see Lane 1966: Part III) to the holders of effective political power. These protection rents, under the aegis of mercantile capital, bear a superficial resemblance to the rent exacted by the controllers and detainers of land in the tributary mode. Under the conditions of merchant capitalism, however, they flow primarily from monopolies over the process of circulation and not from a political claim to a portion of the surplus-product as such. We are no longer dealing with the political monopoly of a landlord class, but with a political grant of power to a class of middlemen which is economically empowered to capture monopoly rent in circulation from the peasantry, and permitted to exact a protection rent to secure their economic monopolies.

Taking a wider perspective, the combination of protection rents and asymmetrical returns to the peasantry under conditions of market monopolies serves to underwrite a significant layer of the "middle classes" engaged in the circulation of peasant produce and dependent upon it. In turn, these "middle classes" facilitate the expansion of the mercantile network into the hinterland, thus enlarging also the circulation of commodities produced outside the peasant zone of production. Just as the controller of peasant produce is often brother to the local political boss, or even identical with him, so he is also kin to the local store-keeper, or that very same person. Singly or together they represent a considerable portion of these "middle classes" which, together with the peasantry, represent the cynosure of conservative thought, the defenders of the nation against international capital and the working classes. They are the significant segment of that "petty bourgeoisie" which at the same time inhibits the expansion of capitalist relations of production, and yet lives in their interestices.

Finally, it should be remembered that the peasant—in exchange for his personal freedom and the right to private property—must pay taxes to the state.

Under the conditions set by the tributary mode, economic rent and political tax were indeed one and the same thing, oweable to the tribute-takers by non-economic compulsion. In the states affected and transformed by the capitalist mode, the realm of economic exchanges and obligations is structurally and ideologically separated from the operation of the state apparatus. Capitalized rent in the land market and monopoly rents in circulation are thus separated from obligations which are payable to the state.

If political decisions to curb, delay, and divert the effects of the dynamic of capitalist development had a major part in the institution of freehold peasantries, it is also true that peasantry—as a class "in itself", though not much "for itself"—now confronts the state as arbiter and manager of both its economic and political fate. The state not only demands taxes and soldiery; it is also the arena where major internal and international decisions affecting the relation of industry and agriculture are fought out. Price policies, subsidies, tariffs and taxes all affect the relation of peasant produce to non-peasant commodities, and thus the persistence or sacrifice of peasant livelihood. There is some irony in the thought that while the nation-state relied strongly for its consolidation upon the peasant/middle-strata alliance, it may now—in the stage of its decline—willingly sacrifice the peasantry to the massed incursion of capital into agriculture. The international movement of agricultural technology, the operations of the World Bank, and the formulation of international marketing arrangements may all hasten the day when capital would finally wipe out differential rent through the introduction of "factory farming" and advanced transportation technology, and absolute rent would decline to zero, in the face of an ever-rising organic composition of capital. Yet peasantry may still survive in the interstices of the world system, as it survived for a while in the interstices of the nation-state. In fact, in the face of the radioactive clouds, some of these—as in the high Andes—may be the only survivors.

NOTES

1. In Marxian terminology, total capital outlay consists of constant capital (c), paid out for machinery and materials, and variable capital (v), paid out to buy labour power. Constant capital is so-called because its value (i.e. the socially necessary labour time required to produce it) remains constant during a given cycle of production. Variable capital gets its name from the fact that it produces both its own value (the socially necessary labour-time required for its own reproduction) and a surplus-value. Surplus-value, the product produced by the labour force in the time span above and beyond that required to earn the value of its reproduction, is appropriated by the capitalists. c + v together define what is called "the organic composition of capital". When the predominant amount of capital is spent on v and much less on c, the organic composition of capital is low. When the predominant amount of capital is spent on c, and much less on v, the organic composition is high. The ratio between surplus value (s) and capital (c + v)

constitutes the rate of profit (p). Neither c nor v is an absolute category. Both are historically relative. c at any given time depends on the development of the productive forces, especially on technological development. v is a function of the historically relative and historically changing character of workers "needs". s is dependent, moreover, on the organizational means for extracting surplus-value from the labour force.

2.   At the European end, money was advanced to purchase commodities which could activate the circuits of circulation. These commodities were then exchanged once or several times for other commodities in the tributary formations of the periphery. The circuit of transactions closed again when the desired commodity was sold in Europe. This circuit actually comprised three phases: European capital exchanged for European commodities; European commodities exchanged for peripheral commodities; peripheral commodities exchanged for European capital (see Carmagnani 1975 : 33). The tribute-takers of the periphery took charge of the second phase of the circuit, exchanging their commodities for European ones. The means for maximizing the receipt of European commodities was to increase production of their own commodity by means of a massive supply of labour, massed by political and extra-economic means.

REFERENCES

Amin, Samir (1970) : *L'accumulation à l'échelle mondiale*, Éditions Anthropos, Paris.

Banaji, Jarius (1976) : "Summary of selected parts of Kautsky's *The Agrarian Question*", *Economy and Society*, Vol. 5, No. 1, pp. 2-49.

Brenner, Robert (1976) : "Agrarian Class Structure and Economic Development in Pre-Industrial Europe", *Past and Present*, No. 70, pp. 30-75.

Carmagnani, Marcello (1975) : *L'America latina dal '500 a oggi*, Feltrinelli, Milano.

Cutler, Anthony (1975) : "The Concept of Ground-Rent and Capitalism in Agriculture", *Critique of Anthropology*, No. 5, pp. 72-89.

Edel, Mathew (1976) : "Marx's Theory of Rent : Urban Applications", *Kapitalstate : Working Papers on the Capitalist State*, Nos. 4-5, pp. 100-124.

Lane, Frederic Chapin (1966) : *Venice and History : The Collected Papers of Frederic C. Lane*, The John Hopkins Press, Baltimore.

Marx, Karl (1967) [1894] : *Capital*, Vol. 3 : *The Process of Capitalist Production as a Whole*, Frederick Engels, ed., International Publishers, New York.

Merrill, Michael (1976) : "Cash is Good to Eat : Self Sufficiency and Exchange in the Rural Economy of the United States", *Radical History Review*, Winter 1977, pp. 42-71.

Moore, Barrington, Jr. (1966) : *Social Origins of Dictatorship and Democracy : Lord and Peasant in the Making of the Modern World*, beacon Press, Boston.

Murray, Robin (1977) : "Value and Theory of Rent : Part One", *Capital and Class*, Autumn, No. 3, pp. 100-122.

Rey, Pierre-Philippe (1976) : *Les alliances de classes*, Maspero, Paris.

Thorner, Daniel and Alice Thorner (1962) : *Land and Labour in India*, Asia Publishing House, Bombay.

Tilly, Charles (1976) : "Sociology, History, and the Origins of the European Proletarian", Centre for Research on Social Organization Working Paper No. 148, University of Michigan, Ann Arbor.

Treue, Wilhelm (1970): "Gesellschaft, Wirtschaft und Technik Deutschlands im 19. Jahrhundert", in Herbert Grundmann, ed., *Gebhardt, Handbuch der Deutschen Geschichte*, Part IV, vol. 3, pp. 376-541.

Tribe, Keith (1977): "Economic property and the theorization of ground rent", *Economy and Society*, Vol. 6, No. 1, pp. 69-88.

Weber, Eugene (1976): *Peasants Into Frenchmen*, Standard University Press, Stanford.

Wolf, Eric R. (1977): *Peasants*, Prentice-Hall, Englewood Cliffs.

Defining Peasants: Conceptualization and De-conceptualizations: Old and New in a Marxist Debate†

TEODOR SHANIN

The *Declinatio Rustica* from thirteenth century Germany had six declensions for the word peasant—villain, rustic, devil, robber, brigand and looter; and in the plural—wretches, beggars, liars, rogues, trash and infidels.

J. Le Goff

Peasantry is not a class but a notion.

G. Plekhanov

. . . as though it were a question of dialectical reconciliation of concepts and not of the understanding of the real relations.

K. Marx

There are reasons to define "peasants", and there are reasons to leave the word vague, a figure of speech outside the realm where judicious categories of scholarship dwell. Such a decision is never inconsequential, for this concept, if accepted as such, is reflected in conclusions of immediate analytical and political concern. Ways in which such words are put to use matter.

One can, no doubt, overdo concern with terminologies and be sidetracked into deadening discourse where long words are used only to spin more words, still longer. To avoid it the minds of social scientists must ever be immersed directly in social and political realities. Once in a while a test of a concept

† First published in *Peasant Studies*, 1980, vol. 8, No.4.

and another look at its epistemological roots are indicated, however. The time seems ripe for that now, because, for reasons we shall return to presently, the intellectual fashion of "peasant studies" seems to approach a new stage and a turning point.

A. PEASANTS AS A MYSTIFICATION

To test a concept it is probably best to commence by considering its content in the way sanctified by the "null hypothesis" of conventional statistics, i.e. to begin from reasons why the concept should be ruled out altogether. In that light the claim of validity of the concept, its links to reality, its internal consistency, its theoretical setting, and its possible illuminations can be examined at their harshest. Let us begin at those beginnings, and state them.

Peasants are a mystification. To begin with, "a peasant" does not exist in any immediate and strictly specific sense. Over no end of continents, states, and regions those so designated differ in ways as rich in content as the world itself. Within the same village the rich and the poor, a landowner and a tenant, a householder and a hired "hand" will usually break any continuity of smooth gradations. History, too, adds its dimension of diversity, for even "the same" would not be same in different years, decades, and centuries. A stricter conceptualization of the social context will make it all stand out even more, for to take a few examples, can similar meanings attach to "a peasant" within different periods and societies, be it feudal Burgundy, slash-and-burn bushland of Tanzania, the mercantilized Punjab of today, or the cotton-for-industry-producing Gezira? Finally, general cross-historical and a-contextual terms have a nasty habit of turning into reifications of reality, or worse still, conscious manipulations by smart politicians and prestige-hunting academics. That is why and how peasants become a mystification.

All that is factually true for every one of the four analytical points made. The heterogeneity of the peasants is doubtless. Peasants cannot be indeed understood or even properly described without their more general societal setting, and the same holds true for the historical context (indeed, only analytically can we divide "the diachronic" and "the synchronic" within social phenomena). Finally, the term "peasants" can be used and has been used in mystification. Yet the stipulation of all that is no more than to clear ground for the discussion of the central questions that are at stake here. What is at issue is the way this concept operates within the process of knowledge about societies. Only within that context can the "defining of peasants" be understood. In those terms a "null hypothesis" will be to state that the usage of the concept "peasants" turns social reality opaque to our eyes, or at least does not contribute at all to its illumination. If so, the conclusion at its most consistent would be to get rid of the awkward term, to avoid afflictions it may lead us into. The alternative, i.e. retaining "peasants" in conceptual usage, will have to be clarified and defended.

A major and increasingly significant role in such considerations has been played by the current surge of academic Marxism. Its increasing "globalization" brought peasants anew into the focus of attention. New insights and new vigour of debate have offered us opportunity to consider anew both societies and scholars' thought. Some of the arguments have re-stated, and to an extent re-positioned, the case against "peasants" as a legitimate concept. Others have declared the opposite. Within the marxist conceptual framework a problematic is being explored, the relevance of which will be easily recognized also far outside that camp. Many of the positions taken, conclusions offered, and doubts proffered cross-cut the Marxist/ non Marxist frontiers and battle-lines.

The paper will proceed from the meaning within which the concept is used, through the ways it becomes problematic within the recent Marxist debate, to pose the issue of de-conceptualization at its end. It follows roughly the case against peasants as a meaningful concept which was set out above.

B. PEASANTS AS A GENERALIZATION

Even to argue peasants into the ground, one has to say first what it is all about. More so, if one would like to put that concept to analytical use. So, what do we mean by "peasants"? Let us begin with the students of peasant societies attempting to generalize the content of their studies. Redfield's statement that "peasant society and culture have something generic about it . . . (that it is) . . . an arrangement of humanity with some similarities all over the world" (1956 : 25) and Fei's description of peasanthood as "way of living" (1946) represent well a widespread feeling of most of those who have studied peasants in a systematic and comparative way. Such intuitions should not be disregarded, for they often reflect tacit knowledge rooted in experience. It may as well represent a professional sight-distortion of 'peasantologists', however. To be more specific, the claim (and the guide to any potential test) of peasant specificity can be presented under six characteristics by which peasants have been delineated from 'others'.

First, the economy of peasants has been said to differ by a distinctive blend of extensive self-employment (i.e. family labour), control of own means of production, self-consumption of produce and multi-dimensional occupational expertise (Galeski 1972). Another way to present it is to show how much peasant conditions of productive life necessitate and are shaped by the establishment of an eco-system and a particular balance of agriculture, animal production, gathering, and crafts with a particular stress on growing rather than manufacturing (Wolf 1966; Malita 1971). A different yet structurally similar scheme will appear within pastoral economies (as for example Naderi 1971).

A variety of economically relevant characteristics follow. For example, planning of production and calculation of performance differ consistently from those of a capitalist enterprise. Kautsky's notion of peasants' under-consumption (Banarjee 1976) and Chayanov's (1966) notion of 'self-exploitation' seem to refer to a general problem of poverty and oppression but also to its specific resolutions in forms which do not operate outside the scope of the peasant economy. The actual pattern of land control expressed in family property and "rights of domain" differ from the legal ownership of the contemporary non-peasants (see Wolf 1966). A broad range of occupational tasks is "telescoped" into peasanthood as an occupation. Typical methods of expropriation of peasant surplus by the holders of political and economic power differ from those used against the wage labourers. Inter-peasant and inter-village exploitation show once again specific forms and direction of development. The taken-for-granted links of supply/demand/price movements within market-centred societies change considerably within massively peasant populations (e.g. the movement of wages which is often inversely proportionate to the price of bread). By the accepted standards of calculation, many peasant farms are 'working at a loss' and should "go bankrupt", yet proceed to operate and even to invest (Shanin 1973).

Secondly, the patterns and tendencies of political organization of peasants have often considerably similarity in different regions and countries of the world. Systems of brokers and patronage, the dendency for 'vertical segmentation' and factionalism, the place of banditry and guerilla struggle, even the typical atmosphere of peasant politics and peasant rebellion can be, and indeed have been, meaningfully compared in societies thousands of miles apart in both geography and social space (Wolf 1969; Stovenhagen 1970). That holds true also for the patterns and problems of the political interactions between peasants and both the landlords and the outsiders—representatives of national bureaucracies.

Thirdly, typical and closely similar norms and cognitions have been singled out in peasantries far enough removed to preclude claims of simple dispersion. These patterns both reflect and influence in turn the ways of social life and production. The pre-eminence of traditional and conformist rationalization, the role of oral tradition, specific 'cognitive maps' (e.g. a circular perception of time) can be used as examples (Bailey 1966; Dobrowoiski 1971). Specific patterns of socialization and training into peasant occupation were also traced and related here (Galeski 1972). The same can be said about peasant ideological tendencies and the related patterns of political cooperation, confrontation, and leadership.

Fourthly, the basic and characteristic units of social organization and their functioning have shown considerable similarity all round the globe. In particular, the peasant household, but also the village and the broader networks of social interaction, like a market centre and the localized lowest ring of the state authority, are easily recognizable to peasants, scholars, and political leaders far afield. The typical internal patterns of interaction and/or exploitation within small composite units, which peasants usually share with rural labourers, craftsmen, petty bureaucrats, and capitalists, are distinctive and highly repetitive. So is the general subservient position of peasant social units within broader networks of political, economic, and cultural demination.

Fifthly, one can single out analytically a specific social dynamics of peasant society (in reality the statics and dynamics would, of course, be indivisible). In particular, social reproduction, i.e. the production of the material necessities, the reproduction of the human actors and of the system of social relations, shows patterns specific and generic to the peasants. For example, typical patterns of family property and inheritance customs, referred to above, are central to the reproduction of peasant family farms. The in-family occupational training, as mentioned, is relevant here. The rhythm of life of the peasant household and village reflects powerfully major "natural" cycles, e.g. the agricultural year.

Finally, fundamental patterns and causes of structural transformation have once again been seen as generic and specific to peasants. Theories of structural change have been rightly expressed in a broader-than-peasantry framework of the national societies or of international systems. At the same time peasant specificity has been claimed in the ways those general processes are reflected within, and reacted to by, the peasant communities. For example, commercialization has usually resulted at first in a stage of "agriculturalization" of the peasant, their earlier non-agricultural tasks taken over by industrial mass-production (while the villagers are often boxed into capitalist exploitive networks of agro-business of various types). At the other side of the fence, collectivization has led to a variety of specifically peasant patterns of action and reaction, e.g. the differential patterns of production on the house plot as against the collective field and their impact on the actual social operation of agriculture (Cuong and Ba 1976). The often-repeated surprise at the tenacity of peasant social forms (the "problem of non-disappearance"), and even contemporary 're-peasantation' of some areas, would also belong here.

There is no place here to discuss the scope of comparative evidence presented in support of those generalizations. Let us proceed directly to what such generalizations imply. To begin with the negatives, the use of the generalization does not, of course, imply homogeneity of peasants. Nor does it assume a clear-cut separation of actual categories, of the 1 : 0 variety. Any generalization based on comparison will assume heterogeneity of data as well as "margins" or "hedges" of conceptual ambivalence. The charge number one against peasants as a conceptual entity on the list above is either beside the point or else doubts the analytical essentials of social sicences and not simply one of its terms. The status of peasants as a generalization was well expressed in a recent lecture by Eric Wolf (1977) as that of a "recurrent syndrome" which of course assumes, and indeed necessitates, diversity (often expressed in additional taxonomies). As such, empirical generalization forms an indispensable part of social science. Its danger lies in possible over-generalization, by extrapolating known similarities or sequences simply because these are known. That being said, the very presence of repetitive and massive similarities is a point well worth making, and that is what the generalizations based on comparison between peasants came to signify. It has helped to focus study, to elicit insights and employ methods of enquiry tested elsewhere, as well as to lay out a field for analysis. It does not provide a substitute for it.

The flourishing of "peasant studies" in the 1960s was linked to new attempts to define peasants by exploring the structural logic behind their "peasantness". In that debate the wing of western anthropology which interpreted Redfield's and Fei's intuitions in terms of political economy has met with the West European rural history and the eastern European tradition of peasant studies, both Marxist and non-Marxist. The results of those encounters led to much more than simple generalizations from the empirical , yet did not usually offer fully developed structural analysis either (see Claus 1973).

An example can help, and it may be simplest to use oneself for the whipping boy (Shanin 1971). A four-pronged delineation of peasants was offered a decade ago, incorporating (a) the family farm as the basic unit of social and economic organization; (b) agriculture as the main source of livelihood; (c) village life and the specific culture of the small rural communities; (d) the underdog position, i.e. domination and exploitation of the peasants by powerful outsiders. Within the discourse, all of the four characteristics qualified for fully-fledged peasanthood, while three out of four defined a variety of "analytically marginal groups", e.g. the rural craftsmen with (a), (c), and (d) only. That was done to give coherence to a Reader, structuring comparative data and contributing to the designation of a field. So far so good. It has offered too little in terms of systematic analysis of the structural logic at the root of the generalization presented. That makes it unsatisfactory on several scores.

To begin, the four components of this delineation are insufficient, not because another fifth one has been missed and should be added, but rather because the links between those four were left broadly unspecified. With no doubt the usefulness of the typology is very much subject to the implicit assumption of tendencies/patterns of mutual determination of its elements. That would explain why one can deduce at a pinch a considerable measure of characteristics of each of them, by looking at the other three in depth. For an example, the way peasant operates can tell us much about the character of the rural community, the peasant family farm, and the typical patterns of exploitation of producers within such a society. Yet even an elaboration of these links will still not be sufficient. Hobsbawn has pointed out that the presumption of *heirarchies* of basic elements of social structure is one of the defining characteristics of Marxist social theorizing (1972). Such consistent principles of interpretation are indeed a necessary part of most theoretical systems. A hierarchy of significance (or else an assumption that there is none) was never spelled out in the case reviewed, which opens the door to ambivalent and/or eclectic interpretations.

Furthermore, while defining peasants as a process and typologising patterns of change, the way different elements of this complex equation link into the more general social history were left relatively unexplored (actually a step backward from an earlier discussion) (Shanin 1971 : 238-243, written in 1966). For example, the impact of international trade and of the global political economy on the basic directions of development of peasant agriculture was not even considered. Looking at it "from the opposite side", the impact of specific histories of peasants on the societies they formed parts of, was left altogether out of sight.

Finally, the way the problematic of societal embedding of peasants was presented suffers from all the essential limitations referred to as concerning history, to which a touch of "provincialism" in the sense of a tendency to approach any problematics, so to say, only from the peasants "outwards", can be added. Explainable as it may all have been as "bending the stick the other way" in an argument against the conceptual marginalization of peasants, all that is unsatisfactory all the same.

While this is not the place for a full-scale re-analysis, what was previously left implicit must be brought out here into the open. Peasant specificity reflects interdependence amount the basic elements mentioned, and cannot be simply reduced to any one of them. At the same time, the core of its determining characteristics seems to lie in the nature and dynamics of the family farm as a basic unit of production and social livelihood. Consequently, the very existence of peasants as a specific social entity is contingent on the presence of family farms as the basic units of economy and society. Peasants must be understood, therefore, via the exploration of peasant family farm characteristics, both internal and external, i.e. its specific reactions to, and interaction with, the broader social context. A point to remember, especially within the diverse "western" experience, is that the essence of such a unit lies not in kinship but in production. The world-wide repetition of economic, political, and cultural traits as well as of the typical patterns of dynamics would have to do with the *modus operandi* of the peasant family farms and the specific ways they link and transform. When (and if) an Occam's razor is used, it would be best to accept the operation of family farms as the narrowest definition of peasants, except where there are definite reasons to choose otherwise.

That is essentially the approach to characterization of the peasantry which was at the core of the mainstream of central and eastern European research and political debate during the last century. While presumptions, questions, and conclusions differed, the way the concept was singled out and assumed has cross-cut ideological camps and academic schools of thought. In particular, while a debate raged over the issue of peasants' stability, nobody seemed to doubt where the root of peasanthood lay. Nor was there any criterion by which we might judge and if, in the wake of economic and social transformations, that social entity came to an end. It was the peasant family unit of production and its structural metamorphosis or disappearance which has delineated both. Three generations later this tradition is still fully reflected in the current generation of leading Marxist students of peasants in eastern Europe, for example B. Galeski, V.P. Danilov, A.M. Anfimov.

Contradictory and often remarkably far-fetched interpretations of Marx have rapidly become a major academic industry of the post-1968 period. It is within this type of debate that a call to de-conceptualize peasants has been recently heard, claiming Marx's authority to it. A quick look at his actual views may not be amiss, therefore. Marx's insight and inspiration concerning peasants are very much those of a central European (with the knowledge of eastern European languages and tradition), who was placed within the English milieu of de-peasantized capitalism. In the study in which Marx tackled peasants of his own times most directly, he characterized and delineated "the most numerous class of French society" through the concept of *"parzellen* holding". What is *parzelle* if not the peasant family farm, duly described in the sentences of his text which follow? It is indeed easily placed as the "individual workshop (which) contains the entire economy, forming as it does an independent centre of production" of the earlier period, subsequently commercialized and partly transformed by the capitalist development of France. Or, to de-code metaphorical language, a "potato" within "the sack of potatoes" (as Marx characterized the French peasants) is no doubt the same unit, i.e. a peasant's family farm. The anticipated direction of further development was also made clear. It is the "dissolution of private property based on the labour of its owner" (Marx 1973 : 478-9), i.e. the advance of capitalist development due to restructure society into two fundamental classes, dissolving peasant family production units and thereby the peasantry in the process. To wit, "the production of capital and wage workers is therefore the major product of the process by which capital turns itself into value" (Marx 1964). The mainstream of Marxist social theorizing has consequently approached the contemporary peasantry via the problematic of its capitalist transformation expressed in two major conceptual debates concerning differentiation and modes of production. The issue of peasants' location within history and society was set accordingly.

C. THE CAPITALIST TRANSFORMATION OF AGRICULTURE: THE THREE ROADS

Capitalist transformation provided the major direction of structural change within the contemporary peasant societies. Capitalism means de-peasantation; in the nineteenth century that view was generally adopted by "the educated public", with fairly few exceptions—the reactionary romantics, the strict populists, and some of the "revisionists" in the German Social Democracy. All those were challenged by the united front of the academic economists, and most of the orthodox Marxists. To all those the question was not that of capitalist de-peasantation of agriculture, but only of its form and speed.

The major work which dominated Marxist thought in those times was *The Agrarian Problem* by K. Kautsky. It was (and still is) rich in content and insight into the peasant problematic. It accepted the possibility of some differences in the way capital penetrates agriculture as against the other branches of economy. It pointed to capital accumulation and structural change within German agriculture, and stressed that the reported lack of concentration of land ownership did not necessarily mean a failure of capitalism to take hold there. The prime mover of capitalist transformation of the rural society was industry, which outstripped, subordinated, and finally destroyed peasant agriculture. Kautsky's position has closely followed and elaborated Marx's presentation of the English/Irish example in *Capital* (1976), suitably generalized and advanced.

Lenin's political success eventually made for the decisive influence of his contribution to this debate, as far as the following generations of Marxists were concerned. In the earliest of his books Lenin was still very much a "Kautskian", but the stress clearly differed. To him it was the *inter-peasant* dynamics of "deepening" market relations, the division of labour, and class differentiation which provided the central point of capitalist transformation (Lenin 1968, 1974). His polemics aimed at a wing within Russian populism which believed that the homogeneity and stability of peasant society would abort capitalist development in Russia. The logic of commodity relations and the exploitative capacity of the richer peasants indicated a necessary polarization of the peasants into rich and poor, and eventually into rural capitalists and rural proletarians. The problem of differentiation, its character, speed, and political results have subsequently dominated the analysis of peasant societies within the Third International and the communist movements of "the East". Long stretches of Lenin's 1899 book still appear practically verbatim within many of the studies of diverse societies today.

Only a thin line divides the appreciation of a masterly analytical achievement from religious self-stupification by it. The best way to tell the difference is simply to ask: Was anything substantively new learned during the 80 years which have passed since Lenin's book was published? Indeed, did Lenin himself learn anything new from the 25 years of his own revolutionary experience which followed the publication of his treatise?

To begin with the second of those questions, Lenin's own approach to peasantry underwent a consistent, if slow, change. Already by 1907 he declared his earlier conclusions about the capitalist nature of Russian agriculture, linked to the period of Plekhanov's theoretical hegemony in the Russian SD, as clearly overstated. Lenin moved further (if more implicitly) in the acceptance of persisting peasant traits. That shift underlies and accounts for the changes in the party programmes in 1917 and 1921, and was expressed at its strongest on Lenin's death-bed. Indeed, very cancellation of the first "agrarian programme" of his party already meant that the 1896-98 analysis, directly related to it, could not be sustained. Yet the book was never re-written, and drifted into cononization together with the man himself.

In the last decade attempts to consider anew the differentiation debate have been made both in the West and in the USSR. In particular, massive amendments in the analysis have been suggested by contemporary Soviet historians looking anew at Russian data. Fresh attempts to put to use Lenin's methodology concerning differentiation of peasantry elsewhere (for example in India) have also presented new insights and new opportunities. Yet in most of those studies the basic presumptions of Lenin concerning peasant diffrentiation are treated by many Marxists as very much akin to the laws of nature, with a clear nod of approval from neo-classical economists. The critical comments and/or amendments to the original thesis, now transplanted, centred on the speed of polarization and possible countervailing influences only. Yet one must tackle also the fundamental models and archetypes at the root of the differentiation analysis. How satisfactory is Lenin's theoretical preamble to his 1899 book for the contemporary scene?

The picture emerging from the complex bits and pieces of international comparison seems more complex and multi-directional than the early differentiation model would grant it to be. In the case of the capitalist transformation of agriculture, not one but rather three major directions seem to occur, simultaneously in different regions and parts of the world, and at times, indeed, within the same society. These will be referred to as the processes of differentiation, pauperization, and marginalization.

Without doubt *differentiation* has played an important role in the capitalist transformation of peasant agriculture, and has often represented the most significant structural change in it. The theoretical and factual claims in support of that are valid. It is the interpretation of it as the axiomatically necessary and exclusive pattern of development, which is not.

To begin with te theoretical model, exploitation plus Myrdal's (1957) "circular causation" and "cumulation of both advantages and disadvantages" should lead to an increasing capital accumulation at "the top", i.e. in the hands of the rural and urban rich and/or capitalists. A free market economy is on the whole presumed. Such a process would also, it is assumed, produce jobs for the newly pauperized, turning them into proletarians and extending capitalism in its classical sense. Let us vary one of the components: the surplus value is accumulated neither in the villages nor in towns of the countryside itself, but in a metropolis 5,000 miles away. What will follow is a twisted "polarization" in which the downward trend is not matched by an upward one, i.e. what we face is not differentiation and proletarianization of the majority, but a process of *pauperization* expressed in the phenomena of "surplus population", rural under-employment", the shanty towns' "culture of poverty", etc. It is not a "labour reserve army" which is produced, for nobody is to call on those reserves within the decades to come. Nor can they be called "deviants", "marginals", or other such words assuming exceptionality, for the social grouping referred to is constant and central to such a society.

Is such a variation of the "differentiation model" realistic? Of course, it happens in every colonial society and typifies what is today referred to as "neo-colonialism" and "peripheralization". Is the resulting scenario realistic? Of course, look at Java (Geertz 1963) etc. etc. Does it call for specific conceptual and analytical effort? No doubt, for, to begin with, peasants under such circumstances will neither fully disappear, nor will they remain structurally as before, or else turn rural proletarians in terms of the classical theory of capitalism. Even the ethnography of the scene differs, and so do the political conclusions and anticipations, i.e. the stuff which makes social analysis truly relevant.

To proceed, the optimistic, "youngish" capitalism of the nineteenth century has very much influenced the classical Marxist view of its. It was seen as aggressive, constructive, overwhelming, and supra-energetic in its capacity to spread. Like the finger of Midas which turns everything it touches into gold, so does capitalism turn everything it touches into capitalism. The earth is the limit.

In the light of what we actually find today, all that seems an over-statement by far. The capacity of capitalist centres to milk everybody and everything around is doubtedless; it is their capacity or their need (in terms of optimization of profits) to transform everything around into the likes of themselves. Peasants are often a case in point. In the doubtlessly capitalist Mexico the relative share of the peasants within the population has been decreasing, but their number have kept remarkably steady since 1910. In the no-less-certainly capitalist Brazil, an absolute increase in the number of the peasantry, i.e. actual re-peasantization, has been taking place (Lopez 1976). Even the World Bank's chief (following a considerable change of mind) has recently spoken about hundreds of millions of small producers on the land by the end of the century (MacNamara 1974). What does it all mean in terms of the assumptions of capitalist transformation of peasant agriculture?

It seems to mean that under some conditions peasants do not dissolve and differentiate into capitalist entrepreneurs and wage labourers, nor are they simply pauperized. They persist, while gradually transforming and linking into the encapsulating capitalist economy, which pierces through their lives. Peasants continue to exist, coinciding with agricultural units different in structure and size from the classical peasant family farm in ways partly explored already by Kautsky. Peasants are *marginalized,* the significance of the peasant agriculture within the national economy decreases, its lower production growth turns it into a backwater. The same may be happening to the position of the peasants within "the nation". Peasants serve capitalist development in a less direct sense, a type of permanent "primitive accumulation", offering cheap labour, cheap food, and markets for profit-making goods. They also produce healthy and stupid soldiers, policemen, servants, cooks, and prostitutes; the system can always do with more of all of these. And, of course, they, i.e. peasants, produce trouble for those scholars and officials who puzzle over the problem of their "non-disappearance".

The theoretical problems of conceptualizing this phenomenon can be, of course, removed altogether by either declaring that "agriculture" (largely unspecified) is simply slow to catch up, or else by simply defining everybody as "capitalist", as long as it is linked with the capitalist economy. Outside such grand reductions (whatever the name attached, be it "dualism", "articulation", etc.), the tendency of some types of linkage with capitalism actually to stabilise some specific peasant characteristics was increasingly sensed and singled out as one of the possible major aspects of transformation within contemporary peasant agriculture. Once again, both the model and the scenario can be easily enough validated through evidence of "the Third World" as well as Europe.

To accept marginalization as one of the patterns of *peasant* change under the impact of capitalism is conditional on the resolution of one more conceptual query. When, if at all, does a peasant stop from being a peasant while retaining a family-farm unit of production? To put it specifically, is a Danish family using family labour to drive and supervise a couple of self-owned tractors, four cars, and a super-mechanized farm supported by massive capital investment and profits, but with no wage labourers, to be defined as peasants? If not, where does the divide lie? A current study by Danilov *et al.* (1977) suggests a neat conceptual solution here. He divides the forces of production of the family farm into "natural" (e.g. land or labour) and those which are man-produced (e.g. machinery and equipment), and suggests that we define as peasant only those farms in which production is decisively determined by the "natural" means of production.

The same work, a most recent, original Marxist contribution to the conceptualization of peasants, has also sounded a powerful reminder about the basic limitations of the classical differentiation theories of old. These theories presume a free market economy, and very much abstract from the nature of state intervention. Yet already in medieval China the imperial agrarian reforms successfully removed large land ownership, reversing differentiation processes back to square one. The Soviet NEP represented a different dimension of regeneration of peasants by the state and the revolution. On the other hand, in a number of developing societies the state transformed peasant economy through the imposition of monopolistic centralization of rural exchange, which, while limiting the rural bourgeoisie, established a "gigantic dispersed manufacture", exploitative in its nature; e.g. note the position of the small coffee farmers of Ghana. Such state transformation defined anew the peasants' "place and role within the social structure". All of it well said and no need to spoil it by a superfluous addition or comment.

D. MODES AND PEASANTS: PEASANTS AS A MODE OF PRODUCTION

The second way the peasant problematic has been approached within the current Marxist revival was via the elaboration of the properties of modes of production. The conceptual problems of specificity, i.e. of the "existence" of peasants, can be and have been presented accordingly. Its particular significance lies in the fact of centring analytical attention on what seems to be the kernel of awkwardness of the whole conceptual problematic, i.e. on the issue of peasants fitting into the broader society and history.

Part of the current debate concerning modes of production has been no more than fashionable verbiage, a bid for a place on a platform or for a Marxist badge, within communities where such things matter. Some of it is reminiscent of the worst examples of Functionalism: logical manipulation of elaborated abstractions, cruelly verbose in neologisms, and essentially sterile in advancing understanding of social reality. Yet, besides all that we find some of the most serious theoretical concerns and opportunities. Identification of fundamental units of analysis, their character, flexibility, and changing usage play a crucial role in the way our intellectual maps are shaped and in turn shape social reality. Modes of production are such fundamental units of analysis within Marxist theoretical thought.

Marx's authority still very much designates what the mode of production is assumed to be. His usage of some concepts was often partial, changeable, or implicit, to be distilled from working which find their internal coherence elsewhere.

That is true also of the concept of modes of production. Yet the central characteristics and elements of it are agreed on by most of those who have studied Marx, even though their respective emphasis may vary considerably.

The mode of production represents the general (in the sense of abstract) and the specific (in the sense of a particular historical setting) way the material needs of society are provided for at a given stage of its development. This makes it crucial for the analysis of the whole nature of society's existence and of the characterization of its specificity. It also explains why the exposition of the concept usually begins with the interdependence of the relations of production and the forces of production, i.e. "appears equally as the relationship of individuals to one another and the specific daily behaviour towards inorganic nature, their specific mode of labour" (Marx 1964 : 94) A system of political economy centred at the creation, appropriation, and control of surpluses through the domination of men by men, i.e. an "essential relationship of appropriation (which is) the relationship of domination" (Marx 1964 : 102) provides a central and distinguishing element of a mode of production. A typically patterned dynamics is part and parcel of the concept and is specific to every mode of production. In structuralist terminology a mode of production has therefore both a synchronic and dyachronic dimension, i.e. it represents not only a specifically structured system, but also a historical epoch. It incorporates reproductive processes inasmuch as material goods, labour, and the system of social relations are concerned. It specifies also distinctive patterns of structural change.

The concept of mode of production as defined provides the hard core and/or determinant of a number of further characteristics. The character and extent of such determinations is never simple and is usualy mutual in character. The legal systems of ownership reflect it well (much of Marx's attention was devoted to it). It defines a political economy yet it represents also a patterned consciousness of a type. It reflects the actual relations of production and control, but at the same time shows partial autonomy and capacity to feed back (with its own determining capacity) into the economy *sensu strictu*. The same can be said about a number of basic structures of social control, interaction, and consciousness, of which the modern state is probably the most crucial.

The rejuvenation of Marxist analysis in the 1970s led to a considerable increase in attention to and sophistication of the usage of the concept of mode of production. This shift in theoretical perspective was for a time influenced with particular strength by the work of Althusser and his disciples, in which Marxism confronted and interacted with contemporary French structuralism. The analytical focus moved towards the hidden beneath the observable, the structural, the non-subjective, with the logic of modes of production overshadowing other units of analysis. The intellectual attraction of such preference relates to the intellectual's quest for the more certain and deterministic, expressed as deeper, more objective, more law-bound, and theoretical. It has been terminologically reflected in the way "science", "scientific", and "rigorous" came to be used as major badges of Marxist scholarship (with Marx's *Capital* becoming more "scientific" than his *Eighteenth Brumaire*).

This theoretical language led to the redefinition of the term "social formation" and the sudden rise to fame of the term "articulation", a newcomer to Marxist discourse. Social formation came to signify a specific society—usually a nation-state. It has been defined, then, as a specific articulation of modes of production, of which one plays a dominant role. The essence of social analysis became very much the consideration of the ways modes operate and articulate within societies/social formations:

Once mode of production is accepted as the central unit of social analysis, the scope of the problematic concerning the conceptualization of peasants can be re-stated in the following sequence of questions. The scheme also offers a systematic approach to the problematic of peasants' societal and historical setting, i.e. charges two, three and four of our "null hypotheses".

(a) Is peasantry as such to be constituted as a *mode of production* and, if so, how does it 'articulate' with the society at large? (and if not . . .)

(b) Is peasantry to be seen as *a component* of a specific (and exclusive) mode of production? (and if not . . .)

(c) Is peasantry to be understood as a social entity autonomous enough to relate to, and to transfer between, different modes of production? (and if not . . .)

(d) Is peasantry an "empty word" exposed and nullified by the satisfactory usage of the concept of mode of production?

To begin, are peasants a mode of production? Evidently the answer relates to the way mode of production and peasants are defined. In the terms suggested above, peasants are not a mode of production because they lack a relatively self-contained structure of political economy, i.e. the most significant systems of exploitation and surplus appropriation have been on the whole external to them. It goes without saying that all peasants are not "equal" and that every peasant community displays complex structures of internal "neighbourly" exploitation often linked within networks of "patronage". Yet to most of the peasants, inter-peasant inequality and exploitation is secondary to the extra-pesant one, both in terms of the share extracted and in the way structural dynamics and class structure bear upon them. Indeed, the turning towards decisive predominance of inter-peasant and inter-village structures of inequality and exploitation spells the end of peasantry as such, i.e. as a specific social grouping.

There are two alternative approaches which lead to the categorization of peasantry as a mode of production. The first is to stipulate two sub-types of "mode of production", one along lines suggested above and another one differently defined. That suggestion has been offered in a number of recent studies designating a "secondary mode of production", which differs from a "primary" one by appearing only in articulation with other modes of production but never on its own (see Cardoso 1975). A society (socio-economic formation?) provides therefore the framework within which an exploitative political economy acts as a determining link between the dominant (exploitative) and secondary (exploited) mode of production. A secondary mode of production would represent a linked structure of forces and relations of production, a necessarily incomplete political economy in which the dominant societal conflict and determinations lie at its boundaries. The "rules of the game" of the dominant mode of production would dominate the "formation" as a whole.

The origins (and legitimation) of the concept of "secondary mode of production" and its present usage are in the discussion of the smallholders— "immediate producers" referred to by Marx (1976 : 926) as "a mode of production . . . (which) also exists under slavery, serfdom and other situations of dependency . . . but . . . flourishes where the worker is the free propreitor of the conditions of his labour and sets them in motion himself". The interpretations of this text have varied considerably, from the treatment of the concept as an essentially pedagogic device (i.e. an abstract "point of beginning" set to clarify the dynamics of capitalism), to the assumption of a fully-fledged ("primary") mode of production of independent commodity producers, e.g. in an epoch in US history in which it offered a temporary barrier to the development of capitalism there (see O'Canner and Sherry 1976). The idea of a peasant secondary mode of production falls somewhat in between those polarities. Peasant economy is approached as a sub-category of a broader family of "petty commodity modes of production", their position within society caught well by the term 'tributary society'.

The second alternative is to redesign the term mode of production in an even more radical fashion. Once more, Marx's own text has been used as support. The mode of production is seen here in its most direct and descriptive sense, i.e. as a way of producing, a labour process, a general technological stage of social development, a concept of scope greatly reduced along the lines expressed, for example, in Marx's designation of *agriculture* as a mode of production *sui generis*.

Both of the alternatives delimit peasants as a mode of production (or else do it for mainly peasant "small commodity producers"). What are the heuristic gains and limitations of such an analytical strategy? The delimitation of presentation of peasant specificity within the concept of a "peasant mode of production" provides a possible approach to the theorizing and analysis of a number of issues in question, e.g. peasants' societal setting. Yet, at the same time the cutting edge of the concept of mode of production has been very much subject to its specific designation as a system/dynamics within which production and exploitative appropriation are central and linked. (The same can probably be said about the very contribution of Marxism to social sciences.) A mode of production as a unit of analysis which does not carry these essential characteristics seems to stretch the term to the point of categorizing out of existence its most important analytical insights. On balance, the concept of "peasant mode of production" has too many heuristic limitations to be sustained.

E. PEASANTS AND MODES : TOTALITIES AND UNITS

To proceed to the second question of the sequence concerning modes and peasants, is peasantry a component of an exclusive mode of production? The most likely candidate here would be feudalism, appropriating peasant labour and produce within a mainly agricultural and decentralized economy and society, with landowners-cum-local rulers (cum-knights) at its top. There are considerable doubts from the outset, however. Quite a number of modes of production/"progressive epochs in the economic formation of the society" (Marx 1973 : 504) of Marx's own definition contain the 'something' which he himself and those who study peasants delimit as the core of peasant specificity. Let us remember also that in the *Eighteenth Brumaire, etc.* he used and explored the concept "peasant" in (early?) capitalist France. Peasant households as basic units of production and social living, peasants as a group with considerable structural similarities, or even with an established political self-identity, can easily be spotted within differently structured socio-economic systems from "the Asiatic" (if there is such a "thing") via the massive outskirts of the slave-managed estates of antiquity, within the blossoming (early?) capitalism of Germany, and as far as the Soviet NEP and Poland of today. The only way to insist on peasants as exclusively embedded in the feudal mode of production is to do it by a tautology, i.e. by arbitrarily defining (a) all modes of production containing peasants as feudal; (b) all family production units outside feudalism as not peasants (or else as a conceptual archaeological remainders which share societal space with those who legitimately occupy it, i.e. the wage workers under capitalism). Such procedures limit rather than extend our grasp of social reality in its complexity and contradictions.

In more general terms the diversity of approaches to the way the family farm as a basic unit of peasant economy/society fits into a mode of production can be presented on a continuum between two poles, both represented within works published during the past decade. On the one hand, it is the characteristics of the dominant production unit which exclusively define the broader structure (mode of production? formation? society?); on the other hand, the essential characteristics of family farms, and consequently of the peasant economy, have been treated as exclusively determined by the broader socio-economic system, or by the (dominant?) mode of production.

Consequent to the first approach, to quote, "the household is to the tribal (?) economy as the manor to medieval economy or the corporation to modern capitalism, each is dominant production institution of its times" (Sahlins 1974 : 76). While Sahlins' designation of a household as typically tribal (with peasant family farms dropping out of the scheme) may be misleading, especially within the contemporary world, the logic of a position was spelt out admirably. It has also been explicitly and rightly related to the comparative taxonomy of economic system by Chayanov, and as manifestly put in contradiction with the structuralism of Terray. The fully developed conclusion of such an approach has been expressed already in Thorner's category of peasant economy defined as a "whole economy of sizeable countres", and as "a widespread form of distinctly peasant social units within population, economy, etc. Consequently, a set of characteristics, of which the peasant household as typical unit of production is the most fundamental, defines an economic system and an epoch of considerable length and heterogeneity, for peasant economies existed "long before feudalism, alongside feudalism, and long after it". It is also the drop in the share of peasant family-farm which will make the term "peasant" at some stage inapplicable to such an "economy taken as a whole" (Thorner 1971 : 202-8, 216-17).

On the other hand, different modes of production systems or societies would mean totally different social essences for peasant family farms (and of peasantry generally), even if formal similarities can be traced. Marx's comment that "even economic categories appropriate to earlier modes of production acquire a new and specific historical character under the impact of capitalist production" (Marx, 1976 : 950) are consequently interpreted to mean that "there is no 'peasantry' in general, only specific forms of agricultural production, worked and managed to a greater or lesser degree by household units . . . specific to the mode of production in which they exist. Typologies based upon technique, agronomic and cultural conditions are at best misleading". Or, in the more rounded-up form of the same text, "Peasantry as a theoretical economic category does not exist in Marxism . . . " and should be treated as "a specific agrarian detachment of petty bourgeoisie". The same would necessarily go for specific peasant history or for any of its assumed basic characteristics. At its crudest, one can proceed by certification of orthodoxy-cum-truth, through simple dividing of the conceptual field between Marxist structuralism and a unit-directed "non-Marxist approach", Marx's own writing included.

The best way to tackle these problems is probably to commence by paying closer attention to the broader epistemological issues which present themselves here, i.e. the relations between "totality" and its sub-units. Does a general structure exclusively determine and define its component units or does the sum total of sub-units define the whole? Are there other possibilities? The third question of the above sequence of questions is also relevant here: can peasants be seen as "inter-mode" transferable entities or is such a notion absurd?

The answer lies, at least initially, at the epistemological level. Marxist analysis is without doubt rightly structuralist to the extent of refusal to accept reduction of any totality to the sum-total of its sub-units (and so, by the way, is sophisticated non-Marxist scholarship[4]). The conclusion which cannot be drawn from it is a reduction "the opposite way round", i.e. an attempt at the deduction of sub-units from the characteristics of the whole via the "simple, logical development of general truth". It is the interaction of the whole and its parts in all of their specific, different, and related characteristics, the often contradictory dynamics and the orders of logic of both the totality and its units, which must be grasped at once. Complex as it is, there is no way around it. The often over-employed words "dialectical relationship" will not be out of place here. To exemplify, social classes reflect the contradictions and laws of motion of modes of production, but no deduction of the first from the second (on *vice versa*) can substitute for the specific analysis. Turning back to the peasants, what must be rejected is a misleading question, assuming a fake duality of possibilities. Without doubt, one cannot understand the operation of peasant units of production without their societal context. Nor can one deduce them or reduce them or conceptually dissolve them simply because of that. Deductionism is not a satisfactory answer to Empiricism.

To put it another way, to accept an "inter-mode" existence and possible transfer of the peasant is to bring it closer to the richness and contradictions of reality. To say so is not to claim that peasants under capitalism equal peasants under feudalism, for that is not at issue (and the opposite is, of course, assumed). What it does mean is that peasants represent social and economic specifity of characteristics which will reflect on every societal system they operate within. It means also that peasant history relates to broader societal histories, not as their simple reflection, but with important measures of autonomy. At its simplest, it means that a capital-dominated social formation encompassing peasants differs from those in which peasants do not exist. Once again, the issue cross-cuts the Marxist/non-Marxist frontier, for as the self-critical remark of a leading exponent of the Structural Functionalism school has it, their conceptual crisis was followed by the new "strong emphasis laid on the autonomy of any subsetting-subgroup or subsystem . . ." thereby "problematized"[5]—a comment which would fit some Marxist structuralisms as well. Finally, and most importantly, these conclusions are not simply an exercise in logic, but are central to strategies of research and political action, for it means that peasants and their dynamics must be considered *both* as sucH *and* within broader societal contexts to further understanding of themselves and the society they live in.

To give relief to those who like authority of textual references, all that is, of course, methodologically implicit also in Marx's own work. For example, his consideration of merchant capital and merchants relates them to different modes of production and gives them a part-autonomous history of their own. Merchant capital is neither totally independent of capitalism, nor does it simply reflect capitalism, nor is it only a stage within capitalism. Nor are merchants ahistorical in terms of the society they operate in. Yet, after stating that it is production and not circulation where the "true political economy begins", merchant capital is singled out for study in its relative independence as a clearly necessary part of the process of understanding of the whole.[6]

So, what are peasants, conceptually speaking? To turn once more to the epistemological beginnings, concepts, generalizations, and models are not reality, which is indeed ever richer. That makes a generalized question such as "*Are* peasants a mode of production *or* economy *or* a class?" nonsensical, for those concepts are neither mutually exclusive nor interchangeable; their illumination may be added up. Concepts are tools of analysis, their usefulness and usage subject to the questions asked, the ways those relate into more general theoretical schemes of questioning and its illuminations of reality. No such conceptualization can be total, except for those which are tautological and/or trivial. Furthermore, such a statement does not offer a defence of principled eclectism, for hierarchies of significance are presumed and different concepts show different measures of illumination (or none whatever), especially once the question is determined. It is therefore the way of usuage of the concept and its heuristic results which are central in our case, i.e. when discussing a current debate within a broadly Marxist framework of analysis.

Peasants have entered the Marxist parley as the analytical pre-history of capitalism, as its passive fodder within "primitive accumulation", but in particular as historical classes "for themselves" with, so to say, low "classness", explainable in turn within terms of peasant specificity.[7] The usage and stresses differed in time and context. Peasants appear for ancient or medieval times in the *Grundrisse,* for the more immediate past of England in Marx's *Capital,* but are central to his analysis of actual political history of France, and the political future of proletarian revolution in "countries of peasant majority". "Class for itself" represents here not only a more extensive definition than "class in itself", but also a different level of abstraction, not only as an analytical construct, not only "bearers" of characteristics of a general "matrix", but a social group existing in the direct consciousness and political deeds of its members.[8] Only the

conceptualization of a class as an actor and subject within social history allows
of posing questions as those of class crystalization and de-crystallization,
temporary class coalitions, retreats, victories, and defeats. Class struggle means
on this level not only an objective contradiction of interest, but actual
confrontation of specific organizations, slogans, and men. A generation later
historically-actual peasants gradually took over again from their more abstract
and analytical conceptual brethren "in themselves" as Lenin's writings and deeds
grew mature, politically more profound, deeper into the decisive confrontation
and closer to victory. A similar history for Mao and Tito will some time also be
written. As immediately relevant political analysis took the pride of place,
peasants were transformed from derivations or deductions to armies and actors;
and simultaneously the relative analytical autonomy of class from the mode(s)
and/or society it links into, was increasingly granted. Peasants became a class
indeed, a class even "within a capitalist country"—to quote post-1906 Lenin.[9]

Yet, that is no happy ending, with all doubts resolved and peasants found out
for what they truly are, i.e. "a class". Peasants *are* a class, an economy, a part-
society, and some other "things" we have not yet conceptualized besides. Only
the setting of a problematic makes possible the selection of valid framework of
conceptualization. Moreover, no social reality can be monopolized by and
neatly divided into one, deductively chosen type of unit of analysis with every
conclusion derived from it. Reality is not neat, nor can relevant analysis of it ever
be. Indeed, to dispose of inelegancies is to rid us of the very points where
puzzlement breeds discovery within social sciences.

All that brings us to the last point in both of the suggested lists of the
problematic of peasant conceptualization, i.e. the point of the possible
uselessness and/or unsatisfactory qualities of the term. That is necessary
because, to understand what peasants "are", one must understand what and how
one thinks about them.

F. PEASANTS AS A FASHION

A history of peasants as a conceptual entity or fashion would be a major task in
itself. We shall limit it here to a few aspects relevant to the issue in hand. The
political significance of the concept provided for a periodicity of its very usuage,
ever reflecting social history in its broadest sense, but also some specific
dynamics of academic thought. An upsurge of it took place in what can
roughly be termed the early stages of industrialization and capitalist transformation of central and eastern Europe, i.e. in societies at the close periphery
of the origins of capitalism. It was linked with rapid urbanization, the rise of
nationalist, pupulist, and socialist movements, and so on. It commenced in the
second half of the nineteenth century, and produced by the beginning of the

twentieth most of the relevant conceptual and ideological tools we carry today. Most of it has come into "properly western" thought through the mediation of the central and estern Europeans who wrote in English (e.g. Marx, Znaniecki, and Sorokin), or else through translations (e.g. Weber, Lenin, and Chayanov).

The upsurge came to an abrupt and dramatic end during the 1920 and 30s, flattened by repressions as much as by the advance of the linked ideologies and policies of militant nationalism and rapid industrialization, which placed peasants where witchcraft and home-spun dress belonged, i.e. outside the scope of progressive political and intellectual concerns. Eastern and western Europe have thereby caught up with an earlier dominant western European/US tendency. Modernization and industrialization were assumed both necessary and "a good thing". A basic taxonomy of modern/traditional (with an implicit us/them assumption beneath it) turned peasants terminologically invisible within the general bag of "traditionals" and exotics. During the 1930s and 40s and later, in the fool's paradise of 'the post-colonial' modernization theories of the 50s and 60s, peasants proceeded not to exist, conceptually speaking.

A building up of crises in the "developing societies" and in world agriculture, the collapse of simply-and-quick modernizing prescriptions, China's decision "to walk on both feet", the World Bank's discovery of peasant tenacity, etc., but especially the way Vietnamese peasants defeated the most industrialized country in the world, have brought peasants sharply into focus. A virtual explosion of studies, publications, and debate followed. The structure of the publishing business and academia as business have turned it all into fashion with the laws of motion of fashion-mongering increasingly taking over. It meant a rapid increase in the use of the word as a publishing gimmick (together with naked females and shirts with pictures of Che). It meant scrambling to say something new and career-promoting in a rapidly overcrowding field, much before any actual advance in knowledge would justify it. The stages to follow can be easily enough predicted within the rationale of such academic dynamisms: disenchantment, signs of annoyance with the over-used and trivialized term, discoveries of its "actual non-existence", calls for de-conceptualization, rush to new gimmicks, and often enough an attempt to cash in academically on the de-mystifying of old pets (a couple of books can always be squeezed out of that). We are now rapidly approaching this stage within the peasant fashion cycle. It happened to "articulate" with, and "conjucturally over-determinate", a wave of deductivist Marxism on the western campuses, itself increasingly under attack by those to whom social reality is undeducible, especially so, where Marxism is concerned.

It goes without saying that to see pursuers of fashions go and graze elsewhere should delight those seriously engaged in study. Moreover, in so far as some issues were elaborated and a few dozen scholars have consequently come into the field, the result of the fashion wave could not be entirely negative. That may be, also, the right moment to retire the trivialized and "tired" concept altogether. After all, words such as "peasant" are not holy scripture, and the less complex the terminology the better. For example, how about "the agricultural detachment of petty bourgeoisie" instead, to have it all fresh, neat and clear?

G. RETIRING CONCEPTS : SOME RULES OF THUMB

To answer it, let us proceed to some "rules of thumb" for the de-conceptualization before turning for the last time to the issue of defining peasants. To begin once more with negations, the following can be said in a general way.

(a) No concept should be retired simply on the grounds of its representing only some aspects of reality. Every concept is systematically selective and therefore carries necessary blinds and limitations. To pitch the demands of our concepts too high is to dualize research into, on the one hand, totally empirical facts and, on the other, the totally theoretical and thereby absolute constructs. Both are of little use.

(b) No concept should be retired on purely deductive and/or logical grounds without a thorough investigation of the insights into reality which may be lost through such a de-conceptualization and/or the adequacy of alternative ways to handle those insights.

(c) No concept should be retired to suit a simple division of concepts into "ours" and "theirs" with those "ours" placed in an aseptic world free from any alien admixtures. Marxist concerns and findings must be recognizable both in fact and problematic to genuine non-Marxist analysts and *vice versa*, deep differences expected. Within Marxism itself deductive purism destroys links with reality, which is richer than any conceptualization. One must avoid in particular swings of fashion, through trying too hard to be a Marxist in accordance with the last of them. As with sex, the less hard one tries, the better one's performance.

De-conceptualization is justified for concepts which are devoid of illumination because of misrepresentation of social reality, and/or irrelevance to problems of significance, and/or faulty logical structure and incoherence. All those may exist from the outset, or else come as the result of change in reality, or else following new theoretical grasp or accepted methods of its verification. How do peasants fare in all those senses?

To recollect first the position stated above, the term peasantry does not imply peasants' total similitude all round the world and/or their existence out of the context of a broader, not-only-peasant society and/or their extra-historicity. Those are scarecrows which juveniles take delight in knocking down. Peasants necessarily differ from one society to another and within any one society too; the question is that of their generic and specific characteristics. Peasants necessarily reflect, relate to, and interact with non-peasants; the question is of the part autonomy of their social being. Peasantry is a process and necessarily a part of a broader social history; the question is of the extent of specificity of the patterns of its development, the significant epochs, and strategic breaks where peasants are concerned. The concept peasant is selective; the question is what we can learn only by using it. Peasants are mystification; the problem is when, how and when not.

The simple question, "Do peasants exist?" would, of course, be silly in its setting and reifying in its content; we do not discuss here immediate reality but a generalization, linked to a conceptual model—a meaningfully selective simplification and formalization for the purpose of better understanding. We should concequently put it all in another way by asking what illumination can be gained by the usage of the concept, and what are the built-in blinds of such theorizing.

An example can pinpoint the issue. The defeat of US armed intervention in Vietnam is still fresh in mind, and doubtlessly a social event of most central political significance in contemporary history. It is also the type of "data" against which both understanding and attempts to shape social reality have been and will be tested all round the globe. Can one satisfactorily explain the defeat of the largest/richest/technologically most advanced military-industrial complex without singling out the specifically peasant social structure of 90 per cent of the Vietnamese? A complexity of factors ever operates in such struggles, but that is not at issue. Can one understand what happened considering *only* the international economic system, the capitalist mode of production, Johnson's neurosis, and/or the inter-US. contradictions and protest? Or is it the jungle, brainwash, military tactics, and/or the qualities of the AK47 carbine? Or is it simply the superiority of socialist *Weltanschauung* and the personal devotion of the party cadres? All those played their role, but it is probably enough to compare Vietnam with other areas where challenge to imperialist military might was attempted, to admit the crucial analytical importance of the singling out of peasant specificity in this case (Hobsbawm 1965). Further examples of heuristic gain were quoted or footnoted above in section B. It is by day-to-day work of actual research and political programming and action that the uses of a concept must be judged. And it is by those standards that genealization of peasant specificity is neither devoid of illumination nor irrelevant to major questions of the world we live in, nor incoherent in the structure of its logic. It is without doubt insufficient on its own, but so is of course any other concept, differences in scope excepted. Which should explain why the last of the basic charges against peasantry as a valid concept, that of its mystifying quality, should be answered along the following lines.

"Peasant" is not simply an empty word reflecting prejudices of the *populus,* linguistic frivolities of the intellectuals, or plots of ideological conspirators, even though each of those may be true at times. If retired, this concept cannot be easily substituted (yet?) by something else of similar ilk. Together with concepts such as "capitalism", "proletariat", and, of course, "mode of production", it carries potentials for reification, i.e. can be misleading and can be used to mislead, especially when used naively. It has been rightly said that "the price of using models is eternal vigilance" (Braithwaite 1953 : 93). It is also true that without such theoretical constructs no advance in social sciences would be possible at all.

Peasants are a mystification mainly to those who are prone to become mystified. Typically, it was the brilliant theorist and the indifferent politician Plekhanov between whose fingers Russian peasants conceptually disappeared, only to reappear within Lenin's political grasp and deeds of the Civil War and after. (Some time later Li-Li San and Mao seemed to re-enact this duality). These are the grand deductionists with little contact with reality who fell most easily into the reification trap (and at the other end, those to whom only the empirical counts do the same). The conceptualization of peasant specificity rests on the admission of complexity and degrees of ambivalence, and expresses an attempt to grapple with it all on a theoretical level. It is essentially not an answer but a presumption which helps to elicit specific new answers.

Fundamental issues of social reality can be understood at a fair level of epistemological sophistication or not at all. At the same time, even the strictest rigour of deduction cannot on its own resolve basic issues any more than the correct use of syllogism can prove to us the existence of the world around us. It is in the final resort not "a question of dialectical reconciliation of concepts" but "of the understanding of the real relations" (Marx 1973 : 90) which concepts are to serve. Within the socialist tradition one must add here the commitment to define dimensions of oppression of men by men and ways to struggle against them. Mystification and ideological usages accepted, the concept of peasantry has performed all these services often enough. This capacity is not yet spent.

NOTES

1. In particular, "On Cooperation", "Better Fewer but Better", and the 24/22 December 1923 letter to the Congress, V.I. Lenin, *Selected Works,* Moscow, 1971, pp. 681-713.

2. For example, L. Althusser and E. Ralibar, *Reading Capital,* London, 1970. For recent discussion see A. Foster-Carter, "The Modes of Production Debate", *New Left Review,* 1978, p. 107.

3. P. Hirst, "Can There Be A Peasant Mode of Production?" (MS), p. 7. The final version of it appears as J. Ennew, P. Hirst, and K. Tribe, "Peasants as an Economic Category", *Journal of Peasant Studies,* 1977, Vol. 4, No. 4. The quote comes from pp. 295-6.

4. For example, L. Von Bertlanffy, *Problems of Life,* New York, 1952, A. Koestler and J.R. Smithies, *Beyond Reductionism,* London, 1969. Also see T. Shanin (ed.), *The Rules of the Game,* London, 1972.

5. S. Eisenstadt, "Sociological Theory and an Analysis of the Dynamics of Civilizations and of Revolutions", *Daedalus,* 1977, Vol. 106, No. 4, p. 66.

6. For example, Marx, *Capital,* 1976, Harmondsworth, Vol. 3, Chapters XIX and XX. See also the relevant letter of Engels to C. Schmidt, in K. Marx and F. Engels, *Collected Writings,* Moscow, 1973, Vol. 3, pp. 483-5.

7. See introduction to T. Shanin, *Peasants and Peasant Societies,* Harmondsworth, 1971. For an explanation of a somewhat different view, see Wolf (1977 : 2-4) "Marx . . . Still worked with a homogeneous model of the hypothetical society . . . . The reason this seems to me important is that peasantries are always localised. They inhabit peripheries and semi-peripheries by definition and peripheries within peripheries. And this is perhaps why it is difficult or impossible to speak of the peasantry as a class."

8. A century after Marx, marxist analysis has added fairly little to the basic list of meanings presented by the "class in itself . . . (toward) class for itself . . ." dichotomy. Both sides of this formula carry the necessary defining aspect of an objective and fundamental collective interest within a system of relations of production and exploitation. The second adds a related component of typical group consciousness, self-identification, and class organization. The assumption of crystallization of characteristics of the "class for itself" via class struggle introduced a historiography of necessary stages and offered a major rationalization of political history. For an old, yet the best available, discussion, see S. Ossowski, *Class Structure in the Social Sciences,* London, 1983.

9. The revolutionary experience of 1905/6 finds its expression in new awareness in those writers, e.g. "Agrarian Programme of Social Democracy etc." (1908), Lenin (1968), Vol. 17, pp. 170-2.

BIBLIOGRAPHY

Amin, S. (1974) : *Capitalism and Ground Rent,* Dakar.

Bailey, F.G. (1966) : "The Peasant View of the Bad Life", *Advancement of Science,* December.

Banarjee, J. (1976) : "Summary of Selected Parts of Kautsky : The Agrarian Question", *Economy and Society,* 5 : 26-35.

Braithwaite, R.B. (1953) : *Scientific Explanation,* Cambridge.

Cardoso, S. (1975) : "On the Colonial Modes of Production of the Americas", *Critique of Anthropology,* 4 & 5 : 1-36.

Chayanov, A.V. (1966) : *The Theory of Peasant Economy,* Homewood, Illinois.

Claus, G. (1973) : "Toward a Structural Definition of Peasant Society", *Peasant Studies Newsletter,* Vol. II, No. 2.

Danilov, V.P., L.V. Danilov, V.G. Restyanikov (1977) : *Osnovnye Etapy Razvitiya Krest'yanskogo Khozyaistva,* Moscow.

Dobrowolsky, K. (1971) : "Peasant Traditional Culture", English translation in T. Shanin, *Peasants and Peasant Societies, Harmondsworth.*

Galeski, B. (1972) : *Basic Concepts of Rural Sociology*, Manchester.

Geertz, Clifford (1963) : *Agricultural Involution*, Berkeley.

Hobsbawn, E. (1965) : "Vietnam and the Dynamics of Guerilla War", *New Left Review*, No. 17.

       (1972) : "Karl Marx's Contribution to Historiography", in R. Blackburn, *Ideology and Social Sciences*, London.

Lenin, V.I. (1968) : *Polnoe Sobranie Sockynenii*, Moscow.

       (1971) : *Selected Works*, Moscow.

       (1974a) : *Collected Writings*, Moscow.

       (1974b) : "Development of Capitalism in Russia", Moscow.

Lopez, J.R.B. (1976) : *Capitalist Development and Agrarian Structure in Brazil*, CEBRAP, San Paulo manuscript.

Macnamara, J. (1974) : "Address to the Board of Governors", Washington.

Marx, K. (1964) : *Pre-Capitalistic Economic Formations*, London.

       (1973a) *Grundrisse*, Harmondworth.

       (1973b) : *Selected Writings*, Moscow.

       (1976) : *Capital*, Harmondsworth.

Myrdal, G. (1957) : *Economic Theory and Underdeveloped Regions*, London.

Naderi, N. Afshar (1971) : *The Settlement of Nomads : Its Social and Economic Implications*, Tehran.

O'Connor, J. and R. Sherry (1976) : Debate in *Monthly Review*, Vol. 28.

Pham Cuong and Nguyen Van Ba (1976) : *Revolution in the Village : Nam Hong, 1945-1975*, Hanoi.

Redfield, R. (1956) : *Peasant Society and Culture*, Chicago.

Sahlins, M. (1974) : *Stone Age Economics*, London.

Shanin, T. (1971) : *Peasants and Peasant Societies*, Harmondsworth.

       (1973) : "The Nature and Logic of Peasant Economy", *Journal of Peasant Studies*, Vol. I, Nos. a and 2.

Stavenhagen, R. (1970) : *Agrarian Problems and peasant Movements in Latin American*. New York.

Thorner, D. (1971): "Peasant Economy as a Category in Economic History", in T. Shanin *Peasants and Peasant Societies*, Harmondsworth.

Tung, Fey Hsue (1946) : Peasants and Gentry", *American Journal of Sociology*, Vol. LII.

Wolf, Eric (1966) : *Peasants*, New York.

       (1969) : *Peasant Wars in the Twentieth Century*, London.

       (1977) : "Is the Peasant a Class Category Separate from Bourgeois and Proletarian?" (notes for a talk, 2.3.77), Binghampton.

The Growth of Capitalism and the Peasant Economy : Some Problems on the Transference of Surplus

EDUARDO P. ARCHETTI

In Latin America, during recent years, there has been a real expansion of the studies on peasants and the revival of some theoretical problems originated in the Marxist tradition.[1] This implied a rediscovery of the classics, fundamentally Marx, Kautsky, and Lenin, but also an opening to other trends, especially after the publication of Chayanov's book in Spanish (1974). In connection with this it is important to mention the growing influence of anthropological literature devoted to peasants and the impact of many scholars, working in the French Marxist tradition, who discussed the agrarian question in general and particularly the peasant question.[2] In some circumstances, in Latin America after 1960, theoretical disputes reveal the crisis of models of social change. In the 60s the industrialization model based on import substitutions lost its historical relevance and the capitalist modernization of agriculture did not solve foodstuffs problems in the majority of countries. As a consequence of these two crises, we registered increasing urban and rural agitation; the growth of peasant movements of various types; and the reactualization of plans for land reforms based on the democratic access to the control and ownership of land. Hence, the peasant discussion will appear not only with a theoretical face but also will reflect political preoccupations as well as general discussions on social classes and class alliances which could influence processes of social transformation.

In this paper we do not intend to give a detailed overview of the debate but rather to raise certain issues for discussion. Let us see some of the issues we will be concerned with. In the classical model of capitalist development one of the main assumptions was the even development of sectors and branches of the national economy. At the same time capitalism was defined not only on the basis of the production of commodities, but as a process associated with the growth of wage labour. There, the history of capitalism could be seen as limited by the forms and conditions of growth of wage labour at the level of a social formation. If we admit that the value of commodities is determined by the socially necessary labour time used on producing them, this implies, at least theoretically, that the relative value of different commodities will fluctuate in relation to the labour time. In relation to this it is essential to identify the social structure which implies a quantitative determination of the products under the form of value, and, secondly, to ask for the conditions associated with the labour force as a commodity with a certain value. As in shown by Marx, the development of value supposes the development of labour as both concrete and abstract labour. It is only under the capitalist mode of production that these two aspects are fully developed, because the means of production are a real monopoly of a given class. This means that the means of production are utilized in order to extract human labour independently of the immediate utility of this labour. In this situation the process of concentration and monopolization of the means of production reproduces permanently the form of value of all products including the labour force.

In this model the growth of the capitalist mode of production in agriculture signifies, basically, the dissolution of the ancient forms of property and the emergence of private property and wage relations of labour; the separation of land property from the management of productive process and, in consequence, the distinction between landlords and capitalists; and, finally, the creation of social conditions for introduction of new techniques and technology which increase the productivity of labour. Therefore the rent is conceptualized as a limitation for the equalization of profit rates among the different sectors of the economy. The rent is a superflous phenomenon from the point of view of the total reproduction of the system. However, in the transitional period towards the dominance of the capitalist mode of production, the peasant economy could and does play a crucial role in the process of primitive accumulation of capital, essentially providing industry with the necessary labour force in order to expand capital. Its contribution to the constitution of an internal market for foodstuffs is smaller because the conditions of production of small farms do not permit a rapid change in the productivity of labour. In this scheme the peasant unit of production, almost by definition, is less efficient and functions with higher costs than the capitalist enterprises.

Because this is an analysis of the transitional period it is important to distinguish the short and long run tendencies. In the long run the hypothesis is clear: the capitalist expansion supposes the eradication of peasantry. But in the short run, under the assumption that the reproduction of the labour force depends to a great extent on agricultural non-industrial commodities, and that the absorption of the excedent force does not occur automatically, two things happen: in the first place, part of the reproduction of the labour force takes place in households producing for subsistence, especially through cottage industry, and in the second place, taking into consideration the agricultural sector as a whole, part of the reproduction of the labour force employed in capitalist agricultural enterprises occurs on subsistence plots. These two processes have a tremendous impact on the national economy because a great proportion of the reproduction of the labour force is found in "spaces of non-value" which are, metaphorically speaking, external to the capitalist mode of production.

But history has shown that the short run was even longer than the long run itself. The peasant economy has survived in capitalist developed societies, as well as in other parts of the globe, and in many places its economic behaviour was not so bad. Therefore, the terms of the debate have considerably changed; what we need to explain is not the removal of peasants but, on the contrary, their persistence, their refusal to die. The explanations proposed by different Marxist scholars will turn around three major constraints which are presented with different causal weight. Let us begin with the first argument: in agricultural production there are ecological constraints which hinder the industrialization of the labour process because the different work operations cannot be realized simultaneously, depending as they do on biological rhythms of plants and animals. This implies a basic discontinuity between the process of production and labour time, being the contrary truth for the industry where both overlap temporally. It is easy to conclude that under this constraint the mechanical equipment of a farm will not constitute a "machine system" as in industry. Another implication is related to the forms of labour division, because conditions are created for intensive use of the labour force in a simple scheme of cooperation. The second argument is of a more economic nature: it is postulated that the peasant economy does not function according to the laws of capital accumulation; it is not oriented towards profit maximization, being, therefore, possibly a transference of surplus labour, and sometimes also necessary labour, to the capitalist sector of the economy. The peasant perceives himself as a "worker" who has a right to an "income" which guarantees his reproduction. Under these conditions the economic categories of profit and rent are superfluous for explaining the conditions of reproduction. From the point of view of the capitalist sector and the whole economy it is possible to obtain cheap agricultural commodities, to decrease the cost of the labour force reproduction on the urban sector, and, consequently, create conditions for a higher rate of accumulation in the urban capitalist sector. Finally there is place for politics; it is argued that different sectors of the industrial bourgeoisie are interested in gaining the support of the peasantry. To achieve this it is necessary to maintain the myth of "small property" autonomy.

Obviously in the works of different authors, as was mentioned above, the relations between ecology, economics, and politics will appear in various ways. For some the fundamental explanation is an ecological one, because the discontinuity between productive processes and labour time conditions lowers rates of profit and poses problems on capital circulation more than any capitalist rural enterprises will be pleased to confront. For others, on the contrary, the way the peasants are integrated into the industrial sector is more relevant for explaining the general function of this kind of producer under capitalism. To give a summary of this discussion is not the main aim of this paper, but in order to follow our argument it is important to point out the difference between the ecological and the economic effects when we are discussing the question of surplus transference. To say that the characteristics of the process of work in agriculture determine the rates of profit, and that therefore it is a non-attractive economic activity for capitalist investment, is not to assert that especially for this reason, a transference of surplus value to the industrial sector must necessarily occur. Though these two aspects are related, we find it convenient for our exposition to keep them analytically apart.

We believe that this way of presenting the debate is correct, but it is necessary to define with higher precision the types of articulation of the peasant economy in a context where there is increasing control of national and international industrial capital. At the same time it is crucial to call for further research on the process of reproduction and transformation of this kind of economy. This implies, as a logical consequence, that we cannot define in abstract terms the transference of surplus without taking into consideration different aspects related to this process and the effects on the internal structure of the units of production under study. We believe, therefore, that the micro-passion of anthropologists that, in many cases, is presented as a negative feature, is a decisive factor for reaching a most nuanced picture. Though we accept that the analysis of a social formation means the analysis of both social relations of production and processes of reproduction, from our methodological perspective it is not a question of life-or-death to present the totality. Through a micro-analysis we retain general tendencies and the complexity of determinations at this level, and therefore the concrete form under which they are combined. In other words, the macro-determinations are always present when we are dealing with units of production and households integrated in a social formation.

Accepting that the interplay of the different causes, from the ecological to the political-ideological, will enter into a concrete analysis, we will specifically discuss the question of the transference of surplus from the economic point of view. Our presentation will revolve on two problems: first, the way the peasant economy is articulated or integrated with other sectors through production, distribution, and exchange, and, secondly, the necessity of defining a complex model of the agrarian sector where we are faced not only with domestic economies but also with other types of enterprise. Related to the first point, we will present a short discussion of the impact of types of integration on social and economic differentiation, as well as how this phenomenon could be measured.

Before considering this subject we will comment, briefly, on two assumptions which in the Marxist tradition are related to this kind of analysis. If we recognize that in Latin America as a whole the dominant mode of production is the capitalist one, this implies that the capitalist law of capital accumulation determines not only the conditions for reproduction of the capitalist sector, but also that of other modes or forms of production which are non-capitalist. This logically implies a necessary transference of surplus from the dominated to the dominant mode of production. From this statement another assumption is clearly derived: the persistence of dominated modes and forms of production involves, at the same time, alterations, transformation, and a permanent readjustment to the processes imposed "externally". In this direction the "ideal reproduction" of the peasant economy will face permanently adverse conditions and, therefore, we will find empirically different kinds of peasant economies, different peasantries. The capitalist determination will provoke an internal differentiation of the peasant sector.

However, the problem of surplus transference introduces us fully to the question of the law of value. If we accept that the exchange value of two commodities is something both have in common, independently of the use value, the exchange value is a phenomenal representation of value. The value as such we cannot measure. Moreover, in a capitalist economy the values are transformed into prices: production price and market price. When this occurs, a commodity is exchanged for another following a law of distribution determined by the rate of profit. The individual variations of rates of profit will depend on the organic composition of capital and on changes in supply and demand. A discussion of the utilization of the law of value is necessary in order to grasp, at least theoretically, the problem of surplus transference. Let us now begin with the matter of the paper.

1. TYPES OF INTEGRATION OF PEASANT ECONOMY

If one of the implicit characteristics of the peasant economy is the participation, in one way or another, in a growing mercantile system of circulation, distribution, and exchange, it is a central aspect to define the contexts of this integration. At this level the patient work of anthropologists is extremely worthwhile. In Latin America the capitalist transformation for agriculture and peasants involves dissimilar degrees of integration. We will distinguish two extreme situations, weak and strong industrial integration (see Fig. 1 and 2).

Figure 1 represents a situation in which the agrarian producers find an almost immediate consumption market without entering into a complex network of transformation and distribution. Here we will discover the traditional social actors in charge of commercialization: small merchants, peddlers, usurary merchants; and the traditional places where exchanges take place: fairs of all kinds, and locally and regionally articulated markets. The productive process, i.e. the different means and objects of production produced internally or through local and regional handicrafts circuits, continues to a great extent without industrial inputs. The credit is subordinated to the different middlemen entering in the flow of commodities.

In Fig. 2, on the other hand, we face quite a different situation because the producers are integrated in terms of both inputs and outputs to branches of industry (obviously in the figure the network has been simplified, but we can imagine that for each product the chart will be different). The credit is under the control of financial institutions and banks. At the same time, as a consequence of the incorporation of the means and objects of industrial production, a more sophisticated management of fixed and circulating capital is needed. This will provoke the growth of services of all kinds, from machinery repairs to technical advices.

In between these two forms of integration we will find in Latin American all kinds of intermediate systems. In order to depict the empirical variation, the kind of product and the degree of industrialization reached for each national society is of extreme importance. As an example, let us mention the markets for potatoes and milk in Ecuador. The market for potatoes resembles Fig. 1, and the market for milk and dairy products Fig. 2. The introduction of "products" into the model is sound, not only as a possible indication of kind of integration but also as a means to recognize "consumers": national/international and wage goods/luxury goods being the most relevant categories. Accordingly, the agrarian policy of the state and the financial facilities advanced to the producers will be more easily understood.

Figure 1. Weak industrial integration

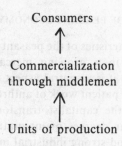

Consumers

↑

Commercialization
through middlemen

↑

Units of production

Figure 2. Strong industrial integration

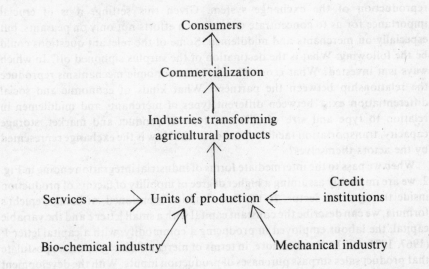

By taking as a point of departure the types of integration, the discussion of surplus transference is qualified. We can presume that in places where weak industrial integration predominates, the surplus is randomly transferred by peasants, and benefits and middlemen operating under the forms of commercialization already mentioned. If one of the central assumptions connected with the exploitation of peasants appears at the level of unequal exchange and the consequent low prices paid, one of the immediate questions is precisely, "Who is taking the lion's share?" One of the main problems is to consider how the law of value functions in the peasant economy, and how the prices are fixed.

Under weak industrial integration we can presuppose that the law of value must be present in its simple form. In such circumstances the exchange of commodities, and, therefore, prices, are derived directly from the socially necessary labour time. If prices do not reflect the amount of labour used in producing the commodities, this is due precisely to the impact of commercialization on the laws of supply and demand. The transference of surplus products does not profit the urban industrial sector in general, but fundamentally and almost exclusively, the sector of merchants. As Mollard points out, there are two additional mechanisms working against the law of value: first, prices do not regulate the amount of social labour because the capital and the workers are not mobile and, secondly, there is a permanent tendency towards a shortage in supply and hence prices fluctuate over values (1977). In this context, the lack of bargaining power on the part of peasants explains the reproduction of the exchange system. Given this setting, it is of crucial importance for us to concentrate our research efforts not only on peasants, but especially on merchants and middlemen. Some of the relevant questions could be the following: What is the destination of the surplus siphoned off? In which ways is it invested? What economic and non-economic mechanisms reproduce the relationship between the partners? What kinds of economic and social differentiation exist between different types of merchants and middlemen in relation to type and size of clientele, type of product and market, storage capacity, transportation facilities, and so forth? How is the exchange represented by the actors themselves?

When we pass to the intermediate forms of industrial integration ending in Fig. 2, we are implicitly assuming a higher degree of mobility of factors of production inside the agrarian sector. In the first situation mentioned, utilizing Tepicht's formula, we can describe the constant capital with a small letter c and the variable capital, the labour employed in producing a commodity, with a capital letter V (1967, 1971, 1973). Furthermore, in terms of mercantile integration we postulate that product sales surpass purchases of production inputs. With the development of industrial capitalism related to agriculture, the constant capital is slowly transformed into C and the variable capital into V. In terms of factor substitution, the traditional peasant-like conversion "land-work" is changed into "land-capital", mainly through purchases of inputs produced by the bio-chemical industrial sector, or into "land-labour", through purchases of inputs of the mechanical industrial sector. At the same time changes occur in the sphere of commercialization where the industrial sector, transforming raw materials into finished goods, plays a critical role.

From the point of view of processes of transformation and integration, it is possible to depict two patterns. In the first the industries producing inputs introduce new technologies which determine the general technological model and the technical norms to be followed. Once this happens, the transforming industry can set up demands on a given quality of products, regular deliveries, specific hygienic conditions of the production process, rational management, and so forth. These demands obviously reinforce the technological package offered by the other industries. In the other sequence, the transforming industries appear first, gradually fix norms and patterns of production, and thereby throw the agrarian producer into the hands of the input industries. In either of these processes the state agrarian policy is to a great extent decisive, since a major part of the basic research needed is carried out at the expense of the national budget. Moreover, the extension service is under the control of state agencies, especially with respect to critical aspects such as vegetable and animal genetics.

We have reached a complex situation of exchanges since it is rather difficult to identify not only the surplus transferred, but also the correct method for measuring it. This scheme is even more complex when we take into account the state price policies and the allocation of different subsidies. The national state appears as an entity regulating the balance among various industrial interests which are, on some occasions, contradictory. The input industry will be interested in higher prices which will guarantee to the producer an optimal rate of reinvestment and capital replacement while, on the contrary, the transformation industry is interested in keeping down, as much as possible, the prices of the products it needs. Having in mind these difficulties and the limitations which arise from a micro anthropological analysis, we believe that some improvements can be made if we can utilize budgets of different producers in order to illustrate problems of profit and rate of profit. Let us discuss this in more depth.

In the situation described previously we postulated that the identification of surplus transferred was less complicated because we assumed, *ceteris paribus,* that the law of value operates in its simple form. At the same time we rejected the usual statement that always, also under this kind of integration, the surplus transferred benefits the industrial bourgeoisie because the cost of reproducing the urban labour force is lowered. When we arrive at a situation of strong industrial integration we face again the same argument that family producers are functional to the industrial sector as a whole. We have shown, however, that this statement must be qualified by making an analysis of the different sectors of industry, and taking into consideration the branches related with the agrarian producers. But what appears immediately as a consequence of industrial integration is precisely the changes produced at the level of organic composition of capital. There is no industrial integration without changes in the proportions of constant and variable capital. This implies, in other words, that a process of capital accumulation necessarily occurs in the sector, and hence the way of reproducing a domestic economy has been tremendously affected. At this point we can accept that the capitalist law of value properly begins to function because there is a real mobility of "capital" (this is relative because the "land-capital" is still not mobile). And when there is a mobility of factors it is possible to calculate rates of profit. In order to increase sales it is essential to increase purchases; in order to keep an adequate rate of investment and capital replacement it is necessary to increase sales; in order to increase the organic composition of capital it is convenient to get credit; and so forth. The family producer enters into a circuit which for many authors is a "forced process of capital accumulation". As a consequence of a general increase of labour productivity in the agrarian sector, crises of over-production are permanently generated in societies where this model predominates, creating a situation of wild competition where the most mechanized, the most capitalized enterprise will survive.

We may conclude by making some comments on the thesis of the functionality of peasant economy. Obviously, most authors refer to family-labour enterprises functioning in both contexts of integration, and in all the intermediate situations we could find in different countries and regions of Latin America. One of the critical aspects is precisely to point out clearly, when discussing the transference of value, the structural integration they are dealing with. Even in the most typical industrial integration, such as various countries of western Europe, the United States, and certain regions of Argentina and Brazil, what is easily shown in concrete investigations is the efficiency and the competing capacity of family farms. That this kind of farm could be more functional to industrial capitalism than other types based on hired labour force because costs of production are lower, because they utilize more inputs per hectare or per man occupied, or because they accept lower prices which hinder reproduction in accordance with existing rates of profit, is an empirical generalization and not a theoretical assumption. This implies that with careful anthropological studies it is possible to illustrate these processes and tendencies. Particularly through farm and family histories we can grasp demographic structures, investment strategies, values and beliefs, reactions to different contexts and situations, and show specifically when and why the substitutions of factors of production began.

2. TYPES OF INDUSTRIAL INTEGRATION AND ECONOMIC DIFFERENTIATION

From the above discussion we may identify some analytical trends in relation to the question of economic differentiation of peasants. Our main hypothesis is precisely to examine differentiation and type of integration at the same time. Let us examine this closely.

A traditional way of analysing economic differentiation has taken as point of departure the social relations of production within the process of work: the poor peasants sell their labour, the middle peasants use family labour, and the rich peasants systematically buy the labour of others. The underlying argument is that all these processes at the level of the labour market indicate the capitalist growth of the economy, i.e. generalized work relations based on wages, and therefore the consolidation of production and appropriation of surplus value. As the works of Martinez and Rendon show, the presence of wage relations in different units of production does not automatically imply generation and appropriation of surplus value and in some cases, due to the low labour productivity, the net income does not cover the expenses of hired labourers (1976, 1978). In many countries and regions of Latin American it is possible to find the expansion of these kinds of relations, and hence the substitution land-labour is not based on family labour. This situation could be explained from the interplay between demographic factors, relative and absolute shortage of land,

and the presence of a better market for labour outside the units of production and the agricultural sector.

Another criterion frequently mentioned, especially at the general statistical level, is the size of the different units of production. As we have pointed out before, the land is a productive factor of extreme importance in agricultural production, but in order to measure differentiation this indicator is not enough, because what is produced, and how, is more relevant to our purposes. Obviously this statement does not deny the influence of size on viability and general conditions of reproduction. The argument is usually presented in the following way: the smaller the size of farms, the less utilization of family labour force, higher tendencies to temporary and permanent migration, smaller agricultural incomes, and less chance for technological transformation. This is true if we can show that under these conditions it is impossible to realize the surplus at the level of the *agricultural* reproduction of the unit of production under consideration. Hence, one of the crucial aspects of economic dfferentiation is precisely to grasp this process, taking as a point of departure the analysis of budgets.

We will not refuse to accept the great complexity of social relations of production in various parts of Latin America, which makes it difficult to utilize the usual classification poor/middle/rich peasants. This we take for granted. Our discussion will not be relevant to the question of the reproduction of these complex units of production, but rather to the question of how to tackle, through budget analysis, the problem of transference of surplus. We will not discuss in this paper the global reproduction of a household economy but only the reproduction of agricultural producers, in other words their ability to sustain a process of accumulation in the urban sector where the capitalist mode of production is dominant. At the same time, since we recognize the existence of various kinds of peasant enterprises, due to different types of industrial integration, we need to standardize our criteria. Finally, admitting that any measure of differentiation in agriculture depends on bad and good years and that this must be explicitly referred to, we would like to distinguish between forms of differentiation. Since we are interested in a structural differentiation, we will utilize organic composition of capital in order to measure this differentiation, and in order to show a more conjunctural differentiation we will use rates of profit.

From our presentation of industrial integration we may see that we, in fact, obtain different units of production in accordance with the empirical combinations of $C + V + S$, where C is constant capital, "dead work" transferred to commodities in the process of production, V is variable capital referred to living work creating value and equal to the socially necesary labour time needed to reproduce labour power, and S is the surplus created by living work. In this sense C acquires a decisive importance in order to differentiate structurally different types of units of production. Generally C includes two different types of "capital": circulating capital and fixed capital. A given capital is fixed or circulating in relation with the role played in the process of production. If it functions as a means of production, and therefore determines the physical productivity of labour, it is fixed. If, on the contrary, it is no more than a material element which, once transformed by labour, is found in the final product, it is circulating. The fixed capital (machines, tools, equipments) correspond to the category "means of labour", while the circulating capital is identical to the "objects of labour" (seeds, fertilizers, insecticides, pesticides). Hence, the proportion of fixed and circulating capital will indicate the type of industrial integration and the constraints suffered by the producers under consideration. A first type of differentiation will arise from the degree of organic composition of capital, the relation $C/(C + V)$. The type of organic composition will be obtained through the relation Fixed capital divided by Circulating capital.

However, this last relation poses quite dissimilar problems to the units of production and their operators. The introduction of circulating capital only involves, in principle, a continuous mercantilization of these economies. The introduction of fixed capital, however, implies a long-run economic logic where rates of depreciation and strategies of investment entail a different way of making accounts. In this sense it is relevant for us to investigate these structural changes, and the effects on the internal organization of the farm and on the economic ideology of the social actors.

We can argue, and with reason, that the inner logic of the family farm eliminates, as a conscious category, the rate of profit, the idea of profit. But if we postulate the integration of this economy in a capitalist environment, and at the same time develop the argument of transference of surplus, it is legitimate for the observer to discuss the limits of reproduction in relation to the rate of profit. Furthermore, the increasing process of industrial integration modifies the functioning of the law of value, making it possible to operate with this category. To say that this kind of economy is functional because it reproduces itself under the accepted rate of profit is an appeal to measure or, at least, to try to measure the existing profits and the rate of profit. Hence, we will differentiate the units of production in accordance with the existing rate of profit. We do not need to abandon the formula used for measuring the structural differentiation, and we can calculate it in the following way: $S/(C + V)$. Usually the cost of production is calculated by taking the circulating capital plus the rate of depreciation of fixed capital, but here C must be defined in another way. We must therefore consider the total fixed capital, and not only the amount which is depreciated each year. This would indicate the "conjunctural" differentiation of the producers.

We will try to summarize briefly the preceding arguments. In the first place, we depicted the functioning of the law of value in relation to the types of industrial integration. We then postulated that this would provoke an economic differentiation between family producers. This was the second theme discussed. We derived from the formula of exchange value the organic composition of capital and the rate of profit as indicators for measuring differentiation, the first being more structural and the second more "conjunctural". This implied for us a restatement of the question of value transference in terms of differential rates of profit, and not in terms of absolute S transferred.

Before taking up the last point of our paper let us remember that until now we considered the agrarian sector composed exclusively of family producers. Since this is not so for many countries and regions, we need to discuss the internal composition of the sector and the impact on peasants, and the problem of the transference of surplus.

3. THE INTERNAL STRUCTURE OF THE AGRARIAN SECTOR

Many discussions on the transference of surplus value have a high level of generality and abstraction and, generaly speaking, are based on two assumptions: (1) the peasants constitute the agrarian sector, and (2) they produce according to the technical conditions existing in the social formation. Until now we presented our arguments with these two assumptions in mind. But obviously, in Latin America the agrarian sector is not only composed of family producers but, metaphorically, by all kinds of producers. In order to simplify the presentation, let us assume that we will find different empirical combinations of family producers and capitalist enterprises. Margulis has correctly pointed out that the question of value transference cannot be tackled without a more concrete examination of the specific kind of producers involved in satisfying a given demand. Logically this will affect the constitution of prices and, moreover, the values. The average prices in some situations will be determined by capitalist enterprises, and in others by peasant farms (1977).

This could be empirically much more complicated if we take into account the different markets for different products. There is no global market; there are *markets*—just as there is no agrarian sector but different *products*. Combining markets with products with kinds of enterprises, we will grasp variations which will modify our main arguments on the necessary transference of value by peasant producers to the capitalist urban sector of the national economy. Why is this so?

The authors who emphasize that the peasant producer *always* transfers part or all of his surplus to the industrial capitalist sector take as point of departure that the price of production is determined by this kind of producer. We pointed out that this is true when the demand is, generally speaking, not satisfied, and when prices are not *political prices*. This implies that when these two constraints are not present in a given situation, the peasant could find market prices higher than his production prices. But even if this could happen the family farm would accept market prices which do not permit the realization of the existing rate of profit. In this way, finally, the crucial argument is developed: the peasant economy operates under the law of unequal exchange, because his logic of reproduction is not capitalist.

Margulis' framework of analysis is rather different (1977). First, he postulates that the capitalist enterprise in the agrarian sector will produce with lower production costs than the peasant enterprise. This is due to the impact of the different rates of organic composition of capital on the productivity of labour, and hence on rates of surplus value. Secondly, as a logical consequence of this statement, it is necessary to investigate, and to determine empirically, the part of the demand satisfied by each kind of producer. In relation to this we have the following empirical situations:

(a) the agrarian capitalist sector determines the average production price, and this being lower than the peasant's price, the latter does not transfer surplus if he sells under the individual value;
(b) the peasant sector determines prices, and this being higher than the capitalist prices there is an extraordinary profit which favours the capitalist producer.

We may conclude that in the second situation the industrial and urban capitalist sector will pay higher prices than in the first situation, because the peasant producers are functional to the agrarian capitalist enterprises and not to the whole national economy. A conflict between the different capitalist interests can be expected. We believe that Margulis has drawn our attention to a very important point that is often forgotten in the debate: the Latin American peasants are not the only agrarian producers. Obviously in the second situation the peasants would transfer surplus, but not to the capitalist industrial sector. This aspect is rarely mentioned in the current analysis of the functionality of peasant economy. Working from the hypothesis that we have one peasant sector confronted by the industrial sector interested in putting down the costs of labour reproduction, we get a rather simplified view of the reality of the agrarian sector of many Latin American societies. In this connection the problem of transference of surplus must be examined in accordance with the internal structure of the agrarian sector.

4. CONCLUSION

We saw that the peasant economy is integrated through different exchange systems: merchants or industrial networks. In relation to transference of surplus to industry in general, we need to specify the role of traditional middlemen and agribusiness, and to measure the amounts alienated by the latter. Though we operated with a model of a peasant sector, we did not assume homogeneity with respect to types of family farms. When the process of industrial integration is achieved, the family labour force or the size of plots does not essentially determine the economic strategies. The organic composition of capital tends to increase, and in this way the general laws of reproduction are the capitalist laws of capital accumulation. Agriculture has been reduced to a branch of the industrial sector. This model is more complicated to depict when, as we saw in the arguments advanced by Margulis, we have both capitalist farms and family farms.

The importance of this kind of analysis is related to the problem of social classes in the agrarian sector and the viability of models of peasant transformation and integration in the industrial economy. A system of production, as we pointed out at the beginning of our paper, is conditioned to a large extent by power relations, forms of domination, and types of conflict existing in a given society. Though we might find only peasants or only traditional landlords or only capitalists in some sectors, in one branch or in one product, this need not limit us exclusively to the economic level. The concrete analysis must allow us to capture the political and ideological levels in order to conceptualize a system of social classes in their complex determinations.

We may conclude that for an adequate comprehension of the impact of capitalist growth on the peasant transference of surplus, we must increase investigations, controlling in an explicit way contexts and productive situations. We believe that it is possible to follow the given methodological paths:

(a) to determine, in the first instance, the type of producer or branch of agriculture under consideration, and thereby characterize types of markets;

(b) once this has been done to specify the internal composition in terms of kinds of enterprises (for many countries in Latin America this information is now available);

(c) to carry out concrete studies of types of producers and the way they are integrated, presenting with accuracy the context of industrial integration;

(d) finally, to discuss the question of transference of surplus in relation to (b) and (c); (b) could permit us to compare costs of production between different units of production, and (c) would provide the actual forms of transference from the given mechanisms of production, circulation, and exchange.

This would imply, at the same time, that we define wth a greater precision the way in which the law of value operates. In this manner the current generalization of the necessity of peasant surplus transference for the reproduction of the whole industrial sector could be re-examined through the analysis of the contexts of production of value. To avoid over-generalization we must accept that the transference of value and the extreme functionality of peasant economy to capitalist accumulation is not a necessary and sufficient assumption. We propose, therefore, the consideration of concrete processes before a general theory is presented.

Finally, with this purpose in mind, considering types of units of production in accordance with industrial integration, it will be possible to redefine dissimilar situations in many countries of Latin America. In this context it is crucial to present the processes of peasant economic differentiation in relation to the growth of capitalism. Confronted by all these problems we believe that the anthropological methodology offers us a very fruitful way of carrying out research in order to make more systematic comparisons.

NOTES

1. The reader interested in this debate will find some of the main arguments in the following literature: Archetti and Stolen (1975), A. Bartra (1976), R. Bartra (1972, 1974a, 1974b, 1976), Coello (1975), Contreras (1976), Diaz Polanco (1977), Flichman (1977), Margulis (1978), Martin del Campo (1978), Martinez (1976), Martinez and Rendon (1978), Murmis (1974), Pare (1978), Rello and Montes de Oca (1974), Sorj and Samaniego (n.d.), Warman (1975). It could be very interesting to follow the Mexican debate in *Comercio Exterior,* Vol. 27, 12 (1977) and Vol. 28, 1 (1978).

2. In that respect, without attempting to present an exhaustive bibliography, we will mention Amin and Vergopoulos (1974), Blanc (1977), Bye (1974), Cavailhes (1970), Clavaud *et at.* (1974), Gervais *et al.* (1965), Gretton (1972), Lambert (1970), Mollard (1977), Ossard (1975), Perceval (1969), Postel-Vinay (1974), Servolin (1972). The Italian Marxists have also been concerned with these problems and a useful introduction to the current national debate could be found in De Vecchis and Varotti (1975).

REFERENCES

Amin, S. and K. Vergopoulos, 1974, *La question paysanne et le capitalisme,* Paris : Anthropos.

Archetti, E. P. and K. Stolen, 1975, *Explotacion familiar y acumulacion de capital en el campo argentino,* Buenos Aires : Siglo XXI.

Bartra, A., 1976, "Sobre las clases sociales en el agro mexicano", *Cuadernos Agrarios, 1.*

Bartra, R., 1972, "Compesinado y poder politico en Mexico : un modelo teorico", *Revista Mexicana de Sociologia,* 3-4.

1974 a, "Sobre la articulacion de los modos de produccion en America Latina", *Historia y Sociedad, 5.*

1974 b, *Estructura agraria y clases sociales en Mexico,* Mexico : Ediciones Era.

1976, "Introduccion a Chayanov", *Revista Nueva Anthropologia, 3.*

Blanc, M. 1977, *Les paysanneries francaises,* Paris : Jean-Pierre Delarge.

Bye, P., 1974,. *Accumulation de capital et dynamique des industries agricoles et alimentaires,* Grenoble : I.R.E.P. Universite de Grenoble.

Cavailhes; J., 1976, "L' analyse leniniste de la decomposition de la paysannerie et son actualite", *Critique de l'Economie Politique,* 5.

Chayanov, A.V. 1974, *La organizacion de la unidad economica campesina,* Buenos Aires : Nueva Vision.

Clavaud, F. et al., 1974, *Quelle agriculture pour la France?,* Paris : Ed. Sociales.

Coello, M., 1975, "Caracterizacion de la pequena produccion mercantil campesina", *Historia y Sociaedad,* 8.

Contreras, A. J., 1976, "La ley del valor y proceso de formacion de precios en las economias capitalistas y pequeno-mercantil", *Cuadernos A De Vecchis, F. and A. Varotti, 1975, Il Marxismo e la questione agraria in Italia,* Rome: Savelli.

Diaz Polanco, H., 1977, *Teoria marxista de la economia campesina,* Mexico: Juan Pablos Editor.

Flichman, G., 1977, *La renta del suelo y el desarrollo agrario argentino,* Mexico : Siglo XXI.

Gervais, M. et al. 1965, *Une France sans paysans,* Paris : Ed. du Seuil. Gratton, P., 1972 *Les paysans francais contre l'agrarisme,* Paris : Maspero.

Lambert, B., 1970, *Les paysans dans la lutte des classes,* Paris : Ed. du Seuil.

Margulis, M., 1977, *Contradicciones en la estructura agraria y transferencias de valor,* Mexico : El Colegio de Mexico-Centro de Estudios Eco nomicos y Demograficos.

Martin del Campo, A., 1978, "Algunas ideas sobre la estructura agraria mexicana : una vision no convencional", *Estudios Rurales Latinoamericanos,* vol. 1.2.

Martines, M.de, 1976, "El empleo de trabajo ajeno por la unidad campesina de produccion" en R. Stavenhagen (ed), *Capitalismo y campesinado en Mexico,* Mexico : Sep-Inah.

Martinez, M. de and T. Rendon, 1978, "Fuerza de Trabajo y reproduccion campesina", Mexico : El Colegio de Mexico.

Mollard, A., 1977, *Les paysans exploites,* Grenoble : Presses Universitaires de Grenoble.

Murmis, M., 1974, *Tipos de capitalismo y estructura de clases : elementos para un analisis de la estructura social argentina,* Buenos Aires : La Rosa Blindada.

Ossard, H., 1975, "L'agriculture et le developpement du capitalisme", *Critique de l'Economie Politique,* 5.

Pare, L., 1978, *El proletariado agricola en Mexico,* Mexico : Siglo XXI.

Perceval, L., 1969, *Avec les paysans pour une agriculture non capitaliste,* Paris : Ed. Sociales.

Postel-Vinay, G., 1974, *La rente fonciere dans le capitalisme agricole,* Paris : Maspero.

Rello and Montes de Oca, 1974, "Acumulacion de capital en el campo mexicano", *Cuadernos Politicos,* 2.

Servolin, C., 1972, "L' absorption de l'agriculture dans le mode de production capitaliste" in *L'Univers politique des paysans,* Paris : Armand Colin.

Sorj, B. and C. Samaniego, n.d., "Articulaciones de modos de production y campesinado en America Latina", Lima: Pontificia Universidad Catolica.

Stavenhagen, R. (ed), 1976, *Capitalismo y campesinado en Mexico,* Mexico : Sep—Inah.

Tepicht, J., 1967, "Economia contadina e teoria marxista", *Critica Marxista,* 1.

1971, Les complexites de l'economie paysanne", *Information sur les Sciences Sociales,* 8:6.

1973, *Marxisme et agriculture : le paysan polonais,* Paris : Armand Colin.

Discussion

J. Vincent: I have a question from Dr. Satya Sharma to Dr. Wolf. In this presentation you talked about, in passing, the outcome of arresting capitalist development. Could you possibly comment on how one can arrest capitalist development?

E. Wolf: Well, how does one arrest capitalist development? — with difficulty! Maybe I used the wrong term to indicate what I had in mind. I wanted to say that some political coalitions are more propitious to capitalist development than others. Such was the case with the coalition of landowners and industrialists in England. In contrast, in France — after the French Revolution — the peasants took the land; that seizure of land created a multitude of private proprietors, but it retarded capitalist development for a long period of time. This is evident, for instance, in the development of French banking. It was not until the end of the nineteenth century that large quantities of capital, usable for investment purposes, were concentrated in banks. Much regional banking in France was just the proverbial French peasant putting his money into a kind of stocking, to draw small increments of interest. In contrast, in England regional banks developed early and mobilized capital on a very large scale. The juxtaposition of England and France in this case allows one to see that there were political factors favourable to capitalist accumulation in one case, while in the other case the conjuncture of political forces retarded it. I would suspect that there might be still other situations where capitalist development was arrested. For instance, in colonial situations where a *comprador* bourgeoisie becomes an important mediating link between the colony and the industrial capitalist centre, and plays an important role in transferring capital to that centre, the result is retardation of internal development in the colony. That is what I had in mind.

K. Gopal Iyer (Panjab University): You have a case in Bihar also: This Kosi Canal Project, which caters to three districts in Bihar. That is the area with the largest concentration of land, perhaps in India also. Landowners possess as much as 10,000-15,000 acres of land. But the policy of the landlords there is that they take only one crop, in spite of the fact that with their sources of irrigation they could take two or three crops. The main purpose of not taking two or three crops is that if they take more, there are more requirements for workers. Thereby you know their earnings will increase — so here is an example of capitalist development being arrested.

E. Wolf: Let me give another example of the same kind. There are studies of the development of large estates or haciendas in Mexico in the seventeenth, eighteenth, and into the nineteenth centuries, which show clearly that their continuation depended on keeping the supply of maize low, and where the relationship between these estates and "Indian" communities nearby centred on the problem of how much maize each party would supply to the market — because a glut could destroy the other - cause trouble for the other.

C. D. Semani (Lucknow University): We have a very complex type of picture. Even in western U.P., where we have large farms, there are non-capitalist lines, with wage labour. We often find that the commercial crop, the cash crop, is taken by the farmer himself, and for the minôr crop the land is given to the labourers. And a share in the crop is taken by the landlord. We have also instances of capitalist relations with feudal relations, in the same villages, with the same person, within the same household.

E. Wolf: I suspect that occurs in other parts of the world, too. I think offhand of Indonesia, for instance, where Geertz illustrates the case of sugar plantations leasing in land from peasant communities and then periodically returning the land on which sugar is grown to allow the community to grow rice, alternating the cultivation of a cash crop with rice production.

J. Palassi: I have a question for· Prof. Silverman. You seem to end your paper with a note of optimism on Steward's approach to the study of peasants; however, most of the other panelists have espoused a Marxist approach. Do you see a congruence between the two approaches?

S. Silverman: Yes,. I do. I think that in a sense Steward brought Marxism into anthropology without Marx. In relation to the prevailing traditions before him, his taking a materialist perspective represents a real departure. The interest in Marxism as such in anthropology is very recent, so one can't look at the 1940s and ask why they didn't see the truth at that point. But I think that Steward's enterprise was close to that of contemporary Marxists, in that we was looking at the rootedness of behaviour and ideas rather than treating them as arbitrary culture pattern. He brought a method for doing this, too, which requires that one look first at productive systems, and then at social relations, then at forms of culture expression.

I don't know that I intended either optimism or pessimism; it was really a more neutral position. I want to reiterate, though, that the approaches I was talking about towards the end of the paper represent perspectives quite a long way from Steward himself. I think that Steward stimulated the development of materialist approaches, which then went in directions that he never anticipated. Certainly his treatment of Puerto Rico itself, while not quite as provincial as he has been accused of, failed to recognize the systemic relations of capitalist development. Based on the historical work that I've been doing, my opinion is that Steward's influence on the Columbia group in the 1940s and '50s was not so much through his ideas, but through creating an atmosphere that allowed a certain development — which became the perspective that the other panelists have been talking about.

T. M. Pandey: I want to comment on Prof. Silverman's paper. I find your material fascinating. I am still not sure whether I can accept your conclusion, because as I see it, both Robert Redfield and Julian Steward were working in the same tradition. Because of his experience among the Shoshone Indians, Steward was emphasizing, as you say, the economic and political dimension. But Redfield, coming from a different kind of background, was not really very interested in that; he emphasized world-view, religion, and so forth. As I see it, one was emphasizing one aspect of reality and another was emphasizing a different aspect.

S. Silverman: What you're saying is true — of course, ultimately they are in the same tradition, in that American culture anthropology is a tradition, and they were contemporaries. I don't think, though, that the difference between them is merely the selection of emphasis; there were different kinds of assumptions involved. For instance, in Steward there is a sense of causal order, which is lacking in Redfield.

Someone sent me a note saying that Kroeber had made the definitive statement about peasants, which I overlooked. Well, Kroeber made definitive statements about everything, but in his statement on peasants there was no sense of "peasants" as an analytic problem; it was simply a comment. The term "peasants" had been used by any number of people. I wasn't trying to pin down everyone who used the word, but rather to look at the point at which the study of peasants became an analytic problem in anthropology, the point at which "peasants" was used a *concept,* not just a descriptive term in its standard English usage. I think that Steward represents a substantial departure from the tradition that Kroeber was connected with. Although Kroeber appears very eclectic, I think he was really most interested in "value culture", and he put values at the centre of the cultural constellation. But I would not describe Steward's approach as Kroeber's "reality culture". I am not entirely sure where Steward's impetus comes from. Robert Murphy, a biographer of Steward from whom I've learned a lot, believes that Steward's main influence was Lowie.

T.M. Pandey: Well, I don't want to prolong the discussion. But I'm still not entirely clear, because as I see it, the field experience played quite a critical role.

S. Silverman: I think that's perfectly true, because — to quote Murphy again — an anthropologist's teachers are not his professors but the people he studied, and Steward learned from the Shoshone. On the other hand, Redfield perhaps was engaged in a different enterprise that wasn't really defined by his field experience, in that he came out of an interest in ways of life in a more general human sense. He was looking for "the good life", and in that sense he was more of a philosopher than a field worker. In fact, he himself was quite astonished that people treated the folk-urban idea as a great theoretical framework. He said he really hadn't any such clear-cut concept in mind — he only studied what interested him. I think that was an honest statement. The theoretical formulation was secondary to him.

T. M. Pandey: Even later Redfield, say 1948, when he went back to Chan Kom — there is a very interesting statement in the book which he wrote. He said, "And what about factions? It would be ridiculous to say that they are not there — they are very much there, but what can we do about that?" So Redfield, as you pointed out, was very much interested in the structure of the socialization for tradition. The nitty gritty aspect I suppose bored him. He was really not interested in the economic and political climate.

S. Silverman: No, he certainly wasn't. He wasn't interested in what you are calling "reality". I suppose it depends on what one calls reality; it is his privilege to use the term to apply to something else.

(A member of the audience raised the question of the relevance of social class to the work of Redfield and Steward.)

S. Silverman: Neither Redfield nor Steward had any sense of class, but I think there is a useful distinction that could be made in the way each of them approach what we would now see as class problems in their work. For Redfield, the folk-elite distinction was quite divorced from basic economic position. It is a matter of communication of ideas, and a recognition that there is variation within a civilization and communication back and forth between folk and elite variants. Steward wasn't much farther along on the class issue. Although he had a notion of class as one kind of horizontal segment, he never had much to say about it. His real interest was in looking at the differences among peasants *within* a class. His contribution was in recognizing that a peasant who grows coffee is quite different from a peasant who grows tobacco. The issue of class is avoided, in both ways. I would say, however, that if you followed Redfield to his logical conclusion, you would be hard put to arrive at class, but with the Steward line you could get there.

K. Gough: I have a question for both Prof. Shanin and Prof. Wolf. I'm worried about the definition of both peasant and rent — worried in the sense that I want them to help me, and they don't in my situation. I am thinking of the situation in southern India, especially in the irrigated areas, which is very similar to what was described a minute ago. From at least the early nineteenth century and probably much earlier, you have had a situation in which much, if not most, of the wet paddy cultivation has been done by agricultural labourers. they were formerly slaves of the state, and then private debt peons in the late nineteenth century. Nowadays they are mainly casual labourers. However, part of the cultivation is done by tenant cultivators who pay something like two-fifths to three-fifths of their produce as rent and who also employ labourers in peak seasons, for transplanting and harvesting. Some individuals shuttle in and out of these roles frequently. They may be doing one in one season and then another the next season — from year to year they don't know whether they're going to be labourers or tenants. Am I to call the tenants peasants because they pay rent, and say that the agricultural labourers are not peasants because they don't pay rent, even though they surrender the greater part of their surplus to the landlord? And am I then to say that for six months a man is a peasant, and for the other six months he is not? How does your definition help me understand this economy, and how do I characterize this mode of production? I think it recurs over and over again in India, and we really don't have the tools yet to characterize this situation in terms of the kinds of concept that are being used today.

A member of the audience: Could I just give one more example so that I could add my voice to ask this question? A study in Orissa, eastern India, in some irrigated areas showed that what the landlord does is to keep the lease very short. It has to be renewed every season. It has to be paid in cash, in advance of the harvest. Every time the lease is renewed it gives the landlord the opportunity to raise the rent if necessary, or to throw out the tenant. This is irrigated farming, with the use of the new seeds and some other aspects of new technology.

E. Wolf: Let me say from the start that there are problems that the term "peasant" is not going to capture. I sometimes think of this term not as a concept that divides the world into categories so that one then can say 'A is A' and 'B is B', but as a pointer: it points towards a particular set of relationships or particular interests to say, "This is what we want to look at." The term "peasant," to me, is useful the way "culture" was useful when anthropologists first tried to think about what is inherited socially and what is inherited genetically: to delimit a set of phenomena and say, let's pay attention to these and see what causes them, and what conditions might underlie them. The problem that you raised was raised several years ago for me by other people who also know India, and who say that it is very difficult to talk about landlord-tenant-agricultural labourer relationships in terms of European or Latin American peasantry. the kind of easy overlap between family, household and farm unit that fits comfortably for some parts of the world does not seem very productive in talking about Indian agriculture. Many of the functions of organizing the productive process may be in the hands of one person who also furnishes the capital, but the actual labour is done by other groups who are not agricultural labourers except that they do work, that is, they are not necessarily in any kind of wage relationship.

I suspect that at this point the simple term "peasant" doesn't tell us very much any more, and I am not sure where one should go — except to describe the situation very carefully. In general theoretical terms it is something like the point raised before — that there are a number of different systems that interdigitate temporally or spatially, and a number of different social arrangements that interdigitate, with regard to the output of the same crop or a set of related crops. The term "peasant" doesn't really specify enough about how production is carried on, who organizes it, who furnishes the instruments, etc. to be able to cope with the kind of question you raised. I would simply second Shanin's last point in his presentation, that peasant studies are important because they point to sets of realities we want to take cognizance of. Then in the next stage you describe them and analyse them. One certainly shouldn't stop with taking a cover term and throwing it over all those people, and thinking that by using it one had delimited what is going on.

S. Silverman: I would add that the situation isn't any more clear in Europe, which is supposedly the source of the peasant who fits all the definitions. These same problems were raised a long time ago for the whole Mediterranean area. The analytic categories don't necessarily match people, and I don't think they should. I think it's a mistake to worry about who is a peasant. The question is, what are the significant relationships and what are the problems that come out of certain kinds of arrangements, some of which are usefully compared and called peasant production. I don't think we can find people anywhere in the world to whom we can attach the term and all agree that "this is a peasant".

K. Gough: As an Asianist I am glad to hear this. Since most of the papers have been by Europeanists and Latin Americanists, I was thinking we ought to get some challenges along that line.

T. Shanin: First let me say that I agree with that Eric and Sydel have said — we must separate terminology from theory. Not because those things are unrelated but because they are not simply related. Establishing conceptual realities helps us understand empirical realities, but never in a pat fashion. But I would go farther, I think what Kathleen is saying is more challenging than that. She said, "What do I need that concept for?" And in so far as this is a challenge from somebody in the field and the answer is, "You need it for the sake of conferences like ours", the final summary to that would be to drop the damn thing altogether. To me at least, the position which I was trying to define is that the concentration on the family unit of production, as conceptually central to what a peasant is, is directly related to the methodological issues of how to study. Under those conditions the answer to "What do I need it for?" (which I face too, by the way, and I agree with Sydel that the problem is not Indian at all) is that the best tools I know how to use in such cases are budget studies. In so far as I assume conceptually that I deal with peasant reality, the family as unit of production is central, and to study it is to try to pin it down to its basic components which will establish the internal structure of the economy and the interaction of different factors in the economy, of this unit of production which is the family, and ways it changes. This is an example of the way in which defining reality as a peasant reality guides me. Secondly, the very issue you raised — you described people as falling in and out of peasant reality — the issue pinpointed is the dynamics of falling in and falling out. Such reality calls for a specific methodology, e.g. dynamic studies in Russia — and they have tried to use them not long ago in Bangladesh. To make the bridge between the conceptual and the methodological, we use the concept of a peasant. It helps define the methodological side of this dialogue, and would be my major answer to the issue of usefulness, or potential usefulness of the concept.

N. C. Goswami (Gauhati University): I wanted to direct my question to Prof. Silverman. Both of you emphasized the role of the family as the production unit. But I have come across several instances where the grandfather is a neo-peasant as a highlander, the son is a neo-peasant, the grandson is a peasant, and the great-grandson is a city-dweller or an industrialist. I wonder how such families can be included in the category of peasants. In think our whole concept of tribe and caste in India has gone from our earlier writers who always spoke about peasants as two: tribe and caste. Actually, all of them are peasants and there is movement between the two.

T. Shanin: I wanted to put a question to Sydel and partly to Eric, because they were both involved in the creation of peasant studies in America, about which I know only little. Sydel described the development of peasant studies within American anthropology. Now, within the field that she described, there were four authors who published massive and analytical studies on the subject-matter of peasantry, and whose writings were available in English. These were Marx, Lenin, Znaniecki, and Sorokin. All four have one thing in common — their roots in eastern and central Europe, injecting into the Anglo-Saxon linguistic realm and scholarly tradition the experience of what I tried to describe in the eastern European blossoming of peasant studies. The question is, did this influence, directly or indirectly, the development of anthropology, or was this left out by the ghetto-like walls which so often separate disciplines?

E. Wolf: I think if American anthropologists have read Marx, they have read him for very different purposes than peasant studies. To use myself as an example, I may have read Marx earlier than some of my professional colleagues, but I did not read him as a source of information on peasants. In fact, his considerations about peasants apper very marginally in *Capital* 3 and the *Grundrisse*. The notebooks on the Russian material are still not available. One read Marx for a picture of how the capitalist system worked rather than for peasantry.

Znaniecki (and there my knowledge is quite limited, although I met him personally) was a very problematic figure for American sociology. American anthropology had no connection with him. I'd be surprised if there were any American anthropologists who had read him. In sociology what was of primary interest was not his peasant studies, but this method of going after the life history of migrants. Sorokin was a problematic figure for American anthropology because he knew everything, and as he nastily said at one point, American social science consisted of latter-day Columbuses who were continually rediscovering America. To some extent that charge is true, except that one must have reference to different intellectual traditions of American social science than Sorokin. We all had to read *Social and Cultural Dynamics,* and I will confess that I was never able to get through that thing. You have to have a mind set that allows you to get to this comprehensive theory covering everything, and that we did not have. I think that Sorokin therefore doesn't have the importance in American social science that he probably ought to have.

S. Silverman: I did read Znaniecki as an anthropology student both at the University of Chicago and at Columbia; I also read Doreen Warriner and rural sociology. It's not that this work was unknown, but it was placed into a particular theoretical framework — one which saw these cases as a certain kind of society or culture that was basically defined by small communities and that represented certain patterns of social relations. It's not the presence or the absence of the information that is the issue; it's the theoretical tradition into which it can be fed. It's what one reads into the material, and not what the material contains, that makes a difference in the development of a tradition.

S. Adnan (University of Chittagong): I have some misgivings about the discussion which has been trying to pin down the household as a production/consumption unit, regarding it as one of the analytical keystones with which we define the peasantry. By and large, the production/consumption unit is no longer the modal form of peasant economic organization in many contemporary societies. What tends to supplant it, as consequences of net polarization amongst the peasantry, could perhaps be termed the income/consumption unit. To take an example, approximately 50 per cent of the rural households in Bangladesh are functionally landless, and tend not to have a productive unit of their own. The individual members of such households work in productive units belonging to others, and in the general case, are linked to several distinct employers, possibly in as many different sectors of production. It is only the incomes of the individual working members which merge into a common family pool for subsequent redistribution; the loci of production and consumption thus need no longer be congruent. However, even though it ceases to be a production/consumption unit, because the household nevertheless continues to be the *site* of the social and biological reproduction of labour power, this change does not necessarily represent a total mutation in the structural role of the household in the peasant economy.

I would, in addition, like to propose a more general framework for the operationalization of some of these concepts of peasant socio-economic organization, and also of economic class. To do so, one needs to bring in a certain amount of quantification. It is possible, for example, to apply the marxian criterion of labour utilization to work out analytical classes, using data on the pattern of labour use of each household under consideration. One could then define appropriate 'cut-off' points differentiating more-or-less homogenous strata in terms of (a) their use of family labour in own production and (b) the extent to which they hire in, or hire out, labour power (i.e. the appropriation of surplus labour, or its reverse). There are of course inherent difficulties in this procedure, particularly with respect to the additivity of labour units, between family labour and wage labour, as well as between surplus labour appropriated in distinct forms of production — capitalist, precapitalist or otherwise. These problems could, however, be further explored for possible solutions.

One particular merit of this approach is that it allows for comparability between distinct samples, as against the stratification patterns based on land-holding magnitudes, given diversity in the sample areas in terms of ecology, land-man ratio, cropping pattern, etc. I would also add that in trying to operationalize one's terms, one is faced with the problem of classifying those specific functional groups in rural society, who are not necessarily agriculturalists, but who are nevertheless integral parts of the agrarian economy and the concomitant social division of labour. In particular, groups such as craftsmen or fishermen are participants in the critical circuits of localized exchange without which purely agricultural systems could not reproduce themselves. In considering this somewhat *broader* notion of the *peasantry,* the problem of class analysis could again be analytically handled if a certain degree of quantification were brought in. Thus, division of economic activities into sectors, and within each sector into roles in production organization, allows a two-fold classificatory scheme which could be made more sensitive by using the labour utilization criterion described above to differentiate in terms of economic classes. (This would be particularly helpful in distinguishing between different types of agricultural tenancy — e.g. the instances of 'reverse tenancy', with the tenant as the dominant contracting party — which would otherwise by lumped together.) Where the economic activities of the members of a given income/consumption unit range beyond a single sector, or a single role in production organization, indices of dominance could be devised to evaluate the compound class-status of such a household.

K. Gough: I think that's extremely relevant from the point of view of Dr. Mencher's introduction this morning, where it was pointed out that the whole scene that this conference is addressing itself to is the question of peasant consciousness and political movements. I think you're moving us in that direction very nicely.

S. Silverman: There is nothing in what either Shanin or I said, in looking at domestic organization, that implied that this described the household as a totality, or that peasant production was the exclusive activity of the household. On the contrary, that's exactly the kind of assumption I was trying to get away from.

G. Iyer: Coming to the point raised earlier, I think that the term "income consumption", rather than production/consumption, suits certain categories in the Indian situation also. For example, when we look to the category of agricultural labourers, income consumption criterion appears to be more relevant. For example, in U. P. there is an atrocious form of bonded labour system. Many of the female agricultural labourers belonging to scheduled castes are very beautiful. They attracted the attention of the commercial prostitutes, who induced the men to send some of their women to brothels and free themselves from bondage. The result of this is that the women were sacrificed to free the husbands. So here income consumption is important.

In the category of rich peasants, there the production/consumption unit becomes more relevant again. From an academic standpoint, it is important to categorize peasants because we want to understand peasant societies, at least within a regional area. From the point of view of mobilization, say for those who have a commitment to the peasantry, who want the agrarian movement to progress at a faster rate, one should really have an understanding as to what the various classes among the peasantry are. This will identify who are the enemies and who are the friends.

A member of the audience: It should not be surprising that those members together collectively find a strategy to reproduce themselves under conditions which are continuously changing, and that in the process they send out labour in many forms. But the point, I think, is that the household is a unit that people use to organize their claims on subsistence and to organize reproduction, which is really the consumption that people do in order to get their labour reproduced. It's the household itself which then becomes the focus for people bringing together those different production relations.

T. Shanin: I think this question of who is a peasant gets much more specific as we try to pin down the dynamics of it. There are many forms of working in agriculture and not all of them are peasant. Chayanov knew that peasants are involved in wage labour as well as we do. But he was using it a *model* of household. Therefore, if we attack him over that we have to attack him over methodology of use of an ideal type. The study of agricultural labour has produced a set of methods used in Russia in the 1920s.

B. N. Varma (CUNY): My comment is about the future of peasantry. Despite Shanin's contention in his paper that the paradigm of modernization has collapsed, I remain unconvinced. I think there is a way out, I have myself written a book on it recently. I hope there is a new paradigm somewhere.

You should look at the empirical issues in the development of the peasantry. Peasants are becoming farmers; peasants are becoming work brigades in the socialist countries; and peasants are moving through middlemen stages, if they move at all. The essential point is to keep in focus the macro-problem of change.

How does one look at the role of the peasants in the evolution of societies? How are peasants integrated in the evolving socio-political system? There are two points of view here; one, the progress of peasants from pauperization to revolution; and the other, as enunciated in the conventional functionalist theory, that peasants become farmers or, if they move to the cities, get converted into underclasses, if they cannot change their beliefs and attitudes. In short, if the peasants will exist in the future, they have to take either the socialist route as in the socialist countries or the capitalist route for their survival.

My other comment concerns the problem of the development of law that was discussed in one of the papers. I think that in the context of the peasantry, it is terribly important for us to remember that Karl Marx took note of the distinction between possession and proprietorship of land. However one may read the Marxian thesis, it is now clear that he was partial to his own world-view in assessing the situation with regard to the ownership of land in India. In my forthcoming book, **The Sociology and Politics of Development,** I have documented eight kinds of rights in land that have existed in India. A capitalist society necessarily multiplies and complicates the rights of ownership, such that in the United States, there are 400,000 lawyers to take care of all kinds of legal problems, whereas in the People's Republic of China, only 3,500 lawyers do the job. I think you have to look at the development of law in terms of the process of change. The growth of law has, of necessity, to be different in a socialist society than in a capitalist society.

Hussain Zillur Rahman (Bangladesh Institute of Development Studies): There appears to be some consensus on describing the peasantry as a household unit and as a consumption unit and as a production unit. I was interested to find out whether such a definition can be used as an element of a theoretical construct. Because if a peasantry defined in this manner is an element of the theoretical system, then how are we going to analyse the reproduction of the social system? This would involve analysing these heuristic units, and investigating how females, the reproductive members of the human species, are redistributed among domestic units. But if we don't view these household units as elements of a theoretical construct, but only as units in which investigation can be carried out, then it's alright. For elements of the theoretical construct we can use other units, for example, classes. Other concepts might have greater explanatory value. Following Godelier, if we make a distinction between a method of investigation and a method of exposition, then I suppose the peasant, as defined this morning, would only constitute an element of the method of investigation. If it is not, then I think we would not get very far in analysing a system.

E. Wolf: I'm not sure I got the drift of the question, but what I get from it involves a larger problem — the one mentioned earlier by Shanin, of how you construct a model of the larger totality within which one places the unit of investigation. The models of the larger society always have to be, of necessity, much simpler, much more abstract, than the kind of recording and monitoring that we can do with the particular unit of investigation. The problem is how to construct that larger model and then make sense of the particular unit of observation we are investigating, and put the two together. The terms that we use, such as "peasantry", community, "class", are means for doing this. The fact that these concepts are never neat enough, or tight enough, or well-bounded enough, has disturbed a number of people including myself. I suspect that if you use the term "class", you are going to lose certain kinds of interconnection between people that appear when you look at what some people have called communities — that is, the actual interrelations, transactions that go on in households and between households, that one needs to know something about in order to build a set of questions like those Kathleen Gough asked earlier. All these different possible arrangements can exist in a place — you can have four classes within the same domestic group — so that the concept of class strains out certain kinds of phenomena that only appear when you shift your attention to the smaller unit of observation. In a peculiar way you've got to have what Rayna Rapp on another occasion called stereoscopic vision. You've got to keep both of these things in mind. You've got to have bifocal lenses to keep moving from one to the other continuously. Otherwise, you lose some essential part of the story.

Member of the audience: It was pointed out that what is reproduced are these household units; so if we focus on the household as an element of the theoretical construct, will we be seeing those relations of reproduction?

H. D. Ramen: I would start from the larger picture, as Prof. Wolf described — the necessarily simpler and more abstract understandings of social relations of the total formation — and then try to talk about the question both you and your colleague are raising, about households as empirical, analytical units in which we can see reproduction going on. What's being reproduced are the social relations of the larger formation. Those larger social relations set up the conditions within which smaller units struggle to reproduce themselves. The units in and of themselves are not *sui generis;* they need always to be reconstructed through all those patterns that people pass down, over the generations, in the struggle for existence that brings together the bits and pieces that they get out of those larger social formations. I don't think you can start in that small unit alone, you have always to be looking at it in relation to the larger social order.

S. B. Chakrabarti (Anthropological Survey of India): What is the social anthropological concept of peasantry? What does it really add to the notion of peasantry already existing in some other disciplines?

S. Silverman: Any discipline is a set of problems, a set of questions, a set of sssumptions. The subject-matter of a discipline is not the *things* it looks at but *how* it looks at them. I think the anthropological view of peasants, as opposed to the economic view, is seeing them as only one possible variant in the human condition. The point of looking at peasants is to learn something about variation in human behaviour. What is also anthropological is the essential comparative nature of its view, so that even those of us who know very little about India have no difficulty in understanding the problems you're raising about the Indian material. We come to our material not with an interest in particular people in particular places, but with a concern with problems of social and cultural processes, and this is necessarily part of the comparative approach. I would also add that anthropology is a method, which other disciplines have learned from us just as we have learned how to count from other disciplines. The fact that the anthropologist looks to see what's going on rather than believing somebody else — this is a major contribution to the scientific endeavour.

A member of the audience: I think we really have not come much farther than Redfield. There are basically three things in the field: a population engaged in agriculture as a productive activity, a group of people who labour, and another group who enjoys the benefits of that labour, and many overlapping categories. If we can put this together with what Redfield was saying, we can move closer to an anthropological concept of peasantry.

E. Wolf: I am not sure what the emphasis of your question is. Are you saying that we are ignoring the realm of ideas in focusing on political economy? If so, I suspect you're right. However, I think this was true of Redfield also, in the sense that he didn't really have the tools to get at the value dimension of culture. Very few people have tried to do this, to find out what peasants know about the world, what they know about each other — to do a cognitive inventory of what peasants know; it's absolutely true that there's an enormous amount to be done there. Peasants do know a great deal about the world, and as anthropologists, we know all too little about what they know. Now, methodologically, I am not sure how one goes about this — how to construct a view of the universe of thought which is adequate to the variation in such knowledge; there is the question of social distribution of such knowledge, also the distribution of productivity of new knowledge. How does knowledge enter the system, and at what point, and through whom? Where is it held back, and who act as barriers? This study is really in its infancy; I can think of a few attempts to do it, but they are mostly *ad hoc* and partial. Agricultural extension agents have studied the innovation process for a long time with regard to particular items, but they have never put those things into a larger context of cognition, and certainly have never tried to relate that cognitive set systematically to other factors, such as class background, domestic cycle, age, sex, and other differences. So I think you're right in saying that we don't know enough about it, and I would say we need to think seriously about how to do it, because, to my mind, I don't think we're very good at it.

J. Vincent: I think that is actually an excellent place for me to start to summarize the discussion. (It's nice to know there's still something out there to be done!) I would say that we have focused on five themes that came up in the course of the presentations earlier, beginning perhaps with the history of anthropological theory, of peasants — although it's my impression that we're a bit dichotomized in that, with the United States and eastern Europe being rather over-represented, and it would have been nice to have fleshed out that body of understanding. We moved on next, quite inevitably, to the definition of peasantry. The three quotations preceding Dr. Shanin's paper really crystallize the discussion that we've had. The third point is the question of whether there is an alternative focus, methodologically, to the family farm and the peasant family. And then we moved quite naturally to the question of whether the starting point of analysis might not be class analysis, and the social formation as a whole. I think the Latin American material brings this out a little bit more. Lastly, we were left with that very nice question of what the peasants think, in effect. This reminds me of a statement I read just before I came here today — that what orthodox theory has given us is a study of capitalism without the working class, a study of imperialism without the blacks, a study of division of labour without women, and I thought that maybe what we had today was the study of the peasantry without the peasants!

PART II

SOME SPECIFIC STUDIES FROM EUROPE, AFRICA, LATIN AMERICA, AND CHINA

Peasant Production and Population in Mexico

ARTURO WARMAN

In my work on the peasants of Morelos, Mexico (Warman 1976), I have tried to analyse the inter-action between two different ways of organizing life, of more correctly two modes of production: the peasants, on the one hand, and the conveyors of industrial capitalism : ranchers, farmers, businessmen or government officers, the promoters of modernism and development,[1] on the other. Both modes coexist and depend upon each other; neither can explain or conceive alone; they are like Siamese twins joined by the same spinal cord. However, these twins not only do not look alike, but also hold very different positions: one dominates, while the other, the peasant, defends himself in a thousand ways in order to subsist, in order to remain a peasant. Sometimes he defends himself by dying, paradoxical as it may sound. This happened during colonial times, in the sixteenth century, when the conquerors had to grant and recognize ancient rights to the natives, running the risk of killing the hen that laid the golden eggs, the only source of wealth. At other times, as in the agrarian movement led by Emiliano Zapata, in the beginning of the twentieth century, the peasants defended themselves by fighting, by making a revolution. At still other times, their defence consisted in multiplying themselves, in increasing the number of peasants needed to survive.

On this occasion, I shall try to explain this last strategy: peasant population growth as one of the ways of adapting to a deeper exploitation. I shall present the analysis in general, abstract terms, and the concrete peasants will scarcely appear. However, they will be always present, especially those from the eastern part of Morelos, the real teachers of this lesson.

At the basis of my discussion are the material conditions of agricultural production.[2] To cultivate and to produce are synonyms only in their widest sense of using natural resources through work and for the ultimate end of human consumption. Otherwise, to cultivate is a special way of producing that uses specific resources and combines them in a peculiar manner. To cultivate is to favour and direct a biological process of growth and reproduction self-generated

by plants; whereas to collect or extract—either wild fruit or precious ore—
consists in using resources in the formation of which human beings do not
intervene, although they may decisively influence their conservation; and to
transform consists in changing the shape and combining the extracted or
cultivated resources—the raw materials—through a series of mechanical
operations. Well-known truths, so evident that they are sometimes forgotten.

The cultivator creates the conditions in which humans can use and benefit
from certain forms of energy. Obviously, the most abundant and important is
solar energy, which through photosynthesis is transformed into plant tissue. The
capabilities of this form of energy are enormous and absolutely uncontrollable,
so much so that the sun is adored as a god or accepted as a given fact; sunlight,
from the standpoint of the grower, is simply something that shines there or falls
(according to his conviction about the theories about the roundness of the earth).
Light is a constant flow with no other variation than seasons or day and night,
changes that occur with absolute regularity. Besides, it is a ubiquitous flow,
perfectly dispersed, outrageously equal but perfectly rigid, inflexible, on which
no possible action or property claim can be exercised. The total inflexibility
cannot be understood as the lack of influence; on the contrary, it is a prerequisite
that constrains the use of the other resources. To cultivate consists in adapting
anything that can move in order to better use the perfect and regular dispersion of
light. The most important source of energy for the cultivator is a constant
element to which he must adapt spreading, dispersing, distributing the plants as
widely as possible. Agriculture is basically a dispersing activity.

Water is not much more malleable. Rain, on which most cultivators depend
directly, is also a seasonal and ubiquitous flow, yet variable and whimsical, with a
dispersion that is far from being perfect. It is agriculture's "show-girl" and
although it may seem more accessible (which is why people try to use magic to
handle it), it is perfectly uncontrollable, and the cultivator has to adapt to its
seasonal recurrence in order to benefit from it as widely as possible, making use
of other resources. Under certain conditions—superficial currents and natural
deposits—water appears as a concentrated resource which must be distributed,
spread. In these cases it can be moved, directed, distributed, and even stored with
quite a bit of flexibility, but still within severe limits. For example, and still
sticking to the obvious, water flows downwards and refuses to flow upwards,
unless it is made to do so through very complicated systems that require huge
amounts of energy; therefore, watering can be used in very limited conditions
even though it may cover wide land surfaces and play the central role in socio-
economic organization (Wittfogel 1966).

The construction, maintenance, and operation of hydraulic works require
great quantities of labour and very complex forms of organization. Labour
demand grows more than proportionally in relation to the amount of irrigated

surface, as one approaches the limits of physical and technological possibility. This is a problem that modern engineers frequently face. They know that the cost of irrigating a hectare near the topographical limit of a hydraulic work is much higher than the marginal profit that could be obtained from it. Modern irrigation systems are built at great distances from the physical limits for cost-benefit reasons. Old systems, especially those of the so-called hydraulic civilizations, on the contrary, are often found to approach the topographical limits, since the cost-benefit ratio was differently applied. The physical limitation in handling water or other resources is not, therefore, a rigid frontier. It does have some degree of flexibility according to how it is combined with technology, human work and its organization, and the nature of the socio-economic pattern. But the physical frontier always remains a true limit.

Neither is the soil a model of elasticity. In one of its aspects, its size or its surface, there is nothing to be done and it has to be taken as something fixed and invariable, perfectly located and limited. Only under very special conditions, such as those found in Holland of in pre-hispanic Mexico, is it possible to increase the soil surface through human work. In order to do so, huge amounts of energy are required as well as a very complex organization, for both of which reigns the principle of diminishing returns as the magnitude and the nearness to the possibility limit increases.

In another aspect, soil as the substratum for plant growth can be subjected to limited handling. Its shape can be changed; it can be levelled and terraces can be built in order to allow a more uniform distribution of other resources, such as water, plants, and labour. These practices also contribute to conservation through erosion control. To a certain extent, the quality of the soil can be changed too. It conditions can be modified so that it will physically and organically provide a better substratum for selected plants through periodical ploughing, tilling, and fertilization. Handling of the soil to preserve it and favour selective and continued plant growth—crop specialization—has very severe limits and becomes rational only with respect to other resources.

Plants themselves, the natural outcome of the combination of the resources mentioned and many others, are at the same time a resource and the concrete object of the grower's activity. The cultivator selects plants in order to use and consume them. This selection does not take into consideration how efficient the plants are in using other resources, but their usefulness, basically their edibility, determined and classified more by cultural preferences than by purely nutritional reasons. Cultural preferences not only refer to taste, which exercises a powerful influence, but include. among other criteria, ease of conservation—an essential requirement for a production which is by nature cyclical and not continuous—its combination with other plants and animals in the diet, and under certain conditions its price. This selection almost always causes the cultivator to favour the growth of plants that are at a disadvantage in relation to other plants, weeds, with an apparently marvellous efficiency.

Cultivated plants must substitute or eliminate other plants in order to use other resources more widely. Artificial selection, domestication, affects the balance of the biotic community, in which take place functions not only of competence but also of complement, such as the formation and the fixation of nutrients. The alteration of the balance must be compensated by work, more intense as the selection deviates further from the natural conditions. Plants, although more flexible than other resources, have a limited elasticity by their very nature and by the ways in which they combine with other resources. They are vulnerable and whimsical, they promise and cannot fulfil their promise; they are living beings.

The limited flexibility of basic resources for cultivation is employed in different ways according to the nearness of physical and technological limits that mark the point of diminishing returns for human labour. The handling of plants, with greater flexibility, is the most desired and less onerous alternative. It takes place through agricultural systems of long fallow, especially the so-called slash-and-burn or swidden. The use of fire helps prepare the biotic community, and allows the planting of selected species with only very limited tools and without touching soil water. To operate the system, it is necessary to have abundant land, which has to be fallow to replace the natural vegetation that makes possible the sporadic growth of cultivated plants. Under long fallowing, the yield per cultivated unit of land is very high, but it is low if it is calculated in terms of the total area needed for operating the system. Short fallowing, in which the soil "rests" at least one cycle for each one that is cultivated, is almost always associated with the use of work animals, since the yield per cultivated unit of land is lower, and thus greater surfaces must be covered. On the other hand, the yield of the total area is higher than under the slash-and-burn system. In short fallowing the soil is handled, plants are not too varied and highly specialized, mostly cereals or grains. Partial restoration of the destroyed biotic balance is one of the crucial (but not always achieved) requirements. The introduction of irrigation increases the yield per hectare, and the yield of the total land area, since the soil is used more frequently, in some cases continuously. With irrigation, not only the water but also the soil must be levelled, or terraces must be built to permit regular water-flow, whether animals or only tools are used. Irrigated agriculture uses all resources with more intensity, human work included. The different systems are not mutually exclusive, and can be combined in many ways depending on the last resource, human labour. People, then, obviously hold a peculiar position: they are at the same time an element of energy for production, and the only existing reason for the complicated and arduous process of cultivation. This, too, because it is so obvious, is often forgotten. People are not the human resource of production as a supreme aim, but rather people produce in order to live.

People, as a source of energy for agriculture, are very flexible. They are mobile. They can spread their activity to catch solar energy and rain more fully, or can concentrate it to build a terrace; they can participate in the construction of a huge irrigation project, or start something as delicate as a graft or a transplant. But, besides contributing energy, people decide; they choose those strategies that will favour plant growth for their own purposes, in relation to other resources; they select the option which allows for the greatest productivity in their work, and contribute energy to carry it out. They are a resource with autonomous motion, with initiative.

People do not seem to be among the most powerful or efficient sources of energy. They eat a lot and tire quickly. They have their own law of diminishing returns: the more work they do in a certain period of time, the greater will be the drudgery and fatigue for the worker in the last work units accomplished, the marginal ones. Everyone can verify this observation empirically, which can also be expressed in other ways: labour productivity diminishes the nearer it gets to the worker's limit of physical endurance; or in a more personal manner: the last pull yields less, and sometimes the string snaps. To increase labour efficiency, people have created implements. Some of them, tools, allow the concentration of energy of fulfil specialized functions, but are inert in themselves. Others, on the contrary, working animals and machines, are substitutes for human force, and obtain their energy from other sources. These work reproducers are generally more potent but less flexible than human work, more specialized and in many ways more limited. Reproducers must be taken with a certain reserve, since in the majority of cases they do not substitute for human labour but distribute it more uniformly; their usefulness is more related to the concentration of energy in the critical moments imposed by the seasonal character of agriculture, than to the elimination of human labour. In other words, they allow people to cultivate more intensely in short periods of time, but in exchange require complementary efforts that are apparently greater but that take place at longer intervals.

Draft animals offer a good example for this contention. Their strength is good only for hauling or for bearing loads. When the agricultural system requires a good deal of handling of the soil, such as specialized non-irrigated cultivation of cereals, the hauling capacity of the animals and the plough allow a small team of people to work a larger surface than they would if they only worked with tools. The energy of the animals is only used intermittently for about ten weeks of the year, but they require year-round care. They need food, which in some cases implies increasing the cultivated area and even introducing forage crops. When cattle graze freely and occupy a specific area, the latter has to be prepared: watering places, fences, surveillance. In the long run, keeping draft cattle demands more energy than it produces, but the expense is distributed over a longer period and in small instalments which can be the responsibility of people who, by reason of having little physical energy (like children and older persons), or having other simultaneous occupations (like women), cannot fully participate in the work during the crucial period of agricultural activity. To own cattle is like obtaining an energy loan to be paid back with interest, in instalments that may be covered by those who have no full job in the cultivation.

From the combination of resources with very little or no elasticity at all, and human work, autonomous and flexible, a relation appears that seems constant in agriculture that only uses biological energy (also called traditional agriculture). This law, the formulation of which does not originate with me, can be stated thus: the more intense use of agricultural land results in an increase in total production and a decrease in labour productivity. In other words, if production is duplicated in a given surface, the amount of labour necessary to obtain it will grow in a larger proportion, since there is the need for more quantity and more complexity in the tasks of pushing other resources near their limits. And still another way of saying it: if more labour units are invested in a limited amount of land, the average productivity per unit will decrease. Well, and with this I stop insisting: the peasant works more and harder but obtains smaller increases in his production, as long as the territorial area remains constant (Chayanov 1965, Sahlins, 1972).

Evidently, the hypothesis contradicts the generalized dogma that the greatest production — the "scale" that constitutes the efficiency model of capitalism — is a condition to raise labour productivity. It also contradicts the productivity measures that are made through capitalism's optics. In capitalism, work productivity is almost always measured per capita and in long periods of time, while in this essay productivity is measured per work unit in fact invested, per hour of effort. In the first sense, in the capitalist sense, peasant productivity increases with intensification; but in the second one it decreases, because labour demand grows more than production. Sometimes we are shown that modern technology, measured in a lot or a hectare during an agricultural cycle, makes work more productive, more profitable, and better paid; yet at other times, not even this can be shown. In calculating these figures, using business micro-economy, facts are in many senses obscured. The result may be totally contradicted by hidden facts, such as work-day length and its drudgery; what people do when the agricultural cycle — which only covers part of the year—is over; what is happening in non-cultivated or fallow land; or what is the meaning of the monetary units in which productivity is measured in terms of subsistence and satisfaction of needs.

The recent history of rural Mexico shows a constant tendency towards the intensification of soil utilization to increase total territorial production. If we apply the above-mentioned law, we find that the work needed to raise production increases in greater proportion. Data from many different sources fully confirm this fact. The central question is now pertinent: What motivated the growth of production and the more than proportionate increase in the efforts dedicated to achieve it?.

Several obvious answers come to mind. The defendants of liberal capitalism cite their reasoning: peasants produce and work more because they wish to live better, as if the protestant ethic had suddenly fallen on them. The facts contradict this optimistic and naive vision. Contemporary peasants still do not exceed the strictest level of subsistence. All their effort, larger all the time, scarcely gives them enough to stay alive; without speaking of saving, much less of investing, or even counting on reserves for a bad year, for illness, for marriage or death. If anything like this happens, and it always does, one has to borrow and work harder yet in the future. There exists an almost unanimous consensus among peasants that the quality of their daily life has deteriorated: one works harder but enjoys less and even eats worse; everything becomes more difficult; "it's tough going", as they say.[3]

Another obvious reply, that I shall attribute to ecological pessimists, is that peasants produce and work more because they have reproduced themselves irresponsibly, like rabbits. The answer sounds logical because evidently peasants are more numerous, double the number they were twenty years before, but it is completely false. The facts show without doubt that production growth came first and was higher, at least until 1970, than rural population growth.[4] In other words, peasants worked harder before they had more mouths to feed, and no hope of saving or investing, or even the illusion of living with less debts; on the contrary, to pay overdue debts. Peasants are forced to produce more by external pressures. The real price of their products has been falling in relation to the price of the articles they have to buy. They have to buy more things that they do not produce, because their resources have been alienated. They have to pay 100 per cent interest to money-lenders, and each year they have to borrow more money for the benefit of middlemen and merchants. As free labourers, peasants earn the lowest wages in Mexico and only for short periods of time. Salaries are established in terms of complementing peasant autonomous production, and they are below the cost of subsistence and reproduction of other groups in the society. To say it pompously, peasants must pay a fee of increasing exploitation to the benefit of the capitalistic industrial sector, because they are dominated through the market, by the forms of land ownership, bu institutions and by the legal or armed violence that shields them. The mechanisms of domination are another story that I shall not go into now, but evidently, they are a central part of this essay.

The facts firmly suggest that it is domination, the growing exploitation that benefits other groups, that is the principal motivation for the increase in rural population. Thus, rural population growth is not a cause but a consequence, a defensive reaction. Let us go back to the above-mentioned law: to each increase in production corresponds a more than proportionate increase in work expended. Now we can also state it in this way: for each value unit that the peasant transfers to the capitalistic industrial sector, his work effort grows in greater proportion. Every time the price of maize falls relatively, and it has not stopped doing so for the past thirty years, the work needed to compensate the fall is greater than the ratio of price deterioration. Faced with a demand for greater production and a diminishing productivity of labour, the peasant has to increase the size of his labour force. He is forced to reproduce himself in order to increase the availability of labour, so that he can keep intensifying agricultural crops even at the risk of cutting down his level of consumption, his standard of living. The peasant adapts and defends himself from an increasing exploitation through reproduction.

With this a vicious cycle develops and a Pandora's box opens. The rural population must reach the necessary size to saturate the maximum labour demand for crops in a constant process of intensification. The maximum demand is, generally, of very short duration, given the seasonal and variable nature of agricultural production. Water, land, and other resources are not available to give constant employment. The saturation of maximum demand implies "unemployment" for the rest of the agricultural cycle, a remnant labour force temporarily idle, which is characteristic of today's peasant populations. From the standpoint of the dominator, the remnant labour force has a potential for exploitation. "Underemployment" becomes determining under the increased level of exploitation, which again regenerates intensification and, obviously, unemployment that must be eliminated.

The suggestion that exploitation is the most important factor, and has the greatest autonomy in the process of intensification of agricultural production, is mentioned here in its most simplified aspect, but it is the central topic of this paper. It does not imply that its determination is mechanical nor that it operates fatally, and its application is only possible if combined with other explanatory factors. Besides, what is said here specifically for peasants is surely not an original issue: class struggle as the driving force of history is, of course, an old and respectable idea, but devilishly difficult to prove.

NOTES

(1) In this approach I use many sources. The Marxist tradition and Marx's writings must be mentioned. Also the "cultural ecology" tradition, especially Julian Steward's *Theory of Culture Change: The Methodology of Multilinear Evolution* (Urbana: University of Illinois ;Press, 1973). Eric Wolf's writings about *Peasants* (Chapel Hill: Prentice-Hall, 1966), and about Mexican peasants in particular, have played a paramount role in my approach. Clifford Geertz's *Agricultural Involution: The Processess of Ecological Change in Indonesia* (Berkeley: The University of California Press, 1963) had a direct influence in the conception of this paper.

(2) The question is almost the same that Ester Boserup asked in her excellent book *The Conditions of Agricultural Growth* (Chicago: Aldine, 1965). The answer given in this paper quite different.

(3) In recent years many good books, by Mexican and foreign anthropologists, have given enough evidence about the qualitative changes in peasant livelihood. Deterioration of the subsistence level can be easily argued. The data used for this paper were taken from the three collective volumes *Los Campesinos de la tierra de Zapata* (Mexico: SEP-INAH, 1974-76) by Alonso, Azaola, Corcuera, Helguera, Krotz, Lopez, Melville, Ramirez.

(4) The quantitative data are documented by the national census of the twentieth century. However, the qualitative data firmly suggest that the census only reflects a pale image of the processes of intensification and population growth in the rural areas.

BIBLIOGRAPHY

Chayanov, Alexander V. (1965): *The Theory of Peasant Economy*, Homewood: Richard D. Irwin.

Sahlins, Marshall D. (1972): *Stone Age Economics*, Chicago: Aldine-Atherton,

Warman, Arturo: (1976) *Y venimos a contradecir . . . El Campesino de Morelos Y el Estado Nacional*, Mexico: Ediciones de la Casa Chata.

Wittfogel, Karl (1966): *Oriental Despotism* or *Despotismo Oriental, un estudio comparativo del poder totalitario*, Madrid, Ediciones Guadarrama.

Social Conditions of Production
and Technical Change
in Venezuelan Agriculture

HEBE M. C. VESSURI

INTRODUCTION

Recently a well-known economist observed that the technology produced by capitalism, with its sophisticated production techniques, tends to be considered, especially by economists and planners of science and technology, as technology proper without further qualification, as if the older craft techniques did not count (Freeman 1975). Although one cannot but admit that the newer technology presents a revolutionary aspect because it is increasingly linked to science, and because on the level of contemporary capitalist economy one may talk about this technology as a universal category, this ahistorical use of the concept may easily lead to confusion.[1]

Inasmuch as it is a historical phenomenon, technology carries the imprint of the economic and social system within which it was developed. Thus, it may be said that there has been and there is a capitalist use of techniques and, even more, that the capitalist logic of capital accumulation has given specific characteristics to the process of production, including the production of scientific and technical knowledge. Such a process has led to the creation of techniques having specific features derived from the historical conditions in which they were produced and from the functions that were assigned to them within a particular social and economic context.

Under capitalism, technology has been conceptually linked to the notion of progress: technical progress appears as a basic ingredient of capitalist accumulation. But precisely because technical progress does not occur in a social vacuum, but means change or novelty with regard to something prior, which is a complex phenomenon and not a mere technique susceptible of being replaced or modified by another, it seems appropriate to emphasize and explore here some aspects of the social-historical character of the technological dimension. The global "sociological" study of a technical novelty—for example the mechanical reaper in the English farm of the mid-nineteenth century—makes clear that the substitution of horse-powered machines for manual labour on British farms was a rather more complex issue than the naive neo-classical models of factor substitution would allow us to infer (David 1975).

The development of techniques has an influence upon the remaining components of the productive forces and upon many other aspects of human life and activity. Reciprocally, current economic and political conditions affect technological growth, although this is often disregarded in the analyses made. For example, with regard to agricultural technical change, the influence of the landscape inherited from long periods of agricultural settlement, which is a reflection of a precise economic and political organization, is frequently forgotten by technicians; nevertheless it is essential to take it into account when considering technical progress. Indeed, the physical condition of the land and the distribution of existing fields, fences, and buildings must be considered in connection with the acceptance or rejection by the farmers of new production techniques. But in general, it may be argued that its role in the social history of agrarian technology has not been sufficiently appreciated or understood.

This paper is based on the assumption of the reciprocal conditioning between the productive forces, particularly techniques—which are their most mobile and dynamic element—and the historical and social conditions expressed in social, cultural, and productive relations. Thus, my starting point is the consideration of the peculiar nature of agriculture, which allows various forms of social organization and several factor combinations. I then proceed to analyse some of the characteristic social forms in which agricultural production is organized in a particular society—Venezuela—and the technical modalities which distinguish them. Finally, I conclude with a comment on the social tendencies observed in the processes of agricultural technical change reviewed. The goal of the case-studies from which the empirical date are derived was not to formulate models of the different productive systems in order to evaluate them from a socioeconomic point of view and then reach conclusions and recommendations. However, I have tried to put forward some ideas and questions based on these studies, that might be tested by theoretical and empirical investigations.

The choice of cases is never a simple procedure, for it implies either taking theoretical concepts and trying to operationalize them without having developed a methodologically sound way of bridging the gap, or alternatively inducing a theoretical order from the observations of heterogeneous phenomena—which is open to even more objections.[2] Examples of these difficulties are several of the attempts to apply to the Venezuelan countryside, in a reductionist fashion, an "orthodox/marxist" typology of social classes under capitalism, which have failed empirically so often that they are not used in the practice of research or in the implementation of programmes. As a consequence, the theoretical vacuum has been filled almost exclusively by the descriptive categories of the censuses, of doubtful usefulness, for they present innumerable difficulties when dynamic approaches to the social processes in the countryside are attempted.

The existence of such a theoretical vacuum has coincided with an increasing urgency to recategorize the social groups that have developed in the process of capitalization of Venezuelan agriculture. This task has already begun on the conceptual level as well as on the empirical one, through field research, although it is still fraught with limitations and deficiencies.

Although ultimately our interests lie in the knowledge of the behaviour of agrarian social classes in the development process of Venezuelan society, in this paper we approach this problem only tangentially, through the analysis of some of the variations which appear most significant to us in the social and technical organization of national agricultural production. But our emphasis, as has already been said, is on the complexity of the interactions between technological, economic and social factors of the productive forms considered, rather than in the political aspects. At the level of the economic context in which production devolves, existing relationships between productive enterprises and the rest of society are of crucial importance. The types and forms of external linkage determine the access to production factors, technical inputs, and the formation and equally the real impact upon the units of production of different agricultural policies designed by the state, such as credit, prices, foreign exchange policies, etc. All these aspects define what have been called "situations of technical change".[3]

SOCIAL SYSTEMS OF AGRICULTURAL PRODUCTION[4]

Agriculture, because of the features that distinguish it in the use of basic resources, allows several factor combinations and various forms of social organization. These factor combinations and associated forms of social organization constitute cultural complexes linked to agricultural production. This notion is not new. Lewis (1949) showed in relation to Mexican agriculture how the differences between hoe agriculture and plough agriculture were not simply a matter of the use of different tools, but represented two different cultural systems or complexes, each with its associated features and long-range social and economic implications. His argument sought to establish contrasts between the two types in as many aspects as possible. His analysis is my starting point for the study of the nature and articulation of different techno-cultural complexes. But I do not wish simply to identify contrasts between cultural complexes found in a given society. Rather, I am interested in showing the relationships of domination/subordination present in situations in which two or more techno-cultural complexes coexist, as is the case in Venezuela and other developing countries. This interest is linked to two basic observations: that technological change can be treated as either internal or external to a given productive process, and that technological change is not neutral. (I shall develop these ideas further in the final section of the paper.)

If by technological progress we agree to mean increase in yield per hectare[5] we must still recognize that the factors involved in the growth of agricultural productivity are multiple and complex. Among them are environmental parameters, prevailing productive techniques, alternative costs to make possible different levels of potential returns, the organization of the productive process, patterns of social organization, features of the political systems, settlement patterns, and the particular characteristics of the social perception of the physical-natural environment. An exclusive or narrow focus upon any of these aspects would result in a falsifying oversimplification of the phenomena and would obscure the processes that we want to explore.

The anthropological tradition characterized by the comparative study of societies usually implied the analysis of systems of production and subsistence, but often overemphasis upon technological change as a universally valid determinant of social progress resulted in oversimplification of relationships and neglect of the multiple processes which led to more complex forms of social organization. That technological aspects are systematically present in socio-economic phenomena has been repeatedly corroborated, although the historical specifications of that interaction have not been explored in sufficient depth. It is increasingly clear that although in a broad sense technological advancement determines social transformation, the latter manifests itself concretely through the unfolding of social relations, thereby adopting or rejecting particular technological innovations.

Besides, and as regards the technological dimension proper, it is only rarely that changes reflected in increasing productivity of resources are clearly identifiable with particular historical moments. Throughout history there has been a continuing process of technological change through modest individual modifications, small improvements, and adaptive inventions of minor import which *cumulatively* become important. However, we must not exaggerate the continuity of historical development. "Imperceptible changes lead to a very clear diversity; from the seed to the tree there are no jumps; and the continuity of the spectrum does not make its colours the less diverse" (Koyre 1973). The idea of the study of productive systems in terms of their specific exonomic rationales, requirements, limitations, and contributions is framed in this historical perspective: transitions between social systems of agricultural production are inevitably gradual, and even when it is possible to distinguish between them it may be observed that the old systems of production usually persist alongside of the new ones. One of the critical problems in differentiating between productive systems in a synchronic analysis is that of characterizing the differences and the weight of the persisting elements.

In the course of our research (Vessuri 1978) we came to choose four productive systems that were sufficiently differentiated and typical as to produce a representative sample of some of the main variations in the social organization of national agricultural production. The first system we studied was that of the traditional peasants. Then followed the middle producers. Next, the peasants organized by the Agrarian Reform and the agribusiness complexes were to be considered.[6] In this paper we shall refer to the first two systems, about which we already have analysed data (see Vessuri 1978a, 1978b).

From the distinctive features of the systems we studied and from the recognition of their modalities, weight, and dynamism, we extract the following comments.

THE TRADITIONAL PEASANTS

By such we mean the *conuqueros* and the current land beneficiaries whose production is not organized through any of the various organizations of the Agrarian Reform and retains specific features as much for the nature of the crops as for its technology, labour organization, etc. They still comprise a high percentage of agricultural units in Venezuela (almost 60 per cent), amounting to approximately 170,000 units.[7]

At the present time their productive system constitutes one of the basic components of the historical inheritance of Venezuelan agriculture. In this connection we ask ourselves several questions: Is there a peasant-economic rationality? In what does the traditional peasant agricultural productive system consist, in concrete terms? What role does the peasant population play in national agricultural production? What are the conditions and consequences of the current technical progress of agriculture in the life of peasants? What knowledge can be gained from peasant systems of production?

In a brief synthesis we may sketch possible answers to these questions.

(a) *How do peasants operate; What is the rationality of their economic activity?* When we speak of a peasant economic system, the conceptual image we evoke corresponds to that of a traditional culture linked to the way of life of small rural communities and to a specific mode of exploitation of natural resources and human labour. According to classical formulations, the peasant economy is a family economy which does not collect from society a land rent, even in the cases in which there is enjoyment of rural property. The foundation of its rationality is not, according to Chayanov, in capital accumulation, but in minimizing the self-exploitation of the family labour force once culturally defined survival needs become satisfied, and defining in the process norms of "good" or "bad" use of resources. What results is a specific and original form of economic rationality, that we might call "peasant economic rationality", which does not include, among its definitory features, important economic inducements to technical change.

In conditions like the ones in Venezuela today, the most common situation among traditional peasants is distinguished by the interaction between such peasant rationality as we have briefly characterized and the rationality of market-law, which permeates the global economy to which peasants are articulated and which subordinates the peasant production to its dynamic. Their agricultural activity is patterned on the basis of the survival needs of the family.

To that effect, land and labour are distributed in order to ensure, on the one hand, the production of fundamental food crops in the family's yearly diet and, on the other, the production of crops destined to the market or the sale of the labour power of one or more of the members of the family group, by means of which they get the required money to fulfil the functioning and subsistence needs. But characteristically, productive activity does not allow the constitution of a sufficiently large fund of capital so as to dispose of it and devote it to alternative investments.

(b) *In what does the peasant agricultural productive system consist, in concrete terms?* It is a common assumption that the technology of the peasant *conuco* is "backward", by comparison with more "modern" techniques which, were it not for the intervention of special factors, ought to be already in use by the peasants. Frequently, two reasons are given to explain why they are not being used.[8] In the first place, it is said that peasants are bound by tradition to follow ancestral modes of doing things. In its most negative form—that peasants simply cannot conceive of methods superior to those they have traditionally used—this notion has practically disappeared from the technical literature. But it has been replaced by another one which is essentially similar, although more attenuated: namely, that peasants have learnt through sour experience to follow certain paths which it is understandable that they do not wish to change, considering the price they have paid to learn them.

This idea has an element of truth as well as an important error. Even though it is true that usually peasants have acquired their techniques through experience, trying their efficacy and adopting the successful ones, it is mistaken to assume that this peasant pragmatism is indissolubly linked to conservatism. In the history of Venezuelan peasant agriculture, without going any further, many "new" tools, techniques, and organizational aspects of production—such as the generalization of the *machete,* the steel axe, new crop varieties, the use of the plough and chemical pesticides—have been adopted quite rapidly, while other elements, such as the sedentary extensive monocrop, fertilizers, or certain certified seeds, have diffused slowly or have not been accepted at all. Some authors argue that a "negative cultural conditioning" which supposedly retards technological progress is operating selectively. As a matter of fact, it is not negative conditioning that is acting here; rather, the peasant is a pragmatist who is fundamentally concerned about whether or not something works for his own benefit.

Besides, it is an indisputable fact that the technology in use in developing countries, where peasants constitute the majority of the agricultural producers, has evolved in response to a set of incentives designed to promote investments based on imported technology. By and large, "appropriate" technologies do not yet exist as sound, well-tested hardware that can be located in engineering catalogues and plugged into development projects. Costs and risks of innovation have not so far been financed with the intention of benefiting the poor. We could hardly expect a wide peasant adoption of modern technology when their economic capacity does not allow them to incorporate a technology that is not appropriate for the needs of the small non-capitalized agriculture (Weiss 1979).

At this point it is necessary to recognize that the scarce or absent capital and savings capacity of the average peasant are obviously important data of his situation; and the emphasis he places on minimizing in risks and seeking security from possible disaster is a consequence of his lack of material wealth. But poverty by itself is not enough to fully explain his scanty use of agricultural tools.

In the modality we studied, the peasant productive system is characterized by a social organization comprising independent family production units, in plots they occupy as owners, beneficiaries of the agrarian reform, or simply in precarious tenancy. The common practice of these peasants is to attempt to appropriate the patterns of migratory agriculture widespread in the tropics. This consists of a form of minimal farming. The same portion of land is used during a number of years, after which it is abandoned or left fallow for a variable period of time, and the exploitation of another plot is begun. Basically, we have a system of "space rotation", instead of the crop rotation which is common to the farming fields of sedentary agriculture. When the peasant finds himself circumscribed to the narrow and fixed boundaries of a plot of land (as in the case of the beneficiaries of the agrarian reform, for example), he tries to reproduce the ancestral practices. Thus, he subdivides his plot in tiny portions devoted to different crop combinations, and rotates them so that several portions of it are in varying conditions of fallow.

Another outstanding feature of this productive system is the set of crops handled, which are fundamentally those known as tropical food-crops, with regard to which often the only technical knowledge existing for their handling is the one that peasants have through their long experience with them.

The "design" of this productive technology implies the complex combination of multiple crops in space and time, taking maximum advantage of topographic variations, humidity, fertility, etc. of the terrain, and of the differences in the cycles of the wide gamut of plants. The tools used are very simple, mostly house-made—*coa, chicura, machete, escardilla*—which ensure the provision of food and survival of the domestic group throughout the whole year.

All this means that there are no special cultural conditionings hindering a positive reaction to appropriate economic incentives. The recognition that peasants do usually experiment in the process of their work is one of the main arguments in favour of this alternative line of interpretation.

(c) *How does technical change occur in the context of traditional peasant production?* One cannot speak of technical change as if it were an automatic, formal, atemporal process, for it is closely linked to the social and historical contexts in which it is produced. We are frequently confronted by dynamics of technical change generated by the wider societies which envelop and dominate peasant populations, and which are derived from the specific needs of the former. Thus, the processes of technical change such as developed in Precolombian American agriculture are very different from those in the *conuco* of the Venezuelan coffee plantation *peon* during the nineteenth century, or in the plot of the Mexican peasant of the present time.

The circumstances lead us to distinguish processes of technical change that may be exogenous or endogenous to the peasant systems of production. In the former case agents external to the social group detect the opportunity or define the technological problem, and develop or select the techniques that are imposed upon the group. In the latter case, the process of transformation is produced internally, as derived from the economic, ecological, or geographical conditions of the peasant unit, starting from opportunities that are detected in its milieu.

When peasant agriculture is talked about as being technologically stagnated, backward, rejecting technological progress, technical change is being considered as an exogenous factor. Such an approach is partially valid. It results from the wider perspective of the strategy of global economic development of the society. Naturally, confronted with the need for providing urban centres with cheap food, the development of a national labour market, etc., the concept of the necessary technical change to increase peasant productivity does not take into account the latter's nature and is imposed upon it as something exogenous.

But in peasant populations, as in every socio-cultural system, we find a continuous process throughout history of small and large inventions, improvements, adaptations to specific conditions, etc. Experimentation and change are features inherent to any productive process, but when—as in peasant systems of production—there is no stimulus to invention and change beyond insuring the culturally pre-established level of production, we find that the process of creation of technical knowledge is not channelled through specific institutional paths. On the other hand, technical changes that would imply transformational effects of the system are rejected; it might even be asked to what extent the development of adaptive techniques has been the mechanism that allowed the persistence of peasant populations. Since the logic of their productive system implies the search for balanced relationships with the natural environment, the invention and adoption of different technical elements take place in this conceptual framework in a highly selective way. This, as we have already said, is valid for cases of adoption of exogenous innovations. Thus, for example, the substitution of the ox-drawn plough for the *chicura* does not necessarily imply a greater capitalization, but rather it may be done in a given situation to compensate for a specific lack of labour. Or, the change from subsistence crops to commercial crops which is currently taking place under market pressures also takes place selectively, trying to reach (often unsuccessfully) new equilibria between market demands and subsistence needs.

Frequently the problems are due, as was said earlier, to the deficient factor combination made by the peasant when he incorporates elements of modern technology in conditions below the optimum.

While in the capitalist enterprise production, technological change is the result and the basic engine of accumulation, in the traditional peasant production endogenous technical change does not appear to be linked to capital, but rather to other economic and socio-cultural dimensions.

(d) *What role does the peasantry play in the national agricultural production?* What are the conditions and consequences of the current technical progress of agriculture in the life of the peasantry? Venezuelan capitalist development, although uneven and heterogeneous in the various branches of economic activity, has a great dynamism, generating an industrialization process that has specific requirements of agricultural raw materials. This is turn implies that an important portion of the rural labour force has become integrated into the national market; a great proportion of agricultural productive inputs are "industrially" produced; there is a national market in full expansion and a state credit policy of stimulus for the development of capitalist agriculture.

But the impact of capital penetration in the countryside is not reduced to the expansion and consolidation of capitalist agriculture enterprises. It also affects the existing systems of production, integrating them in various manners to its dynamic. Through the guidance and coordination of the state, the capitalist class has sufficiently promoted the landed peasantry so as to avoid their withdrawal from production, particularly the production of certain goods that are especially important in the diet of the labour force, but it has done so in such a way as to prevent their productive activity from entering a process of accumulation. Under current conditions, the peasants are unable to demand for their products a price in which a land rent is included, for they hardly get the equivalent of a subsistence salary. Were it not for these reasons, the differentiation of the peasantry might accelerate, increasing significantly and inconveniently (for the capitalist class) the number of capitalist agricultural units getting land rent, thus affecting the global distribution of the social surplus value. If it is agreed to assume that the reformed peasant sector participates in 9 or 10 per cent of the national agricultural production, it can be estimated *grosso modo* that the total participation of peasant production—reformed sector and traditional sector combined—is between 15 and 20 per cent. Of course, the proportion varies acording to whether we consider the nature of the participation by the vegetal or animal subsectors, and within the latter ones by product, since in general their participation is very low in cattle production, and a specialization can be observed in the less profitable crops.

Hence, the importance of peasant production does not lie in its value or its volume, which we can see is low, but in other factors. One of them relates to its own nature, which is based upon tropical crops. Tropical crops are managed fundamentally by peasant populations, with rudimentary techniques and without major investments of capital or technical improvements, allowing under certain conditions the gradual harvest adjusted to subsistence needs and providing cash money as a result of a growing participation in food markets. Throughout history the basic diet of the Venezuelan people has consisted in large measure of the surpluses of peasant production. Despite the fact that in recent decades that diet has been sharply modified, tropical crops are still an important component of it and they are overwhelmingly provided by the peasant sector (Jaffe Carbonell 1977).

Another reason for the importance of peasant production is that it allows the self-sufficiency of a segment of the national population whose dimensions are not insignificant, and which in turn contributes to the subsistence of workers articulated in different ways to the national labour market, who, in the family *conuco,* find support at times of unemployment or ill health.

However, from what has been said one should not deduce an ahistorical view of the "traditional" peasant, for his viability is the continuously rethought result of his subordinated situation *via-a-vis* the dynamic of capital. The peasant producer who remains on his plot of land instead of becoming an agricultural wage-worker or of migrating into the cities due to the lack of local opportunities and the pressures of growing monetarization of the national economy, is led to devote a progressively larger and larger portion of his land to commercial crops, to the detriment of the subsistence crops. This process does not involve the mere substitution of an agricultural crop for another, but implies changes in the very organization of production. Variable portions of terrain must now be devoted to one or more commercial monocrops, thus modifying the distribution of time and effort in the plot's work at the same time that the peasant has to pay attention to the different technical requirements that accompany the new crops. In this way an increasing series of modifications in his mode of production begins, while he attempts to reach new balances. The exigency of improving the quantity and quality of the products frequently coincides with the diminution of the soil fertility and, consequently, the peasant is forced to resort increasingly to the elements of "capitalist" or modern agricultural technology, in conditions in which owing to his "inefficient" factor combination, they are expensive. He will have to resort to crops that have a demand in the market or to the state supportive credit; he will have to spend on certified seeds, industrial fertilizer and pesticides, animal or mechanical power. His partial inefficient incorporation of some techniques of the capitalist productive system, instead of placing him in the best conditions of accumulation and thus allowing him to achieve an economic autonomy, exposes him to major difficulties. On the other hand, he is confronted with the pressure of usury credits which often force him to sell his labour power to obtain money with which to return the loan he needed to get the necessary inputs for sowing. On the other, since he cultivates much less fertile soils than those usually devoted to commercial agriculture by the capitalist class, he joins the capitalist depredation of the natural environment in his attempt to produce within the frame of limited productive, technical, and economic options.

(e) *What knowledge can be derived from the peasant productive system?* This question is linked to two types of concerns. On the one hand, one might think of the promotion of endogenous technical changes in the peasant economies. By this we mean starting from the knowledge of peasant productive practices to try to improve them gradually, taking maximum advantage of their potentialities. From this point of view the study of the peasant productive system might make a contribution to the recovery of a fragment of the national cultural inheritance, understood as the set of elements of productive know-how which have accumulated in rural communities, sometimes in a secular process, and which form a non-structured collection of endogenous solutions to local problems.

When observing the behaviour of the peasant producer in the context of the peasant community, as we confront his fund of resources and the way in which agricultural techniques develop in a pre-industrial productive system in which new ideas are being continuously introduced, but in which a rapid process of capitalization or of increased well-being is not observed, we acquire knowledge about the total attitude of the peasant population and the response of their productive system to the exogenous stimuli coming from the national society.

But this knowledge is not limited in its range of application to the sphere of peasant populations. And here we can mention the second type of concern. The study of these productive practices suggests new approaches to scientific research. More than furnishing us with particular techniques, the most important contribution of peasant productive systems will be given probably by their "different" ways of seeking solutions to old problems, a fact that might stimulate scientific research in unexplored directions.

The peasant agricultural productive system, in its several modalities, contributes elements for the scientific study of the forms of human intervention in tropical ecosystems. Frequently, the only management models we have about those complex and fragile ecosystems are those of peasant peoples, with their knowledge of the structure of specific ecosystems and of stable relationships in their handling. It is certainly equally frequent that those same people are forced to deny their ancestral knowledge and to adopt other productive behaviours that are "irrational" from different points of view, from the moment in which the wider socioeconomic structure in which they are immersed forces them to destroy the ecosystems upon which their subsistence is based. But this latter circumstance does not eliminate the basic fact that there are alternative socio-economic models of development which are derived from assumptions of a more harmonious relationship of productive activities with the environment.

The importance of some agricultural crops and of certain ecologically adjusted techniques, which are the patrimony of peasant producers and which could help solve not only the problems of that sector but also of the diet of the national society, is already widely recognized.

Finally, a peasant agricultural productive system, like any other productive system, is associated with particular forms of organizing production (social techniques), which must be investigated for their possible incorporation and development into other systems of production.

THE MIDDLE PRODUCERS

In this category are included those producers who participate directly in the management of their agricultural enterprises, and frequently in conditions where, relatively speaking, there is an economic adequacy or proportionality between the amount of land and the size of the enterprise, where the land has an economic role as a production factor, where there is a tendency towards the intensive exploitation of resources and consequently towards the support of agricultural activity upon a base of technological investments, where tasks are not carried out by the family group, capitalist wage-labour is generalized, and finally, where production is fully oriented towards the market economy.

To give some idea of the volume of this category of producers, we may look at the 1971 Agricultural Census. If one considers *grosso modo* as medium-sized units those comprised in the stratum of 20-to-100 hectares, there would be approximately 47,000 units extending over 1,850,000 hectares. According to census figures, middle producers constitute 42 per cent of the families devoted to agriculture, making the most significant contribution of products for direct consumption and inputs for agro-industrial processing, and specializing in the production of rice, sesame, perishable staples, sugar cane, sorghum, peanuts, cotton, potatoes, etc.

This social group has grown considerably during the past thirty years, in the process of development of capitalist agriculture in the country. In 1950 there were 26,000 units between 20 and 100 hectares; by 1961 there were already 40,000, and in 1971 47,000. This of course is valid only in general terms, because for several crops units between 10 and 20 hectares should be included, while for still other crops, the average size of units oscillates between 100 and 500 hectares. Furthermore, it is obvious that the transition between medium-sized and large producers cannot be marked by an arbitrary threshold, but is a continuum in which several indicators must be taken into account. Thus, these figures are mere approximations to the increasing quantitative weight of the social group in time (National Agricultural Census 1971).

With regard to this productive category I have taken as a case study the history of one of the first and most important modern colonization projects—that of Turén (Vessuri 1978b). Because of the nature of the study the conclusions reached, rather than results, constitute a set of hypotheses to be tested by future field work. However, considering questions parallel to those we asked in the previous section about peasant production, some preliminary answers may be advanced.

(a) *What is the economic rationality of middle producers?* It has often been observed that the small and medium-sized commercial agricultural units, which have not been the most progressive modalities of western agricultural capitalism, tend to become the most important ones in the peripheries. Sometimes this special capitalism carves its own way freely and openly; on other occasions, despite the peculiar negative features that the "cooperative" organization adopts in underdeveloped rural situations, they know how to take advantage of cooperative forms;[9] finally, there are situations where the state openly promotes their development, as was the case in Turén.

These farmers seek to function under the same patterns of rationality as large producers, that is, to maximize economic benefit profiting from the advantages of credit, price policies, and available technologies. They present, however, significant differences owing to the smaller economic size of their enterprises and their subordinate relationship to agro-industry, to which they are closely linked in the ongoing process of vertical integration. The medium-sized capitalist farm becomes an anonymous and miniscule cog on the complex gears of international agri-business. It becomes modernized only with regard to those components which are promoted in the local market; this modernization does not allow the units to reach a coherent "modern" behaviour.

This system of production is characterized by the intensification and diversification of the use of land. In general middle-producers are a very dynamic sector, but very sensitive to phenomena occurring in the economy as a whole. Paradoxically, the growth and dynamism of this sector has not resulted in the resolution of the food problem of the country. On the contrary, the country continues to import food in large quantities. The diversification of "modern" production has followed *sui generis* paths, following the demands of agribusiness and not the basic needs of the population. In the process, existing negative social conditions have become more entrenched. Agricultural resources are becoming exhausted more rapidly than with the management typical of traditional peasant production, and poverty and rural and urban unemployment, instead of disappeaing, are also increasing.

(b) *In what does the productive system of the middle producers consist?* Usually the middle producer concentrates on one, two, or three commercial crops that are grown extensively in stable fields.[10] This general feature is accompanied by two others that are closely linked to it: first, the generalized use of the plough and other machinery in agricultural work, and second, the imperative need for utilizing chemical or biological methods at an increasing cost, in order to maintain the fertility of the soil that is used uninterruptedly, or at very short intervals of fallow.

There has been a disproportionate expansion of the machinery stock. Machinery is not taken advantage of in all its potentiality; frequently it is inappropriate for the conditions of the soils, the size of exploitation, the types of crops, etc. and induces elements of inefficiency in the management of production factors.

As an example of a typical capitalist crop, we studied the case of sesame production in Turén, which is grown as a dry-season complement of the main crops (rice and maize). Despite the high degree of mechanization and the extensive features of its production, it does not present many technical requirements for it is a very rustic crop. The choice of sesame for rotation with maize or rice in the cycle of two annual harvests taking place in Turén has been a response to commercial and not to technical reasons. We can see that "entrepreneurial", "modern", or "capitalist" does not necessarily mean "technically optimal or adequate". On the contrary, technique (or better, the technological package that is imposed) brings with it its own "built-in" laws and

its own regulatory functions, which can (and often do) contradict the
contributions of this or the other particular technique. Sesame was never the
exclusive or the main crop of middle producers, but was always the dry-season
complement. Its quality of secondary crop is reflected in the fact that commonly
technical recommendations have not been and are not followed in its production, because it is assumed that sesame is a crop for which one should not
spend, for either fertilizers, improved seeds, or pesticides.

The discussion of the assimilation of new techniques, of which at first sight
those used in the cultivation of sesame could appear to be an example, has been
centred fundamentally on the expenses of capital and labour. But the problems
of integrating techniques with other inputs in the process of production have
received little consideration. In this sense, the cultivation of sesame must be seen
as a way of taking secondary advantage of a stock of machinery and a residue of
fertilizers used for other crops in the agricultural unit. It is only very recently
that, as a consequence of marked reductions in yields, this crop began to receive
more serious consideration as concerns its scientific production.

(c) *How does technical change occur in the context of the medium-sized
agricultural enterprise?* In terms of our analysis of types of enterprises
characterized by specific production relations, and from the consideration of the
economic context within which production devolves, including the economic
policy implemented and the socially accepted channels for developing the
capacity of technical innovation, it appears that technological factors, though
crucial, depend nevertheless upon economic and social requirements. An
increasing demand leads to the adoption of technical innovations. These
innovations form part of a specific productive system (economic and social), and
therefore are more easily adopted by certain types of agricultural enterprises,
due to particular features of the latter. Precisely these features define what
enterprises are capable of generating a surplus, and which ones have objective
possibilities of accumulation. They also determine the interest and the attitude
towards technical innovation. Technical innovation cannot be explained solely
in terms of the individual exploitation units. It will also depend upon the forms
of insertion of the enterprises in the global economic context, their different
situations with regard to the accessibility to factor and input markets, and
whether or not they have an acceptable negotiating power in the product
markets.

The consideration of the organizational aspects of production is directly
relevant to the problem of technical change. Modern agricultural colonization
requires the existence of an efficient central body to carry out the large-scale
works needed, and to provide a frame of technical assistance services to the
agricultural units. Farmers must be organized in some way so as to insure the

provision and maintenance of works such as irrigation, drinking water, production of improved seeds, marketing, credit, research, and extension work. In Turen, given the absence of a flexible and agile management system with clear objectives and orientations, an attempt was made to compensate for the lack of organization among the colonists by the mechanism of state paternalism, which changed according to political ups and downs, and was basically ignorant of the actions required to insure the colony's sustained development. This lack of a central organization made the new family farms very vulnerable in their participation in the process of formation of the national market.[11] Thus, Turén is one more example of the fact that an entrepreneurial agricultural development does not guarantee by itself a sustained growth in productivity. In general the increment of production in Turén, and in the whole new agricultural region, has been more a consequence of the increase in cultivated acreage than of a rise in productivity.[12] It would seem that under current conditions in the agricultural sector (which demands minimal levels of investment, favouring certain credit lines instead of others, etc.), it is the need to engage in the production of commercial crops (although from an ecological point of view, they may not be the most adequate ones) that influences the problems related to productivity.

(d) *What is the role of small and middle commercial production in national agricultural production?* What are the conditions and consequences of the current technical progress in agriculture in the life of medium-sized units? In order to answer this question, it is useful to consider two aspects: The first one relates to the features of the historical origins of producers, and the second one takes into account the conditions and consequences of current technical progress in the agricultural domain in the life of family farms.

(i) In Venezuela, the recent entrepreneurial agricultural development took place under the impulse of state policies of stimulus and support of production. It was the Venezuelan state that, by the end of the forties, in the midst of massive imports of deficient agricultural products financed from oil revenues, set in motion the process of modernization of national agriculture. The sector had been stagnating since the 1920s, due to the prolonged crisis of the price of coffee in world markets. The state favoured the participation in agriculture of new sectors different from the traditional groups linked to the export market, as a pre-requisite for insuring socio-structural bases for the new import substitution era that was beginning to take form. Since then the state policy of stimulating agricultural development has been characterized by the promotion of a dynamic sector of middle producers, upon whom a growing proportion of the national production of food and raw materials for agro-industry was to depend.

The organizational model chosen was that of a colonization programme, which adopted technological features typical of the recent development of capitalism. In contrast to what happened in the temperate and sub-tropical zones of Latin America, mainly in the second half of the nineteenth century and the earlier decades of the twentieth, in Venezuela agricultural colonization as an explicit government policy only began by the late forties (Febres *et al.* 1949), and it already corresponded to an ideal of highly technological medium size enterprises involving substantial capital investments. The aim was no longer to keep the population on the land (as had been the case of Argentina for example), but rather to serve the internal market and the new industries that had begun to develop in the country.

In the attempt to diversify production in a modernizing context, modern agricultural colonization fostered the family agricultural unit of the type generally recognized as "family farm". But in practice the proposed diversification almost always gave place to an industrial monocrop, and the family farm had been subjected to great economic risks, tending to disappear during the crises unless it was supported by state credit policies or by the direct action of industrialists interested in its permanence, but always in a precarious equilibrium, depending on the economic and physical ups and downs of production.

(ii) With regard to the conditions and consequences of current technological progress of agriculture in the life of medium-sized agricultural units, it may be observed that small and medium-sized entrepreneurial units have changed considerably in the course of recent history. It has already been said that some of the most important forces of change came from the technological domain. Agricultural techniques, the abilities the farmer must have, and the kinds and sources of elements employed undergo constant transformations. The type of knowledge required is increasingly acquired through more formal educational channels, thus implying in general the progressive presence of links with elements of the system of research and development in the central countries. The complexity of modern techniques in particular, and the characteristics of capitalist expansion in general, lead to significant changes in the agricultural enterprises and in the farmer's behaviour. The system in which "modern" medium-sized units operate tends towards vertical and horizontal integration of agricultural activities under a unique or minimal control. Production becomes increasingly subordinated to the monopolistic control of transnational agribusiness, which has to do with production, progressing, storage, financing, and marketing of food crops and fibres. Decisions about production and marketing are not made so much by producers and middlemen, but growingly, as by the large agro-industrial groups, upon the basis of their monopolized knowledge of supply and demand conditions in the national and international markets. Production on the basis of contracts is already quite widespread. In such cases the small or middle producer may find himself in a position that has more than a point of similarity with that of the wage labourer. The system of contracts of production that has accompanied the development of entrepreneurial agriculture is one of the mechanisms that stifles the small and middle producers, leading them progressively to a total lack of autonomy.

(e) *What experience can be derived from the use of technology in medium-sized agricultural units?* After thirty years of continuous agricultural activity, producers, technicians, and scientists now know more about the deterioration of soil conditions than before. The development of agriculture in Turen meant a choice of productive activities—agriculture *vs.* forest exploitation—with important ecological consequences. The implantation of large-scale agricultural activity in a tropical ecosystem such as that of Turen meant the end of the forest, with disastrous consequences for ecological regeneration, at a time when the scientific study of such complex processes has scarcely begun. In the course of development of "extra-latitudinal" agricultural activity in zones such as Turén, ecosystems have become increasingly artificial and, frequently, also unstable, augmenting the risk of sudden disasters, such as the appearance of plagues of great magnitude, floods, and droughts. The lack of use of organic fertilizers, and sometimes the abusive and dangerous use of inorganic ones, the non-utilization of traditional systems of rotation of lands for the maintenance of fertility, and the absence of tree-curtains to reduce wind erosion, have contributed to the current situation in which many soils contain dangerously low levels of organic matter, to the point where in some cases they no longer support the current systems of production.

The inappropriate entrepreneurial management of tropical agro-ecosystems was exacerbated in Venezuela by a social phenomenon that has been labelled "venturesome agriculture" by some analysts (Hernandez 1977). Its speculative nature and the lack of consolidation upon the land of a rural middle class are features that grew hand in hand with state support policies during the past twenty-five years. Several waves of speculators, petty merchants, white-collar workers, professionals, etc. turned to agricultural activities with the expectation of making quick money, under the incentives of the generous goverment credit policies and rising agricultural prices. The prevailing approach to the use of land was typical of commercial speculation. There was no care for its conservation or improvement. When the soil became exhausted in one plot they turned to new land and began anew the "mining" activity.

Another aspect of technological behaviour in the medium-sized agricultural unit, about which people are more knowledgeable today, relates to the structural conditions in which modern technology is generated and becomes adopted. Different from what happens in industry, at least as a tendency, modern technological innovation in agriculture does not originate within the decisional apparatus of the farm. The process of research and development is not institutionalized at the level of the productive units, because the features inherent to the organization of agricultural production in this sector lead to the configuration of a more complex institutional framework for innovation. Those features, conventionally defined by comparison with the industrial sector, are : reduced relative size of the enterprises, essentially competitive character of the markets in which they operate, relative difficulty and complexity of biological research, and reduced possibility of appropriation by the adopter of the total benefits of research. (Of course, all these features can be qualified further; see Vessuri 1980).

The example of middle producers shows the need to pay attention to the various motivational sources intervening in the creative and adaptive activity that takes place in the agricultural enterprise. It might well be the case that enterprises were forced to seek technological advancement precisely because of their incapacity to generate and appropriate surplus; or that they were compelled to innovate owing to the demands of other types of enterprise to which their production might be linked. For example, as we have already discussed, the demands by the processing firms upon producers, when the former are the main buyers of the latter's products in the market, is a frequent phenomenon. Agro-industry determines technological changes in the products which it uses as raw materials, in order to achieve the standardization of the product within given parameters of quality, texture, ripening terms, humidity, colour, etc. In such a case, the surplus generated by the technological change which occurred within the agricultural units is not appropriated by the agricultural enterprises, but by the processing industries.

Due to this dependence of Venezuelan agriculture upon agribusiness, its technological profile has socially negative features. Instead of mainly adequating techniques to ecological features and to local needs and opportunities, there results a state of affairs in which there is an attempt to change the natural environment and the socio-cultural organization in order to make them more compatible with the capital-intensive technology being implanted, in response to the requirements of international agribusiness, through its local subsidiaries.

CONCLUDING REMARKS

A premise of our study is that the core of the problem of production can only be grasped through knowledge of the actors and the social relations they establish in be process of production. Unless we place the actors in the centre of our analysis, both as producers and consumers situated in a particular time and place, we shall miss the question that concerns us. As agricultural techniques form part of technocultural complexes, the processes of technological change are not neutral with respect to social relations. On the contrary, they are heavily imprinted by different aspects of the social activity in which they are generated and developed. Thus, prevailing social relations are a starting point for the explanation of the nature, orientation, and intensity of technological changes. In all Latin American countries, and in Venezuela in particular, several cultural complexes related to agricultural production can still be distinguished, characterized (among other aspects) by the use of different sets of productive techniques. Those cultural complexes, being differentially situated in the society, will have unequal powers, and therefore unequal possibilities of dealing with and controlling new technical knowledge.

In recent years, the industrial sector producing agricultural inputs has shown great commercial aggressiveness in Latin America, and has obtained extraordinary benefits. In the process it has penetrated deeply into the agrarian productive structures, increasingly modifying the patterns of agricultural work. The massive mechanization of the Latin American countryside has been basically the result of the thrust of the agricultural machinery industry. As it was frequently supported by specific credit policies, it has led to an exaggerated amount of machinery stock, and often (as in the case of Venezuela) has been characterized by a marked inefficiency in the yields obtained. In general, it may be appreciated that fertilizers, agricultural capital goods, and the processing and transportation of food crops appear as the most typical sources of accumulation in the near future in relation to agriculture, all of which involves economic groups different from those concerned with production proper.

Within the national society, through the analysis of social types of producers it can be readily observed that modern technology, created as it is in terms of a certain type of economic factor, appears to be exogenous to particular productive systems—the peasant system, for example—inasmuch as the latter may be the result of different socio-historical and economic processes.

The persistence of old technologies alongside of new ones is explicable in terms of the specificities of capitalist development within national boundaries. The demands of capital accumulation and those of the reproduction of ther social relations of production act upon the concrete process of production to favour the invention of new techniques or the persistence of the old ones that are adequate for the reproduction of a certain system of positions and functions assigned to the various agents who participate in capitalist production.

But what we found in the case-study of Turén is not an exceptional situation. The foreign technology being imported is not even very adequate to the local ecological and social conditions of Venezuelan entrepreneurial agriculture. Given the intrinsic requirements of the production function, the modern local agricultural enterprise adopts the technological package that is available in the inputs market, which usually is neither ecologically "appropriate" nor economically efficient. Owing to the characteristics of the diffusion of such a technological package, the agricultural entrepreneur tends to accept it as "progressive" and "scientific", although in the medium or the long range his efforts will end in failure, precisely because the technology he uses is not the outcome of the application of science and technology to local tropical ecological conditions, and to indigenous sociocultural and economic constraints.

What results is a much more rapid exhaustion of agricultural resources than is the case with more traditional peasant patterns of usage, along with a complex re-structuring of rural and urban employment, which can hardly be considered an improvement under current social conditions.

As to the relevance of peasant groups in the national society, even in a country such as Venenuela which in the past thirty years has become dramatically "descampesinada",[13] their importance is not diminished by the fact that at the present time they no longer muster a large roll. From the point of view of the production and transfer of scientific and technological knowledge, there is enough evidence that among peasants large repositories of knowledge can be found which are relevant to activities of a technical nature, but have been broadly ignored by R & D systems simply because they did not agree with what has become patterned as the conventional research and development problematic domain (see Herrera 1979 for a recent discussion). There are two main types of reasons for this. On the one hand, there is the need to explore alternative technological paths for tropical agriculture, due to the difficulties it is undergoing at present, not only in the management of the environment, but also in view of the need to insure a basic provision of food for the current and future population. In such an exploration, the experience accumulated by the peasants cannot be disregarded *a priori*, but it deserves to be integrally considered as a technological pattern valid in itself, whose benefits and limitations must be determined in relation to specific objectives.

On the other hand, there is a need to find solutions to some of the peasantry's socio-economic problems, which are acquiring increasing importance in tropical regions. The question posed is that of critically studying the management alternatives for the agro-ecosystems localized in those regions, in order to fully incorporate the population in the production of food and other agricultural crops, trying to reverse the characteristic agricultural pattern that, as we have shown, is currently being implanted, which progressively reduces the demands of rural labour at the same time that the cost of production rises, making substantial segments of the population redundant to the productive process.

The production of tropical crops has allowed up to the present time, under certain conditions, the gradual and adjustable harvest depending on the subsistence needs of the peasant population, and has provided it with monetary income as a result of its growing participation in food markets.

We think that aspects such as these, if they are taken into account to conceive of an intelligent and flexible planning, could contribute efficaciously to increase employment and to consolidate the peasant on the land, insuring for him a better subsistence in a stage of capitalist development of agriculture which may be longer in absorbing him than was previously predicted.

Anthropology can contribute positively to the study of the processes of technological change, as it takes technology as a dependent variable in the analysis of the articulation of techno-cultural systems within the global society. As we have tried to show, an anthropological study of technological change cannot avoid a treatment of the complex, for the dynamic of capitalism at the present time reaches the remotest corners of the world and conditions most developments in which technology is involved. Within such an approach anthropologists should concentrate primarily on the actors, and on the social relations they establish in the productive process.

NOTES

1. Thus, it is preferable to use terms such as "advanced technology", "modern technology", "high technology" to refer to it and, in the same manner, to employ the pertinent adjectives to designate other historical technologies.

2. For a recent treatment of this critical problem within contemporary social science, see Shanin (1978).

3. Piñeiro and Trigo (1977). These authors define the concept in terms of three variables. The first one is the type of main enterprise which defines production relationships and indirectly a social group linked to the process of accumulation, which defines the economic context within which production devolves. The second variable used is the economic policy implemented. These two variables summarize and define the economic and social conditions characterizing a given production. The third variable is defined by the institutional models that a given society adopts for the development of its innovative activity.

4. This section has been largely reproduced from Vessuri (1980).

5. The notion of progress, in this case of technological progress, cannot be deduced from *a priori* principles, but implies multiple contents, socially and historically determined. Despite the common usage among economists, who understand technological progress as those changes which increase the global productivity of the economic system, we find it unsatisfactory to define agricultural technological progress exclusively in terms of physical yields. I explore another dimension of the concept elsewhere (Vessuri 1980). But here it is not necessary to go deeper into the discussion of this problem, for what concerns us here is simply to show the complexity of the intervening factors, even if it means adopting a restricted definition.

6. For reasons typical of the context in which research is carried out by local scientists in under-developed countries, eventually these two studies could not be done because the research-worker had to fill other gaps of research and teaching that were "more urgent" to the employing institution.

7. Estimated figures derived from data of the 1971 National Agricultural Census (I.A.N. 1976) and Martel (1977).

8. We follow here Johnson's argument (1971: 72-73) as regards the fomulation of the problem, though our explanation differs from his.

9. A good example of this was that of the milk-producers of Santa Fe and Cordoba provinces, in Argentina, who joined efforts in the cooperative development known as SANCOR.

10. By stable fields we mean those typical of cereals production, managed under systems of short fallow or yearly cropping. Such an activity being foreign to the traditional handling of lowland tropical lands, it has been recently referred to as an "extralatitudinal agricultural pattern". For a discussion of this topic see Convenio CENDES-CONICIT (1976).

11. Turen appears to have been conceived of exclusively as a centre of production, disregarding in the process the management and distribution aspects. For a long time the lack of a market organization affected the well-being of producers. The official credit entity (B.A.P.) and some industrial firms bought amounts of rice, corn, and sesame in payment for the credits and inputs they had advanced to the colonists. In theory, the rest could be sold in the free market, but local controls were so burdensome that commercial activity alongside of these mechanisms was discouraged.

12. The increment of cultivated land in Portuguesa state was spectacular. From 35 in 1937 the index of increase rises to 1,023 in 1971. (Ministerio de Agricultura y Cria and National Censuses).

13. The figures for rural and urban population have changed sides in the past forty years. Today less than 30 per cent of the national population is rural.

REFERENCES

Chayanov, A.V., (1966): *The theory of peasant economy,* Irwin, Inc., Homewood.

Convenio Conicit-Cendes (1976) : *Que hacer con la agricultura venezolana?* CENDES. Caracas.

David, Paul (1975) : The landscape and the machine : technical interrelatedness, land tenure and the mechanization of the corn harvest in Victorian Britain. *Technical choice, innovation and economic growth.* Cambridge University Press.

Febres, H., Carlos Bello, J. Schunster *et al. La colonizacion en Venezuela, 1830-1957.* Ministerio de Agricultura y Cria. Caracas.

Freeman, Christopher (1975) : *La teoría económica de la innovación industrial.* Alianza, Madrid.

Hernandez, Juan Luis (1977) : Conflicto de intereses en la agricultura venezolana. *SIC.* Centro Gumilla. Caracas. Vol. XL, No. 391, Caracas.

I.A.N. (Instituto Agrario Nacional) (1976) : Diagnóstico de la tenencia y de los beneficiarios de Reforma Agraria. Caracas.

Jaffe Carbonell, Walter and Harry Rothman (1977) : An implicit food policy : wheat consumption changes in Venezuela. *Food Policy.* Nov. 1977.

Johnson, Allen (1971) : Sharecroppers of the Sertao. Economics and dependence on a Brazilian plantation. Stanford.

Koyre, Alexandre (1973) : Etudes d'histoire de la pensee scientifique, Gallimard, Paris.

Lewis, Oscar (1949) : Plow culture and hoe culture : a study in contrasts. *Rural Sociology,* Vol. 14.

Martel, Armando (1977) : De la carraplana al despelote. Caracas.

Ministerio de Agricultura Y Cria. Anuarios estadisticos agropecuarios. Caracas.

Ministerio de Fomento. Censo Nacional Agropecuario, ano 1971.

Pineiro, Martyn y Eduardo Trigo (1977). Un marco general para el analisis del progreso technologico agropecuario : las situaciones de cambio tecnologico. Miscelanea No. 149. IICA (Instituto Interamericano de Ciencias Agricolas), Bogota.

Shanin, Martin y Eduardo Trigo (1977). Un marco general para el analisis del progreso tecnologico. Miscelanea No. 149. IICA (Instituto Interamericano de Ciencias Agricolas), Bogota.

Shanin, Teodor (1978) : La medicion del capitalismo dentro del campesinado. *Estudios Rurales Latinoamericanos.* Vol. 1, No. 2, Bogota.

Vessuri, Hebe (1978a) : El campesino tradicional venezolano : sistema de produccion agricola y cambio tecnico. CENDES-CONICIT. Caracas.

(1978b) : Colonizacion agricola, desarrollo capitalista y tecnologia : el caso de los productores de Turen. *Cambio tecnologico y organizacion social de la produccion agricola en Venezuela.* CENDES-CONICIT. Caracas. Publicacion No. 29.

(1980) : Technological change and the social organization of agricultural production. *Current Anthropology,* Vol. 21, No. 3.

Weiss, Jr., Charles (1979) : Mobilizing technology for developing countries. Science, Vol. 203, No. 16.

The Problem of Arab Peasant Kinship: Superimposed, Structure Collectivity and Descent, Politicized Marriage, and Patriarchal Property Control[1]

HENRY ROSENFELD

For many of us the understanding that tribal society was not "political society", that the longest span of human history — if not consistently one of strifeless harmony, equality based on comprehension of differences, anarchy expressed in individualism without forced restraint — was at least a history without structured domination of one group by another, had provided support for the view that a brother-sisterhood of humankind was indeed a future, possible alternative to the history of class society. "Personal relations", or joint and communal relations, the kinship inherent in the work process, in organizing group activities, in socialization, and in beliefs and ideas among tribal peoples would find expression at a new level. After all, the 5-6,000 years of world history under "political-relations" have also been ameliorated by certain limited, but nevertheless rewarding, ties of kinship; and perhaps today, although this is not specifically my claim, it is in peasant society that kin bonds are strongest and maintain the continuity that links the past with the present, and where we have most to learn about human potential for living in both forms of "relations" at one and the same time.

Now, when we view peasants historically, among other things we say that they were tribal peoples who, as rural cultivators, in one way or another had been incorporated into, or made to serve, state ends. These are long-time and, at least in regard to ancient Middle East state-civilizations, perhaps untraceable processes. But what is clear is that tribesmen, and also different fractionated or dispersed groups, caught up in the political processes of state formation, under threat or the direct implementation of force, or through conquest, were transformed into peasants. The question I ask is, in this process what happens to "kinship" and community? Are they carried over from tribal society, held as an autonomous internal system while the wielders of power continue, with their business of taxation, opression and bureaucratic impositions? Or, over time, do kinship and tribal solidarity simply deteriorate, and in peasant society become "vestigial", or vitiated replicas of what were once the heart of life? And there are other possibilities. Do the folk struggle and thereby retain or reconstruct over time what is viable and possible in "personal" and joint relations? And/or, as I shall suggest, do these "relations" reflect the type of state and its political and economic level — what has been imposed on (generally as administrative-fiscal measures) and what has been transformed irrevocably into, a peasant level of administerized, fiscalized, politicized kin relations? Finally, what is to be visualized as a future possibility, in terms of "personal relations", for such peasants who today, in fact, in most areas of the world, are a rural-dwelling proletariat?

I discuss the problem in regard to Arab peasant society. My field experience is with·Arabs in Israel, and to the degree that their present and recent history can be brought to bear on the problem, they are my point of reference. At this stage in the research, I emphasize as a causal, analytic frame of reference the Ottoman period in Palestinian history, although the form and the meaning of some of the categories to be discussed, the patrilineal descent line, collective land use, the endogamous marriage pattern, factionalism, the men's meeting or guest room, certain kin terminology, and so on, may well have histories as ancient as the origins of peasantry in the area.

THE AGRARIAN FEUDAL-TYPE REGIME AND ITS ADMINISTRATIVE-FISCAL IMPOSITIONS

Before we emphasize certain characteristics of the feudal-type regime which set the framework within which Arab peasantry existed in Palestine, we mention some of the features that led to a transition to incipient capitalism. Extensive tracts were owned by the government in an agrarian society where land was the main form of wealth, and, mainly during the nineteenth century, with the increase in land values, merchants, officials, wealthy sheikhs, both absentee and local, bought up large areas of settled and unsettled, cultivated and uncultivated, land from the government and impoverished peasants, or they received land grants from the state, creating a rentier-effendi class. The 300,000 population in 1800 was mainly rural; peasants were smallholders, grain farmers in the plains and valleys, orchard and vine cultivators in the mountains, using family labour and family-owned work animals. Mountain villages appear to have had greater continuity of settlement than those in the plains. It is difficult to know how many were tenants, sharecroppers, and agricultural labourers and not owners. (One-third of the Palestinian peasants were classified as landless in 1930 — Johnson and Crosbie 1930; Carmi and Rosenfeld 1974 : 472-73.) While an effendi-merchant class received rentals, the state claimed (and government officials, or overlords, tax farmers, and others profited from) crop and property taxes (as well as capitation and other extraordinary taxes). Although we do not know the exact impositions on peasants at different periods of time, they were usually higher than the tithe (*'usher*) of one-tenth of the crop. During the nineteenth century, tax-farming rights bought from the government by merchants, Bedouin sheikhs, and others often yielded them returns of up to one-third and one-half of the crop.[2]

The seventeenth and eighteenth centuries reflected the decay of the feudal Ottoman regime: fewer Turkish dignitaries were invested with control over villages in Palestine, and greater predominance had to be given to tax-farming under local chiefs with kin-military followings; the poverty of the peasantry was severe, extensive areas of land remained unsettled, Bedouins imposed protection — payment dues upon villages, many villagers dispersed to safer areas, to towns, or into nomadic life, numerous villages were abandoned, and the regime transferred peasants, Egyptian and Maghribi Bedouins, descendants of Albanians and Janissaries and others from different parts of the Empire into Palestine (Ma'oz 1968 : 164-65; Hutteroth 1975: 9-11: Abir 1975: 284-85).

For our purposes, the overall system of control over the peasantry during the seventeenth and eighteenth centuries of the Ottoman Empire is best understood in terms of its administrative-fiscal procedures. Clearly, distinctions beyond the scope of this paper[3] are to be made within this time period. However, these differences in administrative-fiscal apparatuses appear to have been essentially a function of the distance from the peasantry to the seats of power and the intermediary functionaries who represented (or failed to represent) the government; the extent of the military and administrative controls under those to whom authority was delegated; the extent to which local groups under local authority could refuse to recognize a superior force in the hierarchy of power.

The basic organization during the seventeenth and eighteenth centuries in greater Palestine was a division into two administrative, territorial-geographical units (the Eyālet of Sidon and the southern *sancaks* of the Eyālet of Damascus, with the boundary between the two *eyālets* south of the Sea of Galilee) under central government representatives (valīs); the *eyālets* or the *sancaks* were divided further into a number of sub-units *(nāhiyes)* or more directly in territorial terms, *mukāta'as.* It is these units, *mukāta'as,* which concern us: they are territorial, administrative, fiscal units and necessarily are comprehended in military terms as well. The government delegated authority over such a unit to whoever best served its interests of tax-collection and preservation of order. In eighteenth-century Palestine, at the level of the territorial unit, the tax-farmer was most prominent.[4]

Thus, it follows that any authority should have been vested in those most capable of serving the central government's interests in the area. The *mültezim,* farming taxes in a certain *mukāṭa'a,* was far better able to do this than the *qāḍi* or his *nā'ib* (deputy). The latter, despite their undoubted importance and considerable social standing, had no means of enforcing their authority. In fact, even the basic division of an *eyālet* into *sancaks* was dependent on the ability of the *sancak* bey to command the military force (feudal or otherwise) necessary to exercise his functions (collection of taxes, maintenance of security, etc.) as governor of the *sancak.* In much the same way, it was the *mültezim* alone who possessed the necessary means of enforcing official policy in his *mukāṭa'a.* It is hardly surprising, then, that the *mukāṭa'a,* which was basically a territorial unit so defined for taxation purposes, came to be considered an ideal administrative unit as well. Authority was vested in the *mültezim* by an official act — the bestowal of the *khil'a* by the *vālī.* He was thus not only responsible for the collection of taxes in his *mukāṭa'a,* but also had to keep the Bedouin in check, build fortifications and other public works, attend to agricultural and commercial affairs, etc. It was thanks only to the fact that he possessed the most effective military force in the area that he was able to carry out all these functions in his *mukāṭa'a* (Cohen 1973 : 122)

THE PEASANTS: SUPERIMPOSED VILLAGE COLLECTIVITY, LEADERSHIP, AND DESCENT

What concerns us is what happens to the peasants and their social organization. We say that what is engendered, necessarily, is a formalized (structured) village unit. "Every village being rated for the Miri in the land-tax book of the Pasha, at a fixed sum, that sum is levied as long as the village is at all inhabited, however few may be its inhabitants" (Burckhardt 1822 : 300). Time and again we read that the villages become collectively responsible for taxes (see, for example, Volney 1798, II: 243-44; Burckhardt 1822: 341, Robinson and Smith 1841, II: 146, Wilson 1906: 291) and order, and it is out of such circumstances that the patrilineage in turn became, as we shall discuss, an administerized-fiscalized structure, superimposed on families, extended families, and incipient lineages of whatever form.

In eighteenth-century Palestine the collectivity imposed on the villagers was structured from top to bottom, as follows:

The *māl-i-mīrī* for any given *eyālet* constituted a single lump sum for which the *vālī* was responsible. He would divide the burden of raising this sum among the various *mültezims* in the *eyālet* . . . The *mültezims,* in turn, would divide the sum for which they were responsible among the different villages making up their respective *nahiyes,* each village being collectively responsible for the sum in question. Within the village itself, the distribution of the tax burden among the inhabitants was left to the *Shaykh al-Balad* [the Shaykh of the village], who would determine how much each individual villager had to contribute towards the sum owed by his particular village. (Cohen 1973: 197)

We stress the exploitative, arbitrary nature of the collection of the taxes, wherein the government was concerned with two aspects: that it collect most of the taxes (not all, which it could not do in any case) and that all villages — as collective units — be included in the administrative tax lists.

> . . . it was taken for granted that each lessee in turn would raise more than he was expected to remit to the lessee immediately above him in the hierarchy. . . . The treasury, concerned only with increasing its own revenues, turned a blind eye to the practice. *(Ibid.)*

And,

> While this [fleeing from the area] freed the peasant from the need to pay taxes, it made at first little difference to the *mültezim,* who continued to collect a pre-determined sum from each village in his *mukāta'a* regardless of the actual amount of land under cultivation at any given time or of the number of villagers left in the village. As long as anyone at all remained behind, the village continued to be collectively responsible for the original sum pledged. *(op. cit.: 200)*

Very often "traditional", seemingly indigenous, folk patterns of behaviour are in reality the outcome of state-sponsored devices of control over the folk. An example is *masha'* land tenure. The *masha'* land use system, according to which in many villages during and perhaps prior to the seventeenth, eighteenth and nineteenth centuries the grain fields were redistributed among and by the peasants themselves every two years or so, has often been likened to the original "agrarian commune" or a "communistic arrangement" (Doukhan 1938: 92), because of the collective features embodied in it. The land was not individually owned, and all household heads having plough animals (in some instances all males alive at the partition) had the right to take part in the lot distribution, or had share rights in the land. Parcels were allotted in different categories of land and changed at each redivision (Granott 1952: 217-270).

In fact, and with all its communal overtones, *masha'* "tenure" was not a form of ownership but of usufruct since the land was in the "miri" or state-owned category. It provided peasants with land without awarding them its title, it provided the state with tithes and the tax-farmers with profits, and it guaranteed uniform cultivation under collective responsibility (Abramovitch and Gelphat 1944: 21-23). Often it was the lineage leaders who acted in the name of family heads during the lot distribution. Since taxes were paid in kind, the same crop rotation cycle imposed a collective schedule on the harvest, and on tax-collection procedures that were usually carried out at the threshing floor. *Masha'* tenure is best viewed, I believe, as a state-imposed collectivity, and may well have been adopted as a measure which suited the heart of Ottoman fiscal policy (Rosenfeld 1958: 1132). The fact that othes (e.g. Poliak 1939) have compared and distinguished between the collectivity in Ottoman fiscal land laws and that found in an ancient Hebrew agrarian commune of believers, leads one to postulate that different agrarian, feudal-type regimes could instigate such "collectivity" at almost any time period.

Moreover, private property in houses, garden plots, water, and work animals remained basic to the regime, and is found within all non-tenant villages. Further, inheritance was equal among all the sons. This parallels the situation in China before 1947, where it has been suggested" . . . that the Chinese state favoured partibility in order to maximize the number of the tax-paying units in the realm" (Wolf 1966: 74).[5]

The nature of peasantry is that in cannot deter the regime which exploits it; taxes and rents are collected, if need be through a military-police force (Volney 1798, II: 245; Buckhardt 1822: 291). Peasants can only lessen the rigours of the regime, by seeking variant exploitative relationships within it or by becoming nomads or robbers on its fringes. The nature of the feudal-type, agrarian regime is that it requires a peasantry to underwrite its existence. It is in these terms that we see Arab village peasant social organization as being superimposed. The regime requires the order that will guarantee the systematic payment of taxes and rentals. For a dispersed rural, in part semi-nomadic, population it attempts to do this by keeping the inhabitants in permanent settlements, and by dealing with them in groups through a local leadership. In the deepest sense, while underwriting its own existence it underwrote the existence of the patrilineage-hamula and its leadership, and other collective formations. While clearly it did not "originate" the patrilineage and its leadership, which under multiple, propitious circumstances in settlement are self-generating, the feudal-type agrarian regime controlled the "circumstances" and related to persons in collective, structural terms. Whether or not it retained an ancient pattern, it *applied* an ancient one, structuring what existed or what potentially could be structured, trimming first leadership, and then descent, and so on, to their design and rendering them much of their content.

Spelt out, for the peasant, locked-in "sub-system", this meant, at least during the period of the Ottoman Empire, that those already grouped into descent lines, or dispersed elements, were incorporated into a total, "model" system of "autonomous" villages. The "system" had a certain kind of "ecological" logic behind it. It was adjusted essentially to extensive grain farming, simple technology, redundant village labour, and no capital investment (at least until the late nineteenth century). This had advantages for the regime: under an organized, controlled "autonomy", the peasant smallholder, tenant, or sharecropper supports himself and takes on the burden of care for the aged, infirm, and helpless, keeps order through leadership and lineage-faction patterns orchestrated by the regime, pays taxes, remains on the land, and replicates the "sub-system" generation after generation.

When the central power weakened, and it had to rely more and more on local elements (local chieftains, tax-farmers, merchants), as it did in the seventeenth and eighteenth centuries, and on the new groups (landowners, merchant-rentiers) produced by the reform measures leading to its entrance into capitalism in the nineteenth century, such groups, lacking a formal state basis for control, built their political forces on a factional base. They contested among themselves for recognition from the Porte and from commercial and other agencies of foreign governments on the one hand, and for support from the villages which they directly or indirectly controlled — and which they linked to themselves through 'patron-client' ties and assumed ties of descent — on the other.

Lineage and village leadership were inseparable from and grew out of the same forces that imposed a structured "autonomy" on the village itself, that is, the patrilineage and its leadership developed in tandem. In fact, it may be worth while to view village leadership not only as the key link in a historical and formal process that led to and joined the lowest administrative-fiscal unit, the collectively responsible village, to the local power groups, but also, due to its advantaged representative position, this leadership equally served as the motor that structured lineages into politicized descent groups contesting for the imposed role itself, and for economic privilege, security, and status. (The manner in which the patrilineage became a contesting politicized unit is discussed in the following section.)

For the overlords, the village *mukhtar* (or *mukhtars*, in large villages with strong lineages) was responsible for the transmission of taxes, at certain times was responsible for the appearance of numbers of conscripts for military service, or for public works, and was accountable for the village registers. The statuses, titles of "sheikh" and "mukhtar", are honorifics for representatives of state power and order within the village. The privileges are in the form of tax reductions, conscription exemptions, the roles of overseer and sharer in extortion, and informer against heads of competing lineage segments.

If and when a village patrilineage flourished, that is, its numbers grew beyond its containment by a local factional combination of lineages, then such a group became the oppressors of others within the village and over neighbouring villages (see Cohen 1973: 8-13, 20-31). The head of such a lineage, representing a political-military force under a kin banner, most often connived with the tax officials, the tax-farmers, and their representatives (Granott 1952: 57-58) profiting from his kin and neighbours. In the process, he could well become a tax-farmer himself, directly assessing the villagers, as he moves his family to town and becomes the patron to his now client-kin.

The *maḍāfa,* the men's guest room, writes large the politicking-factional nature of the lineage, the adaptive political role of leadership and the transitory form of contrived communality. Usually it is a room owned, kept up, partially provisioned with food for guests, and maintained as the receiving room of a lineage or village headman; it is regarded as a collective stronghold, and often the upkeep is apportioned among the household heads. Male family heads of his own and allied lineages sit and exchange talk in the *maḍāfa;* depending on his economic condition perhaps they sip a cup of the headman's coffee. Here the tax-farmer, government officials and their minions, and the gendarmerie sleep, eat, and continue the representative link between the regime and its incorporated groupings as they move from village to village. Daily attendance, as Barth has pointed out (1959a: 54; see also Rosenfeld 1972: 68) is the sign of loyalty. Failure to attend means that a kinsman segment head, or an ally from an attached lineage, has switched his allegiance to another faction and its guest room, or now establishes one of his own, gathers supporters, and claims recognition from the government as its representative, as village leader or contender for the post. In other words, the *maḍāfa* does not symbolize the collective or its continuity. It is a technical structure in the physical and group sense of the words. That is, it shifts as the locus of factional alignments shifts, and it comprises those whose bonds may be solely a matter of expedience.

My point is that the patrilineage-hamula as a descent line was not a historically self-sustaining cooperative or collective in its own right, but rather a highly vulnerable, sustained form without structure. In this sense the Middle East, or Arab, descent line is to be analysed historically, i.e. it appeared under specific conditions. Since the structure was not novel, its pattern was carried from place to place, easily picked up and adapted to another village, another semi-nomadic encampment, another town quarter. Part of the pattern, for example, is composed of exactly such structures as the *maḍāfa,* which carry with them the accoutrements of pure and simple factional "relations": authority received from above, the potential threat to opponents this implies, the collective loyalty demanded by and given to a local headman, the mutual thread and intimidation implicit in rival "guest" rooms.

When we turn to the present century, we can no longer view the village and the patrilineage in narrow fiscal administrative terms. The 'external' state remains definitive for the continuity and form of village and patrilineage structures, but now its concern is more directly in preserving order and maintaining controls, and keeping change—which is immanent under new productive possibilities—to a minimum.

For such reasons the formalistic ahistorical manner of viewing the hamula-patrilineage is unsatisfactory (Rosenfeld 1974 : 243-244). Thus, the structural approach, which for definitional purposes emphasizes the descent line and its branches (Antoun 1972: 69) and the differences between descent lines as measured by the number of its branches (Government of Palestine 1945: 6; Granott 1952: 217), is in itself meaningless, and moreover tells us nothing of the actual development of the Middle East hamula. Further, the listing of a series of current formal characteristics — e.g. that members live in the same residential area, that lands belonging to members are next to one another, that they are jointly liable for a wrong committed by any one of them, that all are entitled to use the *madāfa,* and/or that they have a common name, maintain marriage rights, visiting rights, are sent invitations to feasts, recruit marriage deputations (Antoun 1972: 89-90), etc.—lends to such definitions (and encumbers those who live within the structures with) a pervasive, inclusive, and timeless "clannishness" that we find misleading. Such approaches fail to recognize that social groupings have histories, and require a search for factors explaining their appearance in time, as well as their changed appearance over time.

In fact it is becoming more apparent that whatever distinct structural quality adheres to the hamula does so as the direct effect and intervention of the state itself: ".... for its purpose ... it is the state that emphasises joint responsibility as underlying the hamula, while initiating and exacerbating conflicts between hamulas, thus further fostering the hamula as a distinct structural entity" (Rosenfeld 1974: 243). It has been pointed out that within Israel, Arab villagers have been made into hamula members through the enforcement of the state's registration procedure: "Israeli census takers specifically demanded of Arab villagers to supply them with four names: personal name, father's name, father's father's name and the hamula name. Often the fourth name was fabricated, or created on the spot. This was not a part of the indigenous Palestinian system of address" (Nakhlen 1977: 22). The same intervention holds in campaigning and elections for the village councils: "Repeatedly, state agents interfere in assuring that the slates for village elections are formed along descent lines, or sectarian lines if the village is sectarianly mixed. And repeatedly, the majority of slates get formed on that basis, due to harassment, pressures, rewards and punishments" *(ibid.).* The situation is similar in regard to support of "traditional", that is compliant, leadership: "Today, the feudal elite has disappeared: but the mukhtar, as well as lineage heads and others, still receive special privileges if they can guarantee the cooperation of their kinsmen. The Israeli authorities let it be known that these go-betweens are 'their men', and that such a role brings advantages to the occupant" (Rosenfeld 1964: 231).

In discussing Jordanian-Palestinian villages, presumably in regard to the British Mandatory and the late Ottoman periods, Antoun wirtes that many" ... may have been corporate taxation units, Until recent times, mukhtars in Palestine were responsible for the collection of taxes from the villagers" and that "... the village is a legal corporation in regard to certain criminal actions. When public land ... is defaced or destroyed and the culprits are unknown, the inhabitants of the village suspected are held corporately responsible for the deed" (Antoun 1972: 106, 108; see also Robinson and Smith 1841, II: 346). In brief, Israel, Jordan, the British Mandatory government, and the Ottoman Empire have consistently related to the peasantry in terms of collective units, more often than not creating or fostering structures and collectivities, or recognizing existing amenable ones.

As in tribal societies, the Arab village patrilineages are formed out of nuclear and extended families. (Generally lineages are localized, although there are exceptions, descent lines consisting often of paternal relatives to the 5th, 6th, 7th, 8th or wider degree within a single village composed of several such groupings. Simply, the members of the 'minimal', 'major', and 'maximal' lineage segments occupy contiguous domiciles, usually work adjoining land parcels, and interest in various daily and routine ways.) The Arab village patrilineage-hamula certainly differs from tribal lineages and clans in that, as a politically superimposed structure, it has developed quasi-viable relations of its own at the local, factional "politicking" level only. Without these relations, other features of "clannishness" (joint visiting, co-liability, etc.) prove to be transitory.

In part, the point is that the hamula-patrilineage is not a ceremonial group with a distinct and separate set of beliefs, of ritual, of prayer, of abiding spiritual connection to a father or forefather, or to a symbol representing its origins and historical trajectory, its material objects, its land, its future promise. It is not in any sense of the word an idea-group, motivated by ideological premises or perspectives. As an entity the hamula does not represent, nor does its leadership temporarily hold, a storehouse of private culture passed down from generation to generation. Not does it maintain its continuity in the corporate sense of "one person" (cf. Fortes 1953), as holders of indivisible property. In fact, Arab village genealogies do not represent "legal charters" for rights, privileges, offices, and so on in perpetuity, but rather, when they can be recapitulated, a rather harsh record of factional fortunes and influence, of ups and downs, as the descent line, or a particular leader, has passed into or out of favour with a particular notable family power group.

And in part the point is that the key dimension of the patrilineage-hamula—externally, administratively apprehended—*is* structural. It is regarded as a structure, and it is restructured from without, again and again, for administrative convenience. This is simple enough to do since once they remain on the land, family units are and can be formally linked together. In this sense its structural size, continuity, and status are haphazard, temporary functions of situations and factors over which lineage members and leaders are not in control. Probably earlier villages were small, the lineage groupings not extensive (not only because of the low rate of population growth), and the possibilities of lineage fission under new leadership and dispersal to other areas great. It is simpler for the state to handle small, organized groups than large ones; the figures rarely seem to run to more than a couple of hundred inhabitants. The state is concerned with land under cultivation and taxable units. Large groups are potentially organizable under rebellious sheikhs and town patron-notables.

THE PEASANTS : POLITICIZED DESCENT THROUGH ENDOGAMY AND
FACTION BUILDING

The patrilineage in Palestine is, then, best viewed as the outgrowth of the restrictions and limitations of the feudal-type agrarian regime which, for its ends of tax and rent collection, and the implementation of an administrative order, imposed social and economic collectivity on individuals and families, literally structured them through the recognized principles of descent and leadership and tied them to the land in "autonomous" villages. It is the endogamous marriage "system" which put the flesh of kinship on the dead bones of genealogy and made the patrilineal structure viable. I do not say that the marriage pattern was equally and directly imposed. More likely it developed concurrently with the "structured" patrilineage and out of the same complex conditions that were creating, at one and the same time, separatist elite groups, private estate ownership, incipient classes, and depressed peasants seeking means to defend themselves against the new power groups that were forming.

Marriage here determines the formal bounds, the extent, of kinship. In other words, when there are no ongoing endogamous marriages, there is no longer a descent line *per se*. In brief: the political and prestige potential of a patrilineal descent line was made explicit through preferred (and sometimes prescribed) endogamy, that is by denying female members of the lineage as marriage partners to men outside it. In distinction to tribal lineages, which primarily form alliances between and among lineages and tribal groups, the Arab patrilineage, an (incipient) state peasant formation, protects private property (and sets the groundwork for a factional unit), at the lowest (familial) degrees of patrilateral parallel cousin marriage, and creates alliances between segments of a patrilineage as a political-factional device at the highest degrees (3rd, 4th, 5th, and so on) of paternal cousin marriage. Cousin—"right" marriage is the means by which the patrilineage is structured, or structures itself, as a collectivity in response both to the constraints and inducements of the state and as an initial means for defence and aggression from similar competing patrilineages within the village, and from forces threatening it outside the village.

We find today that 30-70 per cent of the marriages in villages are made within the hamula-patrilineage. Thus, we have horizontal integration through affinal ties *within* the lineage.

> Common descent may and does pull segments of a lineage together in opposition to other lineages, but without the endogamous marriages the Arab village patrilineages would dissolve into extended family isolates. ....
> Because of the divisive effect of differences in property, recognition of common descent in itself is not sufficient to hold more distant paternal kinsmen together. [Individual family head] property separates kinsmen and [preferred and prescribed] marriage recreates the alliance giving the patrilineal kin line a descent importance which it essentially lacks.[6] (Rosenfeld 1968:251)

Competing village lineages, those which seek economic and status privileges from state officials and overlords, attempt to alter their disadvantaged political-economic situation by promoting themselves as an alternative replacement for existing village lineage leadership; in addition to their own endogamous marriages, their main, although not only, means to this end was in establishment of alliances through the giving and taking of women in marriage *between* lineages. In order to offset a growing force, a leading lineage necessarily has to compromise its internal endogamy by taking women from and giving women to other lineages, i.e. by creating allies of its own *(ibid.:*251-257). Often such marriages are themselves the cause for antagonism between co-members of a descent line (Aswad 1971: 78-85), whose loyalties extend to their *faction* and not to the full span of geneologically traceable patrilineal kin. In fact, an operative patrilineal descent span is determined by *current* marriage alliances and factional arrangements. If there are no endogamous marriages within and between segments over time, it is fairly clear that the premise of descent that joins them is *in extremis.*

The other side of the politicking-factional descent line coin is that consecutive marriage alliances between otherwise formally unrelated lineages blur their paternal separateness, and lead to the incorporation of the weaker lineage into the descent line of the stronger. This, then, is the fate of kin units whose 'reason' for existence is their "political" viability (for defence and aggression, and for ties to seats of power). We can state it this way: (endogamous) marriage determines the continuity of the descent line: one's affinals are, generally speaking, paternal kin: one's descent line, i.e., affinals, or kin, are (the base for) a faction. A descent line, of whatever span, is then only an initial means towards creating a unit of some resolution. Such a unit must be a faction and, over a period of a generation, necessarily comprises groups outside it.

Although we do not detail those shared features of the preservation of family and female "honour" and "shame" that seem to be attributes of many Mediterranean societies, or their finer nuances (Peristiany 1965: Schneider 1971: 17-22), we can exemplify the tenuousness of the Arab village patrilineage, its lack of corporateness, and the fact that its quasi-viability is a function of its mainly endogamous, faction-building marriage by pointing out that these equally act upon the structural boundaries of "honour". In those instances known to me from several villages, where a female is believed to have brought shame on her family, it has always been a father or brother who has sought to recover honour. And, where a man has dishonoured a woman, again, for whatever cause, those who apprehend him, or the woman, are the men who are (or were, if she is already married) her potential marriage partners within the descent line, and her father and brothers. In other words, the men involved are not any and all men who can trace paternal descent to the woman, since political antagonists from within the descent line are excluded, and exclude themselves, as do distant relatives. The group defending family honour is, then, neither an abstract descent line nor a rigidly defined one, but (rather more cogently) *part* of the descent line, those who are her potential mates or those who control her marriage by defining who the mates may or may not be—those whose rights in marriage and family property (Rosenfeld 1968: 250), now interpreted as "honour", have been diminished by an offender or offenders. In more inclusive and different fashion, J. Schneider suggests that the particular role of the women emerged from a pastoral way of life, in that "As with honour, the idea of shame serves both to defend or enhance the patrimonies of families and to define the family as a corporate group" (1971: 21). She goes on to suggest that women provide the most "likely symbol around which to organize solidarity groups, in spite of powerful tendencies toward fragmentation ... [therefore] The sanctity of virgins plays a critical role in holding together the few corporate groups of males which occur in many traditional Mediterranean societies" *(ibid.:* 22.).

The situation is similar in regard to the "blood vengeance" group: it may not be the entire putative descent group. Again, its structure depends on current alliance relations, which are equally marriage relationships, among the heads of families and segments. While more than one knowledgeable elder has explained to me the exact descent-generation span ("... through the third patrilineal ancestor", see the case in Antoun 1972: 42) of those upon whom an avenging group will retaliate (exempting "... those linked to the culprit through the fourth or paternal great grandfather", *ibid.*), such hair-splitting distinctions are not observed (see Aswad 1971: 61) in a truly heated settling of scores. Since all formalizations of categories and groupings in vengeance liability (level of retaliation, participation in reparations, etc.) hold within them a certain internal logic, so the above cut-off point seems to be an arbitrary legal device for structuring a non-bounded (lineage) structure.

THE "ORIGINAL" AGRARIAN FEUDAL-TYPE REGIME AND THE KIN-CLASS DICHOTOMY

We turn to some of the possible original, historical processes in superimposed collectivity, leadership, and the structured lineage. In discussing Early Dynastic and late Early Dynastic Sumerian city-states, along with well-defined wealthy land-owing elites, Adams recognizes "the existence of lineage or clan modes of organization, not only in landholding but also in craft and professional groupings"; perhaps they were also mustered as such in militias, and worked together at corvee labour. He raises the problem that concerns us (although here in regard to militias) of the essence of the lineage:

> Now, while there is no evidence that the units [in the militias] were composed of individuals related by descent or that their leadership was internally sanctioned rather than superimposed as a stratum of minor officials ... [and] ... Such widely manifested functions suggested that lineage groupings had not become merely vestigial by late Early Dynastic and Akkadian times but, instead, were still both powerful and important. (Adams 1966: 85, 86).

Adams' time of reference is that of the transition to the state in Mesopotamia from approximately 6,000 until "the emergence of a fully developed class society" about 4,500 years ago. Our introductory question remains: Are we speaking of a certain structural, but equally historical adaptiveness of the lineage, something that "had not become merely vestigial" but which maintained continuity, and/or of a lineage whose structure (and leadership) was even then (as recently) controlled, contained, superimposed by ongoing feudal-type productive and power relations?

Whatever else, distinctions in property holdings and status then also caused rifts within lineage structures; nomadic groups "trickle into the cultivated zones as a disorganized, depressed, landless labour force" (Adams 1966: 54). There were internal tendencies towards stratification of high antiquity within "conical clans". "At the same time, however, they survived the superimposition of new political [state] relationships for a considerable time, retaining loyalties and forms of internal organization that were rooted in kin relationships, while adapting to the needs of the state through the elaboration of a new series of specialized functions (military service, corporate framework for specialized crafts skills, 'serving as units for labour management' for state projects and services)" *(ibid.:* 94).

This is quite possibly true. However, if the present projects some light on the past, and some of my assumptions are correct, then as soon as, or soon after, the early states incorporated tribal groups, then as now, we should be speaking of a structure that consistently was allowed to reproduce itself in order to meet state ends, and whose "kinship" is the end result of that state-made structural unit. That is, the early Mesopotamian city-states sapped the tribal kin lineage of its content once and for all. What remained, and what we find, is a recreated adapted structure fabricating its "kinship", as best it can, out of the structures imposed and maintained by successive regimes.

Moreover, consistent with class-formation—comprising ruling families, high officials, and merchants with private acquisitions of land and/or a privileged position in trade in the early city-states at one end of the scale, and a slave or "unfree agricultural class", free peasants, and semi-free serfs at the other end (Adams *op. cit.:* 103-06) — would be the "internal tendencies toward stratification" (94) within the clan of agricultural workers and peasants. In other words, whatever remained of a clan community was at one and the same time developing classmen within it, developing the everlasting contradiction of clan-peasants.

When the "clan" ramifies and some of the members become merchant-townsmen, bureaucrats, office holders, and so on, then we have local, village peasants being exploited by their ex-kin businessmen and state functionaries while holding on to (or avoiding) these ex-kin as personal, economic, "political" links of survival. There is no place for unequivocal, benign kinship relationships or descent ties that are not a matter of expedience within a *stratified* local, village lineage. Wealthy kin keep their wealth within the extended family through patrilateral parallel cousin marriages, isolate themselves from their descent line kin, move out of the village and become, as said, patrons. By turning the endogamous marriage pattern into a class marriage (Rosenfeld 1968: 252), they terminate whatever prior, meaningful lineage sense had been retained in descent and *kin* marriage rules. In other words, stratification is the process that takes place with the origin of the state, the clan undergoing separation among those who belong to *one or the other class.* What remains of the "clan" at the village, agricultural working level is a depressed class: they are summarily, and from time to time, structured or re-structured according to the patrilineage pattern as and when it suits state purposes. It is an irreversibile process, in the sense that the "older" unstratified clan-lineage cannot be revived once the agrarian, feudal-type state makes its "appearance". Meanwhile the new "clan-lineage" is constantly, "artificially" being imposed and contained by the same state, with (in Ottoman Palestine) the top part of the stratified lineage constantly joining the class element outside the village within which its interests lie—tax-farming, office-holding, and so on—making the village the habitat of the most reduced groups, destined to struggle amongst themselves for honour, recognition, factional links, and ties of clientage. That is, the local patrilineage is a function of those who *have* to remain on the land. Its extensions outside the village lead to those who profit from the lineage, and from the land.

It is tempting to contemplate the possibility that these endogamous and interlineage marriages, that the genesis of factional groupings, was part of a "genuine" tribal, lineage response to the disruption being created within it while being structured into a peasantry. However, it seems more likely, as we have suggested, that the incorporation was a total one, these same factions now competing, by means of the marriage "system", for privilege as defined by state circumstances, and/or as a defence against those whose factional superiority already had gained for them authority over the "autonomous" village. Moreover, these same internally competing segments were composed of "type" families which, despite their structural similarities, are the direct socio-economic opposites of tribal-"type" families. A key attribute of the peasant families is that they are household head, private property-owning (land, work animals, control over family labour power, etc.), that is "patriarchal", families.

THE PEASANTS : PATRIARCHAL PROPERTY CONTROL AND KINSHIP CONTRADICTIONS

Here I briefly mention several of the contradictions property control imposed on descent (Rosenfeld 1964, 1968), before pointing to some of the implications that this and factional marriages hold for the meaning of Arab kinship. For one, nuclear family distinctions in wealth and property holdings offer those who only a generation previous had been in a united extended family alternative marriage and factional paths. For example, men have the right to marry their female paternal cousins,[5] but wealthy patriarchs may deny poor nephews that right, implying their divisive political intentions (Aswad 1971: 84; Antoun 1972: 76; cf. Barth 1954: 68). For another, wealthy men make polygynous marriages, and with numerous children may form a separatist "power" segment. Further, patrilineal kinsmen do not share in the bride-price given for a man's daughter, nor do they donate a share of the payment to a bride for his son. As distinct from many tribal societies, these matters are in the private realm; this includes the possibility of regarding the woman as capital, of setting monetary values on women, and so on. Most telling: a woman who takes her legal property rights through inheritance from her extended family is ostracized from her immediate paternal descent line.

One additional example of the basic contradiction between real property ownership by household heads and the maintenance of descent line and affinal relationship as they reflect on the meaning of kinship, can be taken from the levirate and sororate as practised in the Arab village. Notwithstanding the sentiment sometimes voiced, they do not signify abiding ties of affinity, of long-standing claims between lineages. The levirate is the only possible solution open to a young widow in order to remain with her children; the sororate enables a woman to care for her dead sister's children. Without these practices the children may well be harshly treated as orphans, even while remaining with the framework of their own father's extended family. Moreover, the decision whether or not the woman will marry her dead husband's brother, or replace her sister, is solely her own father's who, as well, collects a bride-price; it is not, in any case, a collective kin matter.

We have regarded descent and collectivity in the Arab village as having been superimposed, endogamous marriages as providing descent lines with their quasi-viability, marriage within the patrilineage and with other lineages as a device for developing a political faction, certain institutions such as the *mādafa* and institutionalized forms of behaviour such as family honour and vengeance as having a marriage claim—"political" character, and have noted that these, while formalized and structured, are also tenuous and shifting as they follow factional pressures. Moreover, at the heart of the extended family there is patriarchal private property which stands in contradistinction to whatever collective, joint, or equalitarian premise is implicit in the unlineal descent group. In brief, the patrilineage has developed out of state "political relations", with which it is inseparable.

Where, then, is there "kinship", where "personal relations"? Kinship, of course, is present. It is exactly the outcome of what has been superimposed in descent line collectively, and then activated through aggressive-defensive in-group marriages; it is mainly familial and includes affinal ties to wherever they extend. This same "kinship", however, is equally entwined in the divisive property and factional relations that stem from the state itself, and which are cause for incessant conflict between kin.

For example, the extended family remains as a unit under its patriarch. However, at his death sons divide his property equally. Married brothers may remain together for several years, but continuity of such an extended family is impossible for clear structural (property) reasons: each must pay the bride-price for his own son's marriage. Moreover, each measures his nuclear family's labour power against that of his brothers', and those who believe they contribute more opt to take their share of the property as soon as possible and begin private careers (Rosenfeld 1958). When living *as* an extended family, the family *is* a kin unit in regard to work, raising children, eating, building, visiting, family honour, arranging marriages, and so on. However, when brothers separate, or sons leave fathers, the structural reasons for doing so (property, differences in labour power, etc.) are often expressed acrimoniously: one brother accuses another of keeping separate money, of continuously failing to send his wife or daughters to joint labour; women are accused of beating another's children, of cursing one another's fathers; the son of an "unloved" first wife has already left his father and is bitter towards his half-brothers, and so on. The extended family separates and many of the routine practices of "kinship behaviour" terminate, even though the now nuclear families continue to live within the same or adjoining courtyards; work, child care, eating, acquiring the bride price, are no longer joint matters.

If its conflicts are not severe, kinship ties and subsequent sympathetic behaviour are reconstituted in new extended families at the next generational level; that is, a man leaves his brothers, but his sons marry their daughters, his daughters their sons. However, in numerous instances kin ties are not reconstituted. The contradiction between kinship and private property, inheritance-ownership, means that a full range of relationships between all extended family members is impossible to maintain generation after generation.[7]

When we consider that marriages have been institutionalized within an endogamous pattern in order to meet factional ends, then it must be realized that this was the objective reality of marriage, and not kinship or "personal relations" as such. Similar to the divisive effect that individual property ownership had on kin relationships, that it is private and separatist, so the possibility of gaining status and authority through the proper endogamous factional marriages held equal potential for undermining kinship relations. For example, a series of endogamous marriages created a kin force, set an individual career in motion. But in the nature of a political career, additional polygynous marriages, within and outside the immediate descent line, were necessary in order to bolster and expand the opportunity. This led to animosity among paternal relatives, and also diffused the original kin solidarity. Or, for example, as is well known, authority gained as a government representative by means of one's kin must also be employed against the same kin; equally, the favours and privileges to be dispensed by local authority are given to some kin, withheld from others, given to allies, denied to patrilineage members, etc.

TOWARDS TOMORROW'S "KINSHIP"

Kinship is viewed by the villagers much as anthropologists view it, formally, structurally, in terms of marriage and descent, and in such terms do the villagers set their expectations and elaborate assumptions about mutual aid, support, respect, cooperation at work, in gaining a livelihood, in politics, and so on. However, the reality of Arab peasant existence concerned the contradictions inherent in maintaining kinship alongside private property and in combining descent line continuity with descent line and non-descent line factional marriages. In other words, the narrow factional dimension of descent that was further undercut by private property, meant that individuals vacillated between self-interest and kinship assumptions, making the latter insecure and unreliable.

Without being able to bring technical proof that the 'Arab-type' peasant patrilineage had been superimposed by the state on the tribal kin formation it destroyed, it nevertheless seems clear that the descent line that has formed has been fostered by a succession of agrarian, feudal-type regimes into a formal, collectively responsible unit. And from within, the patrilineage-hamula organized itself for aggression and defence as a separatist factional group, finding the narrowest, most restrictive and isolating of the dimensions of kinship, politicking, for its pivot.

This leads us up to our final question. Why has not there been an awareness on the part of Arab peasants of the mainpulative role of the state and its power groups, and of the reflexive manipulations of peasants that could, themselves, possibly cut across the engineered aspect of descent, of competitive factional marriages, and so on? Until recently, the answer seems to be that people "believed" in descent and the patterns of honourable behaviour that descent exacted, in the mythologies of prestigious groups, in delegated authority and its reflected privileges, and the sense of anchorage that came from connections, even illusory ones, with those in power. And such consciousness was justifiable because within the agrarian, feudal-type political economy there were no alternatives to such social organization and patterns of behaviour and, perhaps most important, there were no alternatives to a unit(patrilineage) that provided a degree of defensive-aggressive security in a hostile social environment. That all were a depressed, declassed peasant class, a fact that could not fail to be conceptualized, was not sufficient in itself to spark a search for an alternative class avenue to the regime above them, and the ongoing factional divisiveness within which they were destined to live. The choices open were within the level of the existing contradictions. For peasants, the choice was between private property aggrandizement and loyalty to the descent group, between private property and amicable family relations, between the patrilineage and factional demand within and outside it. For those who were part of the feudal-type (Ottoman) power structure, it was between a rent-tax overlord, merchant-trade system with depressed peasantry at its economic base, or capital investment in agriculture and work plants towards the creation of a rural and urban working class at its economic base, with that path being taken only hesitatingly, if at all, during the end of the last and the beginning of the present century.

The final question is, how are uncontrived "personal relations" to be engendered out of present circumstances: The patrilineage-hamula, manipulated from above and from within, is a disaster and has created a false consciousness of the integrity of kinship. Whatever definition we give to "kinship" and to "personal relations", we would not equate them with the view that all those with whom there are no marriage ties are factional enemies, and all those with whom there are not ongoing marriage ties are to be regarded with suspicion. Nevertheless, there appear to be two possible, related paths that could lead to a deepening of existing kin mutuality, and the development of a new perspective on personal relations. Thus, in Israel, for example, there is no longer a peasantry. The majority of men are workers who return daily to their home villages. Often they are skilled labourers, and certainly sophisticated in the ways of the work market and the social and political conditions in the country. There is also a small middle class. There is no urban effendi-rentier-merchant class. The point is that there are no factional ties leading to urban power groups outside the village in class-structured Israel. Rather, for its purposes of control over the Arab national minority, at a certain level the state succeeds in manipulating local lineages and leaders and in encouraging factional disputes among them. Equally, many villagers lend themselves to the preservation of those factors that foster the continuity of a residual peasantry and internal conflicts.

One realistic alternative to the administered, factionalized lineage is the *fraternity* among persons within social movements and political parties that cut across lineage divisiveness. Recently, a country-wide political movement for national and individual rights was successful mainly due to organized Arab working-class support; this in the face of the government's ongoing attempt to counter it with force, and the ideology of hamula particularity, sect, and religious separateness. In other words, the factionalism of the lineage is replaced by critical political activity that centres on class and national problems. Perhaps this may reflect itself in alternative marriage opportunities, ties of friendship, womens' and workers' movements, etc.

The other, related, path may prove that endogamous marriages need not in themselves instigate factionalism. The reality of such marriages was in their being part and parcel of a total state-peasant agrarian feudal-type system which, as said, no longer exists. If modern industrial and agricultural exterprises were present in Arab villages, as they are in Jewish communities in Israel, and if opportunities for the Arab intelligentsia were open in all fields, advanced education easily available to members of both sexes, this would go far to eliminating existing features of residual peasantry. Under such circumstances, the state would find it more difficult to structure individuals into units, and kin marriages might well be as personally rewarding as any other.

NOTES

1. In part, the research for this paper was supported by a grant from Wenner-Gren Foundation and in part by funds from the Faculty of Social Sciences at the University of Haifa at the Hebrew University of Jerusalem.

2. For a partial bibliography see Rosenfeld (1964).

3. It is also beyond the scope of this paper to point out the administrative-fiscal similarities between the Ottoman regime and the regimes that preceded it: the Mamluks, the Arabs, Byzantium, the Roman Empire, as systems of control over the peasants.

4. Another system, that of the *emanet,* had become rare in eighteenth-century Palestine. Here the administration of the *mukāta'a* was entrusted to an "emin" "... whose function it was to collect all taxes in the *mukāta'a* and remit them *in toto* to the state treasury. In return for this the emin would receive a fixed salary ..." Meanwhile, a modified tax-farming system *mālikāne,* designed to overcome defects in the *iltizām* (tax-farming) system was introduced during the eighteenth century. It was believed that since *multezims* held their leases over territorial units for only a year or two (subject to reversal by the Porte), they ruled over their peasants "tyrannously", causing peasants to flee the land and "... damage and loss (of revenue) is caused to the state treasury". The new system, among other things, granted rights over the *mukāta'a* for life. (See Cohen 1973: 180-82).

5. Wolf goes on say: "Even more decisive, however, may have been the interest of the state in preventing the build-up of large landed monopolies by officials" *(ibid.).*

6. Barth puts this in a slightly different fashion: "Indeed, it seems appropriate to characterise the content of descent relations as part of politics rather than kinship; and where the territorial estates at the base of these politics are removed, the whole unilineal organization disappears and kinship and local life take on a highly bilateral character" (1973: 18). Also, it is directly in such political terms that Barth has seen parallel cousin marriage as creating agnatic bonds (1954: 168).

7. Here we can make an observation concerning kin terminology and its correspondence to what we shall call a property-ownership designating terminology which, practically speaking, divides all villagers into two separate moieties. The term *'amm,* paternal uncle, which stipulates not only the specific relationship, but is also a term of respect *('ammi* — my paternal uncle) for all elders within the descent line, and those from other descent lines with whom there are marriage relationships and amiable relationships, designates as well those who are property-holding heads. Such "paternal uncles" *('umūm)* may or may not be in the category of the elderly, or simply older, males *(ikhtyār),* but they are never in the category of youths *(šabāb).* However, among the *šabāb* there can be men who in fact are paternal uncles to nephews but, since they have not come into their inheritance rights, do not enjoy full household head status and respect terminology. Therefore, a household head property owner in his twenties will be a "paternal uncle" as a sign of respect to many in his descent line and to others, and he will not be called a youth, *šabb;* meanwhile, a man in his thirties and perhaps in his forties who has not become a "patriarchal" head may be in the twilight zone of jokingly being called either *šabb* or *ikhtyār,* and may well not be called a paternal uncle as a sign of respect.

REFERENCES

Abir, Mordechai (1975): "Local Leadership and Early Reforms in Palestine, 1800-1834" in *Studies on Palestine During the Ottoman Period*. M. Ma'oz, ed., Jerusalem, The Magnes Press.

Abramovitch, Z. and J. Gelphat (1944): *The Arab Economy. Tel-Aviv, Hakibbutz Hameuchad (Hebrew)*.

Adams, Robert McC. (1966): *The Evolution of Urban Society*. Chicago & New York, Aldine/Altherton.

Antoun, Richard T. (1972): *Arab Village*. Bloomington/London, Indiana University Press.

Aswad, Barbara C. (1971): *Property Control and Social Strategies : Settlers on a Middle Eastern Plain*. Museum of Anthropology. Anthropological Papers No. 44. Ann Arbor, The University of Michigan.

Barth, Fredrik (1954): "Father's Brother's Daughter Marriage in Kurdistan" *Southwestern Journal of Anthropology* 10: 164-171.

           (1973): "Descent and Marriage Reconsidered" in *The Character of Kinship*. Jack Goody, Ed. Cambridge, Cambridge University Press.

Burchardt, J. L. (1822): *Travels in Syria and the Holy Land*. London, John Murray.

Carmi, Shulamit and Henry Rosenfeld (1974): "The Origins of the Process of Proletarianization and Urbanization of Arab Peasants in Palestine" *Annals of the New York Academy of Sciences* Vol. 220, Article 6: 470-485.

Cohen, Amnon (1973): *Palestine in the 18th Century*. Jerusalem, The Magnes Press.

Doukhan, Moses J. (1938): "Land Tenure" in *Economic Organization of Palestine*. Sa'id B. Himadeh Ed. Beirut, The American Press.

Fortes, Meyer (1953): "The Structure of Unilineal Descent Groups "*American Anthropologist* 55: 25-39.

Government of Palestine (1945): *Survey of Social and Economic Conditions in Arab Villages 1944*. Special Bulletin No. 21. Department of Statistics.

Granott, A. (1952): *The Land System in Palestine*. London, Eyre and Spottiswoode.

Hutteroth, Wolf (1975): "The Pattern of Settlement in Palestine in the Sixteenth Century : Geographical Research and Turkish *Defter-i-Mufassal"*, in *Studies on Palestine During the Ottoman Period*. M. Ma'oz, ed., Jerusalem, The Magnes Press.

Johnson-Crosbie (1930): *Report of a Committee on the Economic Conditions of Agriculturalists in Palestine and the Final Measures of Government in Relation Thereto*. Government of Palestine.

Ma'oz, Moshe (1968): *Ottoman Reform in Syria and Palestine 1840-1861*. Oxford, Oxford University Press.

Nakhleh, Khalil (1977): "The Hamula as a Political Concept?" (Paper presented at the annual meeting of the American Anthropological Association).

Peristiany, J. G. (ed.) (1965): *Honour and Shame*. London, Weidenfeld and Nicolson.

Poliak, A. N. (1939): "Towards a History of the Fellah's Economy" *Cooperative Economy* 7: 1-2 (Hebrew).

Robinson, E. and E. Smith (1841): Biblical Researches in Palestine, Mount Sinai and Arabia Petrea. Vol. v. London, John Murray.

Rosenfeld, Henry (1958): "processes of Structural Change within the Arab Village Extended Family" *American Anthropologist* 60: 1127-39.

——— (1964): "From Peasantry to Wage Labor and Residual Peasantry : The Transformation of an Arab Village" in *Process and Pattern in Culture : Essays in Honour of Julian H. Steward.* R. A. Manners, ed. Chicago, Aldine.

——— (1968): "The Contradictions between Property, Kinship and, Power as Reflected in the Marriage System of the Arab Village" in *Contributions to Mediterranean Sociology.* J. G. Peristiany, ed. Paris, The Hague, Mouton.

——— (1972): "An Overview and Critique of the Literature on Rural Politics and Social Change" in *Rural Politics and Social Change in the Middle East.* R. Antoun and I. Harik, eds. Bloomington/London, Indiana University Press.

——— (1974): "Hamula" *Journal of Peasant Studies* 1: 243-244.

Schneider, Jane (1971): "Of Vigilance and Virgins : Honor, Shame and Access to Resources in Mediterranean Societies" *Ethnology* 10: 1-24.

Volney, M. C-F. (1978) *Travels Through Egypt and Syria in the Years 1783, 1784 and 1785.* 2 vols. New York, J. Tiebout for E. Duyckinck & Co.

Wilson, C. T. (1906): *Peasant Life in the Holy Land.* London, John Murray.

Wolf, Eric R. (1966): *Peasants.* Englewood Cliffs, New Jersey, Prentice-Hall.

Political Consciousness and Struggle Among an African Peasantry

JOAN VINCENT

There is among many scholars an assumption that capitalism means de-peasantization. "Peasants", as Shanin puts it, "have entered the Marxist parley as the analytical prehistory of capitalism" (1978 : 30). This paper deals with the capitalist creation of a peasantry in Teso, eastern Uganda. It is, perhaps, of particular interest because Uganda provides one of the rare cases where the making of a peasantry, its creation and transformation, have occurred within living memory. This makes the process peculiarly accessible to the inquiries of the historical anthropologist.

In response to economic crisis after the American Civil War in 1865, capitalist manufacturing interests in England sought new sources for the commodity on which Britain's industrial strength rested—cotton. After two decades in which establishment interests embarked upon exploratory, missionary and commercial ventures in sub-Saharan Africa, a reluctant government, responding largely to increasing urban poverty and social unrest, bolstered by a philosophy of social imperialism, agreed to establish in East Africa the colonial dependencies its industrial system required (Vincent 1981).

Contemporary students of African history are somewhat diffident about using the word 'peasant' (Fallers 1961; Post 1972). Colonial administrators, on the other hand, were under no illusions about what they were doing and were, indeed, often extremely explicit about their objectives in fashioning a peasantry out of a tribal or feudal society. In 1927, for example, the District Commissioner of Teso saw for the first time since he had entered the country women working on the roads. This, he thought, ought to be discouraged and he cited an old regulation to that effect. All the same, he observed:

> This does not prohibit women from volunteering, as was the custom, to pick cotton or other crops at Government farms (near their homes and on daily pay) or to pick cotton at stores, provided they return home each day before dark. Peasant Women in England glean in the fields in the same way. (TDA. VADM 5/3.85.1927)

In the generation prior to this observation of 1927, Teso society and economy had been transformed. Homestead settlements of large, extended families, some between forty and sixty in size, many of them polygynous and living within thorn-ringed stockades to protect their cattle against raiding fellow tribesmen had been replaced by dispersed, largely agricultural households of nuclear families with adult male heads. Unlike elsewhere in colonial East Africa (apart from Zanzibar) census enumerators were early required to count individuals and households rather than village clusters or tribal representations. With the advent of Christian schooling, many young boys were removed from the family labour force and women's work in agriculture increased as their menfolk took over herding duties—a process accentuated by the introduction of obligatory cultivation of cotton as a cash crop. The imposition of taxes, fees and fines led to food surpluses being marketed locally at the small centres established by the colonial administration and there was a marked decline in long-distance trading and in domestic industry as labour power was re-directed into the needs of the local, colonially-administered peasant economy. Asian, Arab, and Somali traders entered the region as middlemen. Corvée labour was required to open up the district wich canals, roads, and a railway. With the small towns that developed, a salaried bourgeoisie of chiefs and petty civil servants emerged as a nascent ruling class resting upon the exploitation of the labour power of a largely docile peasantry. Meanwhile, the colonial administration, suffering the contradictions of the process, came to lament the increasing individualism of the Teso population.

It is the contention of this paper that a peasantdom was introduced in Teso to pin down and immobilize a largely pastoral African population so that cotton production might be undertaken on a large scale. The peasant family that emerged in the African savanna was as much a product of cosmopolitical capitalism as the urban families of British industrialism. It is today generally agreed, following Wolf (1966), that a peasantry is characterized by three sets of productive relations: those between the producer and the land; those between the producer and the market; and those between the producer and the state. This paper deals solely with the third of these relationships, asking, first, what was the relationship between the agricultural economy and the restructuring of the Teso population between 1907 and 1927; secondly, given the nature of this relationship, what form did political consciousness and the peasant struggle take?

THE AGRARIAN ECONOMY

The agrarian economy of colonial East Africa was based upon the role in the modern capitalist system of four territories—Uganda, Kenya, Tanganyika, and

Zanzibar—as dependent suppliers of primary agricultural products. The demands of European (and American) industrial economies led to the emergence of specialized forms of agricultural organization adapted to production for world markets. These, along with new systems of land ownership and class relations, were based on a relatively small number of export crops (Paige 1975): coffee (Kenya, Tanganyika, Uganda); tea (Kenya); sisal (Tanganyika); cloves (Zanzibar); and cotton (Tanganyika, Uganda). Following Paige, the four types of agrarian economy that developed, each based on export agriculture, each regionally based, may be summarized as follows:

Dependecy	Product	Dominant Agricultural Mode
Zanzibar	Cloves	Commercial hacienda; mercantile and colonial settler state
Tanganyika	Sisal	Plantations
Kenya	Coffee	Sharecropping migratory labour
Uganda	Cotton	Small-holding peasantry

While this typology of the four East African dependencies is a useful starting point for the analysis of agrarian change, it must be pointed out that, to a greater extent than is usually appreciated (and, certainly, to a greater extent than can be incorporated here), agrarian transformations in Uganda were harnessed to the interests and needs not only of its own industrial and commercial centres in Bunganda and Busoga, but also to those of the white settler colony in neighbouring Kenya. Industrialism in Uganda's heartland and capitalist farming in the Kenyan white highlands rested upon the backs of a labouring peasantry in up-country Uganda.

THE SMALL-HOLDING PEASANTRY

In Teso, a relatively infertile region lying east of Lake Kyoga and the Nile in eastern Uganda, cotton was introduced in 1907. Cotton production may be fostered in two principal ways: on plantations with a considerable outlay of imported capital (as in Tanganyika, German East Africa) or on plots of land that remain in the ownership of the indigenous people. The latter system was adopted in Teso. How, then, to characterize the small-holding political economy as a type?

The first, and perhaps dominant, feature is that there develops no agrarian upper class. The land is owned by those who work it. There is, however, a substantial commercial and industrial upper class whose power and income is based on the control of processing machinery, storage facilities, transportation, and finance capital (Paige 1975). In Teso this was represented by the middlemen and financiers who controlled the marketing of the cotton crop. As the twentieth century proceeds, this power and wealth passes out of the hands of British and Asian capitalists into African hands. Yet, just as the colonial expatriate upper class was extra-local to Teso so, too, non-Iteso and absentee Iteso emerged as the dominant capitalists in the post-colonial era.

The smallholder, then, can be considered as a worker in an agricultural system controlled by urban financial interests. "The small-holding of the peasant is now only the pretext that allows the capitalist to draw profits, interest and rent from the soil, while leaving it to the tiller of the soil himself to see how he can extract his wages" (Marx 1963 : 127). He is a labourer who happens to control a small piece of land from which he "extracts" his wages. This is important within the colonial African situation. Ida Greaves has pointed out that a critical distinction between a protectorate (such as Uganda) and a colony (such as Kenya) is that in the latter European capital adopted a *system of colonization* whereas in the former it adopted a *system of cultivation*. This meant that within a protectorate "the native labour supply has always been a factor of supreme importance" (1935 : 29). Indeed, given the conditions in Teso, where land was plentiful and labour difficult to mobilize (unlike Scott's (1976) Asian peasant economies) the system might well seem analogous to the 'putting out system' of agrarian domestic industry in Europe (M. Meggitt, personal communication). Certainly in Teso, as there, its success relied very heavily upon the extraction of women's work.

In Paige's analysis of social movements and export agriculture in the Third World, the smallholder engaged in cash crop production lies at the stable, conservative end of a continuum of agrarian revolution, a continuum which would appear to have considerable validity for East Africa given that the hacienda or estate system, characteristic of Zanzibar and Buganda, lies at the 'revolutionary' end. He suggests that distinctive forms of social movement are associated with each type of agricultural organization fundamentally as a result of "the interaction between the political behaviour associated with the principle source of income of the upper and lower agricultural classes. Combinations of income sources are associated with particular types of agricultural organization and lead to particular forms of social movement" (1975 : 70). Grossly to sum up a detailed and intricate analysis, a commercial hacienda system leads to an agrarian revolt; industrial plantation systems to reform labour movements; decentralized sharecropping systems to revolutionary socialist movements; and colonial settler systems to revolutionary nationalist movements. As for the small-holding agriculural system, he notes:

A combination of noncultivators dependent on income from commercial capital and cultivators dependent on income from land leads to a *reform commodity movement.* Such a combination of income sources is typical of small holding systems. *The reform commodity movement is concerned with the control of the market in agricultural commodities.* It demands neither the redistribution of property nor the seizure of State power. The typical tactic of such movements is a limited economic protest. The greater the sensitivity to markets of small holding systems, the greater the probability of a reform commodity movement.

(1975 : 70; emphasis added).

This is, indeed, exactly what happened in Teso in 1920.

The reform commodity movement, expressed in the boycotting of the cotton markets, was spearheaded not by peasants but by their colonially appointed chiefs (Vincent 1977;1981).

In Teso, as in Uganda and East Africa generally, the concept of the peasant was used by colonial administrators and post-colonial development planners and agronomists alike. For both, there was a sense of evolution, of progress, in one case from tribalism, through feudalism to the modern era of 'peasant farming'; in the other, from tribal pastoralists and cultivators to peasant cultivators and thence to peasant farmers and capitalist farmers. The policy of "betting on the strong", to use Wertheim's phrase (in East Africa this was generally referred to as aiding "progressive farmers"), was a recognition both of the internal differentiation that had developed with the penetration of capitalism into the countryside and of the desirability that this gradualist trend in agrarian society should continue. There is a considerable tension in the writings of both administrators and development officers with respect to advancing "individualism"—a contradiction that, perhaps, partly accounts for the focus of many social anthropologists during the development decade of the sixties on the individual, manipulation, and strategies of change in Third World peasant societies. (Critiques of this body of writing may be found in Alavi 1973; Vincent 1978; Worsley 1974.)

This emphasis, which gives primacy to subsistence cultivators becoming producers for a market, underplays the simultaneity with which the creation of a peasantry and the creation of a rural proletariat occurred in many parts of East Africa. It neglects the very engineering of that infrastructure upon which marketing depended: the massive deployment of labour, forced and coerced, for the building of roads, railways, and canals as well as for the construction of administrative townships, trading centres, agricultural stations, factories, and godowns essential to the development of the modern agrarian economy. Contrary to earlier assumptions and expectations, a closer analysis of the period from 1907 to 1927 in Teso district revealed that it was not cash crop production (taxation agriculture) that brought Teso's population into the modern world system but wage labour.

In Teso during these formative years this took several distinctive forms;

1. cotton cultivation
2. routinely controlled government labour
3. labour for private employees
4. migrant labour out of the district
5. military conscription

Each needs to be discussed in turn although it must be appreciated that all forms of labour affected all families to various degrees in different parts of the district. This becomes significant when the matter of reproduction of the peasantry is raised. Given that pastoralism and other elements in the indigenous, diversified economy deteriorated, that cotton demands remained constant, and that infrastructural wage labour demands decreased, the characterization of the emergent peasantry must clearly be seen as involving sequences or phases of agrarian survival. Not surprisingly, perhaps, many might feel today that the agricultural development of Teso has brought in its wake more "dwarf farmers" (Lenin 1910) and paupers than progressive capitalists.

LABOURING MEN

Cotton cultivation was introduced in Teso by requiring the compulsory planting of a half acre by every household. Seed was provided; instructions given; experimentation carried out to determine the best spacing of rows and plants, the time of planting, and so on. Later spraying with insecticides was provided at a subsidized rate as was the use of ox-drawn ploughs. Marketing was carried out by middlemen, first buying agents and then lorries being sent out into the countryside to collect the picked cotton. Buying was carried out at government-authorized markets, both the marketing season and the price being controlled. Later flexibility crept into the system with respect to the acreage planted, but clearly little was required of the enterprise of the cultivator but the employment of his land and labour. Since cotton is labour-intensive at the same time as millet cultivation (the main staple) the burden of cash crop production was considerable. It was borne by men, women and children "freed" as it were from the pursuits of the diversified economy—pastoralism, fishing, the growing of a variety of food crops, domestic industry and regional trade—by the colonial bias towards cotton production. The competition for labour between cotton and food crops . . . contributed to the famines that repeatedly struck the district, the most severe in 1919 when over 2,000 died in a six-month period.

Yet the labour demands of cotton cultivation were slight compared with those in other spheres. As early as 1910, missionaries complained that they were unable to hold open air services in the villages "owing to the constant occupation of the men, and women to some extent, in the cultivation of cotton, clearing roads and other Government work" (CMS 1912). Bishop Tucker of the Church Missionary Society attributed Uganda's population decline to the rigours of the government's labour demands. Three related categories of routinely controlled labour mobilization may be distinguished; the most gruelling and extensive was that involved in economic infrastructural development—road-making and the bridging of the swamps, and the clearing of the Agu canal which was built to link the administrative heartland of the district with Lake Kyoga and the Nile route. Steamers on the Nile carried Teso's cotton to Namasagali whence it was transported to the shores of Lake Victoria and thence to Mombasa for shipment to Liverpool and Bombay. Later rail replaced marine transport in eastern Uganda but, by that time, Teso was established as the main cotton-producing region of East Africa, responsible for sixty per cent of Uganda's agricultural exports.

One of the chief results of the amassing of large labour gangs to work on roads and swamp clearance in Teso was the spread of disease and epidemics. Plague and smallpox were pervasive; spinal meningitis became endemic; venereal disease increased. Cultivation suffered, further contributing to the famine conditions that were recurrent throughout the district for the first half of the century.

A second category of labour was employed in establishing the administrative infrastructure of the district, building government rest houses and growing plots of food crops at the camp sites. Every household in each neighbourhood and parish, administered by a salaried chief, was expected to clear and keep clear broad paths bordering its lands. These paths were to be sufficiently wide to permit access to the vehicular traffic of the cotton traders.

Labour for private enterprise was a third category of government-sponsored mobilization. Indeed, as Greaves has pointed out, to make a distinction in colonial Africa between private and public enterprise is virtually meaningless. "Since other industries have been introduced with the sympathy if not the assistance of the Government, official measures for obtaining labour do not discriminate between public and private employers" (1935 : 112). In 1917, for example, a labour draft of 1,700 men per month was supplied by the administration to the cotton ginneries. When to this *levee* is added others—a thousand men working on the roads in one country, for example, or 38,000 porters engaged in relaying cotton to the ports—the massive involvement of the male population in unskilled labour becomes clearer: this out of a *total* population of some 220,000. Under such conditions women's field labour most certainly increased, leaving no family unaffected. One can only ask why, under such conditions, neither class consciousness nor class struggle was generated.

All adult males were subjected to two forms of compulsory labour: *luwalo* which required each year one month's unpaid labour for local authorities, and *kasanvu* which required annually a month's unpaid labour on District-wide projects. The former was considered less burdensome by the Iteso family but it was more open to abuse by the entire hierarchy of chiefs whose nascent class interests were reflected both in the acquisition of land and, more importantly, in the use and abuse of labour. Prior to this the indigenous political system was dominated by Big Men whose power and wealth were more transient but with capitalist agriculture elements of a vertical patronage system became institutionalized in Teso abetted to a large extent by the government's policy of pinning down the Teso pastoralist and fisherman to a parish of residence where he cultivated cotton, supplied labour, and paid taxes. So effective was this process that migrant wage labour out of the district remained slight although youths from the west of the district did, at times, work on plantations and estates in neighbouring Busoga. Some even acquired land as sharecroppers in eastern Buganda where small colonies of Iteso 'settlers' are to be found to this day. By and large, however, movement was restricted and the majority of the Teso population were condemned to remain small-holding cotton producers. As has been universally noted, "the statistical correlation between cotton growing and poverty is startling" (Zimmerman 1936 : 326) and, in Teso, as elsewhere, "Cotton is, and must remain, a Black man's crop" (Todd 1927 : 113).

A final category of labour mobilization involved the porterage required for military expeditions (especially in the early days when the 'pacification' of the Karimoja and Turkana was being undertaken on the Kenyan border) and military conscription in the two "world wars" between 1914-18 and 1939-45. Two particular results may be noted: first, the extensive spread of disease that, combined with internal conditions, contributed to Teso's considerable population decline from 275,500 to fewer than 214,000 in the first two decades; secondly, the impact of the returning soldiers upon agrarian society. Godfrey Wilson's description of Northern Rhodesia in 1941 is equally applicable to Teso. The people of both were:

> members of a huge worldwide community . . . their lives . . . bound up at every point with the events of its history . . . . Their standard of living now depends on economic conditions in Europe, Asia and America to which continents their labour has become essential. Their political development is largely decided in the Colonial Office and on the battlefields of Europe; while hundreds of their one-time separate tribes now share a single destiny. . . . . They have entered a heterogeneous world stratified into classes and divided into states, and so find themselves suddenly transformed into the peasants and unskilled workers of a nascent nation state. (1941-42 : 12)

To sum up the argument thus far: in early capitalist Teso the peasantization and proletarianization of the African population occurred side by side. With the creation of small-holding production units, members of the same families were involved as peasant-farmers and as rural, non-agricultural wage labourers. The peasant farm generated surplus labour power which was utilized by the colonial authorities through coercive force for the infrastructural development of a cotton-producing, cotton-exporting administered district.

Although subject today to excessive criticism (Cavailhe 1976; Etxezarreta 1977; Szurek 1977), Lenin's model of the development of capitalism in agrarian society (1897) fits the Teso case extremely well largely due, presumably, to their similar starting places, i.e. following the redistribution of land in smallholdings in Russia and the egalitarian disposal of land—which was not a commodity—in early colonial Teso. The global needs of capitalism, placing primacy on the production and marketing of cotton, thus generated a peasantry which, in the following years, underwent marked differentiation (Vincent 1974). After the massive infrastructural needs of capitalist industrial agriculture were satisfied, accompanied by the emergence of a rural bourgeoisie of salaried colonial officials who managed the production side of the enterprise, the rural population of Teso was characterized initially by the surplus labour pool of the peasant family farms, then by under-employment and unemployment, and, ultimately, as differentiation proceeded further, by pauperization.

POLITICAL CONSCIOUSNESS AND THE PEASANT STRUGGLE

The population of Teso might be thought to have been extraordinarily docile under these changing and oppressive conditions. Although early resistance took the form of military opposition in the more remote parts of the district, most of the population was obliged to knuckle under to colonial rule. The little resistance that there was took covert forms (Emwanu 1963; Vincent 1981). Nowhere did the peasants revolt.

By and large resistance took two forms. Murder was directed by individuals against local chiefs and their families, and arson was employed in the cotton fields and against government property. At a time when only chiefs were armed, guns were frequently reported stolen or mislaid. Recriminations were heavy including public hangings. A second more common form of resistance was simply to run away from the jurisdiction of the local chief, labour requirements, enforced cultivation, and taxation.

As is often the case in the nascent phases of capitalism (Thompson 1963), alienation took on a religious guise. In Teso a small sector of the population, most significantly those living in the vicinity of trading centres and small townships, joined the Malaki religious sect. This was a movement started in

Uganda around 1913 and introduced to Teso by Kakungulu, the earlier conqueror and administrator of the region for the British. The 1921 Protectorate Census put the number of its followers at around 91,000. The Malaki movement was a clear expression of political dissent. Various components of capitalist development were under attack but especially those that concerned cattle, the land, and the condition of the people themselves. Members of the Malaki movement refused to pay land tax since part of the money went to support European mission doctors. Unlike other parts of Africa where the recognition of increased disease and strain was attributed to European medicine, areas near roads and settlements of dense concentration in Teso failed to generate witchcraft cults. Rather, dissent focused directly on the practices of missionaries, doctors, and veterinary officers. The Malaki sect provided organized political opposition to "European" hegemony. Members were imprisoned for not permitting the inoculation of their cattle against rinderpest, and for not paying taxes. The sect also opposed monogamy and established its own churches, appointing its own ministers of religion to teach the true gospel of Christ. The spread of the Malaki movement was patterned by the uneven economic development of the region; it was not a utopian or millenary movement among the oppressed, excluded from or relatively deprived of the material advantages of western civilization. It was an alternative form of political society mirroring in its sectarian aspect the fact that, in Teso, as in Uganda generally, the authority of the colonial power and capitalism rested visibly on the shoulders of the Christian missions. It flourished where land and marketing relations were most clearly seen to be controlled by aliens (in towns, along trade routes, and near the large estates). Its main thrust was, inevitably, against the state. It, like more violent forms of peasant protest, was aborted by the economic boycott organized by the chiefs.

REASONS FOR THE FAILURE OF REVOLT IN TESO

Paige has suggested that the failure of peasantries in small-holding economies to develop movements of agrarian revolt, or nationalist or socialist revolution, is due largely to the nature of its agricultural system. Data have been provided to suggest that this is a somewhat limited explanation. The comparative stagnation of the Teso economy and the increasing entrenchment of an indigenous bourgeoisie have also to be taken into account. In the years that followed the introduction of capitalist agriculture in 1907 dissent against the system took the innocuous form of letters, from anonymous individuals for the most part, informing the District Commissioner of grievances some against missionaries, most against chiefs. But, through it all, the old indigenous families never lost control over their local followings and—whether chief, councilor, politician, or member of the salariat—patronage remained much the same. The colonial period saw them attaining access to privilege and power by the 1920s and subsequently their consolidation of a capitalist material base, through strategic marriages and the control of access to salaried government positions. Only in an independent private sector would there appear to have been possibilities of alternative African interests developing and within Teso, as we have seen, this was virtually non-existent. Continuous privilege remained in the same few hands. Although the rich grew richer and the poor grew poorer—as was to be expected after the introduction of cotton as an export crop, especially where land came on the market—Teso's population remained proportionately much the same in the non-expanding economy.

The emergent top stratum in the agrarian society—those with education, salaries and opportunities for advancement in this society without a landed class—numbered some 994 individuals in 1921 out of a total adult male population of around 50,000. The bottom stratum of society was made up of a rural protetariat, 'labourers', who numbered some 23,432, a figure approaching 45 per cent of the total. Between the two, the middle sector was made up, first of those who remained in what might be considered their established rural occupations—cultivation, herding, and fishing. Alongside them, literally and categorically, were those who had become the artisans of the industrializing agricultural economy—carpenters, blacksmiths, bricklayers, and others. These numbered in 1921 some 550 (Uganda Government Census 1921).

Possibly it is to the smallness of the artisan and shopkeeper sector that we might attribute the lack of political consciousness in Teso agrarian society. Throughout its colonial history, commerce and trade were largely in the hands of Asians and other non-Iteso, many of them Muslims. The grievances of the peasantry were thus often deflected onto resentment of aliens and intruders. Nevertheless, given that smallholder economies are not characterized by the considerable indebtedness that marks plantations, hacienda and sharecropping regions (although most certainly some existed), this potential for violence did not take on major proportions. Moreover, since many of Teso's alien traders were Muslims with African wives, local racialist antagonisms were muted. Indeed, one of the many contradictions of capitalism under colonial auspices was that the administration saw its role, specifically, as one of protecting the interests of the natives against alien, racialist exploitation. Abuses deriving from antagonistic producer-marketing relations were deflected, therefore, to the local level and solely to Africans. Levelling mechanisms checked Iteso entrepreneurship emergent from below, and efforts of ethnic or religious minorities to attain special recognition (e.g. those of the Bakenyi fishermen in the cotton-centric district) were ruled unnecessary and unprogressive. Nevertheless, it was among Bakenyi tax-payer that Teso's only tax riot broke out in 1955.

Nor, as elsewhere in Africa, can returning soldiers or returning migrants be looked upon as instigators of political movements. The former were easily asimilated by means of a joint administration-ginners scheme, into employment as guards or nightwatchmen. The latter, as we have seen, were extremely few.

Nor were women active in Teso politics in the pre-independence era, although one cannot be too sure of this since women rarely entered the written record in the district's archives and contemporary informants may have understated their role. This might well be accounted for by the demands placed upon them by subsistence cultivation. To this day most field labour is done with hoes alone and there are no forms of animal transportation. Moreover, as in many smallholder economies, while marketing arrangements for the commodity to be exported were excellent, those for the marketing of food crops were abysmal so that there needs be heavy reliance on the domestic unit, family economies, and localized exchange.

It is perhaps necessary to emphasize once again the destructuring of the previously diversified economy; the de-skilling of the Teso peasantry; the heavy labour, tax, and cultivation demands placed on the men, and the burdens of reproduction placed on the women. It is, indeed, commonplace to find that such populations, suffering constant food shortages and riddled with disease, are anything but politically active except where ultimate survival is at stake. Without doubt, too, the severe coercive measures that came immediately into play when any organized political movements were initiated from below contributed not a little to the docility of the Teso peasant.

CONCLUSION

Only further, more detailed, analysis of household economies and family histories can account for the multiplicity of forms that political consciousness and peasant protest took in Teso, its processual nature, and, above all, its continuities and discontinuities. Given that the production of cotton was, perhaps, the only constant throughout the entire period, other factors of political, social, and religious life take on considerable explanatory significance. One is remainded of Stuart Hall's comments on History and Culture, "If you expect there is some moment when His Majesty the Economy is going to stride forth and say, 'Hold on lads, I'm about to determine everything'—if you are really waiting for that moment, then good luck to you—for His Majesty is always not only acting and speaking through other levels, they are the principal languages of his ventriloquism. He constantly speaks in cultural and political and ideological terms" (1978 : 14).

To explain why political consciousness and struggle take the forms they do among the peasantry of Teso it is necessary to reiterate its history of conquest; the imposition and control of a racial division of labour; the use of coercion; the dependence upon women to maintain subsistence; the exploitation of men's labour in unskilled work gangs; but, above all, the unintended demographic consequences of population control for extractive purposes. As Geertz has noted: "Amid the fluctuations of policy, the colonial period consists, from the economic point of view, of one long attempt to bring (a region's) crops into the modern world, but not her peoples" (1963 : 48).

It is considerations such as these that sometimes make it difficult for the African scholar, as yet, to relate his work to studies of peasantry elsewhere. The gradual evolution of a peasantry appears a myth; analyses in terms of household economies and agricultural production alone are inadequate; and peasant transformations appear to be misunderstood. Perhaps a closer study of historical peasantries in terms of regimes of domination and patterns of continental or global trade might bring the two more closely into line. Certainly, this appears to be the way ahead in studies of peasantries in Africa (Palmer and Parsons 1977; Ranger 1978).

REFERENCES

Alavy, H. (1973): "Peasant Classes and Primordial Loyalties", *Journal of Peasant Studies* 1, 1, 23-62.

Cavailhe, J. (1976) : "L'analyse leniniste de la decomposition de la paysannerie", *Critiques de l'economie politique* 23, 110-143.

Church Missionary Society Archives (CMS).

Emwanu, G. (1965) : "The Reception of Alien Rule in Teso 1896-1927", *Uganda Journal* 31, 2, 171-82.

Etxezerreta, M. (1977) : "La evolución de la agricultura campesina", *Agricultura y Sociedad* 5, 51-142.

Fallers, L.A. (1961) : "Are African Cultivators to be called Peasants?" *Current Anthropology* 2, 2, 108-110.

Geertz, C. (1963) : *Agricultural Involution.*

Greaves, I. (1935) : *Modern Production among Backward Peoples.*

Hall, S. (1978) : "Marxism and Culture", *Radical History Review* 18, 5-14.

Lenin (1897) (1967) : The Development of Capitalism in Russia.

　　　　(1910) (1967) : "The Capitalist System of Modern Agriculture", Collected Works, Vol. 16, 427-472.

Marx, K. (1963) : *The Eighteenth Brumaire of Louis Bonaparte.*

Paige, J.G. (1975) : *Agrarian Revolution : Social Movements and Export Agriculture in the Underdeveloped World.*

Palmer, R. and N. Parsons (eds.) (1977) : *The Roots of Rural Poverty in Southern and Central Africa.*

Post, K. (1972) : "Peasantization and Rural Political Movements in Western Africa", *European Journal of Sociology* 13, 2, 223-54.

Ranger, T.O. (1978) : "Growing from the Roots : Reflections on Peasant Research in Central and Southern Africa, *Journal of Southern African Studies* 5, 1, 99-133.

Scott, J.C. (1976) : *The Moral Economy of the Peasant : Rebellion and Subsistence in Southeast Asia.*

Shanin, T. (1978) : "Defining Peasants: Conceptualisations and De-Conceptualisations, Old and New in a Marxist Debate", Paper presented at a panel "Social Anthropology of Peasantry" at the Tenth International Congress of Anthropological and Ethnological Sciences, Lucknow, India. (See above)

Szurek, J.C. (1977) : "Les paysans de Lenine : 'classe' ou 'strate'?" *L'Homme et la Societe*, 45-46, July-Dec., 141-168.

Testo District Archives (TDA)

Thompson, E.P. (1963) : *The Making of the English Working Class.*

Todd, J. (1927) : *The Cotton World.*

Uganda Protectorate Government Census (1921).

Vincent, J. (1974) : "The changing roles of small towns in the Agrarian Structure of East Africa", *Journal of Commonwealth and Comparative Politics* 12, 3, 261-275.

(1977) : "Colonial Chiefs and the Making of Class : a Case Study from Teso, Eastern Uganda", *Africa* 47, 2, 140-159.

(1978) : "Political Anthropology : Manipulative Strategies", *Annual Review of Anthropology* 7, 175-194.

(1981) : *Teso in Transformation : Peasant and Class in Eastern Africa, 1890-1927.*

Wilson, G. (1941/42) : *An Essay on the Economics of De-Tribalisation,* Rhodes-Livingstone Institute Papers 5 and 6.

Wolf, E.R. (1966) : *Peasants.*

Worsley, P. (1974) : "The State of Theory and the Status of Theory", *Sociology* 8, 1-17.

Zimmerman, E.W. (1972) : *World Resources and Industries.*

Cognitive Aspects of Peasant Livelihood in Hungary

TAMÁS HOFER

In the past few years there have been heated debates on the question whether peasantry could be defined as a basic human type, as a peculiar culture. I am in agreement with the views expressed by Sydel Silverman and Eric Wolf at this conference that priority has to be given to those political-economic criteria which determine the existence of peasant groups in a given society. Accordingly, social position and social action have causal priority over the "way of perceiving it" (Mintz 1973 : 96-97, quoted by Silverman).

In the following I will write about the knowledge and the system of measurements and allocation used by Hungarian peasants (or more exactly, by the inhabitants of one village, Átány) in the course of their everyday agricultural work (cf. Fel and Hofer 1969, 1972, 1973, 1974; Hofer 1979). I will take the practical knowledge and the measurements to be a cognitive and partly ideological constituent of their economic activities. These were brought about by a given set of natural, historical, and social circumstances. This cognitive system changed, together with the economic activities of the people of Atany, integrating new elements, but maintaining a certain degree of independence and stability.

Following Karl Polanyi, economy can be taken as an "instituted process of interaction between man and his environment" (Polanyi 1957 : 248). This system of knowledge is an important factor of this "institutedness". It was by means of this cognitive system that the people of Átány perceived and evaluated the peculiarities of their land, climate, plants, and animals, their own labour-power and that of their draft animals, etc. Quantitative rules and traditional modes of measurements helped them to ration labour, food, fodder, etc. according to changing circumstances, and to determine the priorities of their use. This knowledge and system of measurements, among other things, meant that for the people of Átány their own peasant work had a form and style which was consciously recognized, and which differentiated the work done by family production from that done in a non-peasant situation, e.g. similar work done in big manors. However, it was not employed by all people in Átány, but rather was restricted to those owning land.

In the course of everyday routine agricultural work the peasant is constantly faced with choices and decisions. When sowing by hand, should he plough deep or shallow? Should he turn the seeds deep into the ground with the plough, or should be just throw them on the ploughed earth and thinly cover them up with the harrow—or should he divide his seeds, and plant half of them deep and half of them nearer to the surface? Hungary belongs to a transitional climatic zone where three or four years of continental climate are usually followed by one or two years of oceanic climate. Continental years bring cold winters and dry, warm summers, which favour deep planting, while the rainy summers of the oceanic climate favour seeds planted nearer to the surface.

When should the family head, the *gazda,* mow the lucerne and the clover? If it receives rain while drying it loses much of its value, but if he waits too long to mow it the stem will become stringy, the plant will bear flowers and thus lose value as fodder. These decisions then influence the crop's yield, and affect the results of the year's work.

A number of anthropological works dealing with peasant farm management are concerned with those decisions which articulate the relationship of the peasant farm with the outer economic system. How much do they produce for the market, and how much for subsistence? How do they react to changes of prices in markets? In what way do they find a solution to the "peasant's dilemma", i.e. that he has to reconcile maintenance of his family with the demands of the outside world (Wolf 1966 : 12-17)? The decisions mentioned here are on a technological, operational level, and can be clearly distinguished from those economic choices which Raymond Firth places on the managerial and policy levels (Firth 1965 : 28-31, Ortiz 1973). Unfortunately, commonplace characterizations of peasant work as "a simple technology" which can be "ingenious, marvellously fitted to a particular environment, require high levels of skills and performance but still be very simple" (Nash 1966:20), obscure the actual complexity of everyday decisions of organizing work and choosing technology.

TRADITIONAL PEASANT KNOWLEDGE IN ÁTÁNY

Naturally the assembly of agricultural tools available in Átány (situated in industrialized Hungary) was much more complex than that of peasants of other times, or of other economically less developed territories. Nevertheless, there are possibilities of decision-making everywhere with reference to technology, timing, and priority of certain jobs, and it is always necessary to evaluate natural surroundings. This latter is all the more important when technology is of a lower standard. Where today the cooperative of Átány sows a single crop over a vast uniformly deep-ploughed and chemically manured area, a couple of decades ago the peasants who preceded the cooperative were still carefully considering micro-differences in the quality of soil, even to the point of discerning different varieties of both black and "pale" alkaline soils, because with the technology of the time knowledge of these differences could make the difference between success and failure.

One can read about peasant knowledge in the literature on cognitive anthropology. These works, however, put their emphasis on the logic of conceptual differentiation. One can, however, imagine such a mapping of the same knowledge which connects these experiences, used in understanding and evaluating a certain situation, to the decision points of peasant farming. For instance, the people of Átány know several types of grass and weed. They would use this knowledge, for instance, in deciding which pasture to assign to horses, cattle, and sheep, each of which prefers different kinds of grass. Moreover, the quality of hay depends on the quality and moisture-content of the soil of the meadow on which it grows. Moisture-content, however, can change from year to year according to the amount of precipitation. The highest quality hay is produced on dry pale alkaline soils, but the amount of harvest is little. This type of hay is called "sweet" and "fat", and it is given only to the most valued horses. The hay harvest from lower-lying and more humid meadows is more abundant but "sour", and is generally given to cattle. The people of Átány think that every grass and plant "is always there" in the soil, but they do not grow every year. Only those sprout which have had rain and favourable weather "at their sprouting time". As the distribution of rainfall can be part of a yearly changing pattern, one can predict the weather of the following year from the spring sprouting of wild plants. If for instance there is more than average of "bran-grass" (*Erophila verna*), then one can expect a dry year.

Much emotion—feelings of risk, anxiety, and joy—is associated with these everyday technological and organizational decisions of peasant life. Evans-Pritchard found among the Nuer that anxiety for their cattle was a central theme determining their entire lives: "at heart they are herdsmen, and the only labour in which they delight is care of cattle. They not only depend on cattle for many of life's necessities, but they have the herdsman's outlook on the world" (Evans-Pritchard 1940 : 16). Similarly, it could be stated about the people of Átány (and many other peasants) that the central theme of their lives is to tend the plants, so they could grow, and to rear animals which are healthy. Old people fondly recall certain outstanding harvests as their biggest successes, and say that they could not imagine greater joy than when their mares gave birth to healthy foals. On the other hand, the death of an animal, or a hailstorm destroying a crop, meant almost the same degree of disaster as the death or serious illness of an able-bodied member of the family.

THE HOEING OF A MAIZE-FIELD IN ÁTÁNY:

Átány lies on the northern part of the Great Hungarian Plain, and with its roughly 2,500 inhabitants, it is a medium-sized village in Hungary (cf. Fel and Hofer 1969). In 1848 its peasants were freed from serfdom. In the course of the regional specialization of agriculure which took place at the end of the wheat-boom in the 1870s, Átány and the surrounding area continued to produce wheat for the market. As wheat was the main plant for subsistence and for feudal duties in past centuries, the structure of peasant farms changed less with increases in market production than in the case of territories which switched to the production of meat, milk, vegetables, or fruit. In 1868 the compulsory three-course rotation system was partly abolished, then in 1901 completely ended, and in 1927 farm-plots were consolidated, each peasant's holdings being drawn together into one or two plots. In spite of this, until the collectivization (1959) the old ratio of production remained more or less unchanged: one-third of the arable land was taken by winter crops, mostly wheat; another third by spring crops, corn and barley; and the final third, formerly left fallow, was now taken up by fodder plants and cash crops. Barely 20 per cent of the inhabitants could maintain themselves from their land. The rest were either landless or had only a small amount of land, and were thus forced to work on nearby large estates, in towns, or for land-owning peasants in the village. The fields of Átány were cultivated by human labour and by teams of horses or oxen; the ploughs were factory-made with steel breast-boards, and cereals were sown by machine drills and threshed by machine. However, artificial fertilizers were still virtually unknown.

One of the most time-consuming tasks in Átány before 1959 was hoeing crops by hand, and weeding continued to be done by hand even after the cooperatives were established. Plants requiring hoeing (mostly maize) were grown on roughly 30 per cent of the arable land. Wheat was the most important cereal for humans, maize for animals. Pork and lard, together with bread, were the most important element of family subsistence. Poorer people tried to obtain their wheat by working as harvesters on large estates (before 1945), for which they were paid in kind. They obtained maize to fatten their pigs through sharecropping. In May and June hoeing was continually done by poor and rich alike; this was only interrupted by spring sowings and fodder mowing. This common and simple work can serve as a good example of what I have said about portioning and use of knowledge.

Maize had to be hoed three times in the season. The aim of hoeing was loosening earth, weeding, and thinning. It could be sown by seed-drill, or planted in small "nests" made by a hoe, but most often the seed was dropped by hand by a person walking behind the plough. In the latter case, rows were three furrows apart, and seeds were planted at large intervals within each row, 2-4 seeds being planted together. After the first hoeing, two plants would be left. After the second hoeing, only one would be left, and the wild offshoots would be broken off and used for fodder.

In land-owning peasant families the whole family worked together, and often they obtained help by labour exchange. One *hold* (0.57 hectares) could be hoed by four mature persons in one day. Work was organized in such a way that no group would ever be mobilized for a part day's work, but only for one or more full days. Work was apportioned, first among members of the family, by rows. Every adult member worked simultaneously on two rows, while adolescents were assigned one row at a time. If an older or younger member of the work group had difficulty in coping with his or her row, the others would help out. (For instance, the head of the family might have his daughter hoe the row next to his, so that he could help her if needed.)

Shorter and longer breaks followed each other regularly in the course of the day's work. When the family reached the cornfield, which in Átány was strip-shaped, the *gazda* estimated by eye the work to be done that day. This he could do because of his long years of experience in cultivating the same plot, and through his knowledge of the working capacity of the family. When my host, József Kakas, went out to his 19 *öls* (= 34.8m) wide cornfield with his family, four persons altogether, he reckoned that they would do one *hold* (0.57 hectares, 1,600 square *öls*) in one day. Of this they would do 400 square *ols* before breakfast, between 5 a.m. and about 7.30, another 600 square *öls* were to be done each before and after the midday meal. This meant that when József Kakas started his two rows from the left-hand corner of the field he rose only after roughly 22-24 *öls* (40-44 m). In this way he marked out the length of the *pászta*. *Pászta* is that length of the row which they do at a stretch without once standing upright. The *pászta,* however, also marked out that portion of the band-shaped plot of land which had to be completed before breakfast. Reaching the end of the *pászta* they stopped, and if somebody was left behind, the others would turn back into his row to help him. Then the group went back along the rows parallel with those already hoed. Thus, they went to and fro, with short stops at each end, until they completed the portion to be hoed before breakfast.

From breakfast till lunch-time they completed two *pászta*s, but these were shorter, only 15-16 *öls* in length (27-29 m). Thus, they could stand up sooner and turns were more frequent. Between these two *pászta*s there was a break long enough to smoke a cigarette. There was a similar break in the middle of the afternoon's work as well. The lunch-break lasted one hour, and by 5 p.m. they finished work and could start for home. This kind of portioning of work divided the labour, the time, and the land to be worked, and was closely connected with traditional times of meals and breaks. The length of the *pászta* itself varied

The Social Anthropology of Peasantry

according to circumstances. In the case of dry and hard soils, which were difficult to work, it could be shortened, of if they wanted to accomplish more than the average in one day they could make the *pászta* longer, and thus hasten the pace of work.

A work group consisting of strong, young persons, as contrasted with the Kakàs family, would divide the day's work into three units, instead of five. This meant that they took fewer short breaks, and could therefore hoe a larger area during the day. Even those who went out alone to hoe would mark out in advance what they wanted to accomplish during the day. Knowing constantly where they stood, and how much was still to be done, gave them a certain sense of security and the satisfaction of work properly done.

This method of apportioning work, howevr, was lacking when they hoed as day-labourers on a manorial estate (before 1945). Working hours were neither longer nor the expected output greater. Day-labourers, several dozens of them at a time, set out side by side in one row. The overseers went behind them, and from time to time gave them permission to stop and rest. The rest period was neither longer nor shorter than at home. Nevertheless, the lack of the familiar pattern made this work unfamiliar and confused, and the people of Átány did not like it.

The hoes of the members of the family were unequal in size. The biggest was the man's hoe, next the woman's hoe, while the smallest of all was that of the adolescents, "the hoe of the learners". The size of the hoe did not increase or decrease the work to be done. A smaller hoe moved less earth and was easier to handle, but necessitated more movements. Especially strong men used the "vine-stock-covering hoe", bigger than the usual male hoe, generally used only in the sandy soil of the vineyard.

There were also differences in the hoe handles and the way they were attached to the hoe. These were determined by the size and the personal work habits of each person. The handle had to reach to the users' waist. The angle between the head of the hoe and the handle could be altered to fit the posture of the person using it. Some individuals preferred to work in a bent position, and others more upright. This angle could be adapted also to the quality of the soil. A dry, hard soil had to be cut with the hoe, so its setting was closer to a right angle. In a looser, soft soil it was to be drawn, so it had to be set closer to an acute angle. Some people, when switching from softer, black soil to harder pale soil, set their hoe differently, while others retained the same hoe setting and instead made changes in their body position to achieve the same result. A person whose hoe was not right (e.g. the handle too heavy, the shape inconvenient, or the hoe not properly balanced) also had to make adjustments "with her or his body". In any case, the adjustment required additional labour.

Maintenance was also needed during the work. If the soil is wet, it will stick to the hoe and must be cleaned off with a small scraper at the end of each *pászta*.

Sometimes two individuals working side by side would hit their hoes together to clean them. When the earth is especially dry the hoe has to be frequently sharpened; this can be done in the field with a file, but usually the hoe must be beaten with a hammer on a small anvil at home. This job is always performed by men.

Hoeing is tiring, but it is not the most demanding work. The strength needed for the job, in the view of the people of Átány, is derived from food and rest. For hoeing certain "strength-giving" foods were regarded as adequate, but not of the best quality. In winter, which was a time of rest and not of work, they took only two meals daily, conserving the "strength-giving" bacon and meat for other times of the year. From the beginning of work in the spring they took three meals daily. Two meals were eaten in the fields, and these consisted only of cold foods: bread, bacon, sausages, and plum jam. Only the evening meal would be a warm meal, perhaps a soup or a stew. During the most demanding work, the harvest and transporting the crops to the village, the number of meals increased to four. Moreover, the workers were provided with hot food not only at night, but also at noon; in addition, the best bacon and meat were reserved for this time of the year.

In the hoeing of a single plot of maize by a family team, we see the differences between sexes and ages, and the directing role of the head of the family. By simply using their tools, the members of the team also enact their roles in the family structure. Further, we see in the hoeing the system of work organization, which is built simultaneously on units of time, effort, and area. This was also a moral system, since it expressed the norm of the village. To work less would be lazy, and to work more would be too harsh.

CONCEPTUAL STRUCTURES IN PEASANT WORK PROCESSES

The knowledge required to hoe maize was part of a coherent body of knowledge regarding certain themes. The consideration of soil characteristics expressed in maize hoeing was part of a theory of soils in the thinking of Átány peasants. They possessed extensive knowledge of soil types, distinguishing many variants of the black soil, the paler alkaline soil, and the sandy soil of the vineyards. They also classified soils as "cold" and "warm", which also takes into account the degree of moisture. Maize thrives best on "cold" black earth, but the system of crop rotation may sometimes require that maize be sown in a warm soil. The villagers have also a theory about the productive strength of the earth, and how this is modified by its winter "rest" or resting in fallow, by ploughing, hoeing, and manuring, and how much "strength" is taken from the soil by various plants. This knowledge was transmitted predominantly in verbal form, in statements and rules. A significant part of the peasant's agricultural knowledge is, however, not verbalized, and is connected to work movements, and to experiences with particular tools. For example, in the spring the peasant goes to the field and cuts the soil with his hoe, to see whether it is dry enough for planting. If a peasant buys a new plot of land, it will take five to six years before he is sufficiently acquainted with its nature to make this test accurately. During this time, he will probably experience both wet and dry years, and will experiment with manuring and with different crops. (It was not exceptional'for a family to have as many as 15 different kinds of crops sown in any given year.)

Peasants are interacting with the earth, their crops, their animals, and their tools. By this means they assess their work capacity and gain and store knowledge about agricultural processes. Thus, studying the peasants' implements provides a means of learning peasant cognitive maps (Fel and Hofer 1974).

The system of relating time, space, and work is also part of a broader conceptual system which penetrates many other aspects of peasant life. It was a system of measures applied to the evaluation of resources and estimation of yields, the allocation of land, labour, time, food, fodder, and money. It contained different sets of interrelated measurements for farms and households of different size, and marked out the levels of "enough", "too much", and "insufficient". This conceptual system was one of the peasant's basic means of grasping his own economic activities. The measurements formed a flexible system which could be modified according to circumstances, such as good and bad years, family burdens, and the changing demands of the outer world.

The speed of hoeing depended on the weather. If the spring came too late and the rain was heavy, the work of spring and summer would get behind. If maize and turnips were ready to be hoed at the same time the turnips (or sugar beets) would get priority, since weeds could do more damage to those crops. However, moving hay and fodder takes precedence over all kinds of hoeing. The third hoeing of maize can be postponed, or even neglected altogether, without great effect on the final harvest, but hay and fodder crops must be harvested at the proper time or they will be lost altogether.

The quantity of sausages and bacon taken to the hoeing depended in part on the size of the pigs slain during the previous winter, which further depended in part on the amount of maize produced in the previous year, that is, whether or not they had favourable weather and did the hoeing properly three times.

This example shows the constant interplay of the spheres of production and consumption in the thinking of the peasants. The work of the whole year did not aim at a summarized "income", but it was a bundle of many different branches, in which each branch had a definite task or use for the family. The maize was used to fatten the pig (and was given to chickens, horses, and cows as well). The pig gave fat, bacon, meat, and sausages, processed by smoking, which supplied the power to work through the whole following year. (It was complemented by poultry, slain in the course of the year. In a well-to-do house a sheep might also be slain in autumn). Pigs were butchered around Christmas-time. When a pig was butchered, the peasants viewed it almost like a map of the most important work periods of the coming year, because it was decided beforehand which part of the pig should be reserved to be eaten at which period. The four hams were earmarked for the harvest and the time of transporting the crops to the village, the spinal bacon was set aside for spring work in the vineyard (for it could be easily toasted on a spit in the vineyard), the leaf-lard was kept for the spring ploughing, while the most delicious bacon (of the belly) was also saved for the harvest.

Even the money coming into the house was part of this system. It was "earmarked", as Mary Douglas (1967 : 119) would say, for particular purposes— as if it actually had labels attached to it indicating its use. The sums gained from the sale of wheat and animals constituted "the money of the farm", which was controlled by the household head and was destined to buy tools, animals, the upper garments of men, and the footwear of the whole family, and to pay the taxes. "The money of the household", obtained from the selling of milk, eggs, fruit, vegetables, and poultry, was handled by the mistress of the house. This served for the purchase of salt, spices, paraffin for the lamp, dresses for women, and underclothing for men. The woman of the house would also give pocket-money from this fund to a bachelor son, so that he could visit the local pub. Some families had special customs, for instance the Kakas family regularly purchased the blue vitriol necessary for spraying the vineyard solely out of the sale of their surplus beans.

IMPLICATIONS

The foregoing account of the agricultural knowledge of Átány peasants calls attention to the cognitive component of peasant economic systems in general. Through analysis of the peasants' agricultural knowledge we might gain access to the conceptual world in which they do their everyday work and make their operational decisions. Furthermore, we might approach the social and economic characteristics of peasant societies from a new angle.

At first glance, it seems obvious that peasants understand their agricultural job. Acquisition of knowledge about farming is part of the general socialization process in peasant families. Usually, the skills and the knowledge of husbandry are transmitted to young people along the same lines of inheritance by which land and equipment descend to members of a new generation. Ownership of land has a crucial importance in determining an individual's position in village society, and numerous anthropological studies deal with the distribution and transmission of property rights among peasants. Much less attention was paid to the distribution of agricultural expertise in the same societies. Hungarian examples indicate that the distribution of knowledge might also show great inequalities, and that these differences have an impact on the social position of individuals, too.

In Átány, on a closer inspection, we can discern at least three different types of agricultural training and expertise, connected to three different strata of the local society. The whole cycle of agricultural work was known and practised only in families of land-owning peasants who also owned draft animals. They could have a car, and could do the ploughing and harrowing with their horses and oxen. The sons of these families could learn how to rear and breed the "big animals", horses and cattle. The experience and the knowledge of villagers without animals were more limited: they did only manual work, and had at best a cow and/or a pig in their courtyards. Finally, farm-hands on large estates who lived with their families outside the village in manors, had an even more limited range of experience.

Since the different grades of peasant skills could be acquired only by growing up in peasant families of sufficient standing, the training of the children had an impact on their later careers. The lack of the appropriate skills and knowledge hampered poor people's attempts to climb up into higher layers of the local society. Before World War II, in Hungarian villages there was a general trend of downward mobility, facilitated by the fragmentation of holdings through equal division of property among heirs. If a peasant managed somehow to buy land and draft animals, he often got in trouble with his newly acquired horses or oxen. It was risky for an inexperienced man to keep horses, since inattention or a mistake could lead to their injury, illness or even death. On the other hand, servants living on large estates tried to improve the career chances of their sons by hiring them out as farm-hands to land-owning peasants in the village, and thus help them acquire at least some of the villagers' agricultural skills. (For lack of space I cannot discuss either individual differences in knowledge and skills, or the role of personal competence in specific tasks such as the healing and curing of animals, manufacturing of tools, etc.)

Skills were learned in families, but the whole body of agricultural knowledge was somehow consolidated and levelled out by the village as a local society. Looking for the mechanisms of these integration processes (which nevertheless left many individual differences untouched), we may refer to some circumstances of the work activities. At the time of our research, Átány already had lost most of its former characteristics as a corporate community. No communal restrictions limited the free use of the individually owned parcels. However, most of the farms had a similar sowing plan with the same main crops. In maize-hoeing time, nearly everybody in the village was working in the maize fields. Everybody could see who reached their plots early and who arrived late, whose plot was weedy and whose was clean. The fact that everybody's work performance was exposed to public scrutiny furthered conformity to common standards.

Public opinion did not, however, favour traditional practices without qualification. Taking again the example of maize, we can observe the rapid spread of several innovations which were facilitated by the visible, open demonstration of their advantages in the fields: introduction of new species with bigger yields around 1910, introduction of hoeing three times instead of two around 1927, the use of cultivators from 1940 on, etc. Taking the size and the basic structure of Átány farms (with a combined subsistence and market orientation) as given, as determined by political-economic factors, in this frame the Átány peasants' cognitive system showed a remarkable capacity to incorporate technological innovations. This attitude can be contrasted with economically more backward communities where the cognitive system worked as "defensive ignorance" (Wolf 1955).

The example of the hoeing of a maize-field shows, on an elementary level, how social, moral, and symbolic connotations are attached to the shapes of tools, to work movements, and to the division of time into units of work. Doing their daily work, the actors could have the moral satisfaction of acting properly, in accord with the norms of the village. Further, hoeing in the particular way described became an expression of their peasant identity. Dissimilar experiences with hoeing in non-peasant situations, in large estates for instance, might have reinforced this feeling. On a more general level, we can state that the agricultural technology and system of management utilized in peasant farms served as a cultural idom which distinguished peasants and non-peasants, and among the peasants land-owning and landless strata.

In Átány, prestige was won first of all by the ownership of fine and well-tended horses who raised their heads proudly and stepped delicately. An informant said: "We proper peasants knew about the horse; we raised the good colts. One could recognize a true-born peasant by his bearing when driving through the village—by the way he held the whip in his hand" (Fel and Hofer 1969 : 386). Here clearly a notion of style and of aesthetic value appears. Reference is made to the acquisition of peasant skills through socialization in land-owning families. According to the informant, a man who was not born into a team-owner family could never learn the proper style of rearing horses. In 1945, several landless villagers received land in the course of the agrarian reform, and some of them managed to buy horses. The "true-born peasants" never ceased to criticize them for the lack of the proper Átány style in their driving.

Only land-owning, self-sufficient peasants could practise the art of apportioning food, fodder, and other material means for a whole year. Families in other strata tried to imitate this sophisticated system of planning, evaluating, and allocation, with limitations. The landless day-labourers undertook harvesting for payment in kind to secure wheat for the whole year, and acquired maize through sharecropping in order to feed pigs, so as to secure lard, bacon, and meat for the year. Farmhands on manors, bound by a yearly contract, had even less opportunity to practise long-range planning, saving, and economizing with reserves. They got their wages in kind at the end of each quarter, but they often did not have enough to eat in the last weeks of the quarter.

For the land-owning peasants, the urban way of provisioning was even more distasteful. Átány people who became workers in urban factories had to "take the flour from a paper bag", and had to go to the shop to get new supplies. Land-owning peasants, however, formerly reserved the wheat for the whole year, going to the mill four times a year for grinding. The flour for bread and the fine flour for noodles and cakes stood in sacks, and the mistress of the house took a portion for a week, out of which she baked the bread and supplied her family continually. Cooking from the paper bag would have been just as formless and strange for her as hoeing in the endless fields of the manorial estate.

CONCLUSION

These data reveal that Átány was a highly stratified local society in the mid-twentieth century, and that the life-style of land-owning peasants served as a model for a large part of the landless population (cf. Fel and Hofer 1973). In the process of integration into an industrializing national economy, peasants were keenly aware of the differences between peasant and non-peasant life-ways.

Agricultural work processes were imbedded into conceptual structures with positive social and moral connotations, which gave the villagers the consciousness of acting in a right and proper way when tilling the soil. The work processes were part of a positive self-perception and self-identification of the peasants. They thought that their work in the fields was of fundamental importance for the existence of society, and regarded their practical knowledge as at least equal in worth to that acquired from books. The relative independence and self-sufficiency of land-owning families was highly valued. Átány peasants not infrequently expressed pity for the ethnographers visiting them, because they did not "eat bread grown on their own soil" (Hofer 1979 : 91).

In spite of the self-assurance and pride of the "people of the soil", their life in fact depended to a high degree on forces beyond their control. The harvest was "in the palm of God's hand"; the unpredictable climate of the Hungarian basin could heavily damage or destroy the crops. During the period of field work in Átány, a strict state control was imposed on private farms and a system of compulsory delivery of agricultural products was introduced. The self-assurance and pride in the minds of Átány people was complemented by a consciousness of being nearly defenceless, and exposed to the blows and pressures of the surrounding world.

This duality of self-perception appears at other places and at other points in the history of peasants. I quote a historic example, a chapter of William Langland's allegorical poem *Piers Ploughman*. Written in the 1370s, it is considered by historians as an expression of the new class-consciousness of English peasants on the eve of the big uprising. In Book V a motley crowd of people—knights, clergyman, ladies, merchants, and beggars—are moving about a large field, trying to find "Truth", who is conceived as a person. Nobody knows where to look for him. Then a peasant, Piers Ploughman, steps forward and cries: "I know Him, as well as a scholar knows his books." He explains further that it was Truth who taught him how "to plant ... how to ditch and dig, sow and thresh and herd the beasts". It means that the peasant's work *per se* has a moral quality, and even, therefore, is superior to all other trades and occupations, and that the peasant's knowledge is equal in value to the learned knowledge of scholars (Langland 1966 : 77).

REFERENCES

Douglas, Mary (1967): Primitive rationing: A study in controlled exchange. In Raymond Firth (ed.), Themes in economic anthropology, London: Tavistock. A.S.A. Monographs 6. 119-147.

Evans-Pritchard, E.E. (1940) : The Nuer. Oxford: Oxford University Press.

Fél, Edit and Tamás Hofer (1969): Proper peasants. Traditional life in a Hungarian village. Chicago: Aldine. Viking Fund Publications in Anthropology 46.

—— (1972) : Bauerliche Denkweise in Wirtschaft und Haushalt. Eine ethnographische Untersuchung uber das ungarische Dorf Atany. Gottingen : Otto Schwartz.

—— (1973) : Tanyakert's, patron-client relations and political factions in Atany. American Anthropologist 75. 787-801.

—— (1974) : Gerate der Atanyer Bauern. Budapest : Akademiai Kiado, Brede : Royal Danish Academy of Sciences.

Hofer, Tamás (1979) : Hungarian ethnographers in a Hungarian village. In, George M. Foster, Thayer Scudder, Elisabeth Colson, Robert V. Kemper, Long-term field research in social anthropology. New York : Academic Press, 85-101.

Firth, Raymond (1965) ; Primitive Polynesian economy, London : Routledge & Kegan Paul.

Langland, William (1966) : Piers Ploughman. Translated into Modern English with an introduction by J.F. Goodridge. London : Penguin Books Ltd.

Mintz, Sidney (1973) : A note on the definition of peasantries. The Journal of Peasant Studies Vol. 1, 91-106.

Nash, Manning (1966) : Primitive and peasant economic systems. San Francisco : Chandler.

Oritiz, Sutti Reissing (1973): Uncertainties in peasant farming. London: The Athlone Press, London School of Economics Monographs on Social Anthropology, No. 46.

Polányi, Karl (1951) : The economy as instituted process. In Karl Polanyi, Conard M. Arensberg, Harry W. Pearson, Trade and market in early empires. New York : The Free Press. 243-270.

The People's Commune and the Socialist Transformation of the Chinese Peasantry

TSE KA-KUI

The purpose of this paper is to provide a perspective on the nature and direction of transformation of the rural people's commune in China. I shall begin with an examination of the Chinese formulation of the imperative of eliminating the "three major differences" (between town and country, worker and peasant, mental and manual labour) in socialist transition, relating it to the classical Marxist formulations of the question and the historical experience of the Soviet Union. This will be followed by an analysis of the basic structure and internal dynamic of the people's commune system with a view to clarifying its role in serving as the basic unit for the "proper handling" of the contradictions between the peasants, the collective, and the state, as well as in facilitating the narrowing of the "three major differences".

THE "THREE MAJOR DIFFERENCES": THEORETICAL AND COMPARATIVE PERSPECTIVES

The launching of the Great Leap Forward and the formation of the people's communes marked a critical turning point in the Chinese road to socialism. A hallmark of the Great Leap Forward strategy was the attempt to simultaneously develop agriculture and industry, central and local industry, advanced and indigenous technology ("walking on two legs"), and to narrow the "three major differences" (between town and country, worker and peasant, and mental and manual labour). The most important surviving institution specifically designed to accomplish this gigantic historic task is the rural people's commune, instituted on a nation-wide scale in 1958 at the height of the agricultural collectivization campaign.

The formulation of "eliminating the three major differences" as a central task in socialist transition was a novel formulation; it was systematically put forth for the first time only during the Great Leap Forward. It signifies a major departure from the Soviet theory and practice of "socialist transition", and constitutes a characteristic feature of the Chinese approach to socialist revolution and socialist construction. Although there has emerged a growing body of literature devoted to the analysis of the variety of measures and policies relating to the gradual elimination of the "three major differences" in China, there have been few attempts in the West to examine the theoretical significance of this formulation in terms of the Marxist theory of socialist transition. In this part of the paper, I shall briefly examine this vital theoretical question.

To the founding fathers of scientific socialism, the division and opposition of town and country, industry and agriculture, in their modern forms, are the critical culmination of the division and specialization of labour which, though it did not begin with capitalism, was developed within it to an extraordinary and transforming degree. The specifically capitalist development of the productive forces involves not only a massive shift of human and material resources in favour of urban concentrations, but also a conquest over the countryside, which becomes "ruralized", since it by no means represented an exclusively agricultural milieu in the past. From being a centre of all kinds of production, the country becomes "agriculture", i.e. a seperate industry for food and raw materials, separated in turn into various specialized types of farming, districts, etc.

In *Capital,* Marx shows that capital first seizes control of the productive process *outside* the town: "in the country side, in villages lacking guilds". This corresponds to the first historical form of capitalist control of production, that of manufacture, in which the subsumption of labour to capital remains external and formal. With the advent of machine production capital seizes hold of the real substance of the labour process, dynamically reshaping and diversifying all branches of production by the technical-organizational transformation of the productive process. The removal of all fetters on the mobility of labour and the separation of one secondary process after another from agriculture (given the corresponding revolutions in transport) open the way to an accelerated, permanent urbanization based on the "concentration of the motive power of society in big cities" (Marx 1976) and the subordination of agriculture as merely one branch of industry. The dominance of the town is no longer externally imposed: it is now reproduced as part of the accumulation process, transforming and spatially reallocating rural production "from within".

The progressive character of the separation between town and country, industry and agriculture in the historical epoch of capitalism was unambiguously recognized in the writings of Marx and Engels. But to them, the unprecedented growth in production under capitalism also creates the necessity and conditions for ultimately combining the two forms of production and eliminating the distinctions between town and country. As Marx put it:

In the sphere of agriculture, large-scale industry has a more revolutionary effect than elsewhere, for the reason that it annihilates the bulwark of the old society, the "peasant", and substitutes for him the wage-labourer. Thus the need for social transformation, and the antagonism of the classes, reaches the same level in the countryside as it has attained in the towns. .... The capitalist mode of production completes the disintegration of the primitive familial union which bound agriculture and manufacture together when they were both at an undeveloped and childlike stage. But at the same time *it creates the material conditions for a new and higher synthesis, a union of agriculture and industry on the basis of the forms that have developed during the period of their antagonistic isolation.*

(Marx 1976: 637, emphasis is mine.)

In *Anti-Duhring,* Engels has also written:

Only a society which enables its productive forces to mesh harmoniously on the basis of one single vast plan can allow industry to be dispersed over the whole country in the way best adapted to its own development and to the maintenance and development of the other elements of production. Accordingly, the abolition of the antithesis between town and country is not merely possible. It has become a direct necessity of industrial production itself, just as it has become a necessity of agricultural production and of public health to boot. Only the fusion of town and country can eliminate the present poisoning of air, water and land, only such fusion will change the situation of the masses now languishing in the towns, and enable their excrement to be used for the production of plants instead of for the production of disease.

(Engels 1976: 385)

The abolition of the antithesis and division between town and country has been a classic objective of revolutionary socialism since Marx and Engels' days. The *Communist Manifesto* called for "the combination of agriculture with manufacturing industries; the gradual abolition of the distinction between town and country". Engels spoke of socialism as "abolishing the contrast between town and country. which has been brought to its extreme point by present-day capitalist society". To Marx and Engels, "the antagonism between town and country can exist only within the framework of private property. It is the most crass expression of the subjection of the individual under division of labour, under a definite activity forced upon him—a subjection which makes one man a restricted town animal and the other a restricted country animal, and daily creates anew the conflict between their interests." (Marx and Engels 1977:69).

Lenin, writing at the turn of this century, has argued that the separation between town and country is "one of the most profound and most general of the contradictions of the capitalist system" (Lenin 1965: 229). After the October Revolution, he repeatedly affirmed the long-term goal of eliminating the differences between town and country, worker and peasant, mental and manual labour. In *A Great Beginning,* he wrote,

> Clearly, in order to abolish classes completely, it is not enough to overthrow the exploiters, the land-owners and capitalists, not enough to abolish their rights of ownership; *it is necessary also to abolish all private ownership of the means of production, it is necessary to abolish the distinction between town and country, as well as the distinction between manual workers and brain workers.* (Lenin 1975: 172, emphasis mine.)

In another text written in the same year, Lenin put in more forceful terms the central importance of eliminating the differences between the worker and the peasant in socialist transition:

> We say that our goal is equality, and by that we mean the abolition of classes. Then the class distinction between workers and peasants should be abolished. That is exactly our object. A society in which the class distinction between workers and peasants still exists is neither a communist society nor a socialist society. True, if the word socialism is interpreted in a certain sense, it might be called a socialist society, but that would be mere sophistry, an argument about words. .... One thing is clear, and that is, that as long as the class distinction between workers and peasants exists, it is no use talking about equality, unless we want to bring grist to the mill of the bourgeoisie.   (Lenin 1965: 358-359).

Let us recapitulate our discussion thus far. To Marx, Engels, and Lenin, the separation and antithesis between town and country, mental and manual labour predated the emergence of the capitalist mode of production, but has since been greatly accentuated under it. The reproduction of the capitalist mode of production entails the continuous reproduction of this antithesis. The capitalist development of the productive forces, however, also laid the material foundations for the ultimate elimination of the antitheses and distinctions between town and country, industry and agriculture, mental and manual labour. One of the primary tasks in the period of "transition to communism" is precisely the gradual elimination of these differences.

It is important, however, to note that underlying this formulation is the basic assumption that the accomplishment of this historic task is premised on definite material conditions, the most important of which is the attainment of a sufficiently high level of development of the productive forces in the society concerned. This raises a number of fundamental but often neglected issues: In a society with a low level of development of production but in which the party of the proletariat has nevertheless seized state power, is it possible and/or necessary to eliminate the "three major differences" without having attained a high level of development of the productive forces? Or, to put it another way, are there any contradictions between the rapid development of the productive forces and the gradual elimination of these differences in such a society? To the extent that the capitalist socialization of the production process is a contradictory process involving the sharpening of the "three major differences", what does a specifically *socialist* socialization of the production process entail? In what ways do the "three major differences" inherited from the old society manifest themselves as class differences and class contradictions in a "socialist" society? And what are their implications for the nature and forms of the class struggle in the entire epoch of socialism?[1]

These are some of the issues that emerge from our examination of the classical Marxist formulations concerning the elimination of the "three major differences". Hardly any of these have been addressed by Marx or Engels as such, since they had not witnessed the victory of *any* proletariat revolution in their lifetime and thus these issues have not been posed to them in a practical way. The October Revolution was the first victorious proletarian revolution, and Russia at the time of revolution was characterized by relatively low level of development of the productive forces. Nor did Lenin live long enough to theoretically and practically confront these issues; he died scarcely three years after the end of the Civil War and the promulgation of the NEP.

The mid-1920s witnessed a great industrialization debate among the Bolshevik leaders over the strategies—and the possibility—of socialist construction in an economically backward and isolated Russia. None of the questions formulated above, however, received any serious attention by the protagonists in this debate. To almost all of the latter—including Preobrazhensky, Bukharin, Trotsky, and Stalin—it appears axiomatic that in a society with such a low level of development of the productive forces as in Russia, the question of eliminating/reducing the "three major differences" was hardly on the agenda. It seems that an unquestioned assumption generally held by the Bolshevik leaders was that the rapid development of the productive forces necessarily entails the widening—at least temporarily—of these differences, and that it is only after the creation of a solid material base that these differences could in turn be gradually eliminated. This is particularly evident in Preobrazhensky's formulation of the "law of primitive socialist accumulation", the basic logic of which Stalin adopted *in toto* in his subsequent agricultural collectivization campaign. According to

Preobrazhensky, the rapid industrialization of the country necessarily entails the "exploitation" of the non-socialist, petty-bourgeois (i.e. primarily agricultural) sector by the state-controlled sector (industry). The Soviet state is to mobilize the maximum possible economic surplus from the former so as to finance an accelerated programme of industrialization. Under such circumstances, Preobrazhensky recognizes, the tensions between town and country are bound to be acute, while the worker-peasant alliance may be seriously undermined. In the subsequent forced collectivization campaign under Stalin, the worker-peasant alliance was completely shattered. The peasantry were ruthlessly expropriated and compelled to offer their "tribute" to the state, which became possible only after the strengthening of an immensely repressive state apparatus. Rapid industrialization in the Soviet Union was achieved at the cost of sharpening the contradictions between town and country, industry and agriculture.

The historical experience of the Soviet Union also shows that these contradictions tend to reproduce themselves over time, and the development of the productive forces to a high level does not in any way automatically contribute to their resolution. The widening of the "three major differences" leads inexorably to the emergence of new vested interests which may prove to be powerful obstacles for further advance on the path of socialist transition.

It is instructive here to consider the position of Stalin on the "elimination of the three major differences" in the post-World War II era, in which the Soviet Union has already been transformed into a major economic and military power. Stalin wrote in 1952,

> Take, for instance, the distinction between agriculture and industry. In our country it consists not only in the fact that the conditions of labour in agriculture differ from those in industry, but mainly and chiefly, in the fact that whereas in industry we have public ownership of the means of production and of the product of industry [i.e. ownership by the whole people], in agriculture we have not public, but group, collective farm ownership. It has already been said that this fact leads to the preservation of commodity circulation, and that *only when this distinction between industry and agriculture disappears, can commodity production with all its attendant consequences also disappear.* It therefore cannot be denied that the disappearance of *this essential distinction* between agriculture and industry must be a matter of paramount importance for us.
>
> (Stalin 1972:2, emphasis mine.)

In this formulation, Stalin underlines the continued existence of the distinction between industry and agriculture in terms of the differences in the *conditions of labour,* and the fact that this distinction is manifested in the coexistence of two forms of ownership in the USSR, ownership by the whole people and collective ownership. The reproduction of these two ownership forms, Stalin stresses, constitutes the basis for the preservation of commodity circulation. In so far as the realization of the communist society implies the disappearance of commodity production, the epoch of socialist transition must necessarily involve the process whereby the conditions for the continued existence of commodity production are progressively eliminated, which necessitates among other things the abolition of the distinction between industry and agriculture, between the ownership of the whole people and collective ownership. This formulation as it stands is consistent with the positions of Marx, Engels, and Lenin outlined above.

However, a closer reading of the text *Economic Problems of Socialism in the USSR* shows unambiguously that this pronouncement by Stalin is purely incidental. Nowhere in the text—or in any of his other writings—did Stalin attempt to pursue this analysis, and more significantly, to spell out the necessary measures to be implemented in order to gradually eliminate the distinction between industry and agriculture, between ownership by the whole people and collective ownership. In fact, in the same chapter of the text, there are a number of other formulations which are overtly at odds with the quotation above and which apparently reflect more faithfully Stalin's point of view. Consider the following remarks:

> Of quite a different character is the problem of the disappearance of *distinctions* between town (industry) and country (agriculture) and between physical and mental labour. This problem was not discussed in the Marxist classics [sic]. It is a new problem, one that has been raised practically by our socialist construction. ..... Some comrades assert that in the course of time not only will the essential distinction between industry and agriculture and between physical and mental labour disappear, but so will ALL distinction between them. That is not true. *Abolition of the essential distinction between industry and agriculture cannot lead to the abolition of all distinction between them.* Some distinction, even if in-essential, will certainly remain, owing to the difference between the conditions of work in industry and in agriculture. .... But this indicates that my previous formulation was unprecise, unsatisfactory. It must be discarded and replaced by another formulation, one that speaks of the *abolition of essential distinctions* and the *persistence* of inessential distinctions between industry and agriculture, and between mental and physical labour.   (Stalin 1972: 27-9,
> emphasis mine.)

Stalin distinguishes here between "essential" and "inessential" distinctions. The crucial point is of course what constitutes the *distinction* between the two types of distinction. Stalin nowhere makes this clear. *What Stalin fails to confront theoretically and practically is the problem of eliminating one of the most essential distinctions between industry and agriculture, namely, the distinction in the forms of ownership between the two.* Instead there is a tendency on Stalin's part to subsume this essential distinction under the category of "inessential distinctions". Elsewhere in the pamphlet, *Economic Problems of Socialism in the U.S.S.R.,* Stalin mentioned in passing the question of "how the two main forms of ownership will ultimately become one", and considered that "this is a question which requires separate discussion". Mao Tse-tung in his critique of the text seized upon this vital issue and commented sharply, "Stalin is avoiding the issue, having failed to find a method or suitable formulation on the transition from collective to public ownership". (Mao Tse-Tung 1977: 145)

THE CHINESE APPROACH

It has been pointed out that to Lenin, among other Bolshevik leaders, the abolition of the distinction between workers and peasants is a primary task in the epoch of socialist transition, and that the material prerequisite for the accomplishment of this task is the development of the productive forces to a sufficiently high level. There does not seem to be any disagreement between the Bolshevik and Chinese leaders on these points. The crucial and fundamental difference lies in the ways the respective parties approach and "handle" the *contradictions* between the worker and the peasant *in the very process of developing the country's productive forces.*

China on the eve of the socialist revolution, like the Soviet Union at a comparable period of time, was predominantly an agrarian society. Rapid industrialization of the country, again as in the case in the Soviet Union, has to rely to a substantial extent on savings from the agrarian sector.[2] There exists therefore an objective contradiction between the interests of the peasant masses and the state's ever-increasing needs of marketable surplus for industrialization. As revealed in the Wan-sui documents[3], one of the most important lessons Mao drew from the Soviet experience of socialist construction is that this contradiction constitutes by far the most dangerous and weakest point in the entire period of socialist transition. Mao reproached Stalin for his failure to recognize, much less resolve, this contradiction. In the Soviet Union under Stalin, the development of the productive forces—on the basis of "primitive socialist accumulation"—was a contradictory process involving the accelerated growth of industrial production on the one hand and the suffocation of the agricultural sector on the other, with the result that the "three major differences" were widened and the peasant masses condemned to a passive and alienating role in socialist construction.

In China, the Great Leap Forward and the formation of the people's commune ushered in an alternative strategy of simultaneous development of agriculture and industry, heavy and light industry, central and local industry, with a view to minimizing the central procurement of rural resources and releasing the productive enthusiasm of the peasant masses. Industrial production, which had hitherto been concentrated in the big urban centres, was decentralized on a massive scale to local—country and commune—levels. Heavy industry continued to be a priority sector in the national economy, but light industry was also to develop at a great pace, while both heavy and light industrial products were to gear more closely to the demands of the agrarian sector.

The cornerstone of this new strategy is the proper "handling" of the contradictions between the state, the units of production (primarily the collective farms), and the individual producers (primarily the peasants) (Mao Tse-tung 1977: 384-420). The individual peasant is seen to be torn between the desire to increase his personal income and the need of the collective to maximize its accumulation; the collective is torn between the desire to maximize its own income, and the need of the state to maximize capital formation. Mao maintained that the interests of the individual, the collective, and the state were in the last analysis isomorphic, and hence the contradiction was *not* antagonistic. What made it difficult to resolve was the bureaucratic organization of decision-making which, concentrated at the centre, obscured this identity of interest from the people. The state bureaucracy was regarded as the biggest obstacle to the cultivation of understanding among the people of the dialectical identity of individual and communal interests. The solution was to minimize bureaucratic responsibility for accumulation and centralization of resources, and to limit taxation and procurement in order to leave most of the savings from increased production in the hands of the collectives/localities so that the latter might have the initiative and responsibility for the development of both local industry and agricultural mechanization.

According to the Chinese formulation, there do not exist any contradictions between the rapid development of the productive forces and the reducing of the "three major differences"; indeed the latter is held to be a necessary condition for the former. By decentralizing existing industrial capacity to local levels, and at the same time allowing the retention of a substantial proportion of rural savings in the countryside, the Chinese believed that agricultural production would be greatly promoted, and in turn the basis for rapid development of industry would be created. Industrial undertakings located at the doorsteps of the rural producers, which gear closely to the latter's needs, would enable the peasants to better appreciate the symbiotic relationship between agricultural and industrial development.

Both heavy and light industrial products are generally over-priced relative to agricultural ones, that is to say, the exchange of values of products between industry and agriculture is far from equivalent. Although the terms of trade between town and country have improved in favour of the latter since liberation, it is still primarily through the unequal exchange between agriculture and industry that the state accumulates funds for industrial development. As Mao has written in *On the Ten Major Relationships,*

> Our policies towards the peasants differ from those of the Soviet Union and take into account the interest of both the state and the peasants. Our agricultural tax has always been relatively low. In the exchange of industrial and agricultural products we follow a policy of narrowing the price scissors, a policy of exchanging equal or roughly equal values.
> (Mao Tse-tung 1977: 291)

In this formulation, Mao underlines the fact that the state has followed a policy of *narrowing* the price scissors, which implies that in most cases exchange between industry and agriculture is *not* based on equivalent values. On first consideration, it may seem that what Preobrazhensky has envisaged as the process of "primitive socialist accumulation" is also evident in China, and further that the Chinese measures are even more faithful to Preobrazhensky's initial conception of primitive socialist accumulation than those carried out under Stalin, in that the major mechanism for accumulation is "manipulative pricing". This is, however, only a very superficial observation. The essence of Preobrazhensky's formulation is that in order to finance rapid industrialization, the maximum possible resources are to be channelled to the state sector from the private sectors (mainly agriculture), the assumption being that the socialist transformation of the latter has to await the attainment of a high level of development of the productive forces in the country. In China, on the other hand, the crux of the policy since agricultural collectivization was to minimize state procurement of agricultural surpluses and to leave the grass-roots collective units more leeway in accumulating resources for "self-reliant" development. "Manipulative pricing" in China could only be understood in terms of the triangular relationships between agriculture, light industry, and heavy industry which can be expressed as follows: increased agricultural production through collective effort and collective accumulation at grass-roots levels; expansion of light industries (which are granted high profit margins) oriented towards peasant needs, thereby improving the latter's standard of living and stimulating the productive enthusiasm. With rising agricultural productivity, greater capital could be raised for heavy industry development and the collective units are in a better position to consume agricultural and capital goods.

We may now move on to examine the role of the people's commune in facilitating the narrowing of the "three major differences", focusing primarily on the progressive transformation of the ownership system in the countryside.

THE PEOPLE'S COMMUNE SYSTEM

One of the primary conditions for eliminating the class distinctions between the worker and the peasant—which are manifested in the distinctions between town and country, industry and agriculture—is the elimination of the distinction between the two coexisting forms of ownership of the means of production: ownership by the whole people and collective ownership. The continued existence of these two forms of ownership is due primarily to the still marked differences in the levels of development of the productive forces in the respective sectors. In the Chinese Marxist conception of socialist transition, one of the principal tasks in this historical epoch is to gradually raise the level of collective ownership in the countryside until one form of ownership, ownership by the whole people, comes into being for the whole country. The accomplishment of this task depends primarily, but not exclusively, on the pace of development of the productive forces in the countryside, as well as of industrial development of the economy as a whole.

In China, the entire process of socialist transformation of agriculture—which is coextensive with the whole epoch of socialism—is conceived in terms of three principal stages. The first stage was the transformation from private to collective ownership of the agricultural means of production, a process which includes the progressive phases of the formation of the mutual aid team, the agricultural producers' cooperatives, and the collectives (1952-58). The second stage began with the introduction of the people's commune (1958), the development of which involves the process whereby the level of collective ownership is progressively raised from the team to the brigade and then to the commune level. Full communal ownership of the means of production in the country will mark the completion of this stage. The third stage refers to the transition from full communal ownership to ownership by the whole people, the realization of which necessitates above all the *elimination* of the "three major differences".

The basic features of the people's commune can be summarized as follows. The people's commune is first of all characterized by its huge size. In terms of the number of households it comprises, it is far larger than the cooperatives and collectives which had emerged in the years immediately preceding its formation. The original 26,000 communes were amalgamated from some 750,000 advanced agricultural producers' cooperatives. In 1970, there were approximately 51,000 communes averaging 2,900 households, with 13,000 persons per commune.

Another key feature is that the commune is not only a production unit, but is also the basic organ of state power in the countryside. Before the formation of the commune, the township *(hsiang)* was the grass-roots political unit, while the economic organizations functioned quite separately in the form of agricultural producers' cooperatives. By 1958 the newly formed commune unified the two function, organizing political power on the one hand, and production, distribution, and consumption on the other.

The commune also provides the institutional framework for integrating all aspects of rural life including agricultural, subsidiary and light industrial production; politics and administration; social services such as education, health, and welfare, transportation and communication, finance and commerce; water conservation and basic construction; and defence and military training. The previously existing organizations for production, marketing, education, welfare, and the militia were all incorporated into the commune structure in accordance with the strategy of "comprehensive and simultaneous development".

In terms of the ownership system, the rural people's commune consists of a three-tiered ownership system, that is to say, there are basically three levels of ownership of the means of production *within* the commune: ownership by the commune, by the brigade, and by the team. The lowest level, the production team, is the *basic* level of ownership, which means that it is at this level that the principal means of production for day-to-day productive activities are owned. It is at the team level that commune members are organized to engage in regular productive labour and receive renumeration for their work. The production team serves as the basic accounting unit in the commune, owns and controls most of the means of production in China's countryside, and takes final responsibility for most of the economic decisions made in the rural areas.

The production brigade (which comprises about 10 to 20 production teams), apart from performing the vital functions of coordinating agricultural production of the constituent teams and providing a range of vital social services, also owns part of the means of production in the commune. Typically, production brigades purchase (out of the accumulation fund contributed by the constituent teams) and manage medium-sized agricultural implements such as tractors, trucks, pumps, processing equipment, electricity generating equipment, etc., which are too expensive for individual teams to buy and utilize efficiently. The production brigade also plays a significant role in generating new inputs for agriculture. The construction of irrigation and drainage projects such as small and medium-scale dams, reservoirs, canals, deep wells, etc. is most important. The teams concerned contribute labour and other resources in proportion to anticipated benefits, and when the projects are completed, ownership and management responsibility of the facilities rest with the brigade. In addition, the production brigade also runs small-scale factories, farm equipment, repair shops, grain processing plants, etc.

At the commune level, agricultural as well as industrial production is undertaken. The commune retains ownership of the means of production of these enterprises. Commune agricultural production does not produce a significant portion of basic agricultural commodities, since the team owns and controls most of the labour and land, and is limited mainly to such undertakings as forestry, fishing, animal husbandry, and fruit orchards. Of far more importance are commune-run industrial undertakings, the products of which are closely geared to agricultural production and peasant consumption. Typical commune-run enterprises include: agricultural implement manufacturing and repair shops; grain processing mills; fertilizer and pesticide plants; edible oil presses; brick, tile, and lime kilns; and factories producing light industrial products such as light bulbs, shoes, porcelain, etc. The commune also owns and manages large-scale water conservation projects, hydro-electric stations, tractor stations, and large-scale agricultural implements. With the income generated from the operation of these undertakings together with contributions from the constituent brigades and teams (a certain percentage of the accumulation and welfare funds of the lower levels is transferred upwards), the commune also provides a variety of social services for its members.

At the moment—two decades after the first people's commune appeared in China's countryside—the basic unit of ownership in the commune is still generally at the team level:

> The rural people's commune sector of the economy is a socialist sector collectively owned by the masses of working people. At present, it generally takes the form of three-level ownership, that is, ownership by the commune, the production brigade and the production team, with the production team as the basic accounting unit. (Article 7, *Constitution People's Rep. China,* 1973)

That is to say, after the basic completion of the socialist transformation of the ownership of the means of production and the creation of the people's commune in the late 1950s, there has been *basically* little change in the ownership system in the rural areas. This statement, however, requires two major qualifications. First, since the formation of the people's communes in 1958, collective ownership by the production team has existed within the context of two larger collectivities— the brigade and the commune, which alters profoundly the conditions of operation of the production teams. Second, collective ownership of the means of production is not confined to the team only; both the brigade and the commune also own part of the means of production in the countryside. Although the proportions of the means of production owned at brigade and commune levels in total commune assets are generally rather small, they have been steadily increasing in the past two decades. Further transformation of the ownership system in the people's commune depends to a larger extent on the rate of expansion of productive activities operated (and hence on the increasing amount of means of production owned) at the brigade and commune levels.

It is instructive to note that at the very inception of the commune in 1958, the commune was prematurely employed as the basic unit of ownership—that is, all of the means of production within the commune were owned at this level. At the height of optimism and nation-wide mobilization during the Great Leap Forward, it was believed that the second stage outlined above had been completed and the third stage—the transition to ownership by the whole people—was on the agenda. In the Peitaiho Resolution of 29 August 1958, for example, it was envisaged that

> the transition from collective [communal] ownership to ownership by the
> whole people is a process the completion of which may take less time—
> three or four years—in some places, and longer—five or six years or even
> longer—elsewhere.[4]

Although this optimism had been scaled down somewhat in the course of the movement, the basic assumption was still implicit in the second resolution, the Wuhan Resolution, in December 1958:

> it is possible that socialist ownership by the whole people may be fully
> realized at a somewhat earlier date but this will not be very soon. ... This
> whole process will take *fifteen, twenty or more years* to complete, counting
> from now.[5] (emphasis mine.)

That collective ownership was at first instituted at the commune level, and had very much to do with the attempt during the Great Leap Forward to rapidly transform the natural conditions of agricultural production in China's countryside. After the formation of the Advanced Agricultural Producers' Cooperatives (AAPCs) and before the emergence of the people's commune, a gigantic mass movement swept over the rural areas in an attempt to construct and improve large-scale water-works. Over two hundred million people throughout the country were involved in water-works projects of various sorts. The movement was carried out at the village level, with the AAPCs as the nuclei of work organization. In the course of the campaign the limited size of the AAPCs came into sharp contradiction with the imperative of organizing and coordinating water-works on a large scale. Collective organizations far larger than the AAPCs were called for. The spontaneous amalgamation of the AAPCs in various forms—which subsequently took the form of the people's commune— was primarily a response aimed at resolving this contradiction. The people's commune, with its huge size and high level of collective ownership, was instrumental in facilitating the launching and completion of a large number of water conservation projects.

At the height of the "high tide of socialism in the countryside", the people's commune assumed ownership of *all* the means of production within its confine. The land, labour, and other resources of the AAPCs became the property of, and were centrally managed by, the commune, thus equalizing at one stroke the economic well-being of the constituent units. With the commune serving as the basic unit of accounting, equality of income among the commune members was also attained, but at the expense of the productive enthusiasm of the peasants, since it was now difficult for them to perceive any correlation between individual efforts and remuneration. The politically and economically disastrous consequences of the attempt to institute collective ownership at the commune level were speedily recognized by the Chinese leaders, and in the subsequent readjustments of commune organization the level of ownership was shifted downwards from the commune, first to the brigade in 1959, and then to the team in 1961. From this point on the commune took the form of three-level ownership, with the higher levels owning only those means of production which are too expensive or non-economic for the lower levels to acquire or maintain, or those means of production and facilities that are serving all members of the larger collectivities. The commune and the brigade, however, continue to play an important role in coordinating the productive activities of the constituent teams/brigades, and remain crucial for mobilizing labour and other resources for agricultural capital construction serving a large number of collective units.

It has been pointed out above that, generally speaking, basic ownership at the production team level corresponds more closely to the level of development of productive forces in China's countryside. The relatively small unit enables the peasants to exercise collective control over the means of production and the conditions of labour. It also makes possible an intimate relationship between the team cadres and the ordinary members, which serves to facilitate the democratic management of productive and other activities of the team. Given the technological level of agricultural production in most communes, the team represents a unit large enough for the collective and rational utilization of the productive resources of a relatively large number of peasant households, but small enough for its members to recognize the close relationship between individual productive efforts and collective well-being which is critical for releasing the productive enthusiasm of the peasants.

Collective ownership at the team level is thus considered to be a necessary and indispensable stage of the protracted process of socialist transformation of the Chinese peasantry. Through working and living in a team, the peasants would gradually become accustomed to a collective (in contrast to a private) mode of labour, develop ability and capacity for collective management, and improve their standard of living through collective efforts, all of which are essential for developing the peasant's collective consciousness, and enabling them to gradually cast off the centuries-old small peasant mentality. In short, corresponding to the level of economic and social development in the Chinese villages in the 1950s, basic ownership at the team level represents a collective form of ownership best suited for facilitating the development of agricultural production in the communes, promoting the socialist transformation of the relations of production (which cannot be reduced to the ownership system alone), and transforming the peasant's consciousness.

We have thus far been concerned with what the Chinese have conceived as the "correspondence" between the productive forces and the relations of production; the communes' three-level ownership with the team as the basic level corresponds basically with the character of the productive forces. But contradictions between the two also exist. These contradictions tend to become increasingly acute in proportion to the progress made in the development of production on the basis of the team. Let us elaborate.

In so far as the production team is the basic unit of ownership, it serves as the basic unit of production, distribution, and *accumulation*. Given the tremendous variations in the initial possession of material means of production and labour resources, natural endowments and locations, as well as in the quality of leadership and access to outside assistance of various forms, production and income levels of different teams (even within the same brigade/commune) necessarily vary greatly. To the extent that the crucial decisions on the rate of accumulation were generally made at the team level under the principle of "self-reliance", different rates of development of production (a major index is the level of mechanization) may result even within a single brigade and commune. In so far as this is likely to be a cumulative process, the disparity in levels of production and therefore income among different teams could become very great.[6]

If these inequalities are allowed to be consolidated or enlarged in the course of time, political difficulties in the future transformation of the ownership system will be greatly enhanced. The better-off teams will tend to resist such changes and "defend" the existing system of distribution "to each according to his work" which guarantees their hard-won privileges. Ideologically, the reproduction of these inequalities would also serve to strengthen—not weaken—the importance of material incentives for productive labour, and limit the horizons of the peasants to the material interests of their own small collective unit such as the team. This could constitute another major obstacle in the path towards a socialist transition. In a pamphlet entitled *Teaching Political Economy to People's Commune Members,* it was stated:

> At the present stage the people's communes take the form of the three-level ownership with the production team as the basic accounting unit.... but the disparities between rich and poor teams are relatively great. If this is

allowed to continue for long, bourgeois right will be enlarged, class polarization will result and capitalism will emerge. It is therefore imperative to help the poor teams to raise their production and income to reach those of present levels of the average of advanced teams, and when conditions are ripe, to effect the transition from basic ownership by the team to basic ownership by the brigade and the commune. This is now on the agenda.[7]

In this formulation, some of the likely consequences of perpetuating the existing forms of ownership are highlighted: enlargement of bourgeois right, class polarization, and re-emergence of capitalism. Enlargement of "bourgeois right" here refers primarily to the consolidation of the rights of the small collective units to the possession of their means of production and the relatively privileged levels of income. "Class polarization" can be understood as the differentiation and polarization of *collective units* such as the teams—rich teams becoming richer and poor teams becoming poorer, resembling class polarization in the old societies. When the Chinese speak of "restoration of capitalism", they are stressing a tendency of direction of development. The prolonged "consolidation" of basic ownership at the team level does not necessarily entail the restoration of capitalism as such, but it does represent a stagnation in the process of socialist transformation of the peasantry, and to this extent enhances the danger of retrogression and the ultimate re-emergence of an exploitative system; on the ideological level, it also tends to reinforce "bourgeois" values and habits of thought.

The contradiction between the existing forms of ownership and the development of the productive forces also manifests itself in a number of other ways. There is, for instance, the contradiction between the increasingly social character of the agricultural production process following mechanization and the relatively limited sources of accumulation available at the production team level. Accumulation at the team level has been crucial for financing the mechanization process thus far. But as the scale and sophistication of the machinery to be employed gradually increases, the resources for accumulation available at the team level will no longer suffice. Thus, the relative significance of the team as a primary unit of accumulation will tend to diminish as the process of mechanization proceeds. Without a corresponding change in the ownership system towards a higher level to accommodate this higher degree of socialization of the production process, the contradiction between basic team ownership and the development of mechanized agriculture could become acute, and impede the development of the productive forces in the countryside.

Another manifestation of this contradiction arises from the imperative to constantly expand the scope of capital construction to facilitate the development of agricultural production. For instance, the development of farm mechanization necessitates the gradual perfection of the existing irrigation system, the construction of new networks of roads for tractors and trucks, large-scale land improvement, etc. The undertaking of these tasks requires not only labour and capital resources which individual teams could hardly provide, but also the coordination of a large number of collective units, and sometimes rearrangements of the existing distribution of material resources. All these can sometimes be accommodated within the existing framework of three-level ownership (this is also where the superiority of the commune system lies), but after a certain point the contradictions among the unevenly developed collective units can become so acute that these contradictions cannot be "properly handled" without a change of the ownership towards a higher level.

The preceding analysis serves to illustrate aspects of the dialectical relationships between the ownership system and the development of the productive forces at the present stage of China's rural transformation. How to handle and resolve the contradictions arising from the very process of economic development remains a critical concern of the Chinese leaders. On the abstract level, the primary condition for the "resolution" at the present stage is to raise the level of ownership upwards to the brigade, or in some cases to the commune. The question that emerges is: How can this come about in such a way that it will not jeopardize the productive enthusiasm of the collective units concerned, especially the better-off ones?

One way of approaching it, the negative lessons of which the Chinese peasants have paid a heavy cost, is associated with the notorious expression, "one levelling and two transferring" that is, the brigade simply "levels" the income of the constituent teams—rich and poor alike—through administrative measures, so that they all share the same level of income, and "transfers" the means of production as well as labour resources of all the teams within it to the brigade level for central allocation and deployment. In this way, the brigade replaces the team as the basic unit of ownership, and equalizes the economic well-being of the constituent teams.

But this means that while all teams give up their ownership of the means of production, the richer teams are likely to experience a lowering of their level of income (and the poor teams a rise). Such a process will in practice be contradictory to two basic principles of socialist transformation—mutual benefit and voluntarism[8]—and would thus be detrimental to the productive enthusiasm of the peasant masses. Moreover, to the extent that the better-off teams have attained their existing economic well-being through "self-reliance", such a process of levelling would seriously undermine the continued advocation and application of this important principle. The "communist wind" of "one levelling and two transferring" has blown before, during the Great Leap Forward, and again in some places during the latter part of the Cultural Revolution, and it has since been recognized as politically and economically counter-productive, or what the Chinese have characterized as "left in form, right in essence" (see Tse Ka-Kui 1977).

The more "correct" way of handling these contradictions, according to the Chinese, consists of a two-fold task. On the one hand, the brigade and the commune are to actively promote the development of production of the constituent teams, but particular effort is put into helping the poorer teams catch up with the richer ones. This can be done through the provision of various kinds of assistance to the teams concerned, such as advancing loans and according priority to acquire mechanized agricultural equipment, providing technical assistance in production and in training, offering channels for diversification of the team's productive activities, etc. At the same time, it is also necessary to strengthen political and ideological work in the teams, and to upgrade the cadres' organizing and leadership capacity through such measures as attaching higher level cadres to the teams for an extended period of time, and through retraining team leaders at the more advanced units.

On the other hand, the handling of the contradiction between the existing form of ownership and the development of the productive forces necessitates the rapid expansion and strengthening of the collective economy owned at the brigade and commune levels. This constitutes a critical condition for progressively raising the level of ownership in the people's commune. The expansion of the productive capacity of the brigade and the commune implies that an increasingly significant proportion of total commune (three levels) production is carried out on the basis of brigade and commune ownership, and also that the sources of accumulation at these levels would tend to be enlarged. In terms of distribution of income this implies, firstly, that an increasingly large number of commune members would receive their income from brigade and commune enterprises, and secondly, that the brigade and commune would be in a position to provide a greater range of social and welfare services for their members. Indeed the latter can, in course of time, be extended to such a degree that it outweighs the significance and function of *individually* distributed income.

The significance of these changes is that in proportion to the expansion of brigade and commune production, the importance of the team as a unit of production and income distribution would tend to diminish. At a certain point of this development it would be possible to effect the transition from team ownership to brigade ownership (and later from brigade to commune ownership) in correspondence with the character of the productive forces and the political consciousness of the peasant masses, without resorting to any measure akin to the "one levelling and two transferring" policy.

The expansion of the productive capacity at the brigade and commune levels refers primarily to the extension of industrial and other non-agricultural productive activities operated at these levels (see Table 1, appendix). As the process of agricultural mechanization has begun in China's countryside, the development of these non-farm productive activities becomes increasingly important for two major reasons. First, these undertakings constitute in most cases the principal sources of accumulation for financing the expanding scope of agricultural mechanization. Secondly, and equally significantly, these productive activities provide the major channels for absorbing the increasingly large number of peasants released from mechanized farming.

The development of industrial production by the brigade and commune is of particular importance. By bringing industry down to the countryside, the commune members would not have to migrate to the cities or industrial centres for industrial employment as many peasants in other capitalist and "socialist" countries have done and are doing. Apart from satisfying directly the peasants' demand for agricultural implements and other light industrial products, and thus promoting the development of agricultural production and raising the standard of living of the peasants, the presence of industrial technology at the peasants' door also contributes immensely to facilitate the transformation of the peasants' consciousness. The peasants could see with their own eyes how industry works and what industry could do for them, which enables them to appreciate the relationship between national industrialization and the economic transformation of the countryside. This in turn is important for enhancing the peasants' awareness of the relationships between the interests of the individual, collective, and the state. As Mao has pointed out in *On the Correct Handling of the Contradictions Among the People,* the appreciation on the part of the peasants of the identity of interests between the individual, the collective, and the state on the one hand, and the correct handling on the part of the Party of the contradictions between them, constitute two of the primary conditions for rural transformation. That is to say, there is at once identity and contradictions between the interests of the individual, collective, and the state. To the extent that contradictions exist between them (which is partly the result of an imperfect recognition of the identity of interests), it is necessary to properly handle these contradictions by giving due attention to the interests of the three parties. The successful handling or resolution of these contradictions necessitates among other things the demonstration to the peasants, through political education as well as in concrete material terms, the identity of interests between them. In this respect, the "educational" functions of brigade-run and commune-run industry are of critical importance.

Commune-based rural industrialization is also likely to contribute significantly to the narrowing of the differences between town and country,

industry and agriculture, and mental and manual labour. The gradual industrialization of the people's commune makes possible the retention of the rural
population in the countryside, thus avoiding the types of urbanization found in
other industrializing countries. At the same time, together with the attempt to de-
urbanize the large urban centres and to effect a redistribution of population
across the country, large numbers of former urban dwellers were *"hsisfang"*(sent
down) to the countryside. Of those who thus permanently settled down in the
rural areas, a significant proportion are cadres and education youths. For
example, during the Great Leap Forward, over 1.5 million cadres from urban
areas were sent down to the countryside *(New China News Agency,* 22 February,
1958); most of them were expected to settle there permanently. The total number
of educated youths sent down to the countryside from the beginning of the
Cultural Revolution to 1970 numbered over 5,000,000 (*New China News
Agency,* 3 May, 1970). By December 1975, the figure was reported to be
12,000,000 (*People's Daily,* 23 December 1975). This large influx of experienced
cadres and educated elements into the rural areas is likely to prove to be a
powerful catalyst for changing the face of the Chinese countryside.

We have indicated that the Chinese have envisaged the socialist transformation of the peasantry in terms of three principal stages: the transition
from private to collective ownership, the transition from a low level to a high
level of collective ownership, and the transition from full communal ownership
to ownership by the whole people. It is instructive to indicate here the present
stage of this protracted transformation process.

As we have pointed out above, the people's commune in China today still
generally takes the form of the three-level ownership system *with the team as the
basic unit.* This means that in terms of the principal stages outlined above, rural
China is at the moment still in a relatively early phase of the second stage of
socialist transformation. It is likely to take a considerable period of time before
the second stage will be completed. Even with the completion of this stage, the
form of ownership in the country would still be collective—collective ownership
at the commune level. This already presupposes a gigantic development of the
productive forces in the countryside as well as a profound transformation of the
ideological superstructure, but even then the distinction between worker and
peasant, town and country, mental and manual labour will necessarily persist.
The complete elimination of these differences, the Chinese envisage, will await
the completion of the transition from communal ownership to ownership by the
whole people.

It is possible to say that two decades after the formation of the people's
commune, the differences between town and country, worker and peasant,
mental and manual labour have by no means reduced significantly. This is of
course empirically true. What I have tried to show in this paper, however, is the

Chinese attempt and persistent struggle to reduce these differences, and how they have tried to accomplish this task through the institution of the people's commune. I have attempted to demonstrate, above all, the internal logic of the commune system and its direction of development, which manifests the Chinese preoccupation and insistence that the reducing and ultimate elimination of the "three major differences" constitutes a fundamental task in the epoch of socialist transition.

NOTES

1. It is of course impossible to discuss systematically and extenstivelly all these issues in the scope of the present paper. I have, however, attempted to examine them in considerable detail in my Ph. D thesis, *Theories of Socialist Transition and the Historical Experience of the People's Republic of China,* University of Manchester, 1978.

2. As Mao has put it "There are two things some of our comrades do not think of linking up: the large sum needed to complete both national industrialization and technical reconstruction of agriculture, and the fact that a considerable portion of these funds is derived from agriculture" (Mao Tse-tung 1955:26).

3. This refers to the collections of Mao's talks and writings unofficially published in China during the Cultural Revolution, some of which were subsequently included in Volume V of Mao's *Selected Works.*

4. "Resolution of the Central Committee of the CPC on the Establishment of People's Communes in Rural Areas", translated in *People's Communes in China* (Peking; Foreign Languages Press, 1958), p. 4.

5. "Resolutions of Some questions Concerning the People's Communes", December 1958, in *Documents of the Sixth Plenary Session of the Eighth Central Committee of the CPC* (Peking: Foreign Languages Press, 1958), p. 17.

6. For documentation and analyses of this issue, see W.F. Wertheim and L. C. Schenk-Sandbergen, *Polarity and Equality in China's Countryside* (Amsterdam: Centre for Anthropological and Sociological Studies, 1973); Martin K. Whyte, "Inequalities and Stratification in China", *China Quarterly,* No. 68, December 1976: Ng Gek-boo, "The Commune System and Income Distribution in Rural China", World Employment Programme, International Labour Office, Geneva, 1976, mimeo.

7. The pamphlet was serialized in *Theoretical Study (Kirin), April, May, June 1975 issues. (My translation).*

8. Except perhaps in those brigades and communes in which there is an exceptionally high level of socialist consciousness among the peasants concerned who are politically prepared to "self-consciously restrict bourgeois right".

REFERENCES

Engels, R. (1976): *Anti-Duhring,* Peking, Foreign Languages, Press.

Lenin. V. (1965a): "A Characterization of Economic Romanticism" in *Collected Works* Vol. 2, Moscow, Progress Publishers.

(1965b): "Deception of the People with Slogans of Freedom and Equality" in *Collected Works,* Vol 29, Moscow, Progress Publishers.

(1975): *Selected Works,* Moscow, Progress Publishers.

Mao Tse-Tung (1955): *The Question of Agricultural Cooperation,* Peking People's Publishers.

(1977a): *A Critique of Soviet Economics,* New York, Monthly Review Press.

(1977b): *Selected Works,* Peking, Foreign Languages Press.

Marx, Karl (1976): *Capital,* London, Penguin.

Marx. K. and F. Engels (1977): *The German Ideology,* London, Lawrence & Wishart.

N. A. (1978): *Documents of the First Session of the Fifth National People's Congress of the People's Republic of China,* Peking, Foreign Languages Press.

Stalin, J. (1972): *Economic Problems of Socialism in the U.S.S.R.,* Peking, Foreign Languages Press.

Tse Ka-Kui (1977): "Institutionál Change and Agricultural Modernization: Aspects of the Chinese Theory and Practice" in Steve S. K. Chin (ed.), *The Gang of Four : First Essays After the Fall,* Centre for Asian Studies.

Appendix

Table 1

Data concerning the actual scope of these activities in the average commune in China are difficult to obtain. The following table compiled by Ng Gek-boo at the International Labour Office gives an indication of the situation in some of the more advanced communes and localities.

Localities	Non-agricultural incomes (incl. industry) as a percentage of total income	Year
Huasi Production Brigade, Kiagsu	53.0	1975
Chekiang Province	50.0	1975
Siyou Commune, Shangtung	42.9	1975
Kaihsien County, Liaoning	40.0	1972
Tachai Production Brigade, Shansi	40.0	1972
Suburban Shanghai	38.0	1973
Luchuang County, Kwangsi	38.0	1973
Wangan Commune, Hunan	35.0	1972
Anhsiang Commune, Shansi	35.0	1972
Shuangliao County, Kirin	30.0	1972

Source : Ng Gek-boo, "The Commune System and Income Distribution in Rural China", World Employment Programme, ILO, Geneva, 1976, mimeographed, p.14.

Discussion

T. Shanin : Let me try to express the unifying themes that were presented to us in the papers in this part. To do it fully is, of course, an impossible task. The accounts came from various societies and expressed a heterogeneity of problems. In fact only one thing is general to all papers which I heard or read: the fact that peasant society is changing, that peasants are under the impact of industrialization, and as a result of that, peasants are not, and cannot possibly be, what they were yesterday. That is, of course, general, it's correct, it's trivial, and it's useless. If we have to be more specific, the papers fell into several categories—each of which has internal problems, and I will say what I see these problems to be.

There are, first, those papers which have to do with socialist societies and the problematic of transformation of agriculture and rural life within the framework of state-centred societies committed (at least ideologically) to equality. There were some papers of that nature here, beginning with China, Hungary, and Poland. What was in the air, though it was not raised as such, was the problem of Soviet collectivization: as the first example, experiment if you want, how to look at it. I think what is central here is that there is no doubt about the multi-directionality of development within socialist society. From this point of view, one cannot and should not talk any longer about *the* socialist alternative, but about the socialist alternatives. The richness of this development, the tremendous complexity of it, and the variety of possibilities is a fertile and a necessary field for research in the future. Even if we assume the same central aim, or dream of abolishing the differences between the countryside and the city, we have heard on the one hand about the attempts to industrialize the countryside and to abolish the difference in this way, which Tse Ka-Kui discussed in his paper, and on the other we hear about the development of peasant-workers which is the same thing turned upside down. Instead of moving these industries into the countryside, we have a situation in which the countryside becomes a place of living, while the centres of production are urbanized, and the communication between the two is the way to abolish (*de facto*, not necessarily formally) the differences between the rural and the urban. Each of these was to be studied.

One must add that the fact of multi-directionality should also be related to the fact that the socialist ideology is not a dream of productive development alone, and cannot be just that because it would then lose its socialist content. The socialist aim *was* to increase the wealth and productivity of the nation, but also to secure human justice. For this reason, any consideration of this development, positive or negative, must be measured not only in terms of production units alone, but must also be related to the problem of increasing or decreasing social justice. From this point of view, the point of application of Soviet principles of collectivization in agriculture should consider how much efforts can turn out differently from expectations. The aims of maximizing productivity and the aims of justice are often in contradiction, and this should be stated clearly; any socialist revolution cannot be considered as technological in nature, but social and ideological in nature. That's where the major division between strategists within socialist societies will find one of is major roots.

Turning to the papers which have to do with non-socialist societies, the job of drawing them together is even more complex. I would say that here is where the superiority of anthropology over other disciplines is obvious. I mean an approach to the cultural aspects, the consciousness component of development within different places. I cannot agree more with what was said about the danger of over-stressing productivity. It's obvious that such stresses come from a society which went mad about its productivity. It's also clear that such overstresses come when disciplines are committed to just that, such as economics. I think that in this sense anthropology in particular has an important role to play. It should fight these stresses tooth and nail and push them back, to give a balanced picture of reality. One speaker yesterday said there are two ways in which peasantry can go—one is modernization (everybody getting better off and everything getting nicer), and the other is pauperization and revolution. Pauperization does not necessarily lead to revolution. Many societies with the highest degree of poverty have never produced revolutions and will probably never produce one. What bridges destitution and revolution is consciousness of a certain type. And to understand how consciousness works and operates is to understand when poverty produces revolt and when it produces the opposite, that is, total surrender. Both are possible.

From this point of view may I refer to the book by Scott which I read a short time ago, about the place of moral indignation in peasant revolt, i.e. how much revolt is not the result of poverty, but only some types of poverty—the types of

poverty which clash with traditional values, which clash with what people believe
to be right, producing revolt as defence of justice, not only defence of the right to
eat. On this level of understanding of people's struggles and livelihood, the way
peasants transform or refuse to transform into the new world, the consciousness
component is central, and therefore anthropology has a central role to play
because of its own traditions and characteristics. It was often said, in the circles in
which I moved, which were not anthropological mostly, that anthropologists are
being mad amout culture; overdoing the issues of consciousness. There are points
of strength and points of weakness there, for there are two sides to the coin. It is
up to us to turn points of possible weakness into points of possible strength, by
using them analytically, by using them in a balanced fashion.

A member of the audience: I have a request for a point of information from
Joan Vincent. You said that the peasantry was quite recent in East Africa—three
generations. I wonder how you relate it, if at all, to the indigenous peasantry of
East African kingdoms, and if this has any effect on the more recent
transformations?

Joan Vincent: I think one of the characteristics that marks the study of the
peasantry in East and Central Africa is the smaller number of indigenous African
peasantries. Emphasis must be placed therefore far more on the colonial
capitalist creation of peasantries. Rather than seek out indigenous peasantries in
East African kingdoms, I would look back on the mercantile era of the Indian
Ocean as the era preceding capitalist expansion. And, certainly from the point of
view of Uganda, it is necessary to recognize that an ideology of peasantry was
inculated by the colonial administration. Chiefs were seen to be the equivalent of
a gentry, and the people under them were taken to be peasants and serfs. This was
transplanted from the Buganda scene to the acephalous regions of the north. It
was not an accurate representation of what had happened in Buganda and it was
certainly not applicable in the east. This reminds me rather of Dr. Rapp's point,
that the European peasantry transplanted to the rest of the world isn't a very
accurate representation either. Perhaps the most interesting feature of the
distinction between the mercantilist Indian Ocean and the later colonial
capitalist system comes when you focus on the middle sector as it emerged, and
especially on the role of Asians in East Africa *per se*. It is possible to distinguish
the Muslim Indian traders of the mercantilist system from the Hindu and Goan
Indians of the colonial period by virture of their economic roles rather than on
the basis of religion. Furthermore, by focusing on both the earlier period and the
colonial period not in terms of territorial states, nation-states, or empires, but in
terms of conflicting economic interests, it is possible to establish continuities and
discontinuities between the pre- and the post-colonial periods.

S. Silverman: I'd like to pick up some of the themes of this morning's session,
which will perhaps also address the questions about methodology and models of

analysis that have been raised this afternoon—particularly the comment someone made that in looking at production we are using an ethnocentric model. It seems to me that there is no such thing as an analysis that is not ethnocentric, to the extent that the social scientific endeavour is a product of western civilization. One might even say that perhaps a culture like that of the French, who are more given to communication than the Anglo-Saxons, sees its models as matters of communication or sociability, whereas those of us who are more attuned to the utilitarian world begin with work and production. In my understanding, production is not intended as the ultimate purpose to which societies and cultures are addressed, and there is certainly no implication in the works of any of the anthropologists who have used "production" that represents a commitment to the benefits of progress. On the contrary, there is as likely to be a critical view of the cost of increasing energy harnessing.

The point of looking at production is the simple idea that before you say anything about what people are saying, what they are thinking, what they believe, what they want out of life—the first thing you have to ask is how they are surviving. The materialist approach puts everything else in the context of that issue. This is not to say that people do nothing but produce, but only to ask about the implication of exchange, in relation to the basic questions of survival, of resources, and of work.

As an anthropologist who does not define culture as a matter of consciousness or other subjective phenomena, I think it's an unfair statement of the anthropological contribution to say that we can balance out the picture of reality by adding the dimension of consciousness. One of the points I wanted to make in my paper was that the view of culture as meaning was only *one* way of thinking of culture. An equally important tradition in anthropology looks at culture as context, looks at relations among different arenas of human activity, and at the relations among production, sociability, and meaning. Prof. Shanin gave me a very good example of the limitations of defining culture as consciousness in saying that the difference between poverty that leads to revolution and poverty that does not lead to revolution lies in the consciousness of the peasants. I think this masks the question of what kinds of poverty, under what social conditions, and what kinds of social and political arrangements allow what kinds of possibilities. These are the questions that need to be asked, quite apart from the issue of moral indignation, which I find unobjectifiable.

A member of the audience: We are a society in which production and consumption are a kind of a circle. When we use the concept of production all these things are imputed in this concept. What seems to me dangerous is that we try to use this concept as a kind of absolute.

S. Silverman: I don't agree. I think that production assumes that the means of survival are obtained from nature and there is human interaction in obtaining those means. If you want to add energy, this process does involve energy exchanges. Beyond that, questions of accumulation or exchange or use are quite open. I think the approach through production allows one to ask three questions.

Eduardo Archetti: In a sense the way many anthropologists use these categories—production, non-production, material things, non-material things, economics, non-economics, infra-structure, super-structure, and so forth—is confusing. There is no process of production without ideas, without resource allocation, and if I am just trying to measure and attack another problem related to the transference of resources, maybe I will not succeed, without knowing the categories of the actors, I will not be able to explain this process. On the other hand, if as an anthropologist I try to explain the inner logic of the accumulation of capital, rate of profit, and so forth, the actor will not tell me the rate of profit. I would say that this division between ideas and material things is artificial, and it depends on what we are trying to explain.

R. Rapp (commenting on an earlier question): What happens to the social organization of the peasantry is anything but narrowly economistic. What we have heard about today is marriage systems, clan relations, religious systems. These are all social organizational systems strategies that people use, and they are not economistic, they simply relate to the means and relations of production. And I think there's ample room in there for levels of autonomy, consciousness, culture, ritual, and all sorts of organizational forms that we study as anthropologists. The point is to figure out how to fit them into that larger world-wide context, and it's at that point that we turn to epistemological questions of production, but it's not the same thing as saying that's what we study.

Question (to Dr. Archetti) : Would you explain how substantial surplus is siphoned off from peasant production?

E. Archetti: I left out of my paper the mechanism of domination because this is for another longer paper. But the basis of this system is the land distribution. Through land distribution peasants were forced to enter into the market, as part of their land was alienated and the resources that this land produced had to be acquired in the market. Of course, this is not the only mechanism, you have the mechanism of prices, the mechanism of distribution of technological resources, and you have the intermediate system of merchants and money-lenders. But I would say that the basis of transferring surplus from the peasant to the capitalist society is the land distribution system. It's not the only system at work. It can be taxation in some other places. It's also possible through technology. In certain places where peasants use technology, then we have to establish what we mean by high technology, and we have to establish that there is a difference between high complexity in technology and modern industrialized technology. But in Latin America peasants also use modern industrialized technology. They use machinery and sources of energy other than biological energy. These sources of energy support the system of transference of surplus from the peasant to the capitalist society, again depending on the system of ownership of these resources. The peasants use western technology but they don't own this technology. They don't own the contextual framework for this technology. So modern technology becomes another source of drainage from the peasants to the capitalist society.

Comment from the floor: I want to say that to me the peasant is not a static condition; the peasant has been always changing. What makes them peasants is the pattern of change, not change in itself. The absorption of modern technology in a system of domain doesn't guarantee that the dominated group will become modern: quite the contrary, it becomes a reinforcement of the system of inequality because the modern system is used for only a very short time, thus the peasants have to work more. Modern technology to peasants is only a system of intensification of labour demands and intensification of surplus transfer.

PART III

SOME VIEWS OF
THE INDIAN PEASANTRY

The Evolutionary Status of caste in Peasant India*

GERALD D. BERREMAN

In "Caste as Social Process" (1967 : 354) I wrote that "speculations and inferences about the origins and development of caste systems in India and elsewhere are apparently immune to empirical verification, but the origins of particular castes, the conditions attending their origins, and the consequences of the occurrence of caste systems are not".

This paper contradicts the implications of that statement in that it addresses the place of caste in India in social-political evolutionary sequence. I will not document its origins but I will try to historically situate it, discussing its probable development and the implications thereof for peasant society in India.

I suggest here that caste (*jati*) originated as an intermediate stage of stratification between the pre-state, kin-based inequality of bands, tribes, and chiefdoms (cf. Sahlins 1968), and the non-kin (or supra-kin) class stratification characteristic of state societies (ef. Fried 1960, 1967; Service 1971, 1975). I emphasize the peculiar historical circumstances of the South Asian subcontinent, wherein a great number and wide variety of pre-state ethnic groups or tribes evidently came under the control of early state-organized, stratified, conquering peoples of Indo-Aryan origin perhaps 3,500 years ago (cf. Krader 1978), following earlier, less intense contact with the Indus civilization. Thereafter the indigenous small-scale ethnic/tribal groups were absorbed into the emerging larger and more complex polity as entities ranked (and hence stratified) relative to one another and to the dominant intruders whom they supported through labour, rent, taxes, and the land which had been taken from them. During this time labour became occupationally specialized, and livelihood for many was derived from wages or shares. These social aggregates were ranked economically (by control over productive resources, income, wealth, etc.), but that rank was frequently described in terms of ritual evaluation of the occupations or other activities associated with the various groups. In other

---

* An earlier version of this paper was published in Berreman (1979 : 313-325).

instances rank was derived from the place of residence (e.g. forest or wastelands as contrasted with agricultural areas) or from evalution of tribal or other ethnic origins and affinities. Control of important productive resources, however, remained the crucial criterion for rank and the basis for power, with the exception of some priestly groups whose rewards were described as other worldly but included also the patronage of the powerful.

The Gonds, a culturally and linguistically defined tribal group of central India, constitute a case which illustrates this pivotal role of control over resources in determining hierarchical status within Hindu society (see Furer-Haimendorf 1948 : 4-6, *et passim;* 1974; cf. Fuchs 1968 : 194-228, 79-104). The Gonds' horticulturally cultivated land was alienated by an intrusive agricultural Hindu population in the eighteenth century, and the Gonds were absorbed into the caste system near the bottom of the hierarchy, according to the Hindu view, where they often provided agricultural labour for those who took their land. This was the case, that is, except for those Gonds, primarily in the central part of their territory (the former Adilabad district), who managed to retain control of the land and were accordingly adjudged by the dominant Hindus to be "Raj Gonds"—kingly Gonds—by ancestry, and with Brahmanical sanction were awarded the elevated status of *Kshatriya* in striking contrast to the demeaned status accorded their landless fellow tribesmen.

In considering the evolutionary status of caste in India, two excellent and divergent treatments of its origin come immediately to mind, neither of which takes account of the other: Karve's book, *Hindu Society—An Interpretation* (1961), especially the chapter therein entitled, "Caste— A Historical Survey" *(ibid. :* 50-77), and Gould's essay, *Caste and Class : A Comparative View* (1971).

Karve responds at length in her book to G.S. Ghurye's espousal of the idea that *jatis*—regionally specific, ranked social groups, membership in which is determined by birth—originated from the occupational, genealogical, and organizational fission of Indo-Aryan strata, or "caste categories", termed *varnas* (Ghurye 1952; cf. Karve 1961 : 53-57). Karve advocates an alternative hypothesis which she calls an "agglomerative" theory wherein the Indo-Aryan system of stratification into three major occupational and non-hereditary ranks or *varnas*, namely priests, administrators, and commoners, was grafted onto and above an indigenous Indian pattern of distinct but interdependent and ranked tribes, thus creating a hybrid system of stratification. As Karve says (1961 : 78), ". . . I think that the full-fledged theory of caste very probably represents the working together into a single theoretical system of two separate types of organization present in two societies. Through this formulation of the caste society the two separate societies came to be represented as one society." And elsewhere she notes (1961 : 58), "The union of *varna* and *jati* is a matter of fusion of two systems from two cultures."

Karve is unclear in conveying her view of the nature of pre-Aryan *jati,* for she refers to these ethnically distinct entities as both *jati* and "tribe". What she has in mind is something akin to the contemporary (or at least recent) situation in the Nilgiri Hills in southern India where contiguous autonomous tribes (Todas, Kotas, Badagas, Kurumbas) are to a significant extent occupationally specialized, interdependent, and ranked relative to one another. I am more confident that pre-Aryan ethnic groups were tribes than that they were occupationally distinct or interdependent, and I am skeptical that they were often ranked, at least in any way closely resembling contemporary *jati* or *varna* ranking.

Gould takes another point of view. Utilizing a notion which Ghurye had put forth before him, namely that caste emerged from fragmentation of extant groups through occupational specialization, he regards the key factor in the emergence of *jati* to be the "occupationalization of labor" in which ". . . occupational role and role occupant were identical . . . "(Gould 1971 : 8). This he sees as a universal feature of the division of labour in pre-industrial states: ". . . all occupational stratification systems in preindustrial states were essentially castelike and . . . India merely constituted one manifestation of this general type" *(ibid.).* Gould also notes, but does not much emphasize, that "the old state systems arose gradually out of ethnic diversity as well as technological variety", and ". . . units could be strictly occupationally specialized aggregations (like guilds and certain castes) or they could be whole tribes, parts of tribes, migrant Asiatic nomads, etc." *(ibid.).* But in his view, occupation was primary: ". . . It is clear that I regard the caste system of India as a manifestation of ascriptive occupational stratification . . ." *(ibid.* : 9). I agree that it is partly and importantly that, but I think it is also ascriptive ethnic stratification, with the ethnicity historically assimilated to occupation and occupational rank in some cases, and with occupation historically assimilated to ethnicity and ethnic rank in other cases. Specific castes can be shown historically to have been assigned their rank in each of these ways—always with the proviso that significant differentials in control over productive resources take precedence in rank assignment.

Gould suggests that occupationalization of work was the basis for emergence of stratification in the Middle East, and ". . . ethnic, political and military considerations more than technological elaborations . . ." (Gould 1971 : 9) were its basis in sub-Saharan Africa. In India, it seems to me, it was quite clearly a combination of the two.

An essential feature of that combination, and one that makes caste *(jati)* comprehensible in evolutionary terms, is the fact that castes are kin groups—maximal and putative kin groups to be sure, but kin groups nonetheless in the very real sense that they are composed of people who are regarded as actual or classificatory affinal and consanguinal relatives. Each caste constitutes a

marriage network, ranked relative to all others. The caste, of course, is made up
of smaller kin groupings: extended joint families comprising one or more
households and including several nuclear units and often more than one
generation. These small kin groups in turn are organized into lineages, the
lineages into sibs (or clans), the sibs often into phratries (*gotra*). Segments of
these entities in one village or locality may be organized for many purposes,
including ritual ones, in such a manner as to combine principles of both lineality
and locality in what Murdock (1949 : 66) has termed "compromise kin groups"
(Berreman 1962). Thus, each caste is a maximal kin group of considerable
internal complexity not unlike that to be found in many tribes and chiefdoms. In
fact, many castes have a kind of kin-based role ranking and "conical clan"
ranking (cf. Sahlins 1968 : 20-27) similar to that found in unstratified societies.
Such internal ranking no doubt existed in these entities before they became the
kin strata (the micro-strata composed of putative kinsman) that we call castes.
This internal ranking, however, does not constitute stratification as does the
ranking of castes relative to one another. It has an entirely different character
precisely because it is a ranking among kinsmen, with all the mutuality that term
implies, rather than a ranking of unrelated entities with their conflicting interests
and lack of mutuality.

While a caste is like other prestate social aggregates in that it is a kin-based
group in which inequality is organized and expressed in terms of kinship, there is
this crucial difference: Unlike ranked conical clans found in the chiefdoms
described by Sahlins, and unlike the ranked kin roles of bands and tribes (Fried
1960, 1967), castes are in radical disjunction one from another. The members of
one caste are not and cannot be at all related to those of another, and castes as
social entitites are not even putatively related to one another (except in the
remote, metaphorical sense that the four or five major caste categories—the
varns—are said scripturally to have originated from different parts of a
primordial body). They are ranked as disjunctive entities, not as kinsmen: caste
ranking is the ranking *among* castes and is independent of whatever ranking
occurs *within* them among individuals or roles.

In social evolution prior to the emergence of the state, kinship and rank or
hierarchy were inextricable: hierarchy *was* a ranking among kinsmen. In fully-
developed class-stratified states, kinship was replaced by economics as the basis
for rank. As caste emerged during the process of state formation in South Asia,
kinship and hierarchy *both* were retained as the bases for social organization, but
they were separated. The hierarchy became a ranking among unrelated (and,
because endogamous, unrelatable) aggregates of kinsmen. In place of such
principles of kinship as primogeniture and lineality to determine rank were
substituted tribal or ethnic identity, as Karve (1961: 50-77) insists, and
occupations, as Gould (1971) insists, and also a variety of other economic

relations, including, most importantly, control over land and other productive resources, access to productivity, to income, and to wealth, accumulation of wealth, control over other people, and the like, as I here insist. In short, society-wide ranking was replaced by the ranking of categories of people regarded as being unrelated but each bound internally by kin ties. Kin and role ranking was thus replaced by categorical ranking. The result was the appearance of *kin strata* (or kin classes), which is what castes in fact are, as they also constitute emergent stratification.

It seems to me likely that in many early states, as in India, ranking of social entities that were identified and held together by bonds of common kinship and common culture preceded class strata based entirely on economic criteria. Bounded, culturally distinct groups or aggregates are better prepared than mere categories to claim and sustain the interests of their members within the larger society, whatever their place in the hierarchy of rank, and therefore they may tend more readily to originate or persist as entities.

Marc Bloch has made the point with reference to European feudalism:

> In the absence . . . of a strong state, of blood ties capable of dominating the whole life and of an economic system founded upon money payments there grew up in Carolingian and post-Carolingian society relations of man to man of a peculiar type. The superior individual granted his protection and divers material advantages that assured a subsistence to the dependent directly or indirectly; the inferior pledged various prestations or various services and was under a general obligation to render aid. These relations were not always freely assumed nor did they imply a universally satisfactory equilibrium between the two parties. Built upon authority, the feudal regime never ceased to contain a great number of constraints, violences and abuses. However, this idea of the personal bond, hierarchic and synallagmatic [bilateral, reciprocal] in character, dominated European feudalism. (Bloch 1931 : 204)

These were relations between vassal and lord ("vassalage")—a defining feature of feudalism (cf. Service 1975 : 81-83). Such relations I refer to collectively as "estate" relations (cf. Berreman 1981). Note that Bloch identifies them as existing "in the absence . . . of a strong state" and in the absence of "blood ties capable of dominating the whole life". These are therefore relations that might be expected to occur in the transition between (1) the stateless, subsistence-based, unstratified, kin-organized society wherein blood ties *are* capable of dominating the whole of life and indeed do so, and (2) the territorially-organized, surplus-producing, class-stratified, centrally administered state whose "strength" and economic system dominate. Similarly, because in India castes did not have the mutual isolation found among tribes, which enabled "blood" or kin ties to serve as the basis for ordering relations within them, and because India also did not have a strong state or money economy to regulate stratification, the caste system served these functions there as vassalage did in feudal Europe.

Occupational specialization among castes, together with the *jajmani* system of caste-based patron-client relations in traditional India (cf. Beidelman 1959; Kolenda 1963; Wiser 1936), presents a striking parallel to feudal vassalage in Europe, with the important difference that in India it is kin group or caste vassalage rather than individual vassalage. To paraphrase Bloch, as quoted above: in the absence, then, of a strong state, of blood ties capable of dominating the whole life, and of an economic system founded upon money payments, there grew up in Indian society relations of caste to caste (and, between castes, of family to family) of a peculiar type called the *jajmani* system. The patron family, of superior caste, grants its protection and divers material advantages that assure a subsistence to the dependent, low-caste, client family directly or indirectly; the latter pledges (or is required to make) various prestations and various services and is under a general obligation to render aid. These relations are not always freely assumed, nor do they imply equilibrium between the two parties. Built upon hereditary caste hierarchy, authority, and power, the caste regime always contains a great number of constraints, violences, and abuses. However, the idea of the inter-caste bond, hierarchic, exploitative, and yet bilateral, reciprocal, and hereditary in character, dominates the Indian caste system.

The aptness of Bloch's description of vassalage as a description also of *jajmani* relations among castes suggests that "estate" relations are indeed significantly equivalent to caste relations. They are so not only in function but, I believe, in evolutionary position as well, for both organize and sustain inequality (the former on the basis of individuals and categories; the latter on the basis of extended kin groups) at the watershed between kin-based, unstratified, pre-state institutions of inequality and class-based, stratified, state-organized institutions of inequality. Under significantly similar conditions, equivalent institutions emerged in India and Europe, each bearing the distinctive stamp of its historical and cultural context, and both bearing also the common stamp of their evolutionary and structural context and of their functional burden.

As I have suggested in my argument above, relying in part on Karve, the Indo-Aryans evidently brought ranked occupation—hence early class stratification—to India, where it was assimilated to or imposed upon coexisting, culturally distinct, largely endogamous groupings with perhaps a degree of economic specialization and interdependence within regions. The Indo-Aryans placed themselves and those they could not dispossess of their land in the elite castes—those in the three "twice-born" *varna*s at the top of the hierarchy—appropriating to themselves the land and labour of those they dispossessed. The latter, in turn, had little choice but to assume their assigned, economically enforced, and ritually endorsed social roles and statuses, to perform their assigned tasks, and to contribute the corvee *(begar)* labour, clientship, rents, and taxes imposed upon them in the peasant economy of the emerging state.

Thus, the emergence of caste combined traditional principles of kin organization and ranking with new principles of the ranking of social aggregates according to economic as well as cultural (ethnic) criteria. It is for these reasons that I refer to castes as "kin strata", or "kin classes"—a stage in the development of stratification in South Asia's peasant society. This is a stage in which the ranked groupings and the rank system were regionally, even locally, specific and delimited rather than continental in scope; a stage in which the ranked, occupationalized, kin-based groups were perforce self-contained local micro-strata.

The kin component of caste in India is expressed, emphasized, and reinforced in every institutionalized sphere of life. *Economically* it is to be seen in the sharing of occupation within family and caste, in the organization of work which therefore takes place within and among kin groups; it is seen in the *jajmani* system, whereby inter-caste ritual and economic relations are carried out to a major extent through a system of patron-client relations determined not only by caste, but by family, and are generally passed down from generation to generation within the family. In the *political* realm the kin basis for caste is expressed in the caste *panchayat*s or governing councils: institutions which are made up of heads of families or lineages comprising the local caste segment. It is usually the *panchayat* or combined *panchayat*s of the economically and politically dominant high caste or allied dominant high castes (cf. Srinivas 1959) which govern the village or locality, resolve disputes and punish offenders. In the *religious* sphere the pre-state-like kin basis for caste is manifest in the very nature of Hinduism wherein genealogy is endorsed by, and closely identified with, religious ideology. This is a religion which is oriented to the individual, the kin group, and the caste as closely interrelated foci of supernatural belief and activity, rather than to society, the state, or humanity at large. There is no sacerdotal hierarchy or ultimate authority. The paramount priest for most Hindus is the family priest *(purohit)* who oversees the well-being of the family, family worship, and life-cycle rites of family members. Among the most important deities are household, family, lineage, sib (clan), phratry *(gotra)*, and caste *(jati)* deities (often in that order), whose relevance to the individual is passed down within the household, the family, or more extensive kin group, or is acquired from the kin groups of affines who have come to live with members of those groups. Ancestors and the recently deceased are important foci of supernatural concern for family and kin; it is members of kin groups—family, lineage, sib (clan), phratry, caste (in that order)—whose members participate together in, and contribute to, life-cycle observances and other ritual events. (For case material on kin and caste in religion, see Berreman 1972 : 95-98, 110, 126-133.)

Gould has suggested that it was the Brahman religious elite who, through processes he declines to speculate upon, had become powerful and influential in early India and ". . . invented and propagated a religion that sacralized the occupational order and occupationalized the sacred order" (Gould 1971 : 10), thereby contributing in an essential way to the unique nature of the Hindu caste system. Hindu religion plays a clearly definable role in Indian society as religion does in other complex societies, rationalizing, justifying, and obfuscating social, economic, and political relations within the society (a role, incidentally, which can be, and has been, played also by social science: see my critique of the "Brahmanical" view of caste in social science, in Berreman 1971; cf. Jurgensmeyer 1980). Gould attends to this role of religion (1971 : 10-12), but since I have come to it independently and from a somewhat different perspective over the years, I will briefly present my own discussion as follows.

Hinduism claims to justify the caste system by reference to a powerful and nicely articulated set of concepts : *dharma,* whereby one's religious/moral duty is to fulfil to the best of one's ability the obligations inherent in the status to which one has been born—especially caste (and sex) status. One should not strive for another status even if one were to be successful in achieving it. The concept of *purity and pollution* includes both acquired pollution (whose removal brings relative purity) and inborn, inherent degrees of purity/pollution. The latter accounts for differences in the intrinsic worth among castes by which they are said to be ranked. The degree of birth-ascribed purity/pollution is tied directly to occupation, diet, ritual behaviour, religious and secular perogatives, life style, and other aspects of caste *dharma.* It forms a perfect circle: inborn purity or pollution requires specified behaviours which have inevitable consequences, including degree of inborn purity or pollution in the next life. Purity/pollution is the rationale for caste rank, hence for most of caste members' social, economic, political, and religious experiences and opportunities. In this way, those who are perpetrators and beneficiaries of the purity/pollution hierarchy, and those who are its victims, are each enjoined to bvehave correspondingly and are rewarded and punished accordingly—in this life for being born pure or impure, respectively, and in the next life for the extent to which they have fulfilled (or acquiesced in) their *dharma.* Under this concept it is specifically decreed that high castes (who own most of the land) must not till the soil nor work with their hands, while it is the low (and landless) who are allowed to, and therefore must, do so. The fundamental division of India's agricultural, peasant society into landowners and land workers is thus enjoined and reinforced by ideology and divine sanction. Deviation is, of course, as common in this as in other commandments from on high.

Reincarnation, to which reference has been made immediately above, is a basic tenet of Hinduism which defines the nature and locus of one's *karma*—of the just deserts that follow from the way in which one's *dharma* has been fulfilled or unfulfilled. In the next life, one is rewarded or punished, in effect, by rebirth in a higher or lower, happier or more miserable caste, life-form or situation. *Maya,* commonly translated as "cosmic illusion", is the basic Hindu idea that the suffering and rewards of daily life and earthly existence are in any case illusory and not to be made matters of significant concern. Earthly desires, comforts, possessions, pleasures, and even survival are irrelevant and unworthy goals in an ultimate sense. Release from this mortal coil of birth, striving, and rebirth is all that really matters. The many, of course, suffer in the painful illusions of life, while the very few revel in the delightful illusions accessible to and reserved for them at the expense of the rest. It is worth noting that it is the few, the elites—not the masses—who enunciate and most ardently advocate this credo, a credo akin to the Christian "the meek shall inherit the earth". (In Hinduism, the meek shall advance on the path to release *from* the earth.) Those advocates are in a position to wield the power which enforces the credo—a credo which clearly is not designed to foment or condone revolution or even social mobility.

In short, Hinduism decrees that whatever one's lot in life, it is earned, deserved, inborn, irreversible, and ultimately irrelevant. What is relevant is that one fulfil one's *dharma* so as to move towards personal salvation, the highest goal. Birth is the basis for caste membership and therefore for caste *dharma*. Birth, in turn, is defined by parentage: People of ritually equivalent parentage are themselves ritually and socially equivalent, i.e. of the same caste. For these reasons kin relations are central to the religious-ideological rationale for caste stratification as well as to its more pragmatic aspects. That rationale is advocated primarily by the high-caste beneficiaries of the system. Those whose exploitation it is designed to justify consistently see their status as the result of historical circumstances rather than divine will (Berreman 1971; Jurgensmeyer 1980; cf. Berreman 1972: 209, 253-256). Power is the mechanism by which the system is enforced—the ideology realized—for power and privilege are congruent in caste as in other forms of social stratification.

The relevance of this discussion for an understanding of the role and dynamics of caste in the evolution of peasant society in India may now be summarized, enumerating some points which have been made explicitly or implicitly above.

(1) The caste system in India originated and persisted as a form of institutionalized inequality in which ethnically distinct social entities were absorbed into a status and economic hierarchy as ranked, endogamous, birth-ascribed, kin-based occupational groups—kin strata, in effect—in order to provide land, labour, rent, and taxes for the surplus agricultural production organized by and for the benefit of those who acquired their land through the

exercise of military, administrative, and economic power. The role of the caste system is analogous in significant ways to the system of vassalage in feudal Europe.

(2) The kin-based caste system benefited elites not only by providing them goods and services, but also by effectively fractionating society, preventing or inhibiting development of class consciusness and class mobilization among non-elites by the membership exclusiveness of castes and the mutually exclusive vested interests (status interests resulting in status competition) of castes as localized, kin-based, ranked groups. Caste endogamy prevented the formation of caste alliances through marriage. The kin-and caste-based nature of economic relations, political relations, and supernaturally and ideologically endorsed relations of all sorts, reinforced this fractionation, mutual suspicion, competition, and hence the vulnerability of the landless and labouring castes to those who controlled land and labour. It thereby minimized the likelihood of multi-caste organization for change.

(3) Narrow occupationalization and minimal security of livelihood served this function as well. Non-elite castes held little significant control over productive resources including land and occupation, and therefore were unable to make a living except through the exchange of their labour for elite-controlled goods, at rates determined almost entirely by the elites. There was no production for use sufficient to support the landless castes, who were inevitably clients dependent upon the patronage of the landed castes.

(4) The congruity of kin, caste, occupation, and ethnicity prevented both individual upward mobility and horizontal (occupational and geographic) mobility. In the case of the latter, there was little open social space or occupational space into which mobile persons or groups could move because kin- and caste-based patron/client relations (the *jajmani* system) assured that in any locality there were already established occupational role occupants with firm ties by family and caste to patron families and castes. The the case of vertical mobility, the congruity of caste and occupation in social ranking, together with birth-ascription of both, prohibited mobility. Where horizontal mobility did occur, it was usually at the behest of the elites who simply replaced a client group (often for recalcitrance). When vertical mobility did occur, it was a result of change in the distribution of power and resources which enabled a caste to make good the claim—which every low caste harbours—that in fact it is a high caste unjustly maligned or misidentified as to its ancestrally-determined identity. The circumstances under which such a change occurs may be a new-found occupational monopoly on an essential service, universal adult franchise among a numerically large low-status group, access to legal or legislative power or to powerful allies, new sources of livelihood independent of traditional caste controls, or the like. In the case of either kind of mobility, power is the

mechanism for change; ideology is marshalled to justify the change, i.e. a caste does not move up, its "true" identity is simply "discovered" and acted upon.

In sum, the Indian caste system comprises a unique congruity among kin, status, rank, occupation, class, ethnicity (culture), and power creating a powerful, involute, and total system of stratification. It is a system well suited to agricultural production under an early state organization which sharply distinguished between owners and non-owners of major productive resources. But it is *not* well suited to complex, technologically rapidly changing, urban, industrial organization. As a result of the emergence of the latter kind of soceity, we now see changes in Indian caste towards a familial and narrowly ritual phenomenon, and towards a more broadly defined vehicle for political and economic mobilization in new occupations, technologies, bureaucracies, and politics on the other (cf. Berreman 1976; Freeman 1977; Kolenda 1978; Srinivas 1966). Urban migration offers new arenas for mobilization in pursuit of shared interests, with the result that true class stratification is becoming more prominent, and traditional, localized caste status-striving tends to get left behind in the village (where, let it not be forgotten, 80 per cent of the population lives), and to some extent in village-like urban residential neighbourhoods.

CONCLUDING COMMENT

India is perhaps unique among the world's peasant societies in the degree and consistency with which even the humblest of its peasant agriculturists—those with even the slightest interest in (i.e. control over) land—have at their command an underclass of lower castes who perform agricultural labour and service occupations in support of the agriculturists. To a very major extent, owner and worker, exploiter and exploited, identify their economic interests with their caste interests, and their caste interests with family interests. If family was the first form of class consciousness in Europe, as Rapp has argued in this volume, then I would suggest that caste was the form that consciousness was moulded into early in the history and development of peasant India. Like family, partly because it is in fact an extension of family, caste has been a persistent and portentous form of social organization and consciousness in the evolution of India's peasant and emerging post-peasant society.

But if caste in India is an archaic form of social stratification, as I have suggested throughout this paper, it also seems to many observers to be becoming an increasingly anachronistic one with the emergence in India of industrialization, capitalism, democratic self-government, mass communications, secularism in many spheres, and the striving by some castes, allied castes, caste associations (cf. Rudolph and Rudolph 1960), and caste categories to metamorphose themselves into activist self-interest groups on the basis of common class interests—groups such as political parties and political action groups. A conspicuous example of the latter is the Dalit Panthers, founded in 1972 in Maharashtra but now spread well beyond that state. Originating among the untouchable Mahars, this burgeoning organization of the oppressed (for *dalit* means "oppressed") issued a manifesto in November of 1973, stating that it plans to move beyond the caste of its originators to organize "all scheduled castes and tribes, converted Buddhists, workers, landless labourers, small farmers and nomadic tribes" (Padgaonkar 1974), in short to encompass all of the dispossessed categories—the most disadvantaged class—in Indian society.

During the past 30 years the world has witnessed increasing disparities between rich and poor both among nations and, within nations, among class strata and communal entities (ethnic groups, races, castes, language groups, religions). Monumental confrontations and reactive repressions have resulted, arising from the economic, political, and social competition and conflicts of interest inherent in such disparities. Increasingly these conflicts have been carried out through the mobilization of social aggregates on the basis of shared "primordial sentiments" (cf. Shils 1957). These aggregates are communal groups of various sorts which, by their very definition and recruitment are pre-formed, self-aware, bounded interest and action groups. The consciousness of common interests on the part of their members, unlike that of the members of class categories, need not be created or raised in order to mobilize them, because such consciousness is the essence of their existence. That is, conflicts that are basically economic and political—conflicts of class interest—are assimilated to, and expressed as, conflicts that are cultural, i.e. communal. The conflicts are perceived by individuals through the lens of sentiments shared by their membership group(s), and therefore are responded to in terms of group self-interest rather than in terms of the interests of class or other analytic categories. Such conflicts seem to be increasing rather than diminishing in frequency, intensity, and devastation, although the preponderance of economic, police, and military power in the hands of the privileged, so long as it remains or is believed by most of the population to remain, makes remote the likelihood of widespread mobilization to rectify the inequality that generates the conflict. The locus and definition of such power can and does shift, however, when it is too widely and oppressively exercised, or when the means to initiate change from below come to hand, as several recent regimes have discovered to their dismay.

In this context caste in India, like a number of other characteristics sometimes described as symptoms of the backwardness of that troubled nation, may in fact anticipate the future of an increasingly fractionated and inegalitarian world, and of other increasingly divided nations in that world. In short, the trends we see today in Indian caste, and its relationship to class, may represent our future more accurately even than we have supposed it might represent a contemporary (and temporary) survival of a pre-feudal and feudal past. As castes redefine their roles and rationales, as they mobilize, compete, and conflict in pursuit of their interests in an increasingly industrialized state fully involved in the world economy, we perhaps see a foreshadowing of the form competing interest group processes will take within and among nations on a world-wide scale. If so, it is a sobering prospect, deserving of careful attention and analysis.

REFERENCES

Beidelman, Thomas O. (1959) : A comparative Analysis of the *Jajmani* System. Locust Valley, New York : J.J. Augustin.

Berreman, Gerald D. (1960) : Caste in India and the United States. The American Journal of Sociology 66 : 120-127.

      (1962) : Sib and Clan among the Pahari of North India. Ethnology 1 : 524-528.

      (1967) : Caste as Social Process. Southwestern Journal of Anthropology 23 : 351-370.

      (1968) : Caste : The Concept. *In* International Encyclopedia of the Social Sciences (D. Sills, ed). New York : Macmillan and Free Press. Vol. 2, pp. 333-339.

      (1971) : The Brahmanical View of Caste. Contributions to Indian Sociology (New Series) No. V: 18-25.

      (1972) : Hindus of the Himalayas, Ethnography and Change (Second edition) Berkeley and Los Angeles : University of California Press. (First edition, 1963).

      (1976) : Social Mobility and Change in India's caste Society. *In* responses to Change : Society, Culture and Personality. George A. DeVos, ed. Pp. 294-322. New York : D. Van Nostrand.

      (1978)': Scale and Social Relations. Current Anthropology 12 : 225-245.

      (1979) : Caste and Other Inequities : Essays on Inequality. Delhi : Manohar Books.

      (1981) : Social Inequality : A Cross-Cultural Analysis. *In* Social Inequality : Comparative and Developmental Approaches. G.D. Berreman, ed. New York : Academic Press. *In Press.*

Bloch, Marc (1931) : Feudalism : European. *In* Encyclopedia of the Social Sciences R.A. Seligman, ed. New York : Macmillan. Vol. 6, pp. 203-210.

Freeman, James M. (1977) : Scarcity and Opportunity in an Indian Village. Menlo Park, California: Cumings.

Fried, Morton (1960) : On the Evolution of Social Stratification and the State. *In* Culture in History : Essays in Honor of Paul Radin (S. Diamond, ed.). New York : Columbia University Press. Pp. 713-731.

      (1967) : The Evolution of Political Society. New York : Random House.

Fuchs, Stephen (1968) : the Gond and Bhumia of Eastern Mandla. Bombay : New Literature Publishing Company.

Fürer-Haimemdorf, Christoph von. (1948) : The Raj Gonds of Adilabad : A Peasant Culture of the Deccan. London : Macmillan.

      (1974) : A Central Indian Tribal People : The Raj Gonds. *In* South Asia : Seven Community Profiles. Clarence Maloney, ed. Pp. 202-257. New York : Holt, Rinehart and Winston.

Ghurye, G.S. (1952) : Caste and Class in India. New York : Philosophical Library.

Gould, Harold (1971) : Caste and Class : A Comparative View. Reading, Mass.: Addison-Wesley Modular Publications.

Isaacs, Harold R. (1975) : Idols of the Tribe. New York : Harper and Row.

Jurgensmeyer, Mark (1980) : What if the Untouchables Don't Believe in Untouchability? Bulletin of Concerned Asian Scholars 12 : 23-28.

Karve, Irawati (1961) : Hindu Society—An Interpretation. Poona : Deccan College.

Kolenda, Pauline M. (1963) : Toward a Model of the Hindu Jajmani System. Human Organization 2 : 11-31.

          (1978) : Caste in Contemporary India : Beyond Organic Solidarity. Menlo Park, California: Benjamin/Cumings.

Krader, Lawrence (1978) : The Origin of the State Among the Nomads of Asia. *In* The Early State. H.J.M. Claessen and P. Skalnik, eds. Pp. 93-107. The Hague : Mouton.

Murdock, George P. (1949) : Social Structure. New York : Macmillan.

Padgaonkar, Dileep (1974) : The Dalit Panthers. The Times of India (23 January, 1974) p. 4.

Rudolph, Lloyd I. and Susan H. (1960) : The Political Role of India's Caste Associations. Pacific Affairs 33 : 5-22.

Sahlins, Marshall (1968) : Tribesmen. Englewood Cliffs, New Jersey : Prentice-Hall.

Service, Elman R. (1971) : Primitive Social Organization (Second edition). New York : Random House.

          (1975) : Origins of the State and Civilization. New York: W.W. Norton. Shils, Edward A. (1957) : Primordial, Personal, Sacred and Civil Ties. The British Journal of Sociology 8 : 130-145.

Srinivas, M.N. (1959) : The Dominant Caste in Rampura. American Anthropologist 61 : 1-16.

          (1966) : Social Change in Modern India. Berkeley and Los Angeles : University of California Press.

Wiser, William H. (1936) : The Hindu Jajmani System. Lucknow : Lucknow Publishing House.

Agrarian Conflict and Peasant Movements in Twentieth Century India

WALTER HAUSER

In thinking about modern India we are confronted with the obvious fact that this is an overwhelmingly rural, agrarian society. Many of the people who live in its half million villages are peasants. To use the words of Daniel Thorner (1968), they comprise the "largest peasantry in the non-socialist world". In this social and economic setting, the critical issue for India historically and in the contemporary present has been and continues to be, who gets what from whom on what terms, and at what consequences, on the land? Bernard Cohn (1963) has made the point another way in saying that "the control of land and the distribution of the product of the land were and are central to the social relations and the social structure of the bulk of the Indian population. Land tenure in India was and is, not only about ownership of land, rents and taxes, but about kinship, marriage, ritual, status, prestige, power and authority."

These questions concern interactions at all levels of the society from government, or the state at the apex, through various levels of land controllers, tenure holders, intermediaries, peasant tenants, sharecroppers and ultimately landless agricultural labourers at the bottom of the social, economic, and political pyramid. These interactions all involve accommodation over the distribution of resources, however defined, whether production, revenue, rent, shared crops, or wage payments. The structure of the accommodating process involves control from one level to the next, and it is the flexibilities within that process of control that determine the nature of agrarian relations at all points of the social hierarchy. When these flexibilities do not achieve accommodation, conflict is one of the options open to the actors in an agrarian society. When the tensions of conflict are sufficiently severe this conflict may escalate to agitation and violence, and may ultimately be articulated as peasant movement. Such movements have occurred historically in India, and in the 1930s and 1940s they achieved a range and force to impinge significantly on the provincial and national polity. This paper defines the qualities of agrarian relations in the most local structures of the society that escalated to violence and movement in the central Gangetic plain of northern India in that period. It is meant to discuss general issues and approaches to the problem rather than to state the substance of the case. My forthcoming study of agrarian conflict and peasant movements will amplify and refine the issues raised here.

II

I have been concerned with studying these phenomena primarily inBihar, where the control and conflict syndrome did indeed escalate to agitation and peasant movement, particularly in the 1930s, but also in the decades following, if in somewhat different forms. This work raises the basic question that concerns me, namely, what is the nature of the agrarian social structure and how does its moral and political economy impinge on the political processes of India particularly in its local and regional settings, but ultimately also on the politics of the national centre? I take the term "moral economy" from Scott (1976 : 3), to define the peasant view of economic justice, i.e. which superordinate claims on their product are tolerable and within accepted normative bounds and which are intolerable and therefore outside those bounds. The political economy view, which has been argued recently with great effectiveness by Samuel Popkin (1979; see especially pp. 17-31 and Ch. 6.), sees the peasant as a relatively more active agent of change responding to his specific and long-term interests and needs. While these distinctive perceptions of peasant society are obviously not mutually exclusive, I would suggest that particularly in the Indian setting, elements of both are useful in defining and interpreting social reality. They add another dimension to my original question, "Who gets what from whom on what terms and at what consequences?" namely by asking, "For what reasons do these actions take place?" in a peasant society.

The question of the political economy of rural India is one that was socially and politically important in the nineteenth century; it was critically so in the 1930's during the freedom movement, and similarly since independence in 1947. In other words, there has been and is a continuum of social and political interaction in rural India that is as relevant and critical to the body politic in 1980 as it was in 1938 and 1878. This view is confirmed by my own work which focuses on the 1930s, that of one of our students who has worked on the nineteenth century material (Yang 1976), and from the most recent evidence of the 1970s (eg. Franda 1978: 1-3, and International Labour Office 1979). The similarities in agrarian structures over time are apparent, despite all legislation and reform, as are similarities in peasant response. The political system is fundamentally affected by this issue.

I feel that in order to understand how that political system has functioned over time, we must understand the social structural context of the peasant society in which it ultimately finds its roots. In my earlier studies (1961 and 1963) I was primarily concerned with portraying the organizational characteristics of an Indian peasant movement and its relationship to the Congress politics of nationalism. The movements of the 1930s emerged out of a confluence of particular agrarian conditions and the economic spin-offs of the depression with the pervasive politics of nationalism. I am more interested now, however, in the basic elements of social, economic, and political control in the rural countryside that generated conflict and that escalated into struggles and provided the basis for the peasant movements of the 1930s. What follows then, are my ideas about agrarian social structure and the ways in which the normative expectations and interests of the peasant impinged on the political systems of India. As I have indicated, my work focuses primarily on the northern Indian State of Bihar. I would argue that the data can be extrapolated easily to eastern Uttar Pradesh, which would encompass along with Bihar a current population of approximately 100 million. While I am not proposing any generalized conflict hypothesis for all of India, there is much in what follows that has broader application than the limits of Bihar and U.P.

III

I am convinced, after some years of trying to understand how and why peasants agitated and how peasant movements were organized in India, that we must try to understand the phenomenon "control", from the perception of the controlled. I would suggest that the control of the superordinate landlord controller is viewed by the subordinate controlled peasant as exploitation. In saying this I am neither making a value judgement nor staking an ideological position, but merely stating the reality as I judge it to be understood by Bihar peasant/tenants in the 1930's *vis-a-vis* the superordinate *zamindar* land controllers who sat above them in that social system. I think we need to understand what the world looked like from the ground up, from the perspective of those who were subject to the domination, control, power, and authority of the *zamindar*. We should let them speak for themselves and try to understand them in their terms, not ours.

For the purposes of this paper I do not wish to get involved in the definitional thicket of who is a peasant. Certainly in India the term covers a very broad range of meaning. By "peasants" I mean all those on the land and in the villages who rely primarily on the land and its product to maintain subsistence, which may also, incidentally, include commercial production for the market, and who stand in a subordinate relationship to superordinate claimants of rent or revenue, whether intermediate tenure holders, *zamindar*-type landlords, or the state. The term I use here to incorporate these meanings is "peasant/tenant", although even this does not begin to define the enormous diversity of groups and interests on the land in rural northern India. This layering of social and cultural relations and economic and political interests ranges from substantial peasant tenants at one end of the spectrum, down the scale of tenancies and sub-tenencies to marginal tenants who may also perform agricultural labour on wage payment. The complexity of this social and economic stratification is discussed most effectively for the Indian case by Andre Beteille in his essay on "The Concept of the Peasant Society" (1974/1976). In an effort to get at the effect of this stratification on peasant mobilization, I have chosen to study agrarian relations in Bihar in half a dozen different local settings, involving peasants at different levels of the system. What follows are some generalizations that emerge from this effort.

My first point then is that there are social and functional categories and relationships on the land which, by the nature of land as a source of wealth and status, place people in rural India in a conflict relationship. The landlord, by definition, has access to power through his control of the land. The tenant, by definition, has access to land and its resources only through the landlord. He is in an inferior position. Put in more explicit terms, the landlord controls the primary means of production, i.e. the land, and the peasant/tenant does not. Walter Neale (1969) makes the point effectively when he argues that "land is to rule", that land is an instrument to achieve, maintain, and extend economic control, social status, and political power in the local environment. The evidence from Bihar in the nineteenth and twentieth centuries, and certainly in the 1930s, supports this view. Land was an instrument of maintaining and extending control over land and people on the land. The entire institutional, legal, and symbolic system was utilized to that end. And to the extent that individual or collective claims from peasant/tenants, or agitations of peasant movements, or reforms of government, threatened or appeared to threaten that control, there was built-in conflict. Such claims, agitations, or reforms were, and are, seen to impinge on proprietary prerogatives, hence to impinge on economic and political interests and concomitant social status and social control.

My second point is that these conflict relationships between the superordinate land controllers and their supporters (petty administrators on landed estates and strong-armed retainers) on the one hand, and the subordinate, controlled peasant/tenants on the land beneath them, are expressed in terms of compulsion, coercion, intimation, threat, and harassment, and that the use of force and violence in this exchange is not uncommon. It is rather more accurate to say that in this agrarian environment, violence and the threat of violence are the ultimate weapons for enforcing control.

A corollary to both these formulations is that there is a rich language which expresses perceptions of conflict and intimidation in the minds and experience of the peasants themselves. As someone whose first language is English, working in a rural context where the primary spoken and written language is a very localized Hindi, I am particularly impressed by this phenomenon. I would argue that if rural Bihar in the 1930s was semi-literate, it was far from inarticulate. Peasants do speak, and their leaders speak, and both can be interviewed, and their pleas and petitions on paper tell us much about peasant attitudes and feelings. They suggest a consciousness and a peasant culture that is far from weighted down by the hierarchical value system within which it exists, or the victim of a passive "false consciousness", as Marx and some others would have us believe. There is not sufficient space here to elaborate the research that has generated literally hundreds of vernacular terms defining agrarian society and its coercive relationships as seen by the eyes of peasants and their local and regional leaders.

I referred earlier to the depression crisis of the 1930s that caused a severe economic price/rent squeeze, and that with growing demographic pressures exacerbated pre-existing agrarian tension. My fourth point is that the linked phenomena of tenancy and rent constitute the primary mechanism through which control over land, product, and people is enforced in Bihar. But rent is only the top of the control iceberg, inasmuch as there is an infinite range of permutations of the rent syndrome: the amount of rent, whether in cash or kind, whether it is commuted and at what level, the non-issuance of receipts, the various rent collection cesses, and the enormously complicated and institutionalized collecting mechanism which is inevitably in the hands of or under the thumb of the land controlling *zamindar*, through the *patwari*, or land records accountant.

A related element of the control mechanism that I include under the rent rubric is the servicing of debt which was important in the 1930s, and which recent research by Prof. Pradhan Prasad at the A.N. Sinha Institute of Social Studies in Patna, argues is the primary control mechanism in north Bihar in the 1970s. A similar position prevails in West Bengal, where a recent I.L.O. survey (1979 : 48) holds that usury is *the* primary form of rural exploitation in that Indian State.

Another key element of the rent/debt syndrome, and perhaps the least understood, is what I call the perquisite demand. Anyone familiar with the enormous primary literature of famine reports, settlement reports, and rent reduction reports of the 1930s, the land reform legislation of the same period, the various tenancy inquiry committee reports, as well as the Kisan Sabha (peasant association) literature, has encountered the multiple perquisite demands on the peasant, mostly in the form of illegal cesses and services. Whether they were "customary", to use the term of administration, or not, seems beside the point. The fact is, they were an additional floating demand on production and available resources, always in the determination of the *zamindar* controller, to be used at his discretion. In the reciprocity between unequals of obligations and rights, this perquisite demand put an onerous strain on the legitimacy of the authority of the *zamindar* controller in the eyes of the subordinate, exploited peasant. I refer here to the theoretical formulation of Georges Balandier (1971 : 39) on the concept of reciprocity, power, and authority. In the case of *zamindar* control in Bihar, I would revise Eric Wolf's (1966) "rent capitalism" formulation to incorporate the debt and perquisite syndrome.

Let me re-emphasize each of these elements of the control system, i.e. eviction or its threat, increased rent or its threat, usury perquisites including illegal cesses (or *abwabs*), and forced labour (or *begari*), all defining and enforcing the dominance of the superordinate controller over the subordinate controlled on the land. The ultimate sanction in this relationship was force.

My next point is to suggest that if there was control and exploitation from above in the Bihar system, the peasant/tenant was not a passive bystander. Often enough the peasants plead their case in appeals and petitions to the leadership of the Bihar Provincial Kisan Sabha and other agencies of the system. But if there was conflict in response to control, we must assume that the peasant/tenant was not only making appeals, but also resisting. The term the British administration used to describe this resistance was to talk about the "refractory" peasants. One must presume that government and the controllers would in fact have preferred a passive peasantry. These were, of course, other options open to the peasant. He could leave the village, which happened very seldon in the 1930s. Alternative employment was a limited option within Bihar in that period. Another option was the seasonal pattern of out-migration that is particularly heavy in a number of Bihar districts. But none of these possibilities provided wide-ranging or long-term solutions.

This limited range of non-agrarian opportunities meant that the pressures and confrontations on the land had to be worked out within the rural setting itself. I would argue that there was a dynamic interaction between the controlling demands of the superordinate landlord on the one hand, and the political and economic ability of the subordinate peasant/tenant to resist on the other. There is obviouly an ultimate economic limit beyond which rent exploitation demands cannot realistically go; in other words, peasant misery is not "infinitely increasable ". It is true that the rent/debt/perquisite demand appears to have increased exponentially. But it is also true that while some people on the land could not cope and presumably did not survive, most did. It seems to me that they resisted, and in the process an accommodation was made. The dynamic I describe was one of alternating flexibility and resolution on the one hand, with a countervailing tension and conflict on the other.

I would argue that it is precisely this tension and resistance, what I call the "struggle" or "conflict" option, that generated a peasant movement. When

Agrarian Conflict and Peasant Movements   257

accommodation could not be achieved in the customary push and pull of the superordinate/subordinate relationship, struggle and movement followed. To summarize this argument, I would say that because of, and despite, the tremendous pressure from above, peasants responded to exploitation by sending petitions, making personal and written appears, engaging in struggle and confict to assert their claimed rights to crops and land, and ultimately participating in movements and peasant organizations and achieving in the process immediate local redress and contributing also to a climate of long-term change. An important corollary here is that the local struggle and conflict and the regional peasant movement tended to reinforce one another as awareness and communication moved in both directions. In other words, there is a vertical link, or reciprocity, between the local peasant society and its conficts and struggles and the supra-local peasant movement, that is mutually beneficial.

My next argument in this progression is that despite the nature of the rent/debt/perquisite system and the reactions and demands of peasant/tenants, society and politics were so structured in India in the 1930s to militate against agitation and peasant movement developing into more extended revolutionary forms. This was a function of the intense social and economic stratification of agrarian society which in turn precluded the easy formation of horizontal class categories and their political mobilization. Mobilization and movement were also constrained by the coercive power of the state system. The controls of the power strucure and the linkages between the non-official and official power structures were so complete that sustained, violent uprisings did not occur. Violent confrontations did take place, but rebellion and revolution were not inherent in the political economy of rural Bihar in the 1930s. In this context, it is important to understand that the petty administrative officials, rent collectors, police, etc. are controlled by and manipulated by the *zamindar* landlord, and that the formal arms of administration, including the courts, if not openly corruptible, are utilized and exploited by the *zamindar* to serve his objectives of political, social, and economic control. From the bottom, this overarching control structure appears total, inasmuch as the observable collusion between the informal non-official *zamindar* side and the official lower and middle levels of authority are so pervasive as to meld the structure into one large umbrella of authority as viewed from below. The Hindi word for this collusion is *gatbandhan,* meaning literally "bound together", as in marriage. It appears in the petitions and pleas of the peasants of Bihar with great regularity. It is indeed fundamental to their world-view.

I would also suggest that at times the Congress party itself, both as government from 1937 and as a national movement incorporating wide *zamindar* landlord interests, became in the eyes of the peasant/tenant a part of this power structure. In this sense the Congress functioned in a multiple role, inasmuch as it also provided the nationalist political milieu in which all political activity in the 1930s occurred. But while the Congress created a new climate of awareness, it also discouraged much action by its sheer political dominance and the overriding force of its nationalist objective. What concerns us is that there were other strands in Indian politics and that they performed important roles and functions.

Among these strands were the peasant movements that emerged out of the control and conflict syndrome of agrarian society in the twentieth century, parricularly in the 1930s and after. I would suggest that one of the roles of the peasant movements, or kisan sabhas, was to become the new patron of the peasants, representing their interests on the ground, but more particularly acting as their agent *vis-a-vis* the power structure at all levels. The kisan sabha, as agitational movement and as organization, publicly articulated peasant interests and in particular struggles represented peasant interests in very specific ways, in direct negotiations with landlords, on arbitration boards, and in the courts.

This local action was perhaps in total, cumulative terms the most important achievement of the movements of the thirties. Their long-term influence came in creating a climate of change, through publicity and by direct representation in the legislatures themselves that ultimately resulted in major agrarian reform, i.e. *zamindari* abolition. It is important to understand that thie reform, the abolition of the *zamindari* landlord system, introduced a change in the pattern of land control rather than in the structure of control. The links between these early agitations and movements, and very recent agrarian conflict and atrocities in the northern Indian Gangetic countryside are perhaps less tangible, though the conflict phenomenon itself is an expression of the same structural qualities of control seen before, now penetrated deeper into the social system.

IV

My approach to social and political change in twentieth-century India will be clear from the foregoing statement of my ideas about agrarian society and peasant movements. I think of myself as a social historian concerned with understanding the functioning of politics in society. I follow Abner Cohen (1974) in thinking of political and economic institutions as forming essentially one category. To quote Cohen (1974 : 22-23), "economic interests and political interests interpenetrate each other and act and react on one another. The political and the economic form one category, their common denominator being power relationships." Ralph Nicholas (1967) takes this idea one step further, citing Polanyi, to say that in "peasant societies, most social relations of all kinds are 'embedded' in one another", i.e. the political, the economic, the religious, the legal, and the kinship systems. It is in this holistic sense that I view the world of agrarian relations in India and the movements and politics they have produced. I would qualify this formulation only to make certain that we understand that the interaction and influence of all social institutions on one another is active, dynamic, and ongoing; in other words, that it is in process, that it is historical. Accordingly, we are concerned not only with defining the structure of social relationships in the system, but with understanding the patterns and changes that emerge in these relationships as we observe them over time, and as they may vary and distribute spatially.

I have done this by examining the character of agrarian relations where peasants and land controllers live, namely, in the most local structures of Indian society. Indeed, it is from research in those networks of villages I describe as "struggle" villages, that I have come to apprehend the existential reality of those agrarian relations. It is at this level where conflict over rights in the land and its produce are at daily issue in the lives of peasant/tenants and superordinate estate-holding landlords. I have identified a number of such village networks and have rich data on five or six such settings where conflict led to violence in the 1930s. Several of these case studies provide continuity from the nineteenth century, through the 1930s, to the time of my most recent field work in 1975. Studying the range of occurrence of these localized struggles or conflicts, and the contextual reasons for their varying character in space and time, will permit us to identify the operating factors at work in the local structures, identifying similarities and distinctions in style, and thereby to arrive at a more fundamental understanding of the nature of agrarian relations and peasant response. The sample should enable us to begin moving more confidently in the direction of generalization.

CONCLUSION

At the outset of this paper I cited Daniel Thorner in saying that the inhabitants of India's half million villages comprised the "largest peasantry in the non-socialist world". In that same essay, Thorner (1968) writes that the "foundations of traditional peasant society are being shaken". It is the point of my current research to identify the patterns of peasant behaviour involved in that process of social, political, and economic change.

I have made two main arguments in this paper. First, that the political action of peasants is fundamentally a reflection of the implicit qualities of the agrarian social structure in which it takes place; that conflict over rights to the land and its product in an agrarian society often generate violence, and that local leaders have emerged and responded to these conditions to mobilize movements and have provided the link to the larger networks of regional and national politics. My second argument is that there is a significant continuum in the character of conflict and the political response of the peasantry to conditions of control, from the late nineteenth century, through the 1930s, to the contemporary present.

Both these points have profound implications for the Indian body politic. They speak on the one hand of the quality of conflict over the distribution of limited resources in the local settings, and on the other they suggest that as the polity becomes more democratized over time, the political interests and the political character of the local agrarian society will impinge more directly on all levels of the system. I am suggesting that the question of "who gets what from whom and on what terms, on the land" is a question that engages all levels of government, from the federal centre, through the States, down to the most local structures of the system. Understanding how peasants, landlords, political parties, and governments adjust and respond to these various pressures is likely to inform us about significant aspects of Indian life and society.

A NOTE ON SOURCES

I have attempted to generate data wherever and at whatever level material and human resources might be available. This has meant some work in the private and public papers in the National Archives of India and the Nehru Memorial Museum and Library in New Delhi, and work in the Bihar State Archives, mostly utilizing political and police reports and revenue proceedings. In my 1975 research, however, I focused primarily on the local level. I worked at length in each of the identified village networks, interviewing contenders on both sides of a given conflict, land controllers, peasant tenants, and leaders of both. In some fortunate cases this effort produced a variety of written data, correspondence, propaganda leaflets and pamphlets, posters, and a rich body of judicial case papers. I have also pursued each of these case studies into the local or district record rooms, where an enormous range of social and economic data are available in the local revenue and rent papers generated in the late nineteenth and twentieth centuries, what in Bihar are called the "Village Notes" (see Hagen and Yang 1976). In this process I have identified a large number of peasant petitions and a wide range of pamphlet literature, including speeches, reports, and a variety of other organizational material reflecting the interests and activity of party and peasant associations from the local to the national level. Much of this material is in English, and much of the organizational and unofficial material is in Hindi and local vernaculars. It will be apparent that many of these sources and the various newspapers I have utilized, intersect given issues and problems from several vantage points, providing checks and balances and a depth not available in any one set of documentation.

REFERENCES

Balandier, Georges, (1971) : *Political Anthropology* (New York : Pantheon Books).

Béteille, André (1974/ 1976) : *Six Essays in Comparative Sociology* (New Delhi, Oxford University Press).

Cohen, Abner (1974) : *Two-Dimensional Man : An Essay on the Anthropology of Power and Symbolism in Complex Society* (Berkeley : University of California Press).

Cohn, Bernard S. (1963) : "Comments on Papers of W. Hauser, J.R. McLane, and T.E. Metcalf on Land Tenure", *Indian Economic and Social History Review* Vol. 1, No. 2 (October-December 1963).

Franda, Marcus (1978) : *Agrarian Reform in North Bihar : Operation Kosi Kranti* (American University Field Service Reports, No. 6) Hanover, N.H.

(1978) : *J.P.'s Musahri Project, 1978* (Hanover, N.H.: American University Field Service Reports No. 8).

(1978) : *Rural Development, Bengali Marxist Style* (Hanover, N.H.: American University Field Service Reports No. 15).

Hagen, James R. and Anand A. Yang (1976) : "Local Sources for the Study of Rural India : The 'Village Notes' of Bihar", *The Indian Economic and Social History Review* Vol. 13 (March 1976).

Hauser, Walter, (1961) : *The Bihar Provincial Kisan Sabha, 1929-1942 : A Study of an Indian Peasant Movement*, Unpublished Ph.D. Dissertation, University of Chicago.

(1963) : "The Indian National Congress and Land Policy in the 20th Century", *Indian Economic and Social History Review* Vol. 1 (July-September), pp. 57-65.

International Labour Office, (1979) : *Overcoming Rural Underdevelopment :* Proceedings of a Workshop on Alternative Agrarian Systems and Rural Development, Arusha, Tanzania, 4-14 April 1979 (Geneva).

Neale, Walter (1969) : "Land is to Rule", in Robert Eric Frykenberg, *Social Structure and Land Control in India* (Madison : University of Wisconsin).

Nicholas, Ralph W. (1967) : "Discussion of the Panel on Caste and Politics in Bihar", Chicago, Association for Asian Studies, unpublished Comments.

Popkin, Samuel L. (1979) : *The Rational Peasant : The Political Economy of Rural Society in Vietnam* (Berkeley : University of California Press).

Scott, James C. (1976) : *The Moral Economy of the Peasant : Rebellion and Subsistence in Southeast Asia* (New Haven : Yale University Press).

Thorner, Daniel (1968) : "Peasants", *International Encyclopedia of the Social Sciences* (Macmillan Company).

Wolf, Eric, (1966) : *Peasants* (Englewood Cliffs: Prentice-Hall, Inc.).

Yang, Anand Alan (1976) : *Control and Conflict in an Agrarian Society : A Study of Saran District, 1860-1920.* Unpublished Ph.D. Dissertation, University of Virginia.

Peasant Transformation in a Fringe Village:

A Study in the Process

U.S. MISRA & B.R.K.SHUKLA

This paper is based on two studies, separated by a period of ten years, of a multi-caste agricultural village located 15 km south of Lucknow on the Lucknow-Varanasi road. The village, named Mawaiya, was first studied in 1964-66, and re-studied in 1975. The re-study revealed certain significant changes in the land distribution pattern and occupational structure of the village, which apparantly can be correlated with the proximity of the village to a metropolis and State capital. The most important aspect of these changes is that rapid urban expansion, along with the growing demands of the city for a steady supply of skilled and unskilled labour, and the increasing land-hunger among the rich, has created conditions under which the agricultural land is being removed from the control of the local peasants.

THE VILLAGE

The proximity of the village to the state capital provided an ideal situation for studying the phenomenon of occupational change in the village, over a ten-year period. Mawaiya is a large multi-caste village, with a population of 2,305 persons and 439 households, according to a house-to-house census conducted in December 1964. Hindus (2,243 persons, 430 households) account for 97.3 per cent of the population, and Muslims (62 persons, 9 households) account for the remaining 2.7 per cent. The Hindu castes of Ahirs, Gadarias, Pasis, and Chamars account for about 85.19 per cent of the total village population.

OCCUPATIONAL STRUCTURE

The majority of the people in the village belong to lower castes. A review of the occupations of the various caste groups reveals that members of all groups move out of the village, on a regular or seasonal basis, in search of work. A large number of people have given up their traditional caste occupations and have taken to various types of jobs in the city. In almost all castes there is a high percentage of unskilled labourers who throng to the city for employment, mainly in construction work and road-building activities which are always going on in the city. There are about 55 persons regularly employed in the city, in government or private organizations. Small trade in the form of daily supply of milk, vegetables, etc. to the city markets is also a profession of many people belonging to different castes. Thus, although people claim agriculture as their basic source of livelihood, their subsidiary occupations actually provide strong support to their otherwise very poor agricultural economy. People may have deep sentiments for the land they hold, but they show very little initiative in improving their agricultural income.

LAND DISTRIBUTION PATTERN

About 20 per cent of the households in the village are landless, i.e. they do not possess any land of their own for cultivation (though some members of these households do take land from others on sharecropping). However, the availability of employment in the city during the period of agricultural inactivity compensates to a large extent for the inadequacy of their land-holdings. Approximately 43.74 per cent of households have between 0.1 and 3.0 *bigha*s of land; only 7.29 per cent of households have the maximum amount (above 9 *bigha*s) (one *bigha* = 0.625 acre). Castewise, the largest portion of land is owned by Pasis (about 35.62 per cent of the total cultivable land in the village), followed by Ahirs, Chamars, Gadarias, etc. However, in terms of per capita distribution, the higher castes (Brahmans and Thakurs) are better off than others, with per capita holdings of 4.5 and 1.6 *bigha*s respectively; the comparable figures for Ahirs, Gadarias, and Pasis are 0.8., 0.6, and 0.5 *bigha*s respectively. There are landless households in each caste group, though only Bhurjis and Koris are completely landless.

These facts indicate that the people in the village are by and large small peasants, with partial dependence on land, and greater dependence on subsidiary occupations. Even among those who own some land, not all cultivate it directly, but lease it to the landless or smallholders on a sharecropping basis.

The village land is not particularly fertile, and thus requires substantial inputs and irrigation to produce good yields. Though it might be expected that villages located near important urban centres would make use of the latest techniques of cultivation, this has not been the case in Mawaiya. People are apathetic towards agricultural innovations, citing the doubtful economic viability of their holdings.

When the village was revisited in 1972 and 1975, major changes in the land distribution pattern became apparent. Inspired by the increasing value of urban land, and the prospects of the extension of the city limits in the near future, capitalist interests have started making inroads into the village land-holdings. One rich businessman, and a rich political worker from the area (not belonging to this village), have managed to acquire much of the village land. The former has acquired 73 *bigha*s of land in the vicinity, including as much as 23 *bigha*s of village land (rendering 11 households landless). Another 15 *bigha*s have gone to the political worker, which has deprived 6 peasant households of their small holdings. The buyers of the land have created two large farms, pending the complete urbanization of the area when the land will greatly increase in value. The peasants who sold out received a good price for the otherwise uneconomical land, and were also given assurance of priority of employment by the buyers. This was a potent temptation, since in any case their small holdings did not provide adequate support, and they were obliged to sell their labour in the city. Now they are guaranteed employment, at least during the agricultural season, in the vicinity of their homes. The two new owners have dug their own tube-wells and are using the latest agricultural methods to maximize their production, and they have a regular supply of local labour.

CONCLUSION

The process of urbanization in the wake of industrialization and physical expansion of cities is inevitable, and has been accelerating in India since independence in 1947. The villages at the fringes of large cities have greater exposure to the forces of urbanization. But before a village is engulfed by the approaching arms of the city limits, it undergoes a certain change in land distribution, a restructuring of production relations, and the encroachment of vested interests, leading to what might be called a "pre-urbative" stage in which large-scale depeasantization is the main process of transformation from the viewpoint of the local people. There is also a concomitant ideological change among the former peasants. One interesting aspect of this change is their increased political participation as peasants. Whenever there is a farmers' rally or march in the capital, various political parties hire these people and transport them to the capital to march in the procession. Thus, the former peasants are asked to demonstrate for the protection of their interests as peasants, while they are rapidly depriving themselves of that peasant status.

BIBLIOGRAPHY

Rogers, E.M. (1969) : *Modernization Among Peasants,* New York.

Sing, K.S. (1978) : "Colonial Transformation of the Tribal Society in Middle India", Occasional papers in Tribal Development, Government of India, Ministry of Home Affairs.

Stavenhagen, Rudolpho ed. (1970) : *Agrarian and Peasant Movements in Latin America.*

Turner, E.S. (1950) : *Road to Ruin : The Shocking History of Social Reform,* London, Michael Joseph.

Peasants and Neo-peasants in Northeast India and their New Dimension

This paper discusses some general problems which arise from the interaction of tribal groups and sedentary peasant cultivators in several parts of Assam and Arunachal Pradesh (in the extreme northeast of India), based on a number of years of field work in that region.

WHO ARE THE PEASANTS AND NEO-PEASANTS?

I define tribe as a social and cultural entity which differentiates itself from other similarly composed units. The bond generated through the use of a common tongue or because of occupying the same territory no longer operates among many tribal groups. The Rabha of Assam, for example, are distributed over several districts and their sub-divisions speak differing tongues. One point, however, is remarkable. Every tribal individual strongly feels closely related and inseparably tied to the other fellows of the same tribal group, irrespective of the tongue used or the locality inhabited. There is some emotional attachment to the group name, born out of a tradition of being descendants of the same original ancestors.

A social group is either a caste or a religious unit or a tribe. A tribal group, as long as it does not become integrated into the wider framework of social organization of the soil, is recognized as such; but with its entrance into the larger Indian society, it loses its erstwhile tribal identity, though the same is retained for some time only to recast itself as a unit of caste; e.g. the Deuri, the Miri, the Chutiya, the Rabha, the Kachari, the Dimasa, etc. A process of slow but gradual integration of the tribal units into the nuclear Indian society involves a number of stages, which vary from locality to locality and from time to time.

Merger with peasant society and its economy was gradual and never revolutionary, although it ushered in revolutionary changes in their socio-economic structure. It did not remarkably upset their socio-cultural life. The process of involvement in peasant economy was as slow as it was within the easy grasp of the commoners. It has another far-reaching effect. Acceptance of peasant economy as a way of life persuaded them to identify with the socio-cultural life of the neighbouring peasants who professed non-tribal religion. It circumstantially involved the tribesmen in the caste hierarchy which dominates peasant life in the plains.

The new entrants do not find it very difficult to adjust themselves to the prevailing social and cultural practices around them. This is a linked process in the continuum of changes from a highland society to a peasant one. It involves semi-highland-cum-semi-peasant society on the one hand and peasant economy along with its associated folkways on the other. My emphasis is on peasant economy, which in my opinion precedes religious conversion without the intervention of the baptizing agencies. As stated earlier, settled agriculture involves certain rituals which the tribal fold naturally borrow from the neighbouring peasantry. More often than not the peasants happen to be followers of marginal Hinduism. There is no proselytization, there is no coercion. There was no organized resistance in the operational field of the tribe-peasant-caste continuum till the appearance of the exotic missionary activities in India, and particularly in Assam. Tribesmen, adopting wet paddy cultivation as a way of life, voluntarily merge with the neighbouring peasantry out of social necessity. Neither party likes social barriers standing in the way of free intercourse between the neighbouring groups due to affiliation with a particular non-tribal religion. Moreover, the dividing screen is so thin that a little initiative on the part of the minority group pushes this aside, enabling the two groups to have free social and cultural intercourse. The tribesmen strongly desire to participate in the socio-ritual functions of the peasants, who gladly welcome them under the conditions discussed above.

The materials available so far do not conclusively prove that caste structure is an outcome of rural peasant economy based on settled agriculture. An irresistible correlation between wet paddy cultivation or peasant economy and the principles involved in the caste structure, however, crystallizes itself when we scrutinize the data from the northeastern region of India. There is no group of tribesmen in this region which has not involved itself in the caste structure, in some form or other, after adoption of wet paddy cultivation. Another remarkable fact of this process is that there is a tendency of the tribesmen to abandon their animistic religion after a change to a peasant economy.

From the above discussion it follows that, in the context of northeast India, we find three stages in the process of absorption of tribes into peasantry. The transitional stage, when a tribe comes out of isolation and starts adopting peasant ways though not yet fully merging into peasantry, can be called the neo-peasant stage. Thus neo-peasants combine the characteristics of tribes as well as of peasants. The neo-peasant groups of northeast India are in the process of losing their tribal identities and are on the way to establishing themselves as castes.

CIVILIZATION AND PEASANT LIFE

Traditional Indian civilization was more oriented to rural peasant life, in contrast to occidental civilization, where cities and civilization are inseparable. The ruling classes' emphasis on urban life obviously overshadowed the importanceof the peasants. The British administrative machinery was so geared that peasanthood implied backwardness in contrast to the enlightenment of the urban centres. The educated rural youths also migrated to the urban centres (partly because of white-collar jobs, and partly because of new opportunities for business and commerce). Such a situation generated a feeling of inferiority among the peasants. Accordingly, wealthy peasants encouraged their educated sons and daughters to establish permanent residence in the urban centres, as this residence became an indicator of affluence and prestige. This psychology developed so quickly that the expression *nagaria* (or "town-dweller") came to have a prestige association with civilization, in contrast to *gawalia* or villager. This attitude continues even now. Mahatma Gandhi's insistence that people ought go back to the villages and village industries did not gain adequate momentum, although his 14-point constructive programme emphasized improvement of rural life and conditions.

THE PHILOSOPHY OF PEASANTS

Peasants who are born in poverty, brought up in it, and see it all round, learnto live in the midst of it. The Mahabharata story of Kunti asking for a poverty-stricken life as a gift from Sri Krishna (who was ready to grant her any wish) hints at the clue to coexistence with poverty. Bereft of its spiritual significance, the gross lesson of this anecdote is that concentration on religious and spiritual pursuits is possible only for those who are poor. It simply epitomizes the common desire of the masses, who hardly aspire to a life of affluence. This theoretical basis for an unquestioned acceptance, derived from the unmitigable quest for a peaceful life in the midst of insurmountable material discomforts, is derived from the facts of life.

Do peasants submit themselves to the dispensation of faith, rather than exercising their mental and physical efforts? From a close contact with the rural population of northeast India, it can well be stated that they have an ambivalent attitude. In my view this ambivalence is due to a conflict between their desire for a comfortable life, and their apparent failure to achieve their objective of improved material conditions. This ambivalence is primary, and is due to the fact that they are ill-equipped to harness the rich nature around them to fulfil their material needs. The existing social and cultural variables heighten this disposition. Being helpless against the odds around them they sublimate it through a recourse to the dispensation of fate, an easy anchor. It is not difficult to see how it paralyses their many efforts for a victory over the evil forces which benumb the physical efforts for better conditions of life.

Another philosophical undercurrent is a popular belief in the efficacy of cooperation as against competition. Cooperation within the family is basic as it is a small-scale society which suffers from a lack of dependable technological devices. Day-to-day life among the peasants of northeast India hinges upon cooperation. A spirit of competition for individual gain cuts at the roots of cooperation. Progressive adoption of modern devices has minimized the necessity of cooperation. A sense of security for isolated living, instead of living in a village community, has gradually eroded cooperation, even to the detriment of security of life against depredation. Social ostracism, as expressed in the idiom, *jui panir alag* (i.e. deprived of getting the help of fire and water from the neighbours) emphatically implied cooperation and interdependence among the neighbours in a rural community. This refers to a situation when fire, once extinguished, needed to be borrowed from a neighbour, who might refuse this favour for non-conformity to social norms. Refusal of essential fire and water compelled violators of social norms to fall in line with the rest of society. Nowadays, the availability of match boxes and the multiplication of water sources, in the form of tube-wells and ring-wells, have diminished the necessity of depending on neighbours for these essentials. The disappearance of compulsory interdependence among the village community has opened up new lines of adventure for doing things which are not traditionally sanctioned. These new situations might disrupt unity based on a sense of blindly following the traditions; however, these new situations have opened the door to new ideas from the outside, while encouraging competition among the rural population without any sense of conformity. In these changing circumstances, the principle of service to the community has declined in importance.

PROBLEMS OF PEASANTRY IN NEW DIMENSIONS

Apart from the recurrent and enduring problems of the peasantry, such as land and water, they suffer from an ambivalent attitude towards the vocation of agriculture. Food production is essential for the very survival of mankind. The peasants find themselves in successive generations in progressively deteriorating economic conditions, in contrast to their fellow beings who are artisans or job-holders or businessmen. They find that others devote less time to their work, while their earnings are much higher than those of the peasants. They also suffer from low status due to their relative poverty.

An ambivalence towards being a peasant is evident in unstructured interviews with a cross-section of these cultivators: a great majority desired that their children should follow a non-agricultural profession. They assert that they are unable to educate their children, or even maintain a reasonable standard of life, and this applied to owner-cultivators as well. If a man is a sharecropper, he starves and incurs irrecoverable and unending debts. If he is a day labourer, he barely manages to survive in the midst of constant scarcity. Two square meals a day is an unimaginable achievement for him and his dependents. In contrast he observes that those who have white-collar jobs lead a better life. The life of the artisans is no better, but the average businessman can easily live a comfortable life. The politicians are even more affluent by combining all sorts of professions. The peasants' observation is : if one or two persons in a family are job-holders and the rest engage in agriculture on their own land, they can lead a comparatively comfortable life without running into debts. They do so by a careful and industrious husbandry. On the other hand, while extolling the merits of job-holding for a constant source of income, they also assert the independent nature of agriculture in contrast to the servitude of the white-collar employees.

As the cultivators have to depend entirely on the whims of nature for regular and timely supply of water, they feel tired of scorching sun and abundance of water due to recurrent floods. In their own words, *rode sukai, bane khai* ("Scarcity of rains dries the sown crops, whereas floods destroy the crops"). They suggest that a well-planned irrigation system can solve their problems. They say, "we are in the habit of working hard, but we cannot enjoy the fruits of labour due to the uncontrollable whims of nature". And they add, "Nature destroys the crops but it cannot touch the jobs of the service-holders". Hence they prefer that their children should seek some employment other than the precarious pursuit of agriculture. This ambivalence towards their profession has aggravated the situation among the peasants.

The slogan that "the peasants are the backbone of the society" is empty today, as the peasants have lost faith in their own profession. In addition the society refuses to give them a place of honour and prestige because their profession is food production. Slogans like *Jai Kisan, Jai Hind* ("Long live the farmer(s), long live India") can hardly induce the peasants to sustain unflinching faith in their profession, if there are no concrete steps for controlling nature and assuring the production of more food from contented cultivators. The "green revolution" touched the fringe of the problems in some states, but the northeastern region is yet to be brought under the influence of the same movement. The gentlemen farmers, backed by a well-laid irrigation system, improved seeds, and scientific methods, have brought about a green revolution in India, except for the northeastern region, where devastating floods during the rainy season and scarcity of water during the rest of the year have perpetually weakened the economic strength of the cultivators.

The introduction of Bodo paddy and wheat cultivation in this region, together with intensive cultivation of winter vegetables, has slightly improved the situation. Otherwise a bleak future would have been the lot of the flood-stricken peasantry. The introduction of jute cultivation on a large scale has also partly alleviated the otherwise deteriorating conditions of the peasants. Governmental incentives have persuaded a section of the cultivators to adopt modern means of food production through the use of fertilizers, improved varieties of seeds and insecticides. Some farmers have also adopted improved agricultural technology.

PROBLEMS OF TRIBES TRANSFORMED INTO PEASANTS

Neo-peasants continue to believe in the same philosophy as that of the highlanders for quite a while; however, a modification of this ideal takes place as soon as accumulation of wealth becomes an associated virtue of a new mode of socio-cultural life born out of settled cultivation. Liberal spending on rituals and socio-cultural activities becomes less common in imitation of their neighbours, the settled cultivators who accumulate wealth by frugal habits. Liberal spending on drinking is opposed, partly because of their awareness of the waste of rice in the preparation of country liquor, and also because of the Sanskritization of their ways of life resulting from the gradual conversion into Hinduism, Buddhism, or Christianity. In addition to these influences, the social environment demands frugal habits. "Intelligent self-interest for accumulation of wealth"replaces their tribal philosophy, "Commune before self".

This overriding principle of community interest, which governed all aspects of life in a tribal organization, can be illustrated by a few observations from tribal ethnography collected by the author. Forest lands were made open for occupation by the Mishmis for settled cultivation. The Nepali graziers are well known for their surreptitious penetration into the most interior jungles, in spite of the standing rules regarding the Inner Line territories of Arunachal Pradesh. The graziers were initially asked to clear the forest by felling the trees and raising crops for one or two years without rent. Rents were then to be increased for the subsequent year. These graziers, by virtue of their hard work and agricultural knowledge, raise rich harvests in the initial years, enabling them to accumulate surplus paddy or money, which they then lend to the landowners who have accumulated debts. Ultimately the landowners must transfer large parcels of land to the graziers in payment of this loans.

A close analysis of this phenomenon in several localities of Arunachal Pradesh and Karbi Anglong district of Assam bears out my contention that tribal motto of sharing the prosperity with all members of the group blinds their vision. Their logic is: the non-tribal entrepreneurs should share equally the fruits of their hard labour with the tribesmen, because this is the practice among the tribesmen. In reality the reverse practice takes place. The tribesmen are never invited to share the liberal feasts of drink and meat, as practised by the wealthy Mishmis. Instead, the tribesmen are forced to borrow grains or money against heavy interest. In due course the local inhabitants turn out to be debtors in a large way. An acute situation develops out of continued indebtedness. The landowners eventually become landless. However limited, land is still available for reclamation. Hence the situation in Arunachal Pradesh is not as acute as in the Odalguri area of Assam, where grave social tensions have led to violent clashes between the ethnic, religious or linguistic, and territorial groups. The four-cornered clashes have turned into a battlefield of political parties professing different ideologies. Changes in group loyalty often depend on who wins the dispute, and in all cases the real cause of the dispute is the ownership of cultivable land.

Land is the only capital which any peasant can hope to own. The mental horizon of every cultivator is dominated by a strong desire to own a sizable plot of land for economic prosperity. They have never realized that the peasants have been made strangers in their own homeland by a handful of immigrants from elsewhere with a better technology and richer purses. The peasants may share the same level of productive technology, but the immigrants command more money power.

The story of Karbi Anglong district is not at all different from that of Mishmi Hills. The story of reclamation of waste land is a replica of the one described above. The same ideal tribal philosophy of sharing the prosperity among the members of the community has given birth to a local Karbi leadership in business. A small group of Karbis collectively form a lending unit. This unit starts lending grain and money at the same high rate as any non-Karbi banker. Here again ethnicity attracts clients, who prefer to borrow from their own blood relatives in the false expectation of sharing the ultimate benefits. What happens ultimately is that the Karbi bankers behave nearly the same as the non-Karbi ones, except that their blood relatives are invited to share in feasts and celebrations, whereas the Karbis are not invited to the rare socio-cultural entertainments arranged by the non-Karbi money-lenders.

A TRIBAL REVOLUTION

Peaceful renunciation of the aboriginal mode of techno-economic life is the order of the day in northeast India. This has been the case particularly ssince World War II. Some of the highlanders are still practising the slash-and-burn method of cultivation, but they are fully aware of the benefits of plough cultivation and tractorization, which they observe in government-sponsored agricultural farms in the neighbourhood. World War II, waged on their frontiers and home grounds, produced a sharp realization of their badkwardness, which became glaringly obvious when they were compared with the more advanced soldiers. The highlanders are no longer awed by massive machineguns and heavy war weapons; they are psychologically prepared to gain mastery over such weapons. They realize that wet cultivation alone can help them rise above the level at which they find themselves; because of this realization they are now demanding more and more irrigated land. However, they realize, to their chagrin, that the most fertile lands are already in the possession of plough cultivators, the migrants from the highlands (now rightly or wrongly called the plains people). The basic tension created by the growing demands for more and more cultivable land proliferates and manifests itself in language or ethnic riots.

A recent occurrence in Arunachal may well illustrate this point. Group A clashed violently with group B. The real cause of the conflict is possession of land. Traditionally group B are expert wet cultivators, who do not use the plough. Group A have recently adopted the plough. The traditional rule is that certain well-demarcated areas are the homeland of particular groups into which they do not admit others. Outsiders may come and trade in rented houses, but cannot gain rights over land belonging to insiders. Hence the conflict. To the extent that tribal rights prevail in an area, any outsider settling there may enjoy the right of usufruct only, never rights of possession.

Under modern conditions urban centres have developed in all tribal areas, where different tribal groups have to reside together because of opportunities for employment in the establishments of the administration, business, or industry. Under such conditions they have to live far away from their native land with their wives and children. Facilities offorded by the urban centres for education, medical treatment, and employment opportunities cause them to settle in the newly developed urban centres. Vegetable gardening, poultry farming, piggery, and dairy farming have become lucrative occupations in the vicinity of modern townships. The tribal folk are clever enough to realize the benefits of living near the townships, and some of them are shrewd businessmen. Hence the struggle for more and more land near the urban centres, and the conflict. Under such analterable conditions we have observed a change of ethnic affiliation to minimize the trouble. Political motives based on economic gains do not take long to foment trouble on the basis of ethnic affiliations leading to possessory rights over land. Hence a conflict between the indigene and the non-indigene.

Certain deep-seated tribal laws obviously clash with the democratic egalitarian principles which allow many groups to live together cheek-by-jowl in modern urban centres. Peaceful revolution for economic improvements, it appears, generates other sources of clashes with rival competitors. Traditional tribal life was homogeneous in character and provided no occasion for conflict with rival groups, except in war situations. In a heterogeneous town settlement such new situations demand peaceful solutions.

PEASANT MOVEMENT

A noteworthy feature of the peasants in the northeastern region is that there is no single political platform or party through which the peasants can effectively voice their collective opinion, or control the market for agricultural products. Political or social consciousness, though meagre, is due to the political workers affiliated to the various parties, either national, regional, or local. Worse still, besides such a political party-wise division, there are multiple divisions on the basis of ethnicity, caste, sub-caste, religion, religious sects, language, dialects, and regional affiliation. Such a multiplicity of political affiliations cuts across the common interests of the peasants, making it possible for others to control the destiny of the peasantry.

In a democratically organized society like ours, the peasants fail to extract privileges from the state by throwing their collective weight on the side of the party of their choice at the election booth. The peasants are in an overwhelming majority, yet no peasant leader worth the name has yet made a mark in the socio-political life of India. Those who speak on behalf of the peasants are hardly peasants by vocation. The peasant workers and labourers are organized by political propagandists and workers whose programme includes some of the burning problems of the peasants, but in spite of efforts at removing some of the difficulties, none of their problems has yet been solved to the full satisfaction of the peasants themselves.

Peasant movements for equitable distribution of cultivable land are often condemned by political leaders, if they do not serve the interests of the ruling party. Most of the social tensions in this regard have their roots in land ownership. The tribal peasants are somewhat lavish in their spending habits, and easily run into debts. the clever traders as well as the money-lenders advance money for interest. In due course, their indebtedness compels them to transfer their plots of land through a sale deed. Till the past decade plots were available for reclamation. The cultivators, deprived of their original possession near the plains, migrated to the less healthy regions of the sub-mountain areas only to be displaced again in due course by the money-lenders or traders. A further movement towards the northern or southern hill ranges is prevented by a gradual movement of the highlanders to the foothills in search of wet paddy land. This gives rise to a tension among the migrants, who claim autochthonous rights over the land.

The red herring of Naxalism is a misunderstood peasant movement of West Bengal, reputed to be an armed revolution. The occupation of large tracts of land by *zamindar* landlords or tea garden managers, and the depriving of a large number of needy cultivators from tilling the land for cereal crops, have obviously frustrated the younger generation. In the absence of cultivable land and alternative sources of income, honest people become desperate. Undirected and unstructured desperation may easily bring about dysnomia in the society. This is what has happened in many parts of our country. Whether it is is Telengana or Kerala or Naxalbari, the root cause of the social imbalance is economic. Intolerable inequality in socio-economic life breeds revolutionary attitudes. This is aggravated if the educated youth are unemployed or under-employed; these are the conditions where Naxalite movements are observable. To add fuel to the flame there are other issues such as linguistic differences in education, religious minorities and other subordinate groups such as the Harijans and tribesmen who have for long been deprived of liberty. All such factors collectively keep the Naxalite movement alive in the northeastern region, although in a subdued form until lately. The movement may erupt any time if appropriate measures for land distribution among the cultivators are further delayed or ignored. In our view nationalization of land appears to be the only alternative for solving many of the peasant problems which simmer on the surface.

Agricultural Labour
in Thanjavur

KATHLEEN GOUGH

This paper discusses changes in the relations and conditions of agricultural labourers in Thanjavur district of Tamil Nadu, southeast India, between 1951-53 and 1976, the two periods when I did field work there. (For earlier studies of these villages, see my articles cited in the bibliography; for further studies of Thanjavur villages, see especially Béteille 1965, Sivertsen 1963, Alexander 1975, and Shivaraman 1973.)

As in India generally, the agricultural labourers of Thanjavur have greatly increased over the past quarter century. An intensively irrigated, paddy-growing district, Thanjavur has even traditionally had a high proportion of landless or near-landless labourers. In the district as a whole, male labourers were already 36 per cent of the male agricultural work force in 1951. By 1971 they were 53 per cent, while the agricultural work force had remained at 69 per cent of the total work force, against 70 per cent in 1950.[1]

Women labourers increased correspondingly. They were 52 per cent of the total female agricultural work force in 1951, but were 85 per cent by 1971.[2] Taking both sexes together, agricultural labourers increased from 40 per cent of the agricultural work force in 1951 to 59 per cent in 1971.

Child labour, however, declined considerably over the 20-year period. In 1951, almost all Harijan children over age 7, or some 22 per cent of all children, worked as agricultural labourers. In 1961, 5 per cent of Thanjavur's children under 14 were recorded as employed, no doubt mainly in agriculture. By 1976, when I returned there, few children could be seen working in the fields in Thanjavur.

The decline in child labour is partly attributable to school attendance, for in every village a number of Harijan children now attend the elementary school, while one or two in each village are likely to be in high school. School attendance is not the only factor, however, for many Harijan children now have no work, yet do not attend school because their parents cannot afford books and suitable clothing, or because no one has thought it worth while to send them.

The decline in child labour can be attributed to several other factors. One is the decrease in the number of cattle with the partial introduction of tractors and the increase in bus transport. Formerly, boys and occasionally girls were employed to graze their masters' cattle, but today their services are less often needed. When cattle are grazed, old men usually graze them.

A second, more general reason for the decline in child labour is that both men and women are now so severely under-employed that labourers do not choose to have children competing for work with adults. The agitations of the two parliamentary Communist parties may also have contributed to the decline in children's employment.

Again, there is the fact that whereas formerly most labourers were automatically engaged together with their wives and children in a familial, semi-serf relationship, today both male and female wage workers are often hired independently, sometimes by the year but more often by the day. Finally, the modern increase in the statutory wages of both adult and child agricultural labourers encourages farmers to reduce their labour force as much as possible and to restrict it to adults.

In spite of the decline in the employment of children, the total agricultural labour force including both main and subsidiary workers has increased dramatically. It was 263,030 or 29 per cent of the total work force in 1951 and 541,919 or 41 per cent of the total work force in 1971.

My field studies in two villages, Kumbapettai in the northwest of the district and Kirippur in the east, suggest that agricultural labourers were even more numerous by the mid-1970s. In the first village, Kumbapettai, adult men primarily occupied as agricultural labourers were 51 per cent of the total male work force and 61 per cent of the male agricultural work force in 1951. By 1976 they were 62 per cent of the total male work force and 78 per cent of the male agricultural work force. Women labourers had increased from 72 per cent to 92 per cent of the total female agriculturists in the same period. In the second village, Kirippur, male labourers had increased from 51 per cent to 72 per cent of the male agricultural work force and from 42 per cent to 52 per cent of the total male work force: women labourers, from 78 per cent to 90 per cent of the female agricultural work force.

Whence this great increase in agricultural labour? It is sometimes argued that the increase occurs because agricultural labourers have more children than other people. This, however, is not so, for the Harijan castes, who provide the mainstay of agricultural labour, were 22 per cent of the total population in 1971 as in 1951. It is likely, indeed, that the Harijans' *biological* increase over the twenty-year period has been lower than that of the rest of the population, for more caste Hindus than Harijans emigrate from the district in search of jobs. Like the rest of the population, Harijans present in the district increased by approximately 29 per cent in the twenty-year period. Population increase therefore accounts for only 29 per cent out of the more than 100 per cent increase registered by the total agricultural labour population and its dependents between 1951 and 1971.

The bulk of the increase has to be accounted for in terms other than natural increase. My observations in two villages indicate that the greater part of this increase comprises members of families of former cultivating tenants. Given the general increase in the population, some tenants would have lost their land even if the acreage given out on tenure had remained constant. In fact, however, many landowners have evicted their cultivating tenants since 1952 and have replaced them with wage labour.

Landlords have evicted their tenants for two reasons: first, to avoid granting them fixity of tenure and a higher share of the crop under the tenany acts of 1952, 1956, and 1969,[3] and secondly, in order to manage their own cultivation and profit from using "green revolution" technology, introduced on a large scale since 1965.

In Kumbapettai, for example, 50 out of 218 male agriculturalists (23 per cent) lived at least partly by cultivating leased land in 1976, against 51 out of 185 (28 per cent) in 1952. In 1952, 44 per cent of the cultivated acreage was leased to cultivating tenants, but in 1976 this percentage was reduced to 22. In the same period, the average size of a cultivating tenant's holding had declined from 3.3 to 1.9 acres. In 1952, 20 of the 51 tenants were also agricultural labourers, but by 1976, 28 of the 50 tenants were obliged to do agricultural labour to eke out a livelihood. At least 18 tenants had been evicted from at least 43 acres over the past two years.

In Kirippur, which had lower productivity from being near the "tail-end" of the delta, there was even traditionally a smaller percentage of tenant-cultivators and a higher proportion of peasant-owners. In this village men who were mainly cultivating tenants had declined from 17 out of 182 male agriculturalists (9.3 per cent) to 11 out of 226 (4.9 per cent) in the same period, and their average leased holdings had declined from 6.6 to 3.5 acres. In the village as a whole, 41 per cent of the cultivated acreage had been under cultivating tenures in 1952, but only 17 per cent was with cultivating tenants in 1976. (In both villages, a small percentage was with non-cultivating tenants in both 1952 and 1976, but this category need not be discussed in the present paper.)

A second source of new agricultural labour comes from artisans or other village servants who can no longer make a living in their traditional work. Thanjavur's villages now have very few potters, weavers, or goldsmiths, and some of these have been forced into casual labour in agriculture.

Finally, a considerable number of former landowners have had to sell their land since the 1950s because of debts resulting from inflation, family expenses, and the growing cost of agricultural inputs and of labour. Between 1951 and 1971 the total number of "cultivators" in Thanjavur, including owners and tenant farmers, declined from 388,986 to 347,516. Much of the decline no doubt resulted from the eviction of tenants, who were not separately recorded in 1971. My field observations indicate, however, that the number of owners has also declined. Landowners predominantly dependent on their holdings declined from 42 to 25 in Kumbapettai in the 25-year period, and in Kirippur from 73 to 53. Most of those who sold their land were small rentiers who went to work in cities, but some were peasant cultivators, and a few of these are now agricultural labourers.

As a result of these changes, more agricultural labourers today come from the middle-ranking non-Brahman castes than was the case in 1952. In Kumbapettai, 36 out of 112 male agricultural labourers, or 32.1 per cent, were non-Brahmans in 1952, and 45 out of 171, or 26.3 per cent in 1976, a slightly larger number although a lower percentage. In Kirippur, only 15 out of 92 male agricultural laburers, or 16 per cent, were non-Brahmans in 1952, but 53 out of 162, or 33 per cent, were non-Brahmans in 1976. When evictions occur, Harijan tenants are the first to be evicted and to join the agricultural labourers, but non-Brahmans of the traditional peasant and artisan castes are not immune.

Thanjavur has three kinds of agricultural labourers: *pannaiyals*, regular coolies, and casual collies. The *pannaiyal* relationship, nowadays sometimes called bonded labour, is a kind of debt-peonage which derives from the agricultural slavery that was prevalent in Thanjavur until the 1860s. The provisions of the relationship have been changing through the decades, however, and it is now transitional to capitalist wage work. Regular coolies are of several kinds. All of them are less "traditional" and closer to capitalist wage workers than are *pannaiyals*, although regular coolies are sometimes hard to distinguish from *pannaiyals*. Casual coolies are wage workers hired by the day. I will describe each type in turn.

In 1952 *pannaiyals* were 37 per cent of the male agricultural labourers in Kumbapettai and 61 per cent in Kirippur. By 1976 *pannaiyals* had declined to 9 per cent in Kumbapettai and to 14 per cent in Kirippur. In 1976 *pannaiyals* were engaged only by a few old-fashioned local landowners who farmed more or less traditionally. With the assault on bonded labour during the Emergency of 1975-77, the *pannaiyal* relationship was disappearing, and may be expected to die out soon.

In 1952 the *pannaiyal* relationship had the following characteristics. (a) Payment was in grain, sometimes with a little cash, for each day of work. Harvest payments were more than twice those on other days. (b) Married couples were normally hired jointly, together with their children mature enough to work. (c) *Pannaiyals* were engaged by the year, although some of them were re-engaged for several years. (d) The engagement, on New Year's Day in April, was marked by the landowner giving a loan in cash to the *pannaiyal*. The loan was repaid in paddy, nominally without interest, from the *pannaiyal*'s paddy wages during the

February harvest the following year. Since, however, the price of paddy during the harvest might be only two-thirds or even half of that in the scarce season of April to September, the *pannaiyal* in fact paid from about 50 to 100 per cent interest on his loan. If the master wished, the loan might be carried on or supplemented for another year. (e) *Pannaiyals* received annual clothing, a house site, medicines during sickness and childbirth, and gifts of cash or kind at marriages, births and funerals in the *pannaiyal's* or the master's house and at the agricultural festivals of first ploughing, seed sowing, transplanting, flood tide, and the annual cattle show. (f) *Pannaiyals* might be called to work at any time. Usually, men worked some 280 to 300 days a year in west Thanjavur and about 180 to 200 in east Thanjavur: women, about 240 days in west Thanjavur and 110 to 140 in east Thanjavur. In the slack season of March to June when the irrigation channels were dry, a *pannaiyal* could do odd jobs for anyone with his master's consent. (g) *Pannaiyals* had collective rights in the village common land and produce, in the form of mud, wood, and thatch to build their huts; fish, crabs, and rats from the paddy fields; and certain cooked foods at the village temple festivals. (h) *Pannaiyals'* work and rights were graded by caste. Those from the Harijan castes (the large majority) were mainly engaged in paddy cultivation; non-Brahmans, in garden and dairy work, cart-driving, and overseeing, and non-Brahman women in light field work and part-time domestic work for their masters. The payments of non-Brahman *pannaiyals* ran from one and one-fifth to as high as twice those for Harijans. They could approach their high-caste masters more closely and were less subservient in their mode of address. (i) Each *pannaiyal* family formerly received an allotment of one-sixth of an acre of village wet land, called *pattakkal,* for its maintenance. By 1952, however, this custom had been largely abrogated by the landlords, many of whose holdings were dwindling.

By 1976, the rights and obligations of those few *pannaiyals* who remained had changed with the further marketing of crops and other goods and the further purchase of village lands by outsiders. The *pannaiyal* relationship had also become less servile as a result of agitations by the Communist agricultural labour unions. In 1976 it was rare for a master to strike his *pannaiyal,* whereas in 1952 *pannaiyals* in many villages could still be beaten for misdemeanours. In 1952 erring *pannaiyals* were sometimes forced to drink a pint-vessel of cow-dung mixed with water, an ancient punishment. This custom had apparently disappeared by 1976. In 1976 *pannaiyals* worked more regular hours and were less likely to be summoned for work after dusk. In fact, the *pannaiyal* relationship itself was gradually merging with that of the regular coolie. In some villages *pannaiyals'* daily payments were about one-fifth to one-third higher than in 1952. On the other hand, some *pannaiyals* no longer received medicines or clothing, and some received no gifts at life crises or festivals.

In Kumbapettai in 1952, a *pannaiyal* married couple earned the equivalent in cash and kind of about 55 to 64 *kalam*s of paddy per year from all sources; in Kirippur a *pannaiyal* couple earned the equivalent in cash and kind of about 40 to 52 *kalam*s. In 1976, *pannaiyal* men in Kumbapettai worked between 141 and 272 days a year, the average being 216 days. Women worked 81 to 208 days, the average being 164 days. A *pannaiyal* married couple in Kumbapettai earned the equivalent in cash and kind of anything from about 51 to 70 *kalam*s a year in 1976, depending on the duties allotted. Some couples earned more, for example, because the man was entrusted with the general management of the estate and especially with opening and closing the irrigation channels. In Kumbapettai, therefore, the *pannaiyal* relationship had become a favoured one available to only a few labourers, and labourers could be seen queueing outside landlords' homes at New Year in the hope of being engaged. In Kirippur, the few *pannaiyal*s who remained worked only 90 to 139 days a year for their own masters in the case of men, and 58 to 62 days in the case of women. The annual incomes in cash and kind of these couples from their own masters amounted to the equivalent of only 19 to 24 *kalam*s. Kirippu's *pannaiyal*s, however, were able to work an additional 23 to 92 days as casual coolies for other masters in the case of men, and 67 to 80 additional days in the case of women. This additional labour brought the total annual income of a *pannaiyal* couple to the equivalent in cash and kind of 53 to 54 *kalm*s. Therefore, although *pannaiyal*s in Kirippur complained that they were worse off than their forebears in 1952 because of the smaller number of days worked per year for their masters, the average income of adult couples from all sources appeared to be slightly higher. Lacking much extra paddy earned by children however, the total family incomes of *pannaiyal*s were little if any better than in 1952.

The paddy-value of these incomes becomes more meaningful if we consider the food requirements of labourers. With little food from other sources, Thanjavur labourers calculate that a male agricultural labourer optimally requires 19 *kalam*s of paddy per year as food. This amount yields 9.5 *kalam*s or about 798.7 lbs. of husked rice, or about 2.19 lbs. per day. A woman labourer needs 15.2 *kalam*s of paddy per year and a child of about 8 to 12, about half that amount. A family with two children thus requires a minimum of 49 to 50 *kalam*s per year for food, in addition to cash for clothing, lamp-oil, supplementary groceries, and other necessities. In 1952, children earned their own food at the rate of 6 to 12 *kalam*s per year for a girl or boy aged about 8 to 12, but in 1976 most families received little or no paddy for children's work. Even 70 *kalam*s a year—the highest income of a labouring couple—was therefore very modest for a family of four people.

Regular coolies, like *pannaiyal*s, are engaged by the year. The regular coolie is in fact a more "modern" version of the *pannaiyal*. In Kumbapettai regular coolies were 15 per cent of the male agricultural labourers in 1952 and 12 per cent in

1976. In Kirippur regular coolies were 13 per cent of the male labourers in 1952; they were 6 per cent in 1976. Regular coolies differ from *pannaiyals* in that they are paid in cash except at harvest time, a man is usually hired independently of his wife, and the employer does not expect to call on his children for labour. Regular coolies may be required to do almost any kind of outdoor work[4] and are paid at the same rates for the same operations regardless of caste. The regular coolie's employer may or may not give him a loan. A regular coolie is likely to work an eight-hour day and to be paid something approximating the statutory wage. He receives no clothing, medicines, or gifts at festivals. Today when the village waste land has been largely encroached upon, coolies must often buy their own fuel and wood and leaves for building their huts.

Regular coolies' circumstances vary with their masters' needs. A few, usually non-Brahmans rather than Harijans, are employed as overseers of casual labour. Some supervise the fields for absentee landlords and receive extra pay for opening and closing the irrigation channels. Some masters give a specially favoured coolie a plot of land on lease to "hold" him and ensure his loyalty. Some regular coolies plough and thresh with their own oxen and are paid higher wages.

Like *pannaiyals*, regular coolies are free to work elsewhere on days when they are not summoned by their employers. In 1952, regular coolies, like *pannaiyals*, worked a total of about 280 to 300 days in Kumbapettai in the case of men, and about 220 to 240 days in the case of women. Male regular coolies worked about 180 to 200 days in Kirippur in 1952; women, about 110 to 140 days. In 1976, regular coolie men in Kumbapettai worked 145 to 232 days; women 119 to 180 days. In Kirippur in 1976, regular coolie men worked 104 to 130 days; women, 85 to 115 days.

In 1952, a regular coolie couple in Kumbapettai earned the equivalent of about 55 to 64 *kalam*s of paddy per year, roughly the same as a *pannaiyal* couple. In Kirippur a regular coolie couple in 1952 earned between 40 and 46 *kalam*s a year, if anything rather less than did *pannaiyals*. In 1976, male regular coolies in Kirippur earned the equivalent of 22 to 28 *kalam*s per year; women, 13 to 17 *kalam*s. When both husband and wife were regular coolies, they earned the cash equivalent of about 35 to 45 *kalam*s per year. In Kumbapettai in 1976, male regular coolies earned the equivalent of 38 to 50 *kalam*s per year; women, 8 to 12 *kalam*s. When both husband and wife were regular coolies they might earn the equivalent of 55 to 64 *kalam*s per year in 1976, the same as in 1952. Lacking extra paddy earned by their children, regular coolies tended to be somewhat worse off in 1976 than in 1952. In both villages, however, regular coolies, like *pannaiyals*, were relatively privileged labourers who were declining in numbers.

Casual coolies, the vast majority, are usually the least fortunate. In Kumbapettai, casual coolies were 48 per cent of the male agricultural labourers in 1952, 79 per cent in 1976. In Kirippur casual coolies were 26 per cent of the male labourers in 1952, but 80 per cent in 1976.

Casual labourers are hired solely by the day. Beyond the day's wages, no master has any responsibility for their livelihood. In theory, they are paid a statutory wage which in 1976 varied from Rs. 3 to Rs. 11 (US $0. 375 to $1.375) per day according to the type of work performed. Women's tasks of transplanting and weeding are paid at the lowest rate; men's ploughing with their own oxen, at the highest. Most casual labourers own neither stock nor plough and can give only what is called "body help" for the barest subsistence. Casual labourers were already underemployed in 1952, seldom working more than 200 days a year in west Thanjavur and 180 days in the east. By 1976, the conditions of most of them had deteriorated. Whereas the paddy value of their daily cash wages had increased from about 5.3 lbs. to 6.2 lbs. of paddy per man per day in the 25-year period, by 1976 their numbers were so inflated that the men worked only about 76 to 180 days a year in Kumbapettai and about 60 to 168 days in Kirippur. Casual coolie women worked 119 to 180 days a year a Kumbapettai in 1976 but only 60 to 120 days in Kirippur. Whereas a casual coolie couple might earn the cash equivalent of 37 to 41 *kalam*s a year in Kumbapettai in 1952, such a couple earned the cash equivalent of 35 to 47 *kalam*s in 1976. In Kirippur, a casual coolie couple might earn about 35 to 40 *kalam*s a year in 1952. In 1976, very few such couples who were young and strong earned the equivalent of up to 54 *kalam*s per year, but most earned 36 to 44 *kalam*s, and some, usually middle-aged or old people, as little as 23 to 28 *kalam*s. Unfortunately, I do not know what percentage of the casual coolies earned these very low annual incomes, but my impression was that most of the casual coolies in Kirippur were worse off than in 1952, and most in Kumbapettai little if any better off. Without extra paddy earned by their children, it is clear that the casual coolies found it hard to meet even their food requirements, quite apart from other expenses.

In 1976, even at the peak seasons of transplanting and harvest, when labour was traditionally scarce in Thanjavur and was sometimes imported from other districts, far more coolies arrived for work than were required. In the transplanting and harvest seasons of late 1976, a period of drought when some fields remained uncultivated, it was not uncommon to see from 30 to 90 coolies appear for work for which 20 had been requested. In these circumstances employers would naturally pay for only the number of labourers they had summoned. The labourers who had arrived would simply share out both work and wages.

Since 1952 the public amenities accorded to most labourers have improved in some respects. Most of them now have electric street lighting, dirt roads instead of footpaths leading across the fields to their streets, and newly built wells instead of pools to provide drinking water. Perhaps one-third of the Harijans of Thanjavur now have small tile-roofed dwellings with brick walls built for them by the Dravida Munnetra Kazhakam government in 1969-75. With some effort, labourers may send their children to school. A minimal amount of free medical care is available for some in hospitals. The caste restrictions formerly placed on Harijan labourers have been considerably reduced. They may now walk freely in the streets, for example, and wear shirts and ankle-length instead of knee-length clothing.

On the other hand, the food supply of most labourers was poorer in 1976 than in 1952. In 1952, those Harijans who had come under Communist influence claimed that they were giving up eating field rats in an effort to appear respectable and to be fit to associate with the higher castes. In 1976, however, I found that virtually all Harijans and many non-Brahman labourers and smallholders ate rats. They were unable to afford meat or fish, or even their full rice and sugar rations from the fair-price shops in seasons of scarcity. Several told me that, in general, agricultural labourers could eat two meals a day for only three months in each year, that is, for six weeks during and after each of the two harvests. This was the situation at a time when India had 18 million tons of food grains in storage, and when Thanjavur's paddy production had increased more than five times its population increase in the past quarter century. Although they perform the vast bulk of agricultural work, underemployment has turned Thanjavur's casual agricultural labour force, about 37 per cent of its rural population, into a pool of marginal, malnourished people for whose welfare no-one is responsible. Given its dependent form of state capitalism, India's industry is too stunted and capital-intensive to absorb them.

The Communists of Tamil Nadu have carried out organizing and conducted struggles among Thanjavur's poor peasants and agricultural labourers since 1936. By 1976 most Harijan labourers and tenants were organized into unions in the eastern taluks, while Communist ideas and influence had spread into every village. Unions of the Communist Party of India (CPI) were the strongest in Mannargudi Taluk; those of the Communist Party of India—Marxist (CPI-M) in Thanjavur, Nagapattinam, Nannilam, and Tirutturaipoondi.

The peaks of Communist militancy came in the late 1940s and late 1960s. In 1948, in response to rural inflation, lowered wages, and increased rents in the war and post-war periods, a six-week strike of labourers and tenants occurred in the eastern half of the district. Prolonged agitations and strikes finally evoked the Thanjavur Tenants' and Pannaiyals' Ordinance of 1952, which set the rents of cultivating tenants at three-fifths of the crop and in theory increased agricultural wages by about two-thirds. In 1956 tenants' rents were officially lowered to two-fifths of the crop, and in subsequent years statutory wages have been regulated from time to time. Over the years, it was largely as a result of Communist agitation that the ceiling on land ownership was fixed at 30 standard acres in 1961 and at 15 standard acres in 1972.[5] Partly as a result of Communist pressures, cultivating tenants were legally allowed to register their tenures in 1969, housesites were granted to large numbers of Harijans in the late 1960s and early 1970s, and fair-price shops were opened by the Government of Tamil Nadu for the sale of grains to the poor. During the 1960s there were repeated agitations— against the eviction of tenants, for higher wages, and for the control of inflation.

In the late 1960s communist demands focused on the impact of the "green revolution", introduced with the assistance of the Ford Foundation in 1961. Repeated militant strikes occurred, especially at harvest time, to raise wages and give the labourers an adequate share in the profits afforded by higher productivity under the new technology. At the same time the CPI-M conducted drives against the introduction of tractors, arguing that given Thanjavur's agricultural labour glut, the mechanization of agriculture was unnecessary.[6]

In defence of their privileges, in 1962 Thanjavur's landlords formed an organization called the Paddy Producers' Association. Its explicit goals are higher prices for marketed crops, lower wages, and lower prices for agricultural inputs and machinery. In 1968, prolonged disputes over wages and Communist labour union membership were punctuated by the murders of several Communist leaders and peasants in Thanjavur. On 24 December of that year a servant of the Paddy Producers' Association president was found murdered, it was presumed in retaliation for his repeated attacks on the Communist labourers. On the same night a posse of some 300 landlords and their henchmen, reputedly led by the Association's president, carried out a holocaust in the Harijan settlement of Kilvenmani village, a few miles from Kirippur. The attackers wounded several men with buckshot and burned to death 44 women, children, and old men in a hut. Court cases following these events resulted in the imprisonment of eight Harijans from one year to life on charges of murdering the landlord's servant. The twelve landlords accused of the massacre received verdicts of "not guilty" on the grounds of lack of evidence. In early 1976, however, the Supreme Court reversed this verdict on appeal and gave varying sentences of imprisonment to the landlords.

Since the massacre at Kilvenmani, communist agitations in Thanjavur appear to have gradually abated. Struggles over the eviction of tenants and the introduction of tractors have clearly been lost, although a few rearguard actions continue privately among tenants who are newly facing eviction. With the introduction of tripartite bargaining between the government, the landlords, and the labour unions in 1972, both Communist parties appear to have focused more narrowly on agricultural daily wages, the cash value of which continued to be gradually increased up to 1975.[7] In 1976, I found that although Harijan labourers in east Thanjavur still mainly supported the CPI-M, they were largely quiescent, and in some cases despairing. During 1976, Communist public meetings were held in association with the Dravida Munnetra Kazhakam to protest against the proposed changes in the constitution under the Emergency in India and against the sharing of the Kaveri waters with the State of Karnataka, but in spite of renewed inflation in late 1976, no widespread organizing occurred among agricultural labourers. The three leading Communist peasant organizers in the district had been imprisoned under preventive detention orders during the Emergency. Labourers in Kilvenmani told me that they had abandoned militant actions in favour of peaceful boycotts and arbitration by the party's leaders. Some of Kilvenmani's Harijans had benefitted slightly from small gifts of land by the government as a result of non-violent appeals by the local Sarvodaya association, and from the new huts built for them by the D.M.K. government. Their food supply and underemployment, however, were as woeful as in the neighbouring villages. In Kirippur, in-August 1976, Communists supporting labourers held a one-day strike on their own initiative to demand that the statutory wages be paid for women engaged in transplanting and men in fertilizing the fields, and that landlords owning more than four acres pay coolies' daily wages in paddy rather than money as the price of grain had increased. A demand was also put forward for *pannaiyal*s to be given small plots of wet land or *pattakkal* as in former times. This demand failed, and instead the landlords decided to re-engage their *pannaiyal*s as regular coolies.

None of the Communist labourers to whom I talked appeared to have any vision of a socialist future. When I suggested that all the land should really belong to the peasants and labourers who worked it, the response of Kirippur's Communist Harijan leader was, "You are dreaming".

Focusing on wages as the central issue seems to me to have several disadvantages, although it is probably essential to stave off extreme distress in the short run. First, the emphasis must necessarily be on daily rather than annual wages because three-quarters of the labourers are casual coolies. By the same token, however, slight raises in daily wages do not address the main problem of underemployment. Indeed, they provoke landlords to dispense with as much local labour as possible, and instead to hire tractors with specialized local operators from the nearest town. In some cases absentee landlords even import labourers for transplanting and harvesting from their own villages, paying them less than the statutory wage. Even otherwise, when the wages of 20 are shared among 30 or more people, statutory wage rates have little meaning.

Second, focusing on wage rates alienates the cultivating tenants and smallholders, who are very poor but who themselves employ labourers at peak seasons. It was probably partly because recent Communist policy had focused on wages that the Paddy Producers' Association in 1976 counted every one of Kirippur's poor tenants and smallholders among its members.

The Communists' inability to attract poor peasants and cultivating tenants even casts a shadow on their relations with the agricultural labourers. In 1976 I found that the CPI-M received very little support from the non-Brahman as distinct from the Harijan labourers. The reason for this probably was that the non-Brahman labourers found it more profitable to takes sides politically with those of their kinsmen and street neighbours who owned a little land and themselves employed labourers. The temptation for non-Brahman workers to support their employers is great, for they are often given small favours over the Harijans, for example a small plot of land to lease. If they oppose the employers, the social penalties for them are greater than for the Harijans, for they are often related to members of the land-owning class and live among them. Tragically, one finds that non-Brahman labourers are often coerced or persuaded into acting as strike-breakers against the Harijans, and even as hit-men in the bigger landlords' battles against their Harijan labourers. There are Harijan goons too in some villages who do the violent work of the landlords, but they appear to be fewer than non-Brahmans. The communists' task of organizing is indeed difficult in Thanjavur because of the social gulf that still separates Harijans, living in ghettos outside the villages, and their caste Hindu fellow workers within the main villages. Had the communists been able to offer adequate incentives for tenants and poor peasants landowners, however, the gulf between the castes might have been lessened.

It seems probable that a strong peasant movement in Thanjavur would require the organizers of labour unions to radicalize their short-term demands, and also to offer the peasants and labourers a longer-term vision of the possibilities for land distribution followed by cooperative farming. Among the short-term demands, it seems necessary to include the following:

First, a serious demand might be made to implement the land ceiling act of 1972. At present, the official ceiling is 15 standard acres per family of five. In fact, by dividing their land in the names of all family members, many families own 100 or more acres. Among the formerly great landlords there are still said to be three family estates each totalling more than 3,000 acres and several more of more than 500, whose lands are registered in the names of people most of whom are actually tenants or labourers. Since 1970 the Sarvodaya association has documented and publicized some of these cases (see Vijayam 1973), but more might be done by the labour unions to expose them and demand their liquidation.

Second, a strong case can be made and wide support might be forthcoming for a demand to confiscate the land of absentee landlords. In spite of the "green revolution", absentee landlordism has increased since 1952 as small rentiers have sold their lands to merchants and bigger owners and as salary earners have moved away in larger numbers to the cities. In many villages from half to three-quarters of the land is now owned by absentees. A demand could be made that only those who live and work land in the villages should own it.

It is possible that demands to confiscate land above the ceiling and to get rid of absentee ownership might unite most of the smallholders and tenants as well as the labourers, while alienating only those one or two families in each village who own more than the legal ceiling.

Third, it seems necessary to agitate for the actual distribution of surplus lands to landless tenants and labourers without further delay. Although at least half of Thanjavur's land was formerly under large estates each comprising several hundred to several thousand acres, only 1 to 2 per cent of the total cultivable land has so far been redistributed to the landless. A drive to implement the existing laws and to get rid of absentee ownership might reactivate the alliance between small cultivators and landless labourers. I have calculated that without disturbing the rich and middle peasants who own up to 15 acres per family, it should be possible to distribute 2 acres of irrigated wet land to every landless family in the district. Given Thanjavur's high productivity from irrigation, this is enough to maintain a family.

It might be argued that distributing the land in small parcels would lower productivity and prevent Thanjavur from exporting as large a surplus as is currently sent to other, deficit districts. It is true that in Thanjavur, estates of about 15 or more acres that are cultivated with the new technology and inputs tend to produce up to twice as much as small holdings of less than three acres. The reason for this is that large owners need not stint on hybrid seeds, fertilizers, or pesticides. They can also afford to buy pumpsets to supplement the channel water, and tractors to plough quickly so as to take full advantage of the seasons. The answer to this problem seems to be that if a drive to redistribute the land really got off the ground, it would be necessary at once to introduce village cooperation with respect to the use of pumpsets and tractors and to spread chemical inputs more evenly. This could be done as an interim measure and would accustom the villagers to minimal cooperation, in advance of any move towards cooperative cultivation and harvesting.

It must be admitted that it seems unlikely that these changes will be made under India's present system of dependent state capitalism, in which private profit is of central importance and landlords command political power. The most that the agricultural unions could do at present might be to educate the peasants of all classes about the possibilities for a more egalitarian and cooperative future, and to unite them in a series of interim demands. But such measures might go far to invigorate a people for whom the Communist movement has had deep meaning for the past forty years.

NOTES

1. Figures for the district are taken from the Census of India, 1951, Madras and Coorg, Part I, Report, Madras 1952; the Census of India, 1961, Vol. IX, Madras, Part I — A (ii), General Report, and Part V — A (ii), Scheduled Castes and Tribes; and the Census of India, 1971, Series 19, Tamil Nadu, Part X — B, District Census Handbook, Thanjavur District, Vol. 1. Figures for the two villages studied come from my own censuses of 1952 and 1976.

2. Women agricultural labourers form a higher percentage of female agricultural work force than do male labourers of the male agricultural work force because men are counted as belonging to the "agricultural work force" if they supervise land and obtain most of their livelihood from it, whether or not they work it, whereas women are counted as belonging to the agricultural work force only if they work at least part time on the land as owner-cultivators, tenant-cultivators, or labourers. In the two villages studied there were no women who actively supervised land without working it.

3. These acts are the Tanjore Tenants' and Pannaiyals' Act of 1952, the Tamil Nadu Cultivating Tenants' Protection and Payment of Fair Rent Act of 1956, and the Tamil Nadu Agricultural Lands Record of Tenancy Rights Act of 1969. For the texts of these and other land acts of Tamil Nadu, see K. Venkoba Rao, *Tamilnadu Land Reforms Acts,* The Madras Law Journal Office, Madras, 1975.

4. A few special tasks like carrying away the bodies of dead cattle are still performed by the lowest caste of Parayas. With regard to other tasks, men are chiefly involved in ploughing, levelling, sowing, cutting bunds, fencing, cart-driving, picking up seedlings for transplanting, harvesting, and milking cattle, and women in sowing, transplanting, weeding, harvesting, and collecting cow-dung for fuel. Boys and old men usually graze and wash the cattle.

5. The Tamil Nadu Land Reforms (Fixation of Ceilings on Lands) Act of 1961 fixed the ceiling at 30 standard acres for a family of five. The Act was amended in 1974 to fix the ceiling at fifteen standard acres. For the texts of these acts, see K. Venkoba Rao, *op. cit.*

6. For some of the militant actions of this period, see Mythily Shivaraman, "Rumblings of Class Struggle in Thanjavur", *loc. cit.* 1973.

7. In 1975/76, in different parts of Thanjavur, Rs.8 to Rs.11 was being paid per day for ploughing and carting with the worker's oxen, Rs.5 to Rs.6 for ploughing and carting with the landlord's oxen, Rs.4 to Rs.5 for sowing and plucking seedlings, Rs.3 to Rs.4 for transplanting, Rs.2 and Rs.3 for weeding, and the paddy equivalent of Rs.6 for harvesting and threshing. The new wage rates promulgated by the Government of Tamil Nadu in March 1976 were at the lower end of these amounts, and were lower than those already obtaining in east Thanjavur where labour unions are strongest.

REFERENCES

Alexander, K.C. (1975) : *Agrarian Tension in Thanjavur,* National Institute, of Community Development, Hyderabad.

Beteille, Andre (1965) : *Caste, Class and Power; Changing Patterns of Stratification in a Tanjore Village,* Univ. of California Press.

Gough, Kathleen (1955) : "The Social Structure of a Tanjore Village" in McKim Marriott, ed. *Village India,* Univ. of Chicago Press.

(1955b): "The Social Structure of a Tanjore Village" in M.N. Srinivas, ed., *India's Villages*, West Bengal Government Press, (republ. Asia Publishing House, 1970).

(1965) : "Brahman Kinship in a Tamil Village" *American Anthropologist*, Vol. 58, No. 5, October.

(1971a): "Caste in a Tanjore Village" in Edmund R. Leach, ed., *Aspects of Caste in South India, Ceylon and Pakistan*, Cambridge Univ. Press.

(1971b): "The Green Revolution in South India and North Vietnam", *Social Scientist*, Trivandrum, No. 61, August.

(1973) : "Harijans in Thanjavur" in Kathleen Gough and Hari, .P. Sharma, eds., *Imperialism and Revolution in South Asia*, Monthly Review Press.

(1977a) : "Agrarian Change in Thanjavur" in K.S. Krishnaswamy and others, eds., *Society and Change: Essays in Honour of Sachin Chaudhuri*, Bombay, Oxford Univ. Press.

(1977b) : "Changing Agrarian Relations in Thanjavur, 1951-1976" in *Essays in Honour of Aiyappan, Kerala Sociological Review*, Special Issue, 1977

(1977c) : "Colonial Economics in Southeast India", *Economic and Political Weekly*, Bombay, Vol. 12, March.

Shivaraman, Mythily (1973) : "Rumblings of Class Struggle in Tamil Nadu" in Gogh and Sharma, eds., *Imperialism and Revolution in South Asia*, Monthly Review Press

Sivertsen, Dagfinn (1963) : *When Caste Barriers Fall*, Allen and Unwin.

Vijayam (1973) : *Satyagraha in Thanjavur: A Study*, Gandhi Peace Foundation, New Delhi

Agricultural Labourers in Peasant Societies: The Case of South Asia

The purpose of this paper is to explore the role of landless agricultural labourers in peasant societies, both today and in the past, focusing on the case of South Asia, and southern India in particular. Landless agricultural labourers — that is, people who have no rights to the land on which they work, and little prospect of acquiring any land of their own (except, perhaps, their actual house-sites) — are not reported in significant numbers in discussions of peasant societies for most of the rest of the world. Thus, in Europe, the Americas, Africa, the Pacific, and many parts of Southeast Asia prior to the sixteenth century, there appears to have been a sharp contrast with parts of South Asia, particularly the more heavily populated areas where irrigated rice was the major crop, in which the presence of large numbers of such labourers is documented from a very early period.[1]

I will first discuss the question of the landless labourer in traditional peasant society. I then try to analyse what has happened to the category of landless agricultural labourers in one part of southern India, Kerala, over time; and to look at their present condition in two of the main rice regions of the State. I then come back to the question of the role of the landless in peasant societies, and discuss some of the differences in the life conditions of landless labourers under pre-capitalist and capitalist conditions of production, pointing out the differences and similarities, both from the viewpoint of the individual labourer and from that of the system as a whole.

Writing from a perspective informed mostly by research in Africa and Europe, Joan Vincent has noted that within the category of the landless, we may recognize a continuum from those who are comparatively wealthy craftsmen and shopkeepers, owning no agricultural land but possessing alternative sources of income which keep them well-off, to those she categorizes as beggars and tramps, the destitute who are often not only landless but homeless.

Between these two extremes are those who own land but are unable to exploit it for their own use and those who lack both tenure and use. . . . The process of rural differentiation whereby the richest landowners acquire more land and greater wealth while the poorest lose the use of the little they have has been outlined in some detail for both European and Third World agrarian societies in the course of change. (1977 : 59)

She goes on to note how the four types of landless (the leasing shopkeepers, the wage labourers, the rump peasantry, and the destitute) reflect —

The neglected processes involved in the tranformation of agrarian society: the "peasantization" that occurs as "tribal" or "colonial" peoples enter the world economic system and the "depeasantizing", to use the phrase of Russian peasants themselves, that accompanies "the utter dissolution of the old patriarchal peasantry and the creation of new types of rural inhabitants." Both processes find men in movement socially and geographically in agrarian society in response to the market mechanisms of organizational flow. *(Ibid.)*

It is certainly true that the upheavals that beset India following the colonial take-over had profound effects on every section of the population, and have played a part in the increase in the percentage of people in the agricultural labourer category. However, in order to understand the role of landless agricultural labourers in South Asia, it is necessary to go back further in history. South Asia has been highly stratified on class as well as caste lines, at least since the period immediately preceding the birth of the Buddha, though stratification patterns have not remained constant over time (Mencher, in preparation). It is clear that landless agricultural labourers have played an important role in productive processes, at least in the more densely populated regions, from very early times. It is in this context that one often hears western social scientists comment that there is "no such thing as a peasant" in South Asia.

This of course brings us to the controversial question of how "peasants" or "the peasantry" may be defined. However, my purpose here is not to debate that question. For the present purpose, it really does not matter if some scholars choose to define the concept of peasantry so as to eliminate South Asia both in the past and today, or to eliminate many of its most productive regions. However we define these concepts, it is important to look at the nature of the agricultural processes, as well as the social relations of production, in this region, and how they have evolved over the past two millenia.

In order to understand productive relations in South Asia one cannot ignore the role of caste and class, how the two interdigitate, and how they have evolved. It is difficult to get a clear picture of the role of untouchable landless labour in earlier times, but N. Sastri notes that under the Cholas (tenth century),

> That a considerable element in the population, especially among agricultural labourers, lived in a condition not far from slavery is clear from the literature of the age. [1955 : 555]

He also discusses the wages of those who were not serfs or slaves, and makes it quite clear that day labour was common in this period (*op. cit.* 557-9). He notes further:

> From casual references in the inscriptions, we can dimly perceive the existence of a class of hired day-labourers who assisted in agricultural operations on the estates of other people and received a daily wage, usually in grain. There was no clear line of division between the absolutely landless agrarian labourer and the small peasant hiring himself out in his spare time. . . . In several instances a gift of land for some public purpose . . . is found to include some proportion set apart for the residences of the families of labourers engaged in its cultivation. Such labourers *were not* peasant proprietors by any means, and were nearer the class of hired labourers than tenants; they were entitled to the use of a house-site near enough to the place of their work and to get wages fixed in advance, the proceeds of their labour on land being altogether the property of the institution that owned the land on which they worked. (569-70)

He also points out that tenancy was quite common at that time, and that there is no reason to expect there to have been any difference between methods of cultivation on the lands of public or charitable institutions (for which we have good evidence) and on the lands of private landowners.

For the late Chola period (about thirteenth century), Rajkumar notes the following incident:

> A revolt developed in the face of the refusal by the landlords to raise the emoluments [presumably of labourers]. . . . With the struggle progressing to a stage where blood was shed, the demand was conceded. As a result of this heroic struggle which encompassed 24 villages including Paganeri, the Paraya.[untouchable] people . . . were able to wrest a few rights from their oppressors. (1974 : 31)

While it is extremely difficult to document the percentage of the population in any given region working as landless agricultural labourers prior to the arrival of the British, it is clear nonetheless that it was an early custom, especially in irrigated tracts. Traditional agrarian society in India was at least three-tiered, and in many areas four or five-tiered. The structure of rural areas in some parts of the country was more complex than in others, but certainly in all of the irrigated regions members of the large untouchable castes worked as labourers on land to which they held no rights. Habib, writing about northern India during the days of the Moghul Empire, notes:

> . . . there were those who were absolutely indigent in the fullest sense, the landless labourers. Members of the depressed castes not only undertook work considered abhorrent by the caste peasants, such as tannery, scavenging, etc. but were also in a large measure agricultural workers . . . . Thus Chamars and Dhanuks who had their own prescribed occupations, worked as agricultural labourers. . . . The Caste System seems to have worked in its inexorable way to create a fixed labour reserve force for agricultural production. Members of the low castes, assigned to the most menial and contemptible occupations, could never aspire to the status of peasants holding or cultivating land on their own. (1963 : 120-22)

The scope of this paper does not permit a detailed discussion of the relationship between caste and class in ancient India, which I propose to deal with elsewhere (see Mencher, in preparation), but it is clearly more complex than the preceding quotation suggests. I would argue that, rather than the caste system creating a fixed labour reserve force for agricultural production, it was really the opposite that occurred. That is, in an extremely stratified agrarian society, one of the factors leading to the solidification of caste boundaries was clearly the development of a large reserve force of landless labourers. In a society where land was everything (and it should be noted that even many members of the merchant and artisan castes had rights to land which they had worked by others), to be landless was really abhorrent. Often, they were the earliest settlers of the land, long since conquered by later groups. In any case, caste was (and is) a very convenient device for manipulating and controlling the landless.

In discussing agricultural labour in South Asia, I will be referring primarily to wet rice regions, though at times I will refer to other irrigated tracts of the subcontinent. Wet rice cultivation requires the use of large amounts of labour on small plots of land for short periods of time. It has been noted by Etienne that this kind of cultivation can be carried out in either of two ways, either by cooperative or exchange work teams, or else by making use of an army of agricultural labourers who are available for seasonal employment. In Southeast Asia, especially those areas where has been low population density until fairly recently, the pattern for cultivation has been that of exchange labour. For India, however, it has been traditional (at least for close to 2,500 years) to use agricultural labourers, mostly belonging to untouchable or low-ranking castes or tribal groups. This pattern has continued until recent times.

It is clear that as the caste system evolved, it came to be closely interwoven with the basic social relations of production. Without going into detail on the origins and development of caste in South Asia, it is clear from the literature that caste has not been an immutable system, that it has changed and evolved over time, at least from the period of the Indus Valley Civilization. In early times, South Asia was the home of a large variety of indigenous peoples, as well as a kind of *cul de sac* into which large groups of people moved, in part because of its good environment for agriculture. With tremendous amounts of ethnic diversity in a slowly-emerging stratified society, it is not surprising that some groups came to occupy the lowest rungs of the hierarchy and to be forced to do the most onerous duties. When it comes to agriculture, the most onerous tasks, especially for wet rice cultivation, are things such as applying cow dung, transplanting, fixing *bunds,* harvesting, etc. And it is not surprising that at a fairly early period, landowners and tenants came to use relatively low-ranking groups of prople to do this kind of work, since thir labour was cheap.

In general there was a fairly close correlation between caste and social class during the pre-colonial period, i.e. before the penetration of capitalist relations of production into the subcontinent, and even today there is a partial correlation between the two. (That is, there is a much higher percentage of untouchables among the landless labourers than of any higher caste, in any region. And on the other hand, most of the landless agricultural labourers belonged to the untouchable castes). Habib also notes that, though there was no direct evidence in the Moghul literature regarding the status of the depressed castes, it is noteworthy that many divisions of those castes bear the names of higher castes or clans or tribes, which sugests that they may originally have been servants of those higher-ranking groups (122). I have also noted the same situation in Kerala, where even Marxist untouchables identified themselves as belonging to the house of their traditional landlord — even though they no longer work exclusively for his family, and are in fact his political enemies.

I have discussed elsewhere how the untouchables in southern India were formerly agrestic slaves, and have mentioned some of the late documentation for this (in the late eighteenth and early nineteenth centuries — see Mencher 1974 : 470-2). Not all the landless agricultural labourers were necessarily untouchables, but it is clear that the majority were. For the Chola period Sastri also notes how members of other castes, if they were absolutely destitute, could be sold into slavery, or even sell themselves to pay off debts. Not all of these ended up as agricultural labourers, but certainly some did, especially those belonging to lower castes. Higher-caste slaves probably ended up as household servants of the wealthy.

THE CASE OF KERALA

Traditionally, Kerala agrarian relations were extremely complex and multitiered. However, for the purpose of this presentation, I am only concerned with the bottom levels of the hierarchy. At the bottom of the hierarchy of those having rights to land, especially wet land, were tenants. (The detailed description of the various forms and patterns of tenancy is not relevant to the present discussion.) The bottom rung of tenants were not all of the same size, even traditionally. Thus, there were many Ezhava[2] tenants who had small holdings of one to five acres, which they cultivated mostly themselves with the use of family labour (especially if they belonged to large families with many females). The same was true of some of the small Christian households in the south. However, there has always been a large population of untouchable agricultural labourers in Kerala who had no rights to agricultural land. They accounted for approximately 10.8 per cent of the population in 1911, but undoubtedly their proportion in the population was higher before the sixteenth century, because many untouchables converted to Islam in the eighteenth century in northern Kerala, and to Catholicism in the eighteenth and nineteenth centuries in the south. Apart from the small tenants, however, there were two other groups of tenants at the bottom of the hierarchy. They included higher-caste small tenants)who would not do manual work themselves), and large tenants of the Ezhava, Christian, and Nayar communities. These larger tenants often owned substantial holdings, but did not give all of their land out to lower tenants, preferring to cultivate at least some of it themselves with permanently attached labourers of their own caste (in the case of Ezhava tenants) or of untouchable castes. The hardest agricultural labour in the fields was mostly done by untouchable labourers, who were expected to work from early morning (in some areas they rose at 2 or 3 a.m.) until late at night.

Can one characterize such a traditional society as peasant? I would say yes. To put it another way, if it was not a peasant society, what was it? It certainly was not typical of "oriental despotism", with its reliance on a bureaucracy created to maintain massive irrigation works; at least this was not the characteristic pattern in southern India.

In the pre-colonial period, most of the agricultural labourers belonged either to untouchable castes, or to the caste groups just slightly higher in rank (sometimes classified by the British as depressed classes), such as some of the Ezhavas in Kerala or the Naickers and Padiyachis in the northern coastal plains of Tamil Nadu. This is not to say that before the British there were no poor or landless people of higher caste, but rather that such people did not work as agricultural labourers. Poor Brahmans got employment as cooks for wealthy households or temples, or did other kinds of menial work in temples; members of intermediate groups got employment with well-do-do families, but did not generally work in the fields, except perhaps as supervisors.

In some parts of Kerala, during the colonial period, some of the dispossessed higher-caste people did occasionally take to agricultural field work. As a result of the changes that occurred during the colonial period, plus one might add the past 30 years of so-called development, many people formerly holding land as tenants lost their rights to land, and among the uneducated, some at least were forced to turn to agricultural labour. This has been particularly striking in the extreme north of the State, in the Cannonore region, and in Kuttanad in the south. It did also occur in central Kerala, though for a number of reasons, too complex to go into here, it was considered more respectable to go off and work — even as a sweeper in a hotel in Madras — than to do manual labour in one's own village. Many of the Ezhava and Christian tenants who lost land in the period between 1900 and the late 1950s turned to agricultural labour as their main source of income. This has been less true of Nayars, though one certainly did find some Nayars doing agricultural labour in all parts of the state. In Tamil Nadu, most of the tenants lost their land later. (In the Chingleput area it was in the late 1960s, as a result of the landlords' fear of pending land legislation, but here, as in Kerala, the ranks of agricultural labourers have also been increased by other low caste or intermediate-caste former tenants who had nothing else to turn to.)

Today, in Kerala there are several types of landless labourers. First of all, there are the permanent labourers of particular landlords. The percentage of these in the population varies enormously, but it is clear that this is regarded as a special and advantageous relationship. The number of labourers in this category varies enormously from district to district, but in Palghat district, where I was working in 1975/76 and again in the summer of 1977, we found a fairly high percentage of the labourers in this category (see Table 2).

That it is clearly considered advantageous to be a permanent labourer may be seen from the fact that the various agricultural labour unions (which are attached to political parties) were vying with one another in getting labourers registered as permanent servants of particular landlords, after the labour relations bill was passed in October of 1975. Further evidence is provided by the fact that landlords, on their part, were often trying to keep from having labourers registered as their permanent labourers. Far from being the bonded labour of earlier times, being a permanent labourer of a particular landlord today confers many advantages on a worker. To begin with, he is guaranteed more days of work in the year than a casual labourer, a not-too-insignificant thing in a labour situation where unemployment or semi-employment is rife. Secondly, there is the promise (still unfulfilled) that they will eventually be given some sort of provident fund and other employment benefits usually reserved for factory workers. These are specified in the 1975 bill, but have not been actually brought into force yet, and no one knows if they ever will.

Apart from permanent labourers, there are two other types of rural labour. There are those who work primarily as casual labourers, going out for work on a day-to-day basis, usually within their own village, and mostly in agriculture. This again is a feature of the central and northern parts of the State. Also, in these areas, one finds male agricultural labourers who in fact earn most of their living from non-agricultural manual labour, e.g. in construction work, work on the railway line, or as daily coolies for whoever calls them to do a job, and the jobs vary enormously.

In Kuttanad in Kerala, the pattern is quite different. In this region, there are very few agriculural labourers with permanent employment. The vast majority (over 90 per cent) are casual labourers who go for work wherever it may be found. It is in this area that one finds vast armies of people turning up for such operations as transplanting and harvesting. In the harvest season here, people measure the amount of work time in a given day in terms of fractions of an hour, rather than in terms of days or even half-days. Thus, a labourer might get work for 1-1/2 hours on a specific harvest day. This is considered to be fairly good, since in 1-1/2 hours one can harvest a fair amount, and one gets to keep one-sixth or one-seventh of the amount actually harvested. On the other hand, the numbers of workers are now enormous, especially during the harvest season when the ranks of the agricultural labourers are swelled by women from the coir industry, and even fishermen's wives who need the extra money to survive. These casual agricultural labourers are really a new breed of labourers, who have even fewer ties to the land than attached labourers in the sense that they work for any one, any place. There has been some attempt made to use passes to restrict work in a given locale to local people, but it is only partially successful, and can only work at all with the use of the police to check the passes.

It is not an accident that one finds this system in the area of greatest population density, nor that it is in the area that has been affected most by labour conditions in the tea industry (even though not many Kerala workers went up to the tea estates in the high ranges). It is also the area where agricultural labour unions were started earliest, and where they have a very long history of struggle to maintain a living wage for the labourers.

What proportion of the rural population possesses no land? Rather than looking at the total rural population, which includes shopkeepers, people who commute to nearby towns, people engaged in rural industries such as processing of coir or fishing and the like, it is more useful to look at the landless as a proportion of those involved in agriculture. Table 1 gives these figures for Kerala, based on the 1971 census. A few of those recorded as agricultural labourers might also possess a small amount of cultivable land, but the vast majority in Kerala are landless. (In addition, most of the landless are in debt. In our sample of landless households in the two Palghat villages, only three did not have outstanding loans, and for the two Kuttanad villages taken together there were only 11 households without loans.)

Table 2 presents some general information for the four villages where intensive work was carried out in 1975/76. For the Palghat villages, many of those who had only worked for a few years as permanent labourers had worked previously for someone else; a few (five in the first village) previously had their own land, and some had been casual workers before (see Table 3). A variety of reasons were given for changing their permanent employer, including the employer's selling or losing his land, land partitions; the desire to work closer to home, quarrels with the employer, etc. (This question was irrelevant for the Kuttanad villages.)

In Palghat, labourers all said that they were free to change their jobs, but that there were no other jobs available. The fear of not being able to get another job was the main reason given for not quitting. In addition, seven people said that they had debts and could not leave until the debt was repaid. Apart from the ease of borrowing money, a number of informants (37 in village 1 and 54 in village 2) said that they stayed with their permanent employer because of getting more work, that they got all of the work of their employer. Thus, the economic advantage was the main one given.

It is clear that staying as a permanent labourer in the present context has at least some advantages. In another paper (Mencher 1978c) I have looked at the actual nutritional condition of the agricultural labourers in one village in each of the two regions. Tables 4 and 5 present some of that data. These tables show clearly that even when there is more than adequate food in the shops, the agricultural labourers are without adequate food during a considerable proportion of the year. The permanent workers tend to do somewhat better, though even they are often forced to go hungry at times. Of those working only as casual labourers, the vast majority (especially in the Kuttanad area) say that they are not working as permanent labourers because no one will give them permanent work. The majority said that they would be prepared to be permanent labourers if there were such jobs available. This was even the case for those workers who felt that if they had permanent work they would have to work for longer hours.

Apart from village number 1, where there has been some increase in the amount of available work due to the taking of a third paddy crop in some parts of the village, the labourers elsewhere all said that there has been a significant *increase* in the difficulty in getting work. In Kuttanad, there is really no month in which work can be obtained without considerable difficulty. In Palghat the case is different: Here, hardly any people were without work in the months of January-February, February-March, and again May-June, August-September, and September-October, October-November (see Table 6). As indicated in Table 6, these are the same months in which labourers (especially in village 1) buy less rice.

How typical is this situation for India as a whole? To what extent is it recent, and to what extent is it different from other parts of the country? Clearly there is considerable variation statewise in the percentage of landless labourers, from 4.27 per cent in Jammu and Kashmir (where there have been a number of special projects aimed at providing employment) to about 12 per cent in Rajasthan and what was then Assam, to 55 per cent in Kerala (Table 7). There is on the whole a higher percentage of landless in the irrigated areas, but it is clearly more complex than that. The low figure for Rajasthan is not surprising, considering the large amount of desert in the area, and the fact that most of the land there is rain-fed land cultivated by tenants. The low percentage in Assam is (at least in large part) due to the fact that it included a considerable tribal population, who are much more egalitarian than typical Indian society. In any case, it is useful to look briefly at one other state before concluding my discussion of the present situation. Since I have worked intensively in Chingleput district of Tamil Nadu, let me briefly contrast this region with the Kerala situation.

On the basis of a survey of 1,743 households (all but 23 households in 8 villages) carried out in 1970/71, we found that in 709 (40.7 per cent) of households, the head of the household worked primarily as an agricultural labourer, and the household did not own any land at all. In this area, though the vast majority of the landless work as day-labourers year after year, there is enough movement between the categories of landless labourer and sharecropper to keep the landless somewhat divided politically (Mencher 1974b). As in Kerala, the category of landless is cross-cut by caste. In our 1970/71 study, out of 574 untouchable households, 439 (76 per cent) owned one acre or less of land, whereas in the next higher caste, the Vanniyars (also a large cultivating caste), only 245 out of 451 (54 per cent) owned less than one acre.

As early as 1967, in a survey conducted in five villages in this same district, a significant number of agricultural labourers complained about the lack of work, and clearly there was a strong need felt for an increase in the number of days of employment. Though we did not collect nutritional data in this area, it was fairly obvious even to the naked eye that many people did not get enough to eat much of the time. In visiting agricultural labourer households during the period before the harvest season, it was not unusual to hear women comment about not having lit the fire the previous evening. I have discussed elsewhere the potential political militancy among the agricultural workers in this area, and how two strikes (one successful and one unsuccessful) were fought there (Mencher 1975). However, it is also clear that Tamil Nadu has not had the political organizing that there has been in Kerala. Otherwise, the two areas are quite similar in their stratification patterns and in the social relations of production, even though there are physical differences in terms of ecology, water sources, etc., and cultural differences with a long tradition. (The drier regions of Tamil

Nadu, especially the ones where at present there is very little irrigation, are significantly different. But they are also the areas with much less dense populations.) Gough's paper in this symposium presents an excellent picture of what has happened to the landless category in Thanjavur. In Chingleput, as in Thanjavur, the category of landless has been greatly increased by tenants being forced off the land in the 1960s as landowners came to fear land reform. In fact, in India as a whole, there is much less landlessness reported for the turn of the century than there is today.[3] It is clear that the percentage of landless in the population has increased in most of the country as a result of tenants being thrown off the land, and the various other processes involved with the buying and selling of land in the nineteenth and twentieth centuries.

To some extent one could say that the situation in Kerala is a kind of precursor of what may be coming in other parts of India. In Kerala today we have a landless population that has a long history of, and training in, political struggle. On the other hand, the economy seems to have reached the limits of absorption, given the present social relations of production. Many economists have argued that what is needed is to absorb the labourers into small-scale industry (United Nations Report, *Poverty, Unemployment and Development Policy* by Raj, Paniker, Krishnan, and Krishnaji), and this is certainly a noble idea. However, I am quite skeptical about the possibility of absorbing adequate numbers of labourers by this approach. Some can be absorbed, but not really large numbers. In fact, the Chinese experience has been that rural small industry has not been successful in directly generating employment:

> Raising agricultural yields — and, even more, creating the physical infrastructure that can insure that the high yields will be obtained on a sustained basis — is an extremely labour-intensive business. 'Field capital construction', as they call it in China — land-shaping, terracing hills, building dams and canals, digging ponds — can absorb millions of men, particularly if the jobs have to be done by hand and with simple tools. But the development of farmland and water management infrastructure demands large quantities of such materials as cement, bricks, iron and steel, pumps, various types of irrigation and drainage machinery, and hydro-electric equipment. It is the job of rural small industry to meet these demands and thus help agriculture absorb labour. (Agarwal 1978 : 10)

It is clear that for many parts of India today, especially the major rice regions, it would make more sense to focus on intensifying the use of labour in agriculture. But for this to be meaningful, a basic restructuring of the social relations of production is required. One agricultural economist working in Trivandrum pointed out to me how it would be easily possible to both increase productivity in Kerala and also increase the amount of work available, but that in order to do so the government would have to go completely against the interests of those who own land, especially the medium-to-large landowners.

THE LANDLESS IN PEASANT SOCIETIES

I would like at this point to turn to the more general question again, that is: What is the position of the landless in peasant society? It could be said that many other parts of the world, where there was no landlessness prior to the sixteenth century, have in a sense been catching up with what occurred earlier in South Asia. But being landless is something which has occurred in different parts of the world at different times. Thus, at one time, Romans tilled their fields with the help of slave-like labourers. Later on, this was given up in favour of the use of tenants or serfs, who had some rights to the land they tilled and could not be moved around from one area to another, and thus had greater "freedom" than the former slaves.

However, it is clear that being a landless agricultural labourer under capitalist productive relations is quite different from the situation that prevailed under feudalism. It is no doubt true that, both under pre-capitalist conditions and in the present situation, one could characterize the landless as exploited. However, one must be very careful to spell out the details of the specific situation, rather than simply using the term "exploitation" as a kind of catchword. It is important to look at the differences. In southern India, including Kerala, landless labourers were traditionally attached to particular landowners or tenants. They did get work most days of the year, though their wages were very low and they had to work incredibly long hours. They were obligated to give things to their landlord at certain occasions (e.g. when there was a birth, death, marriage, *tali*-tying ceremony, annual festival, etc. in the landowner's house). In return, they were usually given presents at three main festival occasions in the year, as well as help via loans, or sometimes gifts, when they had crises in their families. Nonetheless, their wages were a mere pittance, and their life situation most pitiable. In addition, they were subject to the most stringent rules of caste which forbade their using footwear, shirts, or other upper garments, or building better houses (if by any miracle they could manage to do so). Altogether their life was at the beck and call of their employers.

There is no question that today in India there are more landless labourers than at any time in the past — not only in absolute numbers, but also in proportion to the rest of the population. Thus, competition for work is much fiercer. Furthermore, in many parts of India today, there are fewer ties of a traditional patron-client type that oblige landowners to give certain things to their labourers (such as clothes at specific times of the year, or help when there is a family emergency, etc.). However, there are advantages, too. Even though their leaders might not be advocating any radical transformation of society (see Mencher

1978a), in some areas, especially Kerala, the labourers recognize that only such a transformation will eliminate the iniquities of their daily living. Further, they have won some concessions. In Kuttanad, the hours of work are now so fixed that a siren blows at the start of work and in the evening, reminiscent of factory whistles. Elsewhere there are no sirens, but work time is nevertheless limited, and labourers have some time for their own life. Furthermore, landowners must be careful how they talk to labourers; even justified complaints must be couched in decent language. This was not the case before. It is clear that there is considerable variation between regions within a state, as well as between states, in the situation of the landless today. One hears reports almost every day of battles between untouchable labourers and land-owning elites. It is likely that this is a result of, or a precursor to, organizing on the part of labourers who have begun to see a way out of being treated badly.

Though the newspapers report atrocities against untouchables almost every day in different parts of the country, in Kerala this has not occurred. Where there has been friction it has been on a class basis, i.e. labourers against a given landlord, or a group of landlords against labourers, and in each case the labourers belong to a number of different communities and castes. This is perhaps one of the clearest indications that I can mention of the fact that labourers in Kerala are at the leading edge of a transition to a new social order in India.

It is obviously very hard to compare the landless of today with those of the past. Our knowledge of their hardships and sufferings today is far greater. Our knowledge of these things 1,000 years ago is much more fragmentary. Nonetheless, I would like to suggest that their situation was not especially pleasant even then, and that whenever they thought there was some possibility of succeeding, rebellions did in fact occur. However, what did characterize the past was the absence of any image of a different kind of society. As Mao has stated, the failure of these uprisings was obviously due to the historical environment in which they occurred, and to the fact that "neither new productive forces, nor new relations of production, nor a new class-force . . . existed in those days" (Mao 1954 : 65-76).

Today, there is at least an awareness on the part of some of the landless of alternative ways in which society could be organized. This is especially true in Kerala, where there has been a long history of leftist education and organizing. At the present time the landless in Kerala are politically far more radical than their leadership, which springs from the middle classes and has recently been pacified to some extent by their obtaining rights to land which they formerly held as tenants, under the new land reform measures. These same measures have for the most part excluded the landless from any meaningful economic gains.

If one wants to include societies such as South Asia, in which landowners of all sizes traditionally depended extensively on agricultural labourers, in one's definition of peasant societies, then the definition must certainly be broadened. I have shown elsewhere how the concept of the family farm, and the picure of a peasant family (either nuclear or extended) doing all their own work and being relatively self-sufficient, is totally irrelevant to the irrigated regions, as well as many other regions of South Asia (Mencher 1978b: Chapter 8). Beyond this, it is clear that in order to talk about the peasantry in a soceity as South Asia, it is essential to place one's discussion in a historical perspective. As I have tried to show, while landlessness is ancient, it has also varied over time.

The question may be asked whether it is meaningful to talk at all about peasant society in the context of South Asia, since it is clearly more complex than the majority of other societies for which this term has been used. Whatever decision may be made on this matter, it is clear to me that one cannot simply ignore the landless, either today or in the past.

NOTES

1. It is important also to note here that one cannot really compare South Asia (or greater India) to a single European country. It would actually be more meaningful to compare it to a region like Europe. Thus there is today, and has been in the past, as much difference between the different parts of South Asia (e.g. Kerala, Tamil Nadu, Bengal, Kashmir, and say Sind) as between England, Italy, Finland, and Czechoslovakia. Yet, in some ways there are similarities between these different European countries. For example, all were traditionally Christian, though converted at different times and adhering to different sects. There were many other similar cultural characteristics which linked them to one another in many ways, even during the Middle Ages. The same was true of the different parts of South Asia as early as the first millennium B.C.

2. The Ezhavas (also known as Tiyyars) are a low-ranking, formerly semi-untouchable caste who traditionally worked as toddy tappers; they constitute close to 27 per cent of the population of the state (between 36 and 42 per cent of the Hindu population, depending on region).

3. For example, in 1901 for Madras Presidency (which included present-day Tamil Nadu, parts of Andhra Pradesh and the northern half of Kerala), there was a ratio of 49 cultivators (including tenant cultivators) to 24 agricultural labourers. The 1971 census for Madras State only gives a ratio of 210 cultivators to 155 agricultural labourers. In other words, in 1901 for Madras Presidency the proportion of agricultural labourers to total people involved in agriculture was 33 per cent, and for Madras State in 1971, the proportion was 58 per cent.

REFERENCES

Agarwal, Anil (1978) : "Lessons from China", *Mazingira : The World Forum for Environment and Development,* No. 7 : 6-11.

Census of India, 1901, Vol. I. Report of Tables.

Census of India, 1971. General Population Statistics.

Habib, I. (1963) : *The Agrarian System of Moghul India (1556-1707),* New York, Asia Publishing Co.

Mao Tse-Tung (1954) : (English ed.) *Selected Works, Vol. 3,* London.

Mencher, Joan (1974a) : "The Caste System Upside Down : or the Not so Mysterious East", *Current Anthropology,* Dec. 1974, Vol. 15, No. 4, pp. 469-494.

(1974b) : "Problems in Analysing Rural Class Structure" *Economic And Political Weekly,* Aug. 31, Vol. IX, 1495-1503.

(1975) : "Agricultural Labour Movements in Their Socio-Political and Ecological Context: Tamil Nadu and Kerala", in *Culture and Society: A Festschrift for Dr. A. Aiyappan,* B.N. Nair, ed., New Delhi, Thompson Press (India) Ltd., pp. 240-266.

(1978a) : "Agrarian Relations in Two Rice Regions of Kerala", *Economic and Political Weekly,* 349-366.

(1978b) : *Agriculture and Social Structure in Tamil Nadu : Past Origins, Present Transformations, and Future Prospects.* Allied Publishers, New Delhi.

(1978c) : "Why Grow More Food: An Analysis of Some of the Contradictions in the 'Green Revolution' in Kerala" *Economic and Political Weekly Review of Agriculture,* Dec. 23-30, pp. A-98-A-104.

(in preparation) : "Caste and Class in India : Origins, History, and Present Situation" (a paper dealing with the origins and development of caste in India from prehistoric times to the present.)

Nutritive Value of Indian Foods (1977) (ed.) : National Institution of Nutrition, Hyderabad

Rajkumar, M.D. (1974) : "Struggles for Rights During Later Chola Period", *Social Scientist,* Vol. 18-19: 29-35.

Sastri, K.A.N. (1955) : *A History of South India,* Madras : Oxford University Press.

Vincent, Joan (1977) : "Agrarian Society as Organized Flow : Processes of Development Past and Present", *Peasant Studies* Vol. VI, No. 2 : 56-65.

TABLE 1

Landless Labourers (1971 Census Data)

	Palghat	Alleppey
As a percentage of total rural workers	52% landless	31% landless
As a percentage of workers in categories I & II (i.e. cultivators plus agricultural labour)	76% landless	66% landless

TABLE 2

General Characteristics of Agricultural Labourer Sample

	Villages in Palghat		Villages in Kuttanad	
	1*	2	3	4*
Total No. of Households in Sample	65	58	50	49
Total No. Members	304	283	259	304
Total Male	153	140	118	168
Total Female	152	143	141	136
Total Male Agricultural Workers	43	65	48	69
Total Female Agricultural Workers	83	89	74	50
Total Other Workers	32	24	17	14
Total Adults	197	198	155	193
Total Adult, Old, Disabled, Unemployed and Student	39	20	16	60+
Total No. Agricultural Labourers With Some Education	18	42	122	107
Total Agricultural Labourers With No Education	113	112	0	10
Total Children (16 or less)	117	85	104	111
Children Working in Agriculture	5	9	0	2
Children Working as Cowboy	4	1	0	1
Children Looking After Younger Children	11	9	0	2
Land Ownership				
(a) No. hh less than 1/10 acre h site	59	17	35	46
(b) No. with 10-50 cents dry land	6	24	15	4
(c) Housesite Over 1/2 acre	—	4	—	—
(d) Housesite Plus 1/2 acre Wet	—	4	—	—
(e) Housesite Plus Over 1/2 acre Wet	—	3	—	—
(f) Housesite Plus Other Dry Land	—	5	—	—
(g) No Answer	—	1	1	—

* These villages are the same as those used for the nutrition study.

+ Analysing these 60 individuals we find that apart from the elderly (18 over age 60), those who are still studying, and those claiming to be housewives, we find 19 individuals (9 males and 10 females) in the age group 17-30 who are listed as having no work. The males include one with a B.A. degree, one with S.S.L.C., five who have completed 8-9 years of school, one with four years of school, and one with one year of school. Among the females there are two with S.S.L.C., five with 8-9 years, and four with 4 years of schooling. This extent of unemployment among young poor people is a striking testimony to the extent of educated unemployed in the area—even though we do find agricultural labourers here who have passed S.S.L.C. (four in this village alone).

Even allowing for the unemployed young adults and those over 60, there remain 23 in this category, which makes it still relatively large in the all-Kerala context. One factor which may contribute to the larger number here is the fact that a large proportion of women in Christian households are listed as housewives — though it is possible that some of the women so listed may move in and out of agricultural work depending on the age of their children, their health, pregnancy, etc.)

TABLE 3

Miscellaneous Data from Agricultural Labourer Questionnaire

1. In village number 1, the vast majority had worked for the same employer for 10 years or less. Close to 25 per cent had worked for less than five years. The same held true for the other Palghat village. Thus, taking up permanent work is not an ancient feature, but is clearly desirable in the present.

2. In village number 1, about half of the labourers answering the question had worked as permanent labourers for someone else earlier; in the second Palghat village about one-quarter had done so. People had changed employer for a number of reasons, some relating to the employer, and some to their own convenience (such as being closer to home).

3. When asked why they remain as permanent labourers, in villages 1 and 2 (in Palghat) several people explained this in terms of being able to borrow money (approximately 1/3 of answers); most of the others explained it in terms of obtaining more work in the fields. It is striking that in villages 3 and 4 (in Kuttanad) when asked if they were prepared to get permanent work, the vast majority of those interviewed said yes. This included labourers who said that permanent workers received less pay, and often had to work longer hours.

4. Of the labourers who answered the questionnaire, 182 said that they did not get enough work, 7 that they did, and 31 gave no answer; 212 said that they were prepared to do more work, 2 said that they couldn't do more, and 6 gave no answer. Clearly, all of the labourers in both areas are very eager for more work. They also all said that other labourers in their families also did not get enough work.

5. In comparing the two regions, it is striking that in the Palghat villages, most of the labourers get their wages on the day that they work, but in Kuttanad this is not the case. The vast majority of the labourers in Kuttanad receive their wages only after the harvest. Thus, they are forced to borrow from local shopkeepers, and then repay after the harvest.

6. Uniformly the labourers in both areas complain about not getting enough paddy from their wages for their own home consumption, though the vast majority (about 2/3) also have to sell paddy after the harvest. Most of what is sold is given to shopkeepers or rice merchants.

7. Reasons given for increase in job security in Palghat area:

	Village 1	Village 2
Government regulations	40	8
Union activity	27	59
Other reasons	7	0

8. Labourers claiming union membership :

	Palghat		Kuttanad	
Village:	*1*	*2*	*3*	*4*
Union members	44	41	5	16
Not union members	18	18	45	33

(Though this seems strange in the light of Kuttanad's reputation as the home of agricultural labour unions, it conforms with the impressions gained by the anthropologist through interviews and participant observation.)

9. Sources of income other than agricultural wages:
    (data from all four villages combined)

    (a) Number of people receiving payments from relatives working outside the village 8

    (b) Individuals receiving extra income from sale of eggs. milk, etc.
         (40 of these are in village number 4) 53

    (c) Individuals receiving extra income from sale of cow dung, occasional coconuts, tapioca, firewood, ash, mud, bricks, etc.......................................48

    (d) Individuals receiving army pensions 3

    (e) Individuals reporting other members of their household who do non-agricultural work (such as rice mill workers, head-load, boatmen (Kuttanad), petty businessmen, etc.) ..37

         (Of these, 17 are daily wage jobs, 9 are monthly wage jobs, and 11 involve other types of wage arrangements.)

TABLE 4

Food Consumption During the Harvest Season*

	Palghat Village (March 76) N= 27		Kuttanad Village (April 77) N = 29	
	Calories	Protein	Calories	Protein
Amount consumed by individuals in household ranking lowest in				
(a) calories	1,472		744	
(b) protein		31 gm		16 gm
Amount consumed by individuals in household ranking highest in				
(a) calories	2,664		2,214	
(b) protein		58 gm		72 gm
Mean per consumption unit	1,894	42 gm	1,448	40 gm
Mean per household	1,925	42 gm	1,429	42 gm
By household, standard deviation	318.98	7.78 gm	331.95	13.86 gm
By household, variance	97,979.88	58.34 gm	106,400.91	185.56 gm

* In calculating the amount of calories per person per day from the amount consumed by a household, we have used the following conversion figures based on the National Institute of Nutrition figures for both this table and the following one: 1 non-working male = 1; 1 male agricultural labourer = 1.6; 1 male worker other = 1.2; 1 non-working female = 0.8; 1 female agricultural labourer = 1.2; 1 female lactating = 1.6; 1 child 0-5 years of age = 0.4; 1 child 5-10 years of age = 0.7; and 1 child between 11 and 15 variable between 0.8 and 1 depending on what the child does. There are many questions about this method of conversion which is based mainly on calories, but for a lack of any more precise measures we have had to rely on this one. (See *Nutritive Value of Indian Foods,* National Institute of Nutrition, Hyderabad, 1977 ed., p.10.) For the harvest season, we have figured all of the agricultural labourers as doing heavy work, even though they might not have had full-time work for all of the seven days under the survey. It may be noted that complete data were collected from each household for a seven consecutive-day period.

TABLE 5

Food Consumed During the Lean or Monsoon Season

	Palghat Village August 1976 N = 26		Kuttanad Village August-September 1977 N = 36	
	Calories	Proteins	Calories	Proteins
Amount consumed by individuals in household ranking lowest in				
calories (if sedentary)*	916		731	
protein (if sedentary)		18		16
calories (if heavy work)	798		669	
protein (if heavy work)		16		15
Amount consumed by individuals in household ranking highest in				
calories (if sedentary)	3,264		2,956	
protein (if sedentary)		67		101
calories (if heavy work)	2,448		2,032	
protein (if heavy work)		50		69
Mean per consumption unit				
(sedentary)	1,873	40	1,412	45
(heavy work)	1,503	32	1,133	36
Mean per household				
(sedentary)	2,022	44	1,545	50
(heavy work)	1,584	34	1,232	40
Standard Deviation				
(sedentary)	711.51	16.89	558.22	25.01
(heavy work)	491.51	11.53	415.31	18.94
Variance				
(sedentary)	486,776.19	274.17	302,957.74	508.22
(heavy work)	232,286.35	127.76	167,690.97	348.95

* Data are presented on the assumption of both a situation of no work, and one with regular work for the agricultural labourers. During the monsoon season there is work available only for a short part of the time. It would be possible to try to figure out the actual situation for each household during the three days when diet data were being collected, but this would be hard to evaluate since it is clear that there is tremendous fluctuation in the amount of work available from day to day and from household to household.

It may also be noted that 1 household in the original harvest sample was missing from the Palghat village, and two such samples were missing from the Kuttanad sample. On the other hand, nine additional households were added to the Kuttanad sample. They are households that could only be reached by boat.

TABLE 6

Relationship Between Work and the Purchase of Rice

Months	Number of Respondents saying they have dificulty to get work Village number				Number of Respondents saying they need to buy rice Village number			
	1	2	3	4	1	2	3	4*
Makaram (Jan.-Feb.)	1	2	11	4	2	10	20	1
Kumbam (Feb.-March)	2	2	17	4	2	22	21	0
Meenam (March-April)	49	30	31	4	44	37	24	0
Medam (April-May)	52	16	29	4	48	35	32	2
Idavam (May-June)	1	4	35	8	1	27	39	6
Mithanam (June-July)	46	32	31	37	44	47	43	16
Karkidakam (July-Aug.)	52	53	37	35	49	50	46	10
Chingam (Aug.-Sept.)	0	17	23	1	1	37	28	1
Kanni (Sept.-Oct.)	1	0	14	9	1	6	26	6
Thulam (Oct.-Nov.)	2	2	12	14	2	22	32	12
Vrichikam (Nov.-Dec.)	52	54	11	23	1	48	34	12
Dhanu (Dec.-Jan.)	48	51	12	9	44	49	28	4

* Note: In village 4, 28 people said simply that they had to buy rice in the months of no harvest.

For most villages, there is a long stretch between Medam (after the harvest) and some time in September. The one exception, village 1, has had the good fortune for the past three years of having three crop seasons; thus people had work for the month of Idavam harvesting the third crop just before the southwest monsoon started in. In general, because of having three crops there was much more work in this village and thus less need to buy rice. It should also be noted that in the two Palghat villages (villages 1 and 2) practically all agricultural operations are paid for in kind. In Kuttanad, nowadays only the harvest wage is normally given in kind, the rest being given in cash.

TABLE 7

Relative Percentage of Agricultural Labourers, 1971

State	Agricultural Labourers as per cent of of total workers		Agricultural Labourers as per cent of workers under industrial categories I — III	Ratio of Agricultural Labourers to Cultivators
	Male	Female	Persons	Persons
Andhra Pradesh	27.73	63.08	51.67	1.18
Assam	10.00	5.36	12.44	0.16
Bihar	33.29	73.61	46.76	0.90
Gujarat	17.65	48.35	33.26	0.52
Haryana	15.78	25.96	24.33	0.33
Jammu & Kashmir	3.12	1.93	4.27	0.05
Kerala	25.10	29.06	55.31	1.72
Madhya Pradesh	19.33	48.70	32.75	0.50
Maharashtra	25.21	51.55	44.11	0.82
Mysore	21.12	49.01	37.69	0.67
Orissa	25.38	52.55	35.54	0.58
Punjab	20.28	10.92	31.60	0.47
Rajasthan	7.63	20.80	12.12	0.14
Tamil Nadu	24.15	54.39	47.26	0.97
Uttar Pradesh	17.18	44.49	25.58	0.35
West Bengal	25.00	44.50	43.11	0.83
All India	21.26	50.46	36.54	0.61

Based on *Census 1971, India, Union Census Abstract.*

The Conditions of the Peasantry
in Bangladesh

SHAPAN ADNAN

The peasantry in Bangladesh operates within the domain of what Hamza Alavi has termed a post-colonial state—a state which is influenced to a considerable extent by external powers, and which retains many of the erstwhile colonial relationships in thinly disguised forms. Such a state is also articulated into the capitalist world economy—into systems of unequal exchange and systems of dependence. The peasantry in these contexts, as in Bangladesh, has to be located with reference to these two domains encompassing the national and the international arenas. In brief, I suggest that this should be the general analytical framework within which the peasantry should be situated.

A second methodological consideration at the outset concerns the unit to study. Even if we take the peasant household as the point of departure, the critical emphasis should nevertheless be upon the relations among households within a socio-economic aggregate, such as a village or a regional populace. In particular, the focus should be on the types of productive forces and production relations characterizing such an aggregate, for it is the macro-social context which defines the constrained choices between which micro-level agents such as the peasant household must operate. An important question here pertains to the causes underlying the reproduction of such relationships over time, and the extent to which such reproduction is supplanted by structural change.

The case of Bangladesh provides a specific instance of the broader South Asian social formation. There is great concentration in land-ownership—approximately 10 per cent of the households own 51 per cent of the land, while something like 50 per cent of the rural households are functionaly landless. Correspondingly, about one-third of the arable area is cultivated by family labour, the remaining two-thirds being cultivated by the labour of classes of direct producers other than the owners—mainly sharecroppers or wage workers.

If we look at the trends over time, focusing upon cohorts of households during their period of existence (i.e. leaving out 'substantive changes' such as partitioning), we note that there has been an aggregative downward shift in the relative distribution of land amongst the peasantry, reflecting an absolute decline in the land-man ratio in the recent past. In terms of transition matrices, a substantial degree of *net* polarization in holding-size distribution is noticeable. Furthermore, the trends in Bangladesh are characterized by a pattern of mobility which is 'compartmentalized' according to different groups of land-holding strata. Thus, for example, the lowest agricultural classes (from the landless to the middle peasants) form a 'compartment' of their own, within which there is considerable upward and downward mobility. On the other hand, amongst the upper reaches of the land-holding strata, ranging from upper middle peasants to rich peasants, we find a separate 'compartment' of inter-temporal movements. While there is considerable inner mobility within each of these 'compartments', there is very little mobility *between* them. Some researchers on Bangladesh have advanced a thesis of 'cyclical kulakism' (similar to Shanin's interpretation of the 'dynamic studies' on the Russian peasantry), but the limited evidence that we have from our own research indicates a far more restricted—indeed segmented— pattern in the land-holding mobility of cohorts. *Prima facie,* the potential of class-based peasant consciousness would thus seem to be considerable.

Against this backdrop, let me go into the changes in the social organization of the peasantry over the recent past. One notes a significant shift in the bases of social affiliation over time. The older forms of social organization are largely based on patrilineal kin-groups, 'federated' into various 'community' groups such as the *shamaj* (typical of the predominant Muslim peasantry, for whom notions of caste are weak). The basis of recruitment into these groups is by birth and, as such, the emphasis lies on ascriptive traits and primordial loyalties. These forms are now undergoing considerable change. One is increasingly confronted with various kinds of patronage groups, factional in structure, stressing transactional ties rather than primordial loyalties. Such groups are based upon, and hence effectively propagate, relationships of negative, rather than balanced, reciprocity (to use Sahlins' terms), and are organized in terms of bilateral relationships between the patron and individual clients, as against multilateral relationships centring on a patron figure, such as the *jajman.*

The patterns of both economic and social change reflect, in their own way, the growing impact of the market in reorienting traditional relationships and command over resources. This in its turn can be related to the subordination of the peasant economy (and society) by encroaching capitalism, working through the arena of the nation-state and the world market. It is crucial to note that the dominance of the extra-agrarian forces of capitalism have not, however, led to the general emergence of capitalistic social-productive class relations amongst the peasantry. The social and economic scenario is thus complex, reducible neither to 'peasant' nor to 'capitalist' paradigms in their pure forms. It is therefore necessary to look further into the complexity of production relations before attempting to speculate on the potentialities of peasant consciousness and politicization.

The prevalent pattern of production organization is essentially 'atomistic'. Apart from those 'owner-operator' households which rely solely on family labour and means of production, the typical pattern is that of one-to-one relationships between households, organized round small units of production, embodying tenural or labour-hiring contracts. Furthermore, use of wage labour is dictated largely by the necessity of supplanting family labour; the objective of production for such employers is distinct from that of maximizing surplus value or attaining the average rate of profit, as would be the case with capitalist producers. Thus, even though 'capitalistic' elements such as the use of wage labour and positive responses to market prices are in evidence, the structure of production is to be analytically distinguished from capitalism. It is therefore not surprising that there is insignificant re-investment of (investible) surplus in agrarian production itself, which could otherwise have led to expanded reproduction, characteristic of self-sustaining agrarian capitalism. There is widespread evidence in Bangladesh, and indeed in many parts of India, that the bulk of the agrarian surplus accruing to a minority of farmers, possessing relatively larger land-holdings, is instead deployed in the familiar avenues of usury, trade, land speculation, and even the political superstructure—for, as it has turned out, money spent on getting elected to offices with command over lucrative 'development' resources is very rewarding as an 'investment'.

All this is very much in the way of describing observable patterns, which recur sufficiently to be significant. We are as yet very far from any adequate theoretical explanation of the specific form of economic rationality, and its conditioning by the pre-existing socio-political matrix, inherent in such behaviour. Current research is only now beginning to grasp the fact that the problem under consideration cannot even be adequately posed in *formalist* terms—whether in terms of neo-classical economics, assuming away social structure so as to be able to operate by way of an "autonomous sphere of exchange relationships", or the sterile application of (misconceived) marxist formulae (e.g. wage labour necessarily implies capitalism). As of now, it is only possible for us to suggest a somewhat intuitive interpretation, in lieu of any analytically rigorous explanatory frame.

The prevalent forms of social and economic organization, based on the existing distribution of the means of production (which in turn implies a certain pattern of class control over the distribution of the agricultural product), can be seen to be such as to allow the stratum of large land-holders to extract a considerable share of the output, without having to participate significantly in the process of production, nor having to invest in agricultural productivity. This would not have been the case under competitive capitalism, where the dictates of the market would have necessarily entailed a concern with efficiency and productivity, on pain of constraining the reproduction of defaulting enterprises. Under prevalent conditions, such considerations can be foregone by large land-holders in favour of manifold avenues of surplus transfer—whether one terms these exploitation or not—through degrees of class monopoly on land-ownership, the informal money market, access to critical inputs such as fertilizers, etc., allowing them varied sources of extraction of inflated levels of (pre-capitalist) ground-rent, usurious interest, mercantile profits, etc. From the viewpoint of the contemporary dominant classes (large land-owners, merchants, usurers, etc.), it would seem that (a) self-transformation into agricultural capitalists is necessary, given existent modes of assured surplus extraction, and (b) the emergence of agrarian capitalism in the ranks of the small, or even the middle, peasantry would be counter-productive, for it would allow the latter to gain in economic staying power, and thus break out of the exploitative relationships underlying the varied modes of surplus appropriation.

In terms of this very brief exposition, and hence somewhat unwarrantedly, one could generalize the effective relationship of the dominant classes to the agrarian structure as one in which the optimization of the returns of the dominant classes, seen from their vantage points, systematically entails a sub-optimal structure of production for the agrarian class formation as a whole. (The 'rate of return' in this context is to be analytically distinguished from the category of the rate of profit under capitalist production.) This in my view, is far from a definitive explanation but, rather, the point from which theorization should begin.

There are at least two issues which merit further enquiry. First, the dominant classes in rural Bangladesh are not operating in isolation: they are buttressed by the state, which resists any realistic attempts at reorganizing production (e.g. through land reform), and they are buttressed by a post-colonial state which itself is kept solvent by international creditors. These relationships are by no means as bland and simplistic as they sound, and the task of delineating their complexities constitutes precisely the substantive content of what I have in mind when I propose that the framework of analysis must situate the peasantry in the context of the nation-state and the capitalist world economy. Secondly, the influence exerted by this ensemble of structures at varied agrarian and extra-agrarian levels in creating and sustaining the fundamental disjunction between the structure of production and the structure of distribution in the agrarian economy requires to be adequately conceptualized. For, unlike a capitalist economy, the eventual distribution of the agricultural product (and hence of the agricultural surplus) is not determined solely by the forces of the 'free' market. Rather, it is substantially mediated by mechanisms of forced commercialization and extra-market institutions structured by the socio-political balance of class forces (e.g. the share of surplus appropriated by the eminently corruptible bureaucracy, self-serving agents of the state, if you like, or the equally tenacious merchant-usurers — both sharing in the distribution of the agricultural product, without, however, having to be involved in the process of production).

In moving on to the question of peasant consciousness and politicization, it is necessary to consider first the conditions of reproduction of the present agrarian structure, underlying its apparent stability. Put another way, given the constraint on the development of productive forces by the disjunction between the structures of production and distribution, what are the factors which prevent the disintegration of the agrarian structure as it presently exists? I would suggest that there are a number of socio-political mechanisms which operate to maintain the present agrarian regime, reproducing the structure of dominance of the ruling classes. First, there is the crucial mechanism of patronage, which allows for a functional degree of discriminatory redistribution amongst factional groups. Thus, a dominant faction will attempt to selectively allocate resources amongst its own clientele (cutting across class boundaries), and such behaviour is replicated for a different subset of recipients, whenever a competing faction rises to dominance. Such discriminatory redistribution in terms of organized multi-class segments of the peasantry points towards mechanisms of *en bloc* mobility rather than mobility conceived in terms of individual households (enterprises) 'competing in the market'. Furthermore, it has the effect of (a) thwarting the growth of solidarity organization and class consciousness amongst the subordinate classes, who are divided in terms of loyalties to competing factional leaderships, and (b) of emphasizing the indispensability of each patron to his respective 'vertical' formation of the clientele. The system operates on a principle of disarming simplicity — the patrons as a class are "united in the strife which divides them". Secondly, the pluralistic nature of social organization allows dominant classes to exploit manifold cleavages amongst the subordinate classes in terms of communal, religious, caste, ethnic, linguistic, or regional segmentation. Issues based on such conflicts are consciously manipulated by ruling classes, whenever necessary, to draw attention away from the class contradictions arising from relationships of economic exploitation. Thirdly, even if any instances of the politicization of the subordinate classes were to arise, an array of repressive mechanisms ranging from legalized to extra-legal coercion are available to dominant classes. Thus local-level power-holders can draw upon the resources of the state (police, para-military, or even military forces), as well as their own private armies, to keep the 'peasantry at bay'. Finally, there are the 'softer' approaches to the manipulation of peasant politicization, diverting it towards manifold expressions of false consciousness — the ideology of social engineering masquerading as 'development' and 'modernization', the populist rhetoric of the post-colonial state stressing 'national growth objectives' to the detriment of considerations of redistribution or social welfare, the invocation of notions of metaphysical equality amongst the exploiters and the exploited (e.g. Allah and the community of the faithful). These varied mechanisms can be seen to be long-run adaptations within the social formation, and amongst the classes exercising hegemony upon it, to insure its continued reproduction.

The issues of peasant consciousness and politicization are far too complex to be discussed here in any great detail. Therefore, I will simply draw attention to two aspects which seem to be salient: that of their relationship to the socio-economic structure, and that of the role of externally initiated political activism in mobilizing such potentialities. With respect to the first, it is to be noted that the atomistic nature of production organization and the individualized contracts between households do not allow the possibility of 'unionization' amongst the classes of direct producers as would, for example, be the case under developed agricultural capitalism. Peasant discontent and militancy thus tends to remain localized and structurally incapable of going beyond the form of the *jacquerie*. At the same time discriminatory patronage systematically reproduces factional divisions amongst the subordinate classes, backed up by the impressive apparatus of repression. (It may be noted here that both the 'development' resources channelled into patronage as well as the 'hardware' of repression are largely supplied by external agencies, principally other interested states and transnational institutions.) It is also in this context that the macro-level pattern of land-holding mobility described earlier serves as a structural, if apparently unintentional, reinforcing mechanism — even the compartmentalized domain of mobility, as observable in Bangladesh, serves to provide the illusion that improvement is possible, even if not probable. From the viewpoint of *individual* households (amongst the poor peasants, if not the landless), even the marginal probability of such advancement, mediated largely by extra-market institutional loyalties, has a 'demonstration' effect which endows peasant perception with a certain stake in the system, even as it presently exists.

Against this, one has to contrast the role of political activism from the left which attempts to conscientize and mobilize the peasantry against the existing order. The problems of such activists, who are not necessarily peasants themselves, in trying to articulate what they perceive as the real interests of the large, exploited sections of the peasantry are complex. In part, they arise from a lack of understanding of the complexities of peasant social organization, symptomatically reflected in a severe under-estimation of the solidarity nature of peasant communities in opposition to all 'outsiders', frequently transcending apparent class divisions amongst themselves. Equally, such activism is plagued by the doctrinaire application of miscontrued Marxism, frequently borrowed uncritically from revolutionary experiences elsewhere, in qualitatively distinct historical conjunctures. To the extent that we know about such literature, the tradition of political activism in rural Bangladesh, and indeed the broader South Asian region, has been characterized by a recurrent failure to grasp many of these complexities which are inherent in any attempt to operate in the context of peasant socio-political organization. One notes here, in passing, the apparent paradox that the tradition of political activism has in its own way suffered from misconceptions about the peasantry, as much as the much-heralded attempts at social engineering by the post-colonial state.

Agrarian Movements
in Tamil Nadu

GOPAL IYER

The purpose of this note is to present a brief panoramic view of the peasantry in Tamil Nadu within a limited historical time span. Taking an ecological approach, the aim is to pinpoint the forms and magnitude of exploitation to which the various strata of peasantry were subjected, their perception of them, the extent and intensity of their involvement in struggles, and their forms of leadership. It also looks at the balance of forces among contending classes and the role of the state. The choice of period for study has been guided primarily by the wealth of materials available. It is to be hoped that many of the questions raised will be answered by other scholars who have worked in detail in particular parts of the state.

BACKGROUND

Tamil Nadu is a South Indian State carved out on a linguistic basis in 1956. During pre-British days it was under powerful Hindu kings, who created a network of irrigation works in the various river valleys, especially in the great Cauvery delta. Some of these irrigation works date back as far as the fourth century A.D. or earlier. However, at no time, and certainly not today, did Tamil Nadu present a picture of hydraulic uniformity. Only one-fourth of the state is wet, while the remaining three quarters comprises dry zones. The variation in the strength of the technical base of ageiculture has had its impact on cropping patterns, crop intensity, and labour demand.

During the period of British rule, two systems of land tenure— *zamindari* and *ryotwari*— existed. The zamindari areas were confined to the districts of Ramnad and parts of Madurai (apart from small pockets in other districts). The ethnic composition of the state included the Brahmans—perched at the apex of the social and economic hierarchy, enjoying an almost total monopoly of the right to education. A number of high-ranking land-owning castes, backward intermediate castes, and a sizeable population of scheduled castes— socially, economically, and politically defranchised, huddled on the outskirts of the village — constituting the rock-bottom.

In the wet regions, the oppressive character of the Brahmanic domination manifested itself in the construction of temples endowed with latifundia which were the exclusive preserves of Brahmans. Scheduled castes were totally deprived of any privilege to seek divine benediction in these temples, while others maintained varying degrees of social distance. There were also temples galore in the dry lands, though these lacked the wealth found in wet areas. These temples helped to provide sacred sanction for the economic exploitation of those at the bottom, and to instill fear in the hearts of any who thought of attacking the status quo.

In the zamindari areas the zamindars were vested with proprietary rights in land. In lieu of the payment of a sum of revenue fixed in perpetuity, they could make their writ run large over the entire estate. The unfavourable ecological conditions, however, necessitated a more favourable land-man ratio to provide a cushion to tide over the recurrent droughts. The zamindars, exhibiting little understanding of the tenants' situation, resorted to rack-renting, eviction of so-called defaulters, and illegal imposts. During the years of favourable monsoons, the poor and middle peasants who constituted the vast bulk of the tenants somehow managed to scrape together enough to make the excessive payments required by the zamindars. But when there were years of drought, they tended to be pushed to financial ruin, which was reflected in the progreessive diminution of their land base during the letter part of the 19th and early 20th centuries. The Communists attempted to mobilize the tenants wherever possible. The consequences of the struggle, however, depended on the intensity of the movement.

Immediately following independence, the Congress Government abolished the right of zamindars to impose and collect rent. By this act, tenants were transfomed into peasant proprietors and brought into direct relationship with the state. The latter, for its part, had the right to impose and enhance revenue, but could not be as arbitrary as the zamindars. Eviction no longer featured as an issue. Some of the former zamindars who had never taken any interest in cultivation sold their personal lands to traditional money lenders. However, in zamindari areas like Madurai, where peasant militancy had not posed a threat to the continued possession of land by zamindars, many of the former zamindars managed to retain relatively large tracts of land. The result of this retention is that today in the Madurai area one finds large landed estates run along capitalist lines by the descendants of the old zamindars.

Many tenants who found themselves transformed into peasant proprietors, with law to back their rights and adult franchise to influence state policies, were slowly weaned away from the path of militancy. Since the base of the communist-affiliated peasant organization in these regions was the landed pesantry, reforms acted as a damper to more militant struggle. For example, in Ramnad district the struggles of peasants underwent a significant metamorphosis after the passage of the Zamindari Abolition Act. The former tenants had improved their economic struggles under Communist leadership. Much of the new blood came from among the victims of the zamindari system. With their newly acquired strong bias in favour of the landed interests it was obviously hard for the leadership to have much concern for agricultural labourers. The one major struggle that the party organized in this district in 1972 centred round the demands for remunerative prices of agricultural produce and withdrawal of the agricultural income-tax (levied on the basis of the area under cultivation and the kind of crops grown there). Some farmers in the process succumbed to police bullets. This, however, did not radicalize their struggle; it only transformed the political battle into a legal one. There has not been any struggle for higher wages for labourers in this region.

As pointed out earlier, the tenant struggle in Madurai was weaker than in Ramnad. Despite zamindari abolition, the concentration of landholdings in the hands of the former zamindars continued, though superficially it was changed (i.e. they came to be registered as ryotwari land holders). The course of the struggle in this district has turned out to be significantly different from the one we have discussed in Ramnad.

THE WET AREAS

The wet areas were paddy growing. The pattern of landholding in this area — especially in the Cauvery delta — was much more inegalitarian than in the zamindari areas. Landed elites, constituting a microscopic minority, owned almost all the land. With traditional techniques of agriculture they were forced to rely on an army of *pannaiyals* (attached wage labourers) and sharecroppers. The divorce between ownership and management was almost total. The *pannaiyals* were drawn from castes occupying the rock-bottom of the social hierarchy. They belonged to one or two untouchable castes, who were subjected to severe social disabilities and made to drudge for as many hours as their masters needed them.

The sharecroppers, drawn from poor peasant castes, were economically and socially a shade better off, but to maintain even this unenviable position they had to avoid all social connections with the *pannaiyals*. Rents were high — up to nearly 80% of the gross output. However, with good weather and a bit of luck, the share-croppers could at least fill their stomachs by supplementing their income with wage labour when necessary. The so-called peasant proprietors used their ill-gotten gains in carousal, and for buying a place for themselves in the next life by bribing the gods heavily through the construction of magnificent temples endowed with vast stretches of fertile land and stocked with gold.

Given such a dismal picture how could the wretched of the earth rise against their savage exploitation and consequent abysmal proverty? The paradox is that they did almost fight the law of gravitation. The spark that lit the prairie fire was the induction of some leaders of the railway workers trade union, of Communist insurgents of Tamil Nadu origin from Malaya. In the late thirties and early forties of this century they resolved to scour the countryside in a clandestine manner and establish contacts with advanced elements among *pannaiyals*. Through a series of small get-togethers they were able to convince quite a large number of their suffering brethren that their wretched condition was not ordained by fate, but was the result of an anachronistic system based on private property that starved and dehumanised the producers in order that the parasitic owners might thrive.

Such nocturnal incursions, however, could hardly be kept secret from the prying eyes of the landlords and their henchmen. Many of the cadres were caught and forced to face the most abominable retribution. This, however, did not deflect them from the thorny path they had elected to traverse. However, as a good tactical measure they concentrated on Kunniyur, a village in east Tanjore in which one landlord's holding of thousands of acres sprawled over a large number of villages. The adjoining villages were also not neglected, and as the first signal of open defiance, they held a public meeting in broad daylight attended by over 1,000 persons addressed by various Communist leaders and cadres. The surging tide of oppressed humanity marching in unison could not be stemmed by landlords on their own. The police were mobilized and once again many of them were beaten, evicted, and threatened with dire consequences. In the situation then prevailing, eviction literally meant condemning the *pannaiyals* to death by starvation, but this was nothing compared with the savage physical torture that many of them experienced.

The movement started expanding very fast. The administration could no longer remain a silent spectator, and in 1944 for the first time the landlords capitulated. A tripartite agreement between the District Magistrate, the *pannaiyals,* and the landlord representatives was signed, prohibiting social oppression and promising some wage increase and reinstatement of the evicted *pannaiyals*. Curiously enough, the agreement was to be binding on landlords only in two *talukas* where the movement had made significant headway. But by 1947, the surging tide of struggle had engulfed almost the whole of East Tanjore. The State legislature passed a law which, though it did not provide for any structural change in agrarian property relations, did at least mitigate some of the barbarous mediaeval practices. *Pannaiyals'* wages were legally determined, working hours regulated, injury to persons made an offence, and above all provision of compensation to *pannaiyals* the masters would like to dispense with. In addition, the handkerchief-sized plots traditionally allotted to them could not be taken back by the landowner.

We have already made a reference to numerous temples and *maths* (religious institutions) owning vast tracts of land. The heads of *maths* and temple trustees could hardly afford to look after the mundane business of bringing the land under the plough. They relied on rent-farmers, known as *mothakuthigaidarar,* who were generally persons with large holdings of their own. They would lease in the entire land of the *math* or temple, and lease small bits out to tenants who usually also worked as agricultural labourers to make both ends meet. The amount collected from the sub-tenants constituted the rent-farmers' profit.

While there was a sprinkling of scheduled castes among the poor peasants, the vast bulk of them occupied a somewhat higher rank in the social and economic hierarchy, though few of them could provide the implements, draught power, or seeds to carry on farming operations. It was the *mothakuthagaidarar* who advanced everything on credit. Once the harvest was over, the sub-tenant would carry the produce to the rent-farmer's house. The rent-farmer would first deduct his advance and then set aside the share accruing to the sub-tenant. The use of false weight was almost universal. The poor tenant, after all the reckoning had been done, would discover that hardly 10% of the gross produce fell to his share. In such circustances there was no need for anyone to convince him of the parasitic claim of the deity, the devotes and the *mathakuthgaidarar*.

Eviction, however, was not common, nor was physical assault. What made eviction rare was the total readiness of the tenants to accede to any demand of the *mothakuthagaidarar*. At least this helped them and other members of their families to work as "free" wage hands and to use much of the labour time at their disposal productively. The thin line dividing the tenants from *pannaiyals* was enough to strike mortal fear to their hearts. In the case of the sharecroppers of private landowners, the terms of lease were no less onerous.

The history of revolutionary movements the whole world over indicates that it is the landed peasantry suffering from a relative sense of deprivation, rather than the landless agricultural labourer wallowing in the quagmire of proverty, who has greater revolutionary potential. Just as till the 19th century history had described peasants as a bulwark against reaction, so has the 20th century so far ascribed the same role to the agricultural labourers. The Tanjore experience stands out both as a confirmation and a repudiation of the experience drawn from history. the Communists first recruited their activists among the tenants attached to temples. There were large-scale evictions, threats and even cases of assault. The tenants, however, stuck to their guns. Since the tenants' struggle and that of the *pannaiyals* almost coincided, it was the massive support from the latter that proved to be decisive for the tenants. As a matter of fact, the Tanjore Tenants and Pannaiyals Protection Act protects both *pannaiyals* and tenants. The tenants got their share of the produce enhanced, their rights more secured, and they were freed from many former abuses.

STRUGGLES AND CONFLICTS

Following the Telengana struggle, which according to Barrington Moore was the second largest one in Asia, the Communist Party of India was outlawed. A phase of severe repression involving indiscriminate arrests, mass tortures, and executions became the order of the day. It gave a severe jolt to the agricultural labourers' and tenants' struggles, particularly in Tanjore. Even though the tenants had been granted a larger share in the gross produce and were protected from other kinds of swindling, they were not given occupancy rights or permanent rights to the land they cultivated, regardless of how long they had been working that land. The landlords, however, feared that if the struggle was intensified some such legislation would be passed. Therefore, following the 1951-52 legislation, many landlords began to resort to large-scale eviction of tenants. Even the *pannaiyals,* though they were spared many of their former ignominies, also suffered in that the tiny bits of land which they were formerly allowed to cultivate for their own use were taken away as a part of the eviction program.

At this point, during the 1950's, the landlords began to form a party of their own to protect and promote their interests. They mobilized massive sums of money, obtained fleets of trucks, and coordinated their activities in order to import labour from areas with acute unemployment or underemployment. While this could hardly reduce their costs in the short run, it definitely had the potential to create intra-class war. With the poor pitted against the poor, the rich could hope to at least maintain control of the situation.

Once the ban on the Communist Party was lifted, the old political faces again appeared on the scene. Though they were able to increase the militancy of the rural poor and the tempo of their struggle, they were no match for the organized power of the landlords, aided and abetted by the state. The struggle did definitely better the conditions of share-croppers and *pannaiyals.* It aslo emerged as a formidable challenge to the authority of landlords. But with the horizontal split of the Communist party into CPI and CPI (M) following the India-China war and other ideological differences, the movement was weakened. The landlords, already an organized force, could now act with impunity. The gruesome murder of 44 agricultural labourers, including women and children, in the village of Kilvenmani, ended the struggle (see Gough's paper in this volume).

THE DRY ZONE

The dry zone of Tamil Nadu differs from the wet zone in terms of the technical base of agriculture, the cropping pattern, the cropping intensity, and the heavy reliance on state credit and power delivery agencies. To harness groundwater resources, the farmers have to put massive investments into sinking borewells, ranging in depth from 40 to 200 feet. Even then the water which these wells provide is more of a protective than productive character. Two successive droughts can depress the water-table severely, requiring the wells to be deepened and more bores sunk to continue irrigation. The energization of these wells and the regular consumption of electricity adds to irrigation costs considerably. The principal crops grown are groundnut, cotton, chilis, cholam (an inferior grain), and other inferior grains.

Except for the last, all other agricultural produce has to find its way to the market and compete with the same commodities grown under more favourable conditions. Another significant fact about this area is that mere ownership of land will hardly ensure a decent survival, since massive investments have to be undertaken, not only by large farmers, but even by the middle peasants. In this situation the peasants and farmers evince deep interest in the price policy of the state, both regarding the inputs they consume and the output they wish to sell. Again in the absence of crop insurance, successive droughts greatly increase the debt burden and therby create a contradiction between the farmers and peasants on the one hand, and the state on the other. It is in this area that rural agitation exhibits a character markedly different from that found elsewhere. Peasants of all strata have been engaged in a sustained and aggressive struggle against the government for the last four years. While there have been several ups and downs, the struggle shows no signs of abatement. The government has taken punitive measures to punish defaulting farmers by disconnecting their electricity lines, thereby adding fuel to the fire.

The agricultural labourers in this area are perhaps in the most unenviable position. Wages are extremely low. The incidence of unemployment and underemployment is fairly high. So is the incidence of bondage. In the face of the solid phalanx of the dominant caste farmers, they have hardly shown any sign of protesting their wretched existence. Political consciousness is the monopoly of those struggling to emerge as agrarian capitalists, though more of them show signs of slide-down than climb-up. Left politics if any is of the extremist type, and one often gains the impression that instead of trying to mobilize the inert masses, they have only been able to communicate with those who are already mobilized.

In the dry districts, Coimbatore stands as a unique case. The base of industrial workers has enough potentialities to strengthen worker-peasant unity. This was partly utilized by the CPI (M) between 1972 and 1974. The agricultural workers in several villages struck for a number of days. The industrial workers actively supported the agricultural labourers, participating in the struggle as well as extending material help to sustain the movement. This helped not only in raising the wages, but also in strengthening the organiziation of agricultural labourers in villages within the proximity of Coimbatore city.

In the dry areas, as we have already noted, we find greater dispersal of ownership of land and consequently a more complex social stratification than in the wet areas. Notwithstanding the land-ceiling legislations, the concentration ratio continues to be very high. In the areas under zamindari tenure, social oppression was not a significant phenomenon; rack-renting and land alienation were the dominant themes. The peasant struggle as such was synonymous with the struggle of the tenantry to contain the exploitative tendencies of the *zamindars*. There were hardly any struggles against social exploitation or lower wages. The abolition of zamindars, and the consequent transformation of tenants into peasant proprietors, mitigated tenant sufferings to the extent that their militancy decreased.

A decade and a half later, agriculture was given a real boost by the huge sums invested by government in exploiting underground water resources and in ushering in the biological and chemical innovations in rice production. In the case of rice, the switch to the new technology has not yet been able to increase production enough to help the smaller peasants liquidate their debts to the state in the form of low interest loans for new inputs. Furthermore, several successive droughts or partial droughts in the 1970's largely offset investments in irrigation and new inputs. In addition, the increasing predominance of commercial crops in these dry zones has also militated against the interests of the peasants. The result has been the eruption of a strong farmers' agitation, fed by the larger farmers, during the past four years which demands the cancellation of debt arrears, reduction in input prices and more remuneration for their produce. The agricultural labourer and poor peasants are almost completely separated from the agitational vertex. The emergence of a strong farmers' lobby, threatening to extend its ramifications over large areas both within and outside Tamil Nadu, has created a dilema for the Communists, who still harbour the hope of winning a majority. Unfortunately, caste-induced inhibitions have yet to go and there has been only insignificant effort so far to forge the worker-peasant unity — the sine qua non of success of many movements. In any case, the final verdict is not yet in.

Discussion

The discussion that followed the papers in this part of the symposium was quite wide-ranging, and tended to skip from one subject to another. I have taken the liberty of trying to put the comments into some sort of a logical order. Furthermore, it was impossible to identify a number of speakers from the floor, as they did not identify themselves clearly enough to be heard on the tapes. Since some of the comments from these anonymous speakers were extremely important and insightful, they have been included, with the editor's apologies to those people who see their comments in print without acknowledgement.

—Editor

Dharma Kumar (Delhi University): I've been trying all my life to find out what I was, and I learned today that I am an intellectual untouchable. No respectable Marxist, populist, neo-classical economist—into which one speaker divided the intellectual universe — would touch me. So, in keeping with my low status, I'll be very brief. And I'll also perform the menial task of pointing out what other people have done. Also, like an economist — that's the other low class I belong to — I'll point out, I'm afraid, some boring statistical details. Now, I agree with a number of speakers on the picture that emerges, for the twentieth century, of general stagnation, particularly in the agricultural sector of the Indian economy, with a growing labour force, and most disturbing of all, growing malnutrition and impoverishment of the poorest. By and large I think I'd agree with that. I'll just make two quick provisos.

One is that it's important not to exaggerate this movement by looking just at the census figures. This is a very well-known trap in Indian economic history. We keep falling into that trap, and I'm distressed that no speaker today has noted the important paper by J. Krishnamurthy in the *Indian Economic and Social History Review,* which shows how the pre-1951 census data have to be reworked. Krishnamurthy shows that there is indeed a growth in agricultural labour between 1900 and 1951, but of a very much lower order than that shown by the raw census data. Similarly, my colleague K. Sundaram has recently published an article in the *Indian Economic Review* on the structure of the rural work force in the period 1951 to 1970/1. Again he corrects the 1950-51 census data, which are particularly bad, for a number of very boring reasons such as problems of definition. He finds that the percentage of agricultural wage labourers in the adult male work force goes up from 21.5 per cent in 1950/1 to 24.25 per cent in 1971 for all of India. The most interesting point he makes is that there is a fall in this proportion in the southern zone. He finds that the southern zone started out with the highest proportion of agricultural labourers, and it's there that the percentage of agricultural labourers in the work force declines, whereas in every other part of India it increases. And he suggests a variety of reasons for this. There may be a number of problems here. I think he has taken a number of very broad considerations into account, and I think it's important to look in detail again at Joan Mencher's work, and the work of other writers who use not the census data but their own primary data. These may show either that Sundaram made the wrong assumptions, or, on the contrary, that the areas studied in detail are not typical of the southern zone as a whole. Until more detailed work is done, I don't think one can generalize. But I think it's extremely important for social anthropologists to contribute to the broader discussions of general trends of economists, because economists may not be making the right corrections or the right assumptions.

My second point is about population and polarization. Now of course I agree that you cannot attribute the growth of landless labour merely to the growth of the population of the landless group, and that you have to look at the entire population. But it seems to me that the growth of population certainly is one factor which increases landlessness, for the simple reason that almost every size class finds itself in the land-man trap, and some fall down the trap. Take the man whose five sons have one acre each; their sons may have ¼ acre each, and eventually they may take to agriculural labour. Agricultural labour will become the mainstay of their livelihood. This is shown by most, if not all, of the studies I have seen on the distribution of land in southern India. I did one myself on Madras Presidency, and I found practically no change in the inequality of land-ownership as measured by Gini co-efficients between 1871 and 1971. There have been other detailed studies, one by a student unsympathetic to my point of view; even he could not help finding in Chingleput that the largest landowners had split their holdings, and that those who employed 40 or more agricultural labourers earlier were employing 4 or 5 in 1976. And you also find these results coming out now in papers on other areas, such as Maharashtra and Gujarat. So I think this whole question of land distribution has to be considered very carefully. Now this is not to say that there hasn't been an increase in poverty, or that population is the

330 The Social Anthropology of Peasantry

only factor. Not at all. It may well be that Kathleen Gough is correct in Thanjavur, and that it was evictions that were much more important. I just want to see the data on that, which I'm sure she'll publish, and I would venture to say that population will be found to be a contributing factor. The importance of it will vary from region to region.

To turn now to broader questions, there seems to me to be a kind of general depression about India, and people are agreed that we won't get what they consider the best solution, which would be a Communist society, nor even the second best solution, agricultural capitalism. We will just stay in this very stagnant position. Again, to make an impressionistic statement—that's not my picture of India. I haven't found it stagnant over the past 30 years, certainly. And I think having that kind of feeling diverts one from some very interesting theoretical issues about political conflict, on which I am really not at all competent to speak, so all I will do is ask some questions. I wonder if we could have more on how caste affects problems of mobilization of labour in various parts of the country, which several speakers touched on today and yesterday. Do sociologists think this is a temporary phenomenon, or does it make the Indian agrarian structure resistant in the much longer run to change? Secondly, again something that's been hinted at by two or three speakers but not directly faced, is how do the specific Indian and Bangladeshi political systems affect the mobilization of labour, the work done by social anthropologists on vote banks and the way the electoral system works in India — the financing of elections — which may be important.

Kathleen Gough: I would like to respond to Dharma Kumar. It is true that I have used census data in my work; it would seem odd not to do so if one is covering a fairly long time span in this century. I have probably not gone into the criticisms of these data sufficiently, and I must do so, but I do not think that it is as faulty or useless as Dharma has suggested. The 1961 census has some real problems because of the unusual criteria for "workers" and especially women workers, but a comparison of the 1951 and 1971 figures for Thanjavur makes good sense to me in the light of my own field work.

When we come to my own village data, I do have reliable figures from my censuses of 1951-53 and 1976, which I took myself from every household. I'm sorry that it's only two villages, but still I think it is quite unusual to have such figures over a twenty-five-year period.

As was mentioned, there has been considerable descent of small peasant owners into the agricultural labouring population. There has also been considerable disemployment among artisans, many of whom have become agricultural labourers. In my second village, for example, a whole street of weavers have stopped weaving and are now mostly agricultural labourers. I could go on and duplicate this for potters, and for many goldsmiths. I cannot say yet what proportion of the agricultural labour force in the two villages comes from such sources.

Now, I agree with Dharma that the increase in labourers does come to some extent from the children of tenants. They cannot all obtain land to lease, so they drop down into the labouring class. That is quite true, and it's different from the actual eviction of tenants; one needs to know how many labourers come from each source. However, I want to say that in a healthy economy that kind of thing would not happen. Some other employment than agriculture would be found for such people. In Thanjavur, industry is too limited and in the case of the new rice mills, for example, too capital-intensive to employ them, and new cottage industries are not coming up to any great extent.

Moreover, all of this does not do away with the fact that tenants are being evicted. My case histories and figures show it, as does the fact that only about a quarter of the land, or less, is now leased out to tenants, whereas about half of it was leased out in 1951. So obviously, we have to look at the whole economy, and at what is happening to Thanjavur in relation to the "green revolution", the reactions of landlords to land reform legislation, and Thanjavur's relations to Indian and foreign corporations that sell the new agriculural inputs, to the World Bank that funds the agricultural extension programmes, and so on. We are looking at the gradual development of capitalism in agriculture, but in a peripheral, industrially stunted economy.

I also agree with Dharma Kumar that there has been *some* rise of new peasants from among the old tenantry; she calls them middle peasants. There are a few of them in the villages I studied; a very few have even become "small rich peasants". They have been lucky enough to get their tenant holdings registered and so to pay lower rents, and in a few cases to buy a little land. But they are very, very few compared with the numbers of tenants evicted, and of newly emerging agricultural labourers. One has to look at the whole class profile over time, and I simply do not think it can be denied that there has been a massive increase in agricultural labour at the expense of the other classes.

Joan Mencher : I would like to answer some of the points which were raised by Dharma Kumar in her discussion of our papers. I do not question her point that there was a large percentage of agricultural labourers at the turn of the century, but I think there is no question that there has been an increase in Tamil Nadu and Kerala which cannot be accounted for simply as a result of increases in the size of the population. I quite agree that the 1951 census is an extremely poor basis for comparison with later years. But if it is unusable for the purposes of proving that there has been an increase in landlessness and an increased improverishment of the population, it is equally unusable to try to prove the opposite. If we want to look at the changes in Tamil Nadu, it is useful to look at what has happened over both long periods of time and shorter periods. For the longer period, it is certainly clear that Tamil Nadu agriculture has been radically transformed by the introduction of electricity, tractorization, the use of new seeds, chemical fertilizers, the introduction of tube-wells and deep bore-wells, etc. (see C.T. Kurien 1978). Kurien, using NSS data, notes that "the major beneficiaries of changes in the ownership of land have been . . . those owning more than 15 acres but less than 50 acres" (Vol. I: 18), and "the changes in distribution of operational holdings have been to the advantage . . . specifically (of) those with between 20 and 50 acres" (*ibid.:* 21). Here, of course, Kurien is talking about operated holdings and not simply the holdings as listed in the official village land record books.

It is clear that the increase in landless has come more from those who were tenants than from those who owned full rights in the land. The period between independence and 1971 was a time when more and more landowners, fearing legislation which might give some sort of permanent rights to tenants, forced their tenants off the lands and took over direct supervision of the land, using daily labour. In some cases, they shifted some former tenants to *al-varam* (a kind of temporary, seasonal tenancy where labourers are shifted from one plot of land to another, and where they are only given a small share of the produce, the landowner providing all of the inputs for cultivation). But in many cases they found that with the new technology, it was more profit..ble to work the land with hired labour, either supervising it themselves or with hired supervisors.

Certainly, there has been a break-up of large old estates as a result of both *zamindari* abolition (immediately after independence) and changes in production techniques, but this has not led to a more equitable distribution. Rather, what this has done is to lead to the emergence of a new type of capitalist farmer, holding 20-50 (or more) acres of double or triple-cropped paddy land in many areas, or similar amounts of land given over to other commercial crops. There has been a marked concentration of the new assets, such as pump-sets and bore-wells, tractors, and rice mills in the hands of this rising class of landowners.

Looking directly at the census information, Ramachandran, in a most informative paper (1980a) points out a number of important things. There is no question that there were a lot of problems of definition involved in comparing the 1961 and 1971 censuses. However, "to correct the data for definitional changes . . . [the census authorities themselves conducted a] resurvey on economic questions" (147). They were looking for "an adjustment factor employing which the 1961 and 1971 Census and participation rates can be made comparable over time and independent of any effect of the difference in the concepts used at the two Censuses" (quoted in Ramachandran 1980a; 147-8). The resurvey quite clearly suggests that the change in the proportion of agricultural labourers to the total work force was even greater than was recorded in the actual census returns. Thus Ramachandran points out: "it is . . . clear that the increase in the incidence of agricultural labourers at the two censuses is no mere statistical aberration, but a reflection of a very real trend in the economy over the decade" (149). He goes on to note that the increase of agricultural labourers as a percentage of total workers varies from one district to another, and to show that in fact it has if anything been higher in the districts that earlier had reported low incidences of agricultural labourers, than even those that had earlier reported large percentages of agricultural labourers, i.e. that there has been, at least in part, a closing of the gap between districts. He then goes on to show from the *taluk*-wise data that the incidence of agricultural labourers in the working population is positively associated with the irrigation index, so that as irrigation has apread or been improved, there has been an increase in the proportion of land cultivated with the help of agricultural labourers rather than tenants (*ibid:* 151-4). He concludes that "the period 1961-71 was marked by a dramatic increase in the percentage of agriculture labourers to the total working population in Tamil Nadu" (154; see also Kurien and James 1979; Rama-chandran 1980b).

Apart from the comments made by Ramachandran, there is one other point which cannot be ignored. That is the extent to which the concentration of land-holdings has come to be hidden. With the expectation of land ceilings, landowners have done everything in their power to hide the actual extent of holdings. Thus, land is put in the name of relatives far and wide, even sometimes dead relatives, dogs, landless labourers who are heavily in debt or under obligation to their landlord, or in the names of females whose household may be difficult to identify, etc. In addition, most of the larger landowners have managed to have their land in a number of adjacent villages, so that their holdings appear in a number of different records instead of just one. Since the villages are not far apart, this really isn't that difficult, and in any case, one can always employ someone else to go and do the dirty work (irrigating the land at 2 a.m. when there is electricity available, or supervising the labourers when it is very hot or rainy).

It has been argued by some that this is partly the result of a small landowner with say 10 acres and maybe 5 sons having to divide and then sub-divide his land among his descendants. However, what is striking to me working in Chingleput, is how among the fairly large landowners, there has not been a tendency to simply divide the land among all the sons, but rather to see to it that other sons are educated and that the family deploys its resources in a more useful manner. Officially, the land might be listed in the names of all the sons, but one will in effect manage the land, one might have a government job with a regular steady income, one might be a lawyer or doctor or engineer, one may be in the agriculture department so that the latest information about new advances is readily available to the brother who stays with the land, etc. Thus, instead of being reduced by partitions, by the 1960s, fairly well-to-do farmers were using their children to establish wide-ranging economic bases and to gain a foothold in a number of different fields. In almost every village the wealthier landowners owned rice mills, or brick kilns, or had branched out into paddy trading in the nearby town, etc. This too is part of the transformation that has occurred in rural areas and an additional reason for the increased inequality. On the other hand, former tenants dispossessed of their land, have only rarely been in a position to educate their sons or daughters to such a degree that they could hope to obtain salaried work.

The picture for Tamil Nadu is not too dissimilar to that found in Kerala. The only possible difference in Kerala has been the change that occurred especially after 1975, whereby semi-skilled (and even more unskilled) Muslim males, and to some extent Christian males, managed to get jobs in the Middle East. That new source of wealth has managed to change land relations to some extent, indeed.

Atul Kohli (University of California, Berkeley) : I wish to make two points. *First,* the argument has been made repeatedly in this session that because India is a complex and diverse nation and society, we should not or cannot make generalizations about it. This is a familiar argument and is, I think, rather absurd. In any field of study, including that of Indian or South Asian society, generalizations can be made at varying levels of abstraction, despite internal variation. India shares much within its diversity — i.e. much which transcends its diversity. Generalizations about the whole — about the shared characteristics and processes — serve valid purposes, just as empirical findings about particular localities and events serve different but equally valid purposes. Both must be empirically derived and/or tested, and their significance in turn carefully analysed. Broad generalizations are perhaps more likely to be carelessly derived and interpreted than specific data. But careful derivation and interpretation of our generalizations and analyses at all levels is exactly what we attempt to do as social scientists. Our response to those who object that to generalize is to do violence to the complexity of the Indian nation or subcontinent must be that we recognize unity in diversity, even as we recognize diversity in unity.

My *second* point concerns the theoretical understanding of peasant rebellions. A theme that has been both explicit and implicit in our discussions has been: "What are the factors which explain peasant rebellions?" or, "What are the conditions under which peasants become rebellious or less than acquiescent?" It seems to me that there are two contradictory, or at least not easily reconcilable, answers. One stresses the social organization of production and changes therein. This analysis emphasizes increasing commercialization and capitalization, with resulting increase in the concentration of property and the disparity in access to goods and services. This generates increasing misery and potential for rebellion among the dispossessed. Somehow, the changes in the organization of production and distribution are thus associated with the appearance of peasant rebellion. The other answer to these questions, not surprisingly, refers to political organization. That is, peasant rebellion becomes likely in circumstances where state mechanisms of repression are weakened. That seemed to be the case described in Dr. Gough's paper on Thanjavur. Even though she does not stress this, both the periods of rebelliousness which she described were periods in which state mechanisms for repression of peasants had been weakened.

These two explanations should be discussed with the aim of delineating the factors which cause rebellions. Social structural aspects have been stressed by Dr. Wolf. I believe that political factors are also important, especially because empirical research seems to bring them out repeatedly. I would like to hear further comments on this point.

Gerald Berreman (University of California, Berkeley): Let me comment on the conditions under which peasants rebel in South Asia. As I have said elsewhere, the frequently alleged quiescence of India's lowest castes ("untouchables"), and of other dispossessed, exploited, and oppressed social groups and categories, is belied by their continual efforts to seek physical, social, and psychological escape from their status and its consequences. For example, low castes universally claim higher *varna* ststus, and they have recurrently embraced reputedly egalitarian religions such as Buddhism, Islam, Christianity, and various reform sects of Hinduism. Most spectacular in this regard are mobilizations for emancipation such as that of the Dalit Panthers recently in the news, and occasional outright rebellion.

When these latter measures are undertaken is precisely when they are regarded by the oppressed as being worth while. And when they are regarded as worth while is *either* when the oppressed come to define their situation as intolerable and hence worth any risk to alleviate it or avenge it, *or* when the oppressed come to define their situation as one which can be effectively changed. The latter is perhaps more common than the former, and is certainly more likely to result in significant change. But it is important to remember that it is the definition of the situation as perceived by those seeking change which is the critical factor in the decision to rebel. The observations of others, or the "objective reality" as defined by others, are irrelevant to the decision to act (although clearly they *are* relevant to the likelihood of success in the act). Conditions likely to lead to this kind of redefinition of the situation of the oppressed uniformly entail a change in their perception of the balance of power: acquisition of the vote, of powerful allies, of empowering legislation, of legal redress, of weapons, of economic resources and security (such as occupational monopolies, union protection, etc.).

In sum, acquiesence to drastically inferior status is not so much (or perhaps at all) a matter of consensus on the system of inequality and its rationale, as it is a consensus on the nature of power relations: who has the power? How, under what circumstances, and with what effect will it be used? When *this* consensus breaks down, rebellion may seem plausible and rewarding. If so, it is likely to be attempted.

Walter Hauser (University of Virginia): We have come now to a very significant part of the total discussion, namely, the social stratification within the peasantry itself in South Asia. This appears to be the dominant thrust of the papers of this session. Most of them have addressed the problem of stratification, ranging from landless labour to the rural power structure and its links with the political process, the way in which the rural power structure is buttressed by the state, the organization by the rural rich in order to gain and maintain control, the organizing and the development of a consciousness among the landless, moving towards strengthening their bargaining power within the system, towards ultimately posing a challenge to the system itself. The social stratification within the peasantry as presented here is the major issue for discussion.

The conclusion that emerges from the studies cited (I am referring particularly to the studies on agricultural labour) is that the only solution to improving the bargaining power of the landless labourers is through their political education. There is a note of caution in the papers, however. Political education must not be only in the direction of wage struggles. It is more important to highlight the nature of the agrarian social structure and the political economy of the nation as a whole, and the need for restructuring the agrarian social structure through land reforms and cooperatives. This point was particularly emphasized by Kathleen Gough when she said that poor peasants, who uneasily move from cultivator status to labourer status, have to fit in somewhere into this total bargaining process. As long as political organizations concentrate only on wage struggles, they leave this very big mass of the impoverished section of the peasantry outside their purview, as a result of which caste can be used as a factor to divide these two very important segments which are really one in terms of their objective conditions.

A member of the audience: I am not an anthropologist. Therefore, as a point of information I would like to know whether this is the right forum for discussing politics and political leaders?

Eric Wolf: Well, I think that it is a reasonable question, and perhaps the answer is that over time the definition of anthropology has widened to include politics and political leaders. There is a movement to widen the field, so that if one works on peasant movements, very definitely questions of politics and political leaders do enter in.

A member of the audience: I would just like to say that several studies on India, particularly in the eastern and northeastern regions, have found that practically the same situation exists, in terms of rent and usury being the most important sources of political as well as economic control, of the state structure buttressing those who exercise these forms of control, and of the plateau that the green revolution has reached because the surplus is not reinvested in agriculture but goes back into usury and electioneering, and various other ways of retaining political control. In this context I would just like to mention that the cooperatives, for example, were stimulated in a very big way to be the major loan disbursing agencies for the green revolution, in order to provide peasants with capital to buy expensive inputs. The major beneficiaries of the cooperatives have been the big landlords in these regions, and they have never repaid their loans, whereas the small peasants have generally repaid their loans. What is most interesting is that even the loans from the cooperatives, which were meant theoretically for the purchase of inputs in order to further stimulate the green revolution, have really gone into usury, and what one could call pre-capitalist modes of control. Whether one could call them pre-capitalist modes, I don't know, that is for the debate — but I would just like to say that what has been stated for Bangladesh is very much existent in large parts of the country. I think what has emerged very significantly from the discussion are the regional differences in a large subcontinent like India, in terms of the agricultural processes and the changes in permutations and combinations of caste and class in the relations of production, and the difficulty of generalizing for the country as a whole, and the need to look in a very detailed way into the regional processes, because, for one thing, I think on the very first day Prof. Shanin, as well as Prof. Wolf, talked of the futility of going in for cosmic views of agriculture which do not take the sub-units into consideration; secondly, this has a direct relevance for political organization in each of these regions — political organization of the labourers as well as political organization of the poor peasants. How you organize, how you see the class formation in each region, will depend upon how you see the class configurations of the society itself, and this differs from region to region. Thus, modes of struggle have to differ from region to region.

S.B. Chakrabarti (Anthropological Survey of India, Mysore): I would like to talk about my area of research in Burdwan district, West Bengal, where the Intensive Agricultural District Programme (I.A.D.P.) was launched in 1962. The categories of sharecroppers, agricultural labourers, and owner-cultivators can be classified into various segments. Among the landowners there are some people who do not live in the village. Landowners who live in the village may be divided into supervisor-cultivators, depending on the nature of their work. They may again be divided into big, middle, and small cultivators, depending on their land-holdings. Some of the landowners, in must cases substantially big owners, have either business or professional assignments or both. Agro-based business dealing in fertilizers, insecticides or trading in food grains or cash crops and the likes are some of the new openings for a flourishing agro-managerial class. Another very important observation is that quite a large number of landowners belonging to the upper stratum have started directly cultivating a portion of their land by hiring ploughs from those who once formed the entire category of sharecroppers.

Among the sharecropprs there are three types: some people own some land (in this case it is noticed more among two groups, i.e. Sadgope and Muslim) and also do share cultivation on others' land; there is a large contingent of landless sharecroppers (mainly coming from the lower castes, i.e. Bagdi, Dule, Bauri, and Charal and the Santal tribal group); the last one is an emergent form of sharecropping locally known as *thika,* i.e. contract. This has appeared after the introduction of *boro* (a high-yielding variety of paddy). In this case a good number of educated and professional people have become share-cultivators. Unlike the traditional share-cultivation where the landowners get 50 per cent of the produce, in the *thika* system the landowners get a fixed amount of paddy (now 3 maunds per 1/3 acre). The cost of this highly expensive cultivation is of course borne by the share-cultivators. Another emergent form of share-cultivation has been that some share-cultivators, instead of owning ploughs or bullocks, get their land tilled by hiring ploughs. For *boro* cultivation, the traditional sharecroppers also engage agricultural labourers for their own cultivation. These latter two phenomena were absolutely unknown in traditional share-cultivation. Another observable impact of land legislation on the traditional sharecroppers in this area is that the landowners are distributing their lands to a number of tenants in pieces at a time on purely verbal terms.

The landless agricultural labourers fall into three categories: annual farm servants, farm servants for a particular period of operation, and those employed on a daily wage basis. Between the sharecroppers and agricultural labourers there are certain overlappings, and also between the smallholders and sharecroppers. I observed that the sharecroppers and agricultural labourers not only struggle with the landlords, but they also compete among themselves for getting work and land from the employer. This is the real trump card in the hands of the landlords of the area, by which they can fruitfully manage or manipulate the situation.

Certain new situations are also appearing in the terms of work of the sharecroppers and agricultural labourers. In the highly techno-economic input-based cultivation, the sharecroppers are expected to bear the cost of seed, fertilizers, insecticides, and water charges for irrigation. Some sharecroppers occasionally work on others' land as labourers on a daily wage basis for a certain period. The introduction of tractors has led to the gradual transfer of male labourers from ploughing the land to transplanting, weeding, and harvesting work. But since the women labourers, specially the Santals, are preferred for transplanting work, they are naturally getting more work than the men. The Santal labourers as a whole are preferred to lower-caste Hindu labourers.

Besides the other points discussed above, the improved method of cultivation, the mechanization of ploughing, and the vast area available for cultivation have together created a condition for the emergence of child labour as well as large-scale migration of labourers into this area from the neighbouring dry districts of Purulia, Bankura, and Midnapur. These outside labourers come on contract to some of the landowners, who use them for a particular period of time. These labourers get some extra payments and create a competitive labour market for a limited period. However, the village employers do not completely cut their connections with the local labourers. They occasionally advance money to them so that they can extract cheap labour from them throughout the season, except in the shortlived period of transplanting or harvesting. In fact the situation is exactly reversed between the peak period of work and the lean period. In the former the landowners are seen literally begging labour from the labouring families, and in the latter the labourers are seen knocking at the door of the landlord begging for loans (in cash or in kind).

Regarding political movements, the peasants are being patronized by both inside and outside political forces. So a discussion of political movements must include the programmes of peasant fronts of all the political parties. This apart, any development plan for the peasants in general, or the rural poor in particular, must also be analysed in proper perspective taking the macro-socio-economic and political dimensions in view. Confusions are apparent among the planners and political thinkers as to who will be the real force for the rural transformation — big, middle, or poor peasant groups; what will be the main strategy — transfer of land to the tenants or occupancy right to the tenants; whether to support increase for the agricultural labourers, or to favour support price for agricultural commodities, or both.

The academic and applied problems, therefore, are how to reach an abstraction on such a challenging task which presents a number of local, regional, and national variables.

Joan Mencher: One of the people who was supposed to participate in the symposium, Prof. Krishnaji from the Centre for Development Studies in Trivandrum, could not be here, and I think the main point of what he wanted to present should be mentioned. One of the main points of Marxist doctrine has been that rebellions often start when there is a collapse of the middle peasantry, and the middle peasantry then serves as a leader for the poor peasantry as well as the labourers. What Krishnaji has documented in this material is how in the Indian state, one of the things that has been consciously done has been to prevent the collapse of the middle peasantry by government subsidies — especially for the wheat areas, and to some extent for the rice areas. The government has provided price subsidies for wheat and fertilizer when prices were high, has subsidized pesticides, and has put tremendous amounts of money into irrigation and other infrastructure. For the case of wheat it has been very powerful, probably because the wheat lobby in Delhi is very strong.

In the case of rice it has been true for everything except price subsidies, and one reason why certain things are happening in Kerala and Tamil Nadu is that at the moment (December 1978) the government has not put forth a price subsidy for rice. If they do, of course, then we will have the same subsidizing of the middle peasantry in the rice regions as in the wheat regions. I do think that this is an important thing to consider in peasant movements in South Asia, and I'm really sorry that he was not able to present his material today.

A member of the audience: There is one problem before the peasant movement today: the strength of the peasant movement today comes from the poor peasant and the agricultural labourers, because the middle peasant by now has been satisfied. The problem before the poor peasant and agricultural labourers is to build up their forces, because of this there is a search for alliances. How to build up a broad front of the peasantry to be able to confront the estate farmer and get maximum benefit? This problem has been confronting the peasant movement and peasant leaders, particularly the CPI and the CPI-M.

Now look at the peasant movements in U.P. and in various pockets elsewhere in the country. The peasant movements are struggles for wages and sometimes for land, and for a share of the land that will be declared surplus in the implementation of the ceiling laws. Now all these struggles have been mercilessly crushed because agricultural labourers have been isolated. The rich peasants and the landowners in the villages succeeded in mobilizing the middle peasantry, including marginal farmers, using caste as a tool to isolate the agricultural labourers and crush them.

Another participant: One of the themes which seems to have come up in the discussion quite a few times so far has been the necessary conditions of peasant politicization. I also would like to take into account a comment by an earlier speaker that we should not be put out by the complexity and diversity of the social formations. Unless we can devise a structural model of peasant organization and then derive from it a model of peasant activism, we are not going to provide any significant generalizations on the matter. My own views on the subject are as follows: I think before we can discuss the conditions of peasant rebellions and movements, there are three basic components which are involved in the generation of such consciousness that we must take into account. First of all, the inner articulation and tendencies of the peasant classes amongst themselves in their relationships between one class and another. Secondly, the perception and strategies of the external activists, who seem to be a recurrent feature in peasant rebellions. And thirdly, the reactions of the state and its external ventures. It is only by studying the conjunction of these three specific components that we can arrive at any analytically formulated treatment of this issue.

Now if we take each of these components one at a time, one of the striking things about the sub-continental agrarian formation is that it is not being differentiated in the manner that the inroads of capitalism would have led us to believe. That antediluvian forms of capitalism persist, rather than the development of extended reproduction. Now this is a function of a number of mechanisms that I don't have time to elaborate on right now, but it is important to remember that there are specific aspects of these processes which are not apparently recognized as relations of production, but which are in fact eminently so. Take, for example, kinship relations which are seen as very ideological ones. One could suggest here that in many of these relationships of conflict and cooperation, kinship relations are functioning as relations of production. So, similarly, a lot of the ideological and superstructural factors which are regarded as somehow being detached from the material relationships, are not really so if you look at them in some depth. What is really important is that agrarian formations are constantly reproducing themselves over time. The question one has to ask is why it is succeeding in this particular persistence. I pose this as a question that we have to answer in order to understand the process of peasant rebellion.

The second component is that of the role of activism. Now this is with us in the history of the peasant movement all across the continent, and it seems that a purely spontaneous movement of the peasantry is very difficult to come across. In which case we should ask, what were the strategies of the activists who came in? What were their perceptions of the problems of the peasantry? Only thus can one begin to trace the problems and inconsistencies in those strategies which then will allow one to analyse the failings of these peasant movements over time.

To come to the role of the state: the state has been analysed *vis-a-vis* peasant rebellion with an allegiance to the *status quo*. In addition, in modern times most of the sub-continental governments have shown an interesting degree of foresight. It has been a degree of foresight which has suggested the degree of reforms within a reformist framework. Now this has been often motivated by a concern that if these reforms were not met, in the case of agrarian relations and land reforms, then polarization or differentiation (which seems to me theoretically overdue) would in fact take place, and would lead to a process of political instability which the existing state would not be able to take care of.

Now it is my suggestion for the future that we need to analyse the necessary and sufficient conditions of peasant rebellions in the subcontinent in terms of the conjunction of these three variables: that we try to build up a general model of such peasant movements which would be sufficiently diversified to take into account regional variations.

*   *   *

On this point, the discussion ended. Obviously many questions remain unanswered. Nonetheless, the discussion did serve to bring up a number of important points. Part IV contains the summing up of the discussion by Prof. Wolf. It was an extremely difficult task to pull together all of the strands of this set of conference papers. What was striking was the fact that they did add up to a coherent whole, and that they do point the way to new and important research. Certain critical questions still remain unanswered, but these are clearly dependent on future events as much as on future research.

—Editor

REFERENCES

Krishna Murthy, J. (1967): "Changes in the Composition of the Working Force Faction from 1901-51", *Indian Economic and Social History Review*, Vol. IV, No. 1

Kurien, C.T. (1978): *Dynamics of Rural Transformation in Tamil Nadu, Madras*, Vols. 1 and 2, typescript (in press, Orient Longmans)

Kurien, C.T. and Josef James (1979): *Economic Change in Tamil Nadu, 1960-1970*, Allied Publishes, New Delhi.

Ramachandran, V.K. (1980a): "Agricultural Labourers in the Working Population of Tamil Nadu: Some Results from the Censuses of 1961 and 1971 and The World Agricultural Census 1970-71", *Bulletin, Madras Development Seminar Series*, Vol. X, No. 3, pp. 145-158.

(1980b): "A Note on the Sources of Official Data on Land Holdings in Tamil Nadu" December, 1980, Madras Institute of Development Studies, Data Series No. 1.

Sundaram, K. (1977): "Structure of the Rural Work Force in the Period 1951 to 1970-1", *Indian Economic Review*, Vol. 12, No. 1, Pp. 15.

PART IV

SUMMING UP

Summing Up

ERIC R. WOLF

Ladies and gentlemen, colleagues and friends, I am indeed appreciative of the honour you have done me in asking me to sum up the course and conclusions of this symposium. At the same time, I must approach this task with some humility, since it will be impossible for me to do equal justice to all the things we have heard and learned on this occasion. I do think that we raised major problems in our discussions, if only because our deliberations grew more heated as we approached the end of our conference. I think this was a good thing: one can remain completely cool and unconcerned about issues which are far from one's heart. Involvement and passion, on the other hand, generate a will to engage and supersede contradictions. Permit me to raise a few of the major themes sounded in the course of our presentations. Some of these themes will prove to be logically inter-connected; others bespeak problem areas for which we do not as yet find adequate solutions.

Let me say something first about the course of anthropological studies of the peasantry. A number of intellectual and political circumstances contributed to the development of peasant studies within anthropology around the mid-century. Cultural relativism yielded to a renewed interest in cultural evolution. Cultures were no longer studied as equally valid — if different — schemata for dealing with the human condition. Instead, there was a renewed search for the dimensions which would differentiate primitives from peasants, members of "simple" societies from participants in more "complex" systems. For Robert Redfield — as for V. Gordon Childe — the significant dimension of contrast was the presence or absence of the city. Redfield modified his views of the folk-urban continuum to permit the distinctive inclusion of the peasant as "a rural native whose long established order of life takes important account of the city" (1953: 31). Others, harking back to Lewis H. Morgan and Friedrich Engels, would re-emphasize the development of classes or the emergence of the state as the chief diagnostic criteria differentiating simple from more complex social orders. The choice of dimension of contrast had important and sometimes unsuspected consequences for field work and theory, as Sydel Silverman showed us in the paper presented at this conference. One choice emphasized qualitative changes in "culture", in human understandings, connected with the rise of the city. The other traced developmental change to shifts in the political-economic ordering of society. Both approaches, however, were evolutionary, envisioning a major shift out of the primitive condition towards something "new and strange".

Another significant stimulus to peasant studies was the rising interest in cultural ecology. The leading influence here was the work of Julian Steward, who located the core of culture in the articulation of culturally organized objects and activities with aspects of the environment. Yet even Robert Redfield, for whom culture was embodied in human "understandings", took account of this new interest by noting "the interrelationships of man and nature . . . natural and artificial" (1955:26). For Redfield, these interrelationships included men's "own view of things" (1955 : 32), since "human mental life has a structure of its own" and the constructs generated are in part "independent of the forms of nature" (1955 : 31).

Still a third anthropological strand of peasant studies focussed less on ecological systems embracing the interaction of man and nature than on the economic action of the peasant producer. In different ways, the major path-breakers in this approach were Raymond Firth and Xoatong Fei. (It is of some interest to note that both these notable contributors were students of Bronislaw Malinowski's, as was Joseph Obrebski, who wrote a long unpublished thesis on a Mecedonian village. It is also worth recalling that Malinowski, together with Julio de la Fuente, carried out one of the first anthropological studies of a rural marketing system.)

Peasant studies received a still further impetus by political developments after World War II. A Latin American poet once wrote that "the strawhat would never, never pass under the archway of history", but in the 1940s and '50s — in widely different parts of the world — country people were indeed knocking on the gates of palaces, demanding to be heard. The peasantry had clearly entered the political process; in a few areas it came to incarnate that process itself. Thinking about the peasant role in rebellions, revolutions, and movements of political liberation led to questions about what kinds of rural people participate in these movements, what kinds of interests drive them on, what sorts of conditions inhibit or further their political action, and who gains what under the impact of different conditions.

Each of these perspectives took a quite different view of the object of study, and each defined that object in different terms. Initially, at least, definitions tended to be couched in typological terms, contrasting the dimensions of folk/urban; land-ownership/lack of ownership; use of family labour/employment of non-family labour; production for subsistence/production for the market. In any developing field, typologies may be used to identify the significant features of phenomena, and to think about the external and internal determinants of these features. They should be treated as half-way stations on the road to knowledge, and not as ends in themselves. Treating typologies as taxonomies merely short-circuits inquiry. It is indeed striking to what extent the field of peasant studies, as evidenced in the papers presented on this occasion, has moved from a fixation upon taxonomy towards a concern with strategic interrelationships within "organized flow", to employ Joan Vincent's term. The papers presented here attempted to locate the connections of people to one another, through their ties to the land, to the market, and to the political system; and they exhibited an increased willingness also to understand these relationships "in flow" in their processual and temporal aspects.

The papers assembled on this occasion spoke to one or another vector at work in such "organized flows". Arturo Warman, as well as Hebe Vessuri (in a paper submitted to the symposium, but unfortunately not presented by the author herself), emphasized the ecological vectors underlying peasant existence, the role of human actors in the management of an energetic system based on the determining and determined role of human intervention in the growth cycle of domesticated plants. Vessuri's paper further contrasted various systems of agrarian management operative in Venezuela, in their social, technical, environmental, and economic aspects, emphasizing technology not merely as the development of material instruments, but also as the deployment of knowledge. Eduardo Archetti traced out the different ways agrarian units of production were connected to the larger system in what he called weak or strong industrial integration — whether the producer, using his own inputs, is connected to the consumer through middlemen, or whether he is connected also to inputs and outputs of branches of industry. My own paper on peasant rent points in the same direction, trying to elucidate the differences between tributary and capitalist rent, and to specify the mechanisms of capitalist extraction of rent under conditions of peasant proprietorship or tenancy. Walter Hauser discussed mechanisms of rent, debt, and the demand for perquisites in twentieth-century agrarian India.

Other papers examined the political framework within which "organized flow" goes forward. Both Gerald Berreman and Henry Rosenfeld — speaking respectively of India and the Middle East — illuminated the ways in which the vectors of kinship were articulated with power exercised within political systems. They reminded us that every ordering, including the ordering of political force, represents a subtraction or elimination of alternative modes of action. Dialectically, one would expect every system of ordering to generate its own suppressed counter-valences and counter-tendencies. Tse Ka-kui spoke of the ways in which the transformation of the peasantry in the People's Republic of China attempted to build upon the successive contradictions generated in the process.

The search for the forces energizing the phenomena of peasantry was carried in a different direction by Rayna Rapp's paper on "peasants into proletarians". It shifts the focus of attention from more usual attempts to follow the peasants in their migration into urban employment, to posing the issue of reproduction as well as that of production. Reproduction here includes the continued genesis of new generations and the need to support them in daily maintenance. Households may carry on these tasks under non-wage, semi-wage, or infra-wage conditions. Even fully-fledged proletarian households, based on income through wage labour, depend upon unremunerated household labour for continuation. There thus exists a very complex interplay between the demand for labour and the support systems for that labour, an interplay highly variable in space and time. This interplay underwrites the reproduction of households; it also ensures the reproduction of the social relations governing the supra-household system.

Rapp's discussion begins with the household, but does not end there, an important caveat to all analytic procedures which take the household, the domestic group, as the basic building block of society at large. The construct is useful, as long as one is mindful of its limitations. We know empirically that the actual processes of work are carried out by people drawn from a plurality of domestic groups, while kinship and its capacity for mobilizing labour and resources are ever dependent upon linkages between households, through the exigencies of exogamy. Hypothetical analysis of the isolated domestic unit is useful as a phase of inquiry, but not at its final point, when the analysis of how the larger system reproduces its strategic social relationships necessarily calls for a grasp of inter-household linkages.

It is especially important to see households and their members involved in a wider web of inter-household and inter-individual linkages when one tries to relate the structure and function of domestic groups to the formation of social classes. Classes are not neatly compounded out of households, nor do generational cycles take place only within the walls separating one household from another. Both the Marxian and the Chayanovite understanding of the socio-economic dynamics of rural populations would benefit from closer inquiry into the ties which connect different households, or which range the members of different households against other members of their domestic groups.

All the approaches presented here share a common interest in looking at the flow of surplus products/surplus labour from the domestic unit that produces it to others, to non-producers who appropriate the surplus. This focus of study is of course akin to the Marxian model of society and development, with its interest in how the environment is transformed to human use in the course of production, how people are organized to effect production, and how surplus generated is transferred from one set of human beings to another. What the Marxian approaches offer is not only a concern with such categories, but a sense of their interrelationship, and the sense that this interrelationship among nature, organization, labour, and surplus-takers has changed over the course of human history. The Marxian approach and the course of peasant studies converge, moreover, in the conviction that to understand peasantry one will also have to grasp the larger socio-political-economic order which subsumes the peasant.

In Marxian discourse this larger socio-political-economic order is explained by reference to the concept of "mode of production", perhaps best understood as a dynamic set of relationships which impart directionality and force to social phenomena. The major variations of class society have been discussed variously as "feudal", "tributary", "Asiatic", "African", and "capitalist". The model of the capitalist mode of production, as worked out by Marx, is perhaps the one with the greatest capacity for ordering relevant facts and with the greatest power of explanation. One needs to be aware, however, what kind of a model it represents. It was set up by Marx explicitly as a simplified and abstract model of strategic relationships between key elements of production, "as if" there were no other relationships in the system except those obtaining between capital and labour, and "as if" the capitalist system constructed on the basis of the initial English experience were isomorphic with the system of the entire world. It is thus an abstract model of how the system works, not an actual history of the development of capitalism on a global scale. One can gain from the Marxian model a sense of the general capitalist dynamic, but the model does not tell why capitalist development differed in England and in Germany, in France and in Italy, in Mexico and in Japan. In order to follow the actual course of capitalist development, one has to see that dynamic at work in different historical and geographic contexts. Another way of saying this is that the capitalist world system — in which peasantries participate — is a system of heterogeneous parts, the constituent units of which are not all of the same kind.

Capitalist development is quite uneven. It was uneven even in its homeland, England, where some regions were quickly caught up in capitalist transformation, while others lagged behind or were put out of the running. The same point can be made with regard to entire continents and subcontinents. Mesoamerica and the Andes were first drawn into the growing mercantile circuits of Europe, then India, then Africa. Plantations and commercial farming were implanted now here, now there, creating peasantries and bringing them into the system at variable moments in time and space.

Not only is the peasantry drawn into the system at different times and in variable fashion, but the capitalist system itself is in some degree predicated on the specialization of its parts. It not only invaded the different world regions at different times, but it turned Malaya into a rubber factory, Egypt into a cotton field, the Guatemala and Chiapas highlands into a coffee plantation, and it specialized the peasantries there in terms of those products. The processes of work and the social relations of work are consequently different in each of these areas; they underwrite different kinds of peasantries, even though there is a general dynamic of the world-wide system which feeds on these heterogeneous differences.

If it is possible to see capitalist development as particularities merging into a universal, it is thus also possible to look upon the capitalist system as paradoxically creating its own unevenness in the process of generalization. For example, the whole South African mining complex, a major contributor to capitalist development in the world, is predicated on labour drawn from the so-called tribal reservations. These tribal reservations are creations of the capitalist system. They were not there before the English, Dutch, and Portuguese reached South Africa; they are modern ways of organizing labour for use in the mines. The ways in which these reservations are set up maintain "tribal" mechanisms. Cultural patterns develop to organize the women and feed the children while the men are away. Eventually, workers come back to the reservations to retire. Men who work in the mines will invest a great deal of their income in organizing prestigeful positions on the reservation where they will go when they can no longer work. Thus, a seemingly non-industrial (though not primitive or pre-capitalist) way of life is created by the very conditions of industrial capitalism in certain regions.

We also touched on the issue of how to think about a "colonial" mode of production. That term refers to the fact — and it is a fact — that the exercise of colonial domination allows the rulers to affect the culture that is dominated. The colonial administration can further certain arrangements and re-arrangements of existing elements which it favours, and discourage and limit alternative arrangements which is does not desire. The ability to thus derange and reorder the dominated society, moreover, brings into being coalitions of allies who benefit by the new scheme of things, and redirects the processes of surplus extraction in favour of some surplus-takers as against others. The fate of the peasantry "on the ground" will be strongly, yet unevenly, affected by these relocations of power and influence. This points up the need to place the various peasantries under study historically, to combine the more traditional social anthropological study of peasants with the insights to be gained from economic and political history.

Permit me to end on a somewhat different note. While the ecological and politico-economic perspectives have gained in strength within anthropology over the past quarter of a century, the gap between these "materialist" approaches and the very different endeavours which have striven to elucidate the human construction of symbolic understandings has widened, not narrowed. The co-chairman of our symposium, M.C. Goswami, has reminded us on numerous occasions in the course of this endeavour of the significance of symbolic systems. Hebe Vessuri pointed to the role of cognition in the growth of technology; Walter Hauser spoke of the "moral economy" of Indian peasantry; and Joan Vincent discussed the historical forces shaping "the politics of the common people" in the development of an African peasantry. Yet, in general, the symposium raised few systematic questions about the relation of society to ideology. Dr. Goswami's reminder should be taken seriously. It is all too easy to reject inquiry into what "the people themselves think and say" as merely epiphenomenal of other, more materially grounded processes. On the other hand, there has been too little concern in peasant studies, as in anthropology in general, with the ways in which structuralism, phenomenology, and semiotics have re-shaped the concepts of "culture", of "world view", of *mentalite'*, and of "consciousness". Inquiry into how human beings transform themselves in the course of transforming nature has taken a path wholly divergent from studies which strive to understand the workings of "mind". Bringing the two endeavours into conjunction remains one of the important tasks for the future.

REFERENCES

Redfield, Robert (1953) : *The Primitive World and Its Transformation,* Cornell University Press, Ithaca.

(1955) : *The Little Community,* University of Chicago Press, Chicago.